THE BUSINESS OF EDITING

THE BUSINESS OF EDITING

Effective and Efficient Ways to Think, Work, and Prosper

Richard H. Adin

Edited and with a Foreword by
Ruth E. Thaler-Carter and Jack M. Lyon

WAKING LION PRESS

ISBN 978-1-4341-0369-7

Printed in the United States of America.

First edition.

Published by Waking Lion Press, www.wakinglionpress.com.

Design and production services by Jack Lyon.

Indexing by Sue Nedrow, www.nedrowindexing.com.

10   9   8   7   6   5   4   3   2   1

DEDICATIONS

Everyone has someone they love and who has shown great patience as projects like this one are brought to fruition. Thus, we make these dedications:

To my true better half, Carolyn, my wife, who shows her love for me every day. Also to our grandchildren, Azra and Ziva, who, young though they are, bring me true joy and remind me how wonderful life truly is. Perhaps someday they will read this book and think I was a literary giant. —*Richard H. Adin*

To my beloved husband "Wayne-the-Wonderful," who couldn't be more supportive of my work; and to my respected colleagues Rich Adin and Jack Lyon, who made my year by asking me to be involved with this book. —*Ruth E. Thaler-Carter*

To my wonderful and supportive clients and customers all over the world. —*Jack M. Lyon*

CONTENTS

Foreword   xv

Preface   xvii

Five Key Resources   xix

I   Roles   1

1   What is Editing?   5

2   Finding a Professional Editor:
     The Needle in the Haystack Problem   8

3   Editor, Editor, Everywhere an Editor   11

4   The WYSIWYG Conundrum: The Solid Cloud   14

5   The Changing Face of Editing   17

6   The Blurring of Roles and the Downward Pressure on Price   21

7   A Rose by Another Name Is Still Copyediting   24

8   Light, Medium, or Heavy?   28

9   The Elusive Editorial Higgs Boson   32

10   Expectations   36

11   The Commandments: Thou Shalt Use a Professional Editor   40

12   The Commandments: Thou Shalt Treat Editors as Partners   44

13   Relationships and the Unwritten Rules   47

14   The Missing Ingredient: Grammar Skills   51

15   Professional   Editors: Publishers   and   Authors   Need
     Them—Part I   54

16   Professional   Editors: Publishers   and   Authors   Need
     Them—Part II   57

II   Tools   61

17   The Professional Editor's Bookshelf   65

18   On My Bookshelf   68

19   It's the Little Things: Hardware   72

20   It's the Little Things: Software   76

21   It's the Little Things: Software Redux   80

22   Editors and "Professional" Resources:
     A Questionable Reliance   88

23   Working Effectively Online I—The Books   91

24   Working Effectively Online II—The Macros   94

25   Working Effectively Online III—Mastering Word   98

26   Working Effectively Online IV—Mastering Macros   101

27   Working Effectively Online V—Stylesheets   105

28   Working Effectively Online VI—The Books   108

29   Working Effectively Online VII—Macros Again   111

30   Are Editors to LinkedIn as Oil Is to Water?   114

31   What Happens When the Cloud Isn't Available?   118

32   Removable Drives and Windows 8   121

33   Author Queries   125

34   Domains and E-mail   129

35   Editing Tools: MultiFile F&R and Search, Count, Replace   133

36   Preparing for Disaster   137

37   Liability Insurance—Nyet   141

38   The Editor's Interest: Copyright or Not   144

39   Editors and Contracts: Editor Beware!   148

40   Contracts—A Slippery Slope   152

41   Nondisclosure Agreements   156

III **Process**   **161**

42   The 3 Stages of Copyediting: I—The Processing Stage   165

43   The 3 Stages of Copyediting: II—The Copyediting Stage   168

44   The 3 Stages of Copyediting: III—The Proofing Stage   173

45   Citing Sources in the Age of the Internet and eBooks   176

46   Symbiosis: The Authorial and Editorial Process   178

47 Artificial or Arbitrary Schedules — 181

48 Schedules and Client Expectations — 185

49 Consistency — 188

50 What an Author Should Give an Editor — 192

51 Losing Money the Paper Way — 195

52 The Logistics of Large Projects — 198

IV Profits — 203

53 Great Expectations: A Recipe for Disappointment — 207

54 Getting Paid: Things for a Freelancer to Think About — 210

55 Thinking About Money: What Freelancers Need to Understand — 213

56 Living in a Dream World: The Professional Editor's Fee — 216

57 The Publisher's Search for Savings — 219

58 The Rule of Three — 223

59 Reducing Fees — 226

60 Killing Me Softly — 229

61 Best-Price "Bids" — 232

62 Wildcard Macros and Money — 235

63 One Price Doesn't Fit All — 240

64 New Year, New Books — 243

65	Thinking About Invoices	246
66	The Ethics of Billing	249
67	Raising Prices	253
68	Lower Your Rate?	257
69	The Demand for Perfection	260
70	What to Charge—Part I	264
71	What to Charge—Part II	267
72	What to Charge—Part III	271
73	What to Charge—Part IV	276
74	What to Charge—Part V	280

V The Career of Editing 285

75	Editing Tests	289
76	Pricing Yourself out of the Market When Applying for Work	292
77	How NOT to Get Work	295
78	The Making of a Professional Editor	297
79	To Post or Not to Post Your Fee Schedule?	301
80	Do You Want to be Acknowledged?	304
81	Burning Bridges	307
82	Difficult Clients	310
83	Veterinarian or Editor?	314

84   What Do Editors Forget Most Often?   317

85   How Do You Know You Are a Good Editor?   321

86   What Makes an Editor a Professional?   324

87   The Ethics of Editing   327

88   Implied Promises and the Professional Editor   330

89   Personal or Emotional Satisfaction and the Job of Editing   333

90   Taking on Too Much   337

91   Losing the Chance   340

92   Why a Company?   344

93   Solopreneur or "Company"—Part I   348

94   Solopreneur or "Company"—Part II   351

95   Solopreneur or "Company"—Part III   355

96   "I Can Get It Cheaper!"   358

97   The Disappearing Client   361

98   Workdays and Schedules   364

VI   The Future   **369**

99   Viewing the Future of Publishing   373

100   eBooks and the Future of Freelance Editors   376

101   The Times are Changing! Will Editors Change With Them?   379

102   The Decline and Fall of the American Editor   382

103 Is Editing a Future Safe Harbor?   386

104 Group Sourcing?   389

105 Missing the Editorial Boat   391

106 Missing the Editorial Boat Redux   394

107 The Editorial World—Will it Pass Editors By?   396

108 Competition Gets Keener: Agents, Authors, and Perseus   400

109 Does the Future of Editing Lie in Tiers?   402

110 The Crystal Ball Says . . .   405

111 Who Speaks for the Freelance Editor?   409

112 One Is the Loneliest Number   412

113 Working Alone—or Not?   415

114 Is the Editorial Freelancer's Future a Solo Future?   418

Want to Know More?   423

About the Author and the Editors   424

Index   426

FOREWORD

Welcome to a definitive perspective on the nature of editing as a calling and as a business. The essays in this book originally appeared as posts on Richard H. Adin's *An American Editor* blog. They have been grouped and resequenced by topic rather than original date of publication, so you may notice a few inconsistencies in references to the author's years in the field. (Those who are interested in the original publication dates will find them on the blog.) The essays have been edited primarily for consistency and to make the new sequence smooth and logical for the reader, whether a blog subscriber or a new reader of this important voice in the profession of editing and the notion of editing as a business.

To continue the conversation by following An American Editor, go to:

http://americaneditor.wordpress.com/

This compilation will prove valuable to new and established editors who are committed to both editorial quality and business success.

–Ruth E. Thaler-Carter and Jack M. Lyon

PREFACE

At one time, editing was a respected profession. It attracted some of the brightest minds, even some who are still celebrated today, such as the famed Maxwell Perkins and Bennett Cerf. But today, editing is viewed differently.

With the rise of self-publishing, the need for professional editors is ever greater, but it is those who most need the services of a professional editor who are least likely to obtain those services. Instead, many authors believe that they can do as good a job as a professional editor themselves, or that crowd-editing is just as good, or that no editing is really needed. The excuses and reasons for not hiring a professional editor are as myriad as the authors.

When families ran the publishing houses, there was great pride in quality production. With the demise of the family-run publishing houses, the idea of editorial quality being the number-one task has declined. Even in the traditional spheres in which editors have worked, the value of editing is being undermined. As the accountants take over the decision-making process, editing, because it provides a hidden value, is among the first services to be cut. This worries me greatly, as it does many of my colleagues.

This sea change in the profession of editing is one of the topics addressed in this book, which is a compilation of essays from my blog, *An American Editor* (www.americaneditor.wordpress.com). The essays discuss the business aspects of freelancing, which, traditionally, is a weakness of freelancers. The essays cover a broad gamut of topics, but each topic is important to succeeding as a freelancer. The idea is to help you become both business-savvy and editing-savvy so you can succeed in this ever-changing world of editing.

What you have before you is the fruit of work done by Ruth E. Thaler-Carter and Jack Lyon. My belief was that the essays were already available on the blog, so there was no need for the book. Ruth and Jack thought otherwise and hounded me until I finally said, "If you want to do a book, go to it. It's your baby, you birth it." And so they did. Perhaps they are right and such a book is needed. Certainly, it is easier to find an appropriate essay. Both Jack and Ruth did a wonderful job sorting and editing my blog essays.

Of course, a book like this is of little value if you cannot find the material you are looking for easily. Consequently, the indexing job—a masterpiece of indexing—done by Sue Nedrow (www.nedrowindexing.com) is greatly appreciated and a wonderful resource. Finding high-quality indexers is difficult, but Sue is an example of such an indexer.

I hope you find this book valuable. If you have any suggestions for future topics that you would like to see in a book or on the *An American Editor* blog, be sure to drop a note to me in care of Waking Lion Press (editor@wakinglionpress.com).

—*Richard H. Adin, An American Editor*

FIVE KEY RESOURCES

Many essays in *The Business of Editing* mention three software programs that increase a freelancer's productivity and efficiency. For more information about these programs, see:

- **EditTools** (www.wordsnSync.com)
- **Editor's Toolkit Plus** (www.editorium.com)
- **PerfectIt** (www.intelligentediting.com)

Each of these programs is available for individual purchase at the listed websites. They are also available as a single package, called **Editor's Toolkit Ultimate**, at a significant discount. For information and ordering as a combined package, visit:

wordsnsync.com/editors-toolkit.php

A fourth, very valuable, resource is the Communication Central conference for freelancers, which is held every year in the fall. Information about upcoming conferences is available at:

www.communication-central.com

Another key resource is the consulting services that are available from Richard H. Adin, Jack M. Lyon, and Ruth E. Thaler-Carter. If you or your company are interested in private consultations with one or more of us, please e-mail consulting@communication-central.com.

Part I

ROLES

"If *you* don't believe you are the greatest, who will?"

—*Richard H. Adin, An American Editor*

One of the many challenging aspects of being a freelance—or even in-house—editor is establishing your role in the profession, the industry, and the interaction with authors or clients. The essays in this section explore this important element of the business of editing, starting with a look at what it means to be an editor and progressing to how editors relate to both clients and projects.

1

What is Editing?

Have you ever wondered what editing really is? Or about what course of study is best for preparing for an editing career?

The practical answer to the latter is that it doesn't matter what you study because education is valuable and broadening; experience matters more. But when backed to the wall, my answer, unlike that of many of my colleagues, is that the best courses of study are philosophy and law.

The reason is because of what editing is. Editing is the art of language compromise, not the art of strict structure application. I suppose a little context would be helpful.

The matter arose in a discussion on LinkedIn in which I suggested philosophy as the best course of study and another member suggested linguistics. Linguistics is a wonderful field and certainly of great interest to editors, but it is a structural field. True, it wonders about word origins as well as how words are used, but its focus is the structure and lineage of language.

Philosophy and law, on the other hand, focus not on structure but on how to think. Both are "argumentative" fields—Does a god exist? If I don't see you, do you really exist? What is my place in society? What role should/does X play in social affairs?—that require thinking about all sides of a question. The difference, I think, between the philosophy-trained thinker and the linguistics-trained thinker is the difference between the average chess player and the chess champion. We all can learn to play chess and even to play it well; few of us, however, can master the advanced thinking techniques required to be a grandmaster.

(Before I stray too far afield, let me reiterate that all education is good and all education can prepare a person for the intellectual challenges of editing. What we are discussing is the hierarchy.)

Much of editing is structure-oriented, such as checking or correcting grammar and spelling, and coding manuscript. Structure is mechanical and can be self-taught or picked up in a couple of courses on, for example, grammar. I grant that it is the rare person who develops that same depth and breadth of knowledge about the structural issues via self-learning or a couple of entry-level courses as would be obtained from the rigors of a university major in linguistics, but how much is really needed for editing, especially as editing is the art of language compromise, not the art of strict structure application?

Over my 30 years as an editor, what I have most realized about some of my editor colleagues is that they are very capable of applying the "rules" of language. Where they are weak, and what I think often distinguishes the good, competent editor from the great editor, is that they are unable to "think" about what they are editing. They are unable to grasp a broader picture by, for example, putting themselves in the shoes of a variety of readers or by analyzing a text from multiple angles. To use another metaphor, most editors are like professional baseball players in that they are the better, more professional, more able players from the pool of would-be professional players, but are not the superstars who are an even more finite group. Baseball fans recall Willie Mays, for example, but how many of his teammates on the 1954 World Series team do we remember?

It is this "thinking" ability that I believe philosophy and law teach but that linguistics and other study disciplines do not. Linguistics will teach us how to ascertain the origins of all the variations of "god," but not to think about what "god" means in the context of the manuscript and as being conveyed to the variety of hoped-for readers of the published manuscript. Linguistics doesn't really teach the art of communication as much as it teaches the science of communication, but editing is (or should be, I think) more concerned with the art than the science.

I am not suggesting that the science of editing is unimportant. Knowing what punctuation to use where and when is very important in making sure that the author's meaning is correctly understood (using Lynne Truss's famous example, is it "eats shoots and leaves" or "eats, shoots, and leaves"?). Knowing whether the right word is being used to convey the intended meaning is equally important, as is choosing among the homophones (does the author mean *to, too,* or *two*?). And good editors do these tasks well and correctly. For the most part, I suspect, this is the job for which most editors are hired. And this is the job for which most education prepares us.

Yet there can be more to editing than just those tasks. And, for many of us, when we suggest rewriting a sentence or a paragraph or reordering paragraphs or chapters, we are embarking on that additional path. As we gain experience, we begin to think differently about language and its use. I know that the editing I did 30 years ago is not as good as the editing I do today; those intervening years have taught me many things and exposed me to many new ways of looking at language. The more I read and learn, the better editor I become.

But even 30 years ago, I had the advantage of having been trained to think analytically. That is the legacy of a philosophy and law education: It is not *what* to think, but *how* to think. What I think about is of little importance to philosophy; the methodology of thinking about it is important.

Editing is a combination of structure and philosophy; it is not one without the other. The more accomplished one is as an editor, the more skilled one is at both prongs. Most of us begin our editing careers strong in one prong but not the other, and we build strength in both prongs as we gain experience. But if asked what is the best course of study for a wannabe editor, my answer is philosophy or law because it is learning how to think that is hardest to master.

Once we have mastered how to think about language, we learn that editing is more the art of language compromise and less the science of applying rules.

2

FINDING A PROFESSIONAL EDITOR: THE NEEDLE IN THE HAYSTACK PROBLEM

On one of the ebook lists of which I am a member, an author asked: How does one find a *professional* editor? On the surface, this doesn't seem like too big a problem, but dig deeper and one realizes that this can be a gargantuan task, like finding a needle in a haystack. After all, there are hundreds of thousands of people calling themselves professional editors, but there is no governing body that issues editorial licenses after proof of minimal competency.

The issue really comes down to how one defines *professional* when speaking of editors—and how we present ourselves in that sense.

In other essays, I have suggested some of the things that separate the professional from the amateur editor. The problem is at least twofold: (a) An author can't easily verify that the editor really owns and knowledgeably uses these resources, and (b) Owning the right tools doesn't turn a person into a professional.

The definition of professional also turns on what the editor is expected to do. A professional copyeditor is not necessarily a professional developmental editor nor vice-versa. Different skills and resources are needed.

As you can see, the problem of defining *professional* and then finding a professional editor is just that—a problem! I am not sure there is an easy or sure way to solve it.

One suggestion that many editors make is to ask about books (or articles or journals or whatever is appropriate) that the person has worked on in the past. The idea is that someone who has already edited 200 fantasy novels would be a professional editor of fantasy novels. I'm not sure that is sufficient. My own experience—I've been editing medical books for 26 years—tells me that all that it proves is that I have edited books, not how well I have edited them, and how well I have edited them is the true crux of the matter. I think past work is one criterion, but what do you do with the brilliant young editor who is just starting out? We all had to start at zero at some point in our careers.

There is something else to note about the past projects list. If a person copyedits only short journal articles, it is possible that their list would be thousands of titles long and, thus, impressive by sheer weight of numbers, especially compared to the person who edits primarily long tomes and, thus, can do fewer projects over the same timeframe. I know this because most of my work is on books that are 5,000 manuscript pages or longer, and it isn't possible to complete such long projects in the same length of time as a 150-manuscript-page project.

Another suggestion was years of experience doing the particular type of work. I admit that I like this criterion better than the past project criterion for a lot of reasons, but the primary one is that it would be difficult to sustain a livelihood as an editor over the course of many years if you didn't have at least minimal competency. This is even more impressive if the person has a couple of long-term clients. But, alas, this, too, is insufficient to separate the professional from the professional-wannabe.

A third suggestion that is often heard is to ask for references. But how telling are they? You have to trust the person giving the reference and have to assume that the person knows the difference between quality and nonquality work. A glowing reference may be because the work went smoothly and was finished on time and on budget, rather than because the work was of exceptional quality—even if the person giving the reference believes it was for superior quality work. There can be a chasm between belief and fact.

A fourth suggestion has been to ask for samples. This raises a host of problems and also doesn't really answer the question. Among the problems it raises are whether the editor has the right to share the work with you. I treat all of my clients' work as confidential and would not share it with anyone without written permission; after all, isn't that how you would want me to treat your work? But a more important problem is determining whose work you are really seeing. If you are being shown or referred to the final version, you do not know what improvements to the manuscript were made by whom, even if you can compare the originally submitted manuscript with the final version. And viewing a copy of the manuscript that shows tracked changes doesn't really indicate a lot, either. If it is the first go-round, the editing will be rougher than the final go-round; if it is the final go-round, you will have missed the important intermediate steps that brought the manuscript to this point and not know whether it reached this plateau through the editor's efforts or despite the editor's efforts.

Of course, there is one final problem with this last suggestion: You really can't evaluate an editor's work without knowing what limitations were placed on the editor by the client or the client's approach to having someone edit their work. I can't tell you how many times in my 26 years I have had authors tell me my job is only to code the manuscript for typesetting, not to make corrections or suggestions.

I could go on for many more paragraphs and I would still be no closer to solving the original puzzle: How does one find a *professional* editor, that needle in the haystack? Perhaps together we can find a viable answer by addressing these questions:

1. How would you find a *professional* editor?

2. How would you define *professional*?

3. How would you evaluate an editor's work?

EDITOR, EDITOR, EVERYWHERE AN EDITOR

A book has many contributors to its success. One contributor is the editor and, in some instances, several editors. Editors are the hidden resource that can help or hurt an author's work.

There are many levels and types of editing—too many to address here. In essence, I think all of the various levels and types of editing are divisible into two broad categories: **developmental** (sometimes known as substantive or comprehensive) and **copy** (or rule-based). Each serves a different role in the book production process, but each is important. (*Disclosure time:* I am an editor of 25 years' experience. I am also the owner of Freelance Editorial Services, which provides independent editorial help to publishers and authors.)

A developmental editor's role is multifaceted, but it is less concerned with grammar and syntax and more concerned with the manuscript's overall structure. The developmental editor addresses these types of questions (and many more):

- Is the manuscript coherent—that is, do its various parts fit together as a coherent whole?

- Who is the author's audience? Does the manuscript present its information logically for the target audience?

- Are the author's ideas presented clearly? Will the audience understand what the author's point is? Are the author's thoughts clearly and logically developed or do they meander?

- Does the author present the ideas concisely—that is, is the author using a shotgun or a laser approach?

- Does the material in each chapter connect with what went before?

- Is the author using jargon or technical terms in a manner that will befuddle the audience?

- Is the work complete? For example, are sources cited where and when needed?

The developmental editor helps the author hone the manuscript for the author's audience. It is not unusual for the editor and author to engage in multiple back-and-forth discussions to clarify text, find missing sources, reorganize chapters and parts, and the like.

Once the author and the developmental editor are satisfied with the manuscript, the copyeditor steps in. The copyeditor's role, broadly speaking, focuses on the mechanics of the manuscript. That focus includes things such as:

- Spelling

- Grammar

- Punctuation

- Style

- Consistency

The copyeditor is the "rules-based" editor. The copyeditor is usually given a set of rules (styles) by the author or the publisher to follow when deciding questions of capitalization, numbering, hyphenation, and the like. It is the copyeditor's job to apply and enforce those rules, and to do so with consistency. In the editorial world, consistency is the law, not the hobgoblin of little minds.

When appropriate, a good copyeditor also questions the text. For example, if the author has referred to a particular character as Sam but now seems to have changed the name to Charlie, the copyeditor will "flag" this change and ask (query) the author about it. Additionally, if the name change is sudden but, from further reading, appears to be correct, the copyeditor might suggest to the author that a better transition is warranted so readers can follow the change more easily.

Unlike the developmental editor, the copyeditor's role is *not* to help organize and rewrite the manuscript. It is to make the "final" manuscript readable by ensuring that it conforms to the language conventions readers expect and the style the publisher prefers. It is to ease the reader's burden, helping author and reader connect.

The ultimate role of the editor—no matter whether developmental or copy—is to help the author connect with reader. A good editor eases that connection; a poor editor hinders that connection. An editor is another eye, another view for the author. A good editor recognizes pitfalls and helps the author avoid them. A good editor is an artist of language, grammar, and the mechanics that help a manuscript take the journey from ordinary to great. When asked to define my role as editor, I usually reply, "to make sure what you write can be understood by your audience."

The final arbiter of how the published manuscript will read is the author. Editors give advice that the author can accept or reject. In the end, the manuscript is the author's; the editor is simply a contributor, but a contributor with special skills and knowledge.

One last note: This description of what an editor does is not a comprehensive description. There are circles within circles, levels within levels, and many more tasks that editors can and do perform. The above is merely a broad view. If you are an author looking to hire an editor, you should discuss with the editor the parameters of the work to be performed by the editor. There is no set, immutable definition of, for example, developmental editing; for any given manuscript, what role the editor is to play is determined by dialogue between the editor and the author or publisher.

4

THE WYSIWYG CONUNDRUM: THE SOLID CLOUD

We've had this discussion about the value and importance of professional copyediting, but it seems that it is a topic that just won't die in the eBook Age. As I have noted before, too many authors believe that they are capable of doing everything themselves while producing a superior product. I admit that, out of 1 million authors (in 2009, more than 1 million books were published), there are a handful who can do it all themselves and even do a very credible, if not superb, job—but it is a handful. As my grandfather used to say about a neighbor who thought he could do it all, "jack of all trades, master of none."

Like writing, editing is a skill. It is a developed skill; that is, experience brings a higher level of editing quality, just as an author's second novel is often better written than the first as the author's experience grows. There is a significant level-of-quality difference between a well-experienced professional editor's skill set and a nonprofessional editor's skill set.

When we look at a sentence, we see what we expect. When we look at thick clouds, they look solid enough to walk on (do you remember being a child and talking about how someday you were going to walk among and on the clouds?), but, as we know, our expectation that they can support us is a false expectation. What we see is *not* what we get—the *WYSIWYG conundrum*! (WYSIWYG stands for What You See Is What You Get.)

The same is true of words on paper (or computer screen). We often see what we expect, not what is really there. If we always saw only what was really there, we could turn out perfect manuscripts every time. But the truth is that, if you hand a manuscript to five different people, each of the five will find something that the other four missed, in addition to what all five do find.

Think about eyewitness identification. This is a field that has been explored by scientists for decades and the conclusion hasn't changed: Eyewitness identification is one of the least-reliable forms of evidence because the eyewitness has certain expectations that unconsciously get fulfilled, even if those expectations deviate from the facts. (If you haven't watched it recently, I highly recommend *Twelve Angry Men* with an all-star cast led by Henry Fonda.)

Professional editors provide a dispassionate look at an author's work. They provide a skilled, experienced eye that is trained to find the kinds of errors that the author, who is intimately familiar with the manuscript, will miss when he or she tries to self-edit. A good author lives with his or her manuscript for months and years, lives with the characters, and lives with the plot. The author knows how the heroine spells her name and whether she is left-handed, the color of her eyes, and all the other important details. Consequently, it is not unusual for an author who is self-editing to miss the extra "r" in Marrta because the author expects to see Marta. Our mind skims over minor errors, converting them into what should be because we have trained ourselves to see it as it should be.

It is this role that the professional editor, the "indifferent" or "dispassionate" set of eyes, fills. The professional editor can stand back—aloof—from what the author has lived with and can note the misspelled or changed name or that, in 20 other instances, the heroine was left-handed but now is right-handed; the sentence construction that the author understands but the reader doesn't. If nothing else, this last item can be the most valuable service the professional editor provides an author—making sure that the story, the plot, the characters can be followed by the reader.

Authors of fiction tend to forget that most readers read a novel once and then never look at it again. They also tend to think that their work deserves the same intense scrutiny that a reader would give to a nonfiction book about the theory of relativity, but novels are intended to entertain, which means nonintense reading. The reader does not want to have to spend time trying to follow the storyline and certainly does not want to study the text to make it understandable. But the author rarely is capable of standing in the reader's shoes because of the intimate relationship the author has with characters, plot, and storyline. The author *knows* where the story should be going and expects it to go there; the reader doesn't know, doesn't have the intimate knowledge needed to draw everything together in some logical fashion. The author's job is to draw it all together for the reader, but if the author can't stand in the reader's shoes, the author can't honestly judge how well he or she has accomplished that task. The professional editor can because the professional editor is disinterested; there is a difference between one's passion and one's job that enables one to stand back and look objectively at one's job but with bias at one's passion.

Professional editors bring many skills that are complementary to the author's skills to the table. These skills cannot be brought to bear on the project by the author because the author cannot separate him- or herself from his or her writing. The author suffers from the WYSIWYG conundrum: *The author sees what the author expects to see.*

The authors who recognize this conundrum and who take steps to have their work professionally edited are the authors who enhance both their readers' enjoyment and their likelihood of success in an overcrowded marketplace. Success is much more than the number of downloads of free or 99¢ ebooks, especially when there is no way to know how many of those downloads actually were read or well thought of. Instead, success is having readers clamor for your books, talk about your books, express a willingness to pay a higher price for your books—all things that a professional editorial eye can help an author achieve by preventing the kinds of mistakes that turn readers away.

5

THE CHANGING FACE OF EDITING

At one time in my career as an editor, my function was crystal clear: Everyone understood and agreed on the role a copyeditor played in the publishing business. But, as the years have passed and the traditional publishing industry has consolidated into six megacorporations whose decisions are made based on bean-counting, what was once clear-cut has become fogged.

This was brought when I was contacted by a client to copyedit a new medical book. The client's inquiry included these points:

"<Name> has recommended you for a new title, which requires copyediting, and we need someone who is a **subject matter expert** in physiology with a strong science background to copyedit this book, as **some sections may need to be rewritten.**

"...

"Language edit required: **Yes** (Many of contributors are not English speaker so will need copyedited pretty closely for language, especially for the chapters written by a non English speaker)"

The project was approximately 600 pages and needed to be completed within three weeks. The client estimated that the editing could be completed in 92 hours. The fee? The standard copyediting fee.

I declined the project for several reasons. Here is my written response:

"I appreciate you and <name> thinking of us for this project, but I don't think we fit your needs for three reasons. First, none of us are subject-matter experts in physiology. We are very experienced medical copyeditors, but that is not the same as having expertise in a particular subject area.

"Second, you mention rewriting sections. That is the job of a developmental editor, not a copyeditor. Although we can do developmental editing, our fee is significantly higher for doing so, especially if English is not the native language of the original authors. Copyeditors work under the guise that the project has already been developmental edited and although they may change a sentence or two for tense or ease of reading, copyeditors do not rewrite paragraphs and sections.

"Finally, if a project needs developmental work (again, especially if English is not the original authors' native language), I think the schedule you propose is too tight for normal working hours. I'm not clear on how you came up with your estimate of 92 hours being needed to do the job, but that equates to approximately 6 pages an hour (using your stated number of pages as 549; we always reserve the right to verify the page count based on our agreement with <client>), which, in my experience over 27 years of medical editing, is much too high if rewriting is required (again, especially if English is not the original authors' native language). Rewriting work under such circumstances more often than not works out to an editing rate of 2 to 3 pages an hour."

I didn't bother emphasizing that the fee was inadequate for a developmental edit, which clearly was the level of editing expected. And it also needs to be remembered that, in addition to doing the editorial work—grammar, spelling, syntax, etc.—the copyeditor also needs to code every element of the manuscript for typesetting, often by applying a template and tags.

This request is typical of the inquiries I am receiving (and have been receiving for quite some time). It is not enough for editors to be proficient in the tools of editing; editors are now expected to rewrite and to have subject-matter expertise.

I have edited thousands of books over the course of my 27 years as an editor, but I don't believe that turns me into a subject-matter expert. True, I have greater familiarity on a broad level with the subject matter, but expertise is gotten by a combination of specialized training and practical experience, not just reading: Simply because I have edited hundreds of medical books does not qualify me to be a doctor.

The demand for greater expertise and for higher-level service is a result of bean-counting. When I began my career, publishers had a budget line for developmental editing and a separate budget line for copyediting. It was expected by everyone in the publishing loop that a project would go to copyediting only after it had been developmentally edited. But in the press to reduce costs and increase profits, the segregation of the tasks has slowly disappeared and now everything that can be called editing is bunched together under the name *copyediting*. (Worth noting is that copyediting is a less-costly budget line than developmental editing, thus the merger of developmental editing into copyediting rather than vice-versa.)

This merger by publishers is also reflected in dissatisfaction expressed by authors over the editing that is done. Authors see the edited manuscript either as proof pages or as marked-up copy (usually using Word's track changes). The real problem is when authors first see the edited version in proof pages, without the benefit of seeing all the work that the editor did clearly defined. Authors tend to see every error that remains as a major error and vocally complain. They forget that the purpose of the proof is to catch the errors that slipped past during copyediting or that may have been introduced during the copyediting and typesetting processes.

The balance is off-kilter. The expectations of authors and publishers soar as the various editorial roles are blended, yet the output of the editors cannot keep up with those expectations for numerous reasons, not least of which are insufficient time allocated by the client to do the tasks and inadequate compensation.

It isn't clear to me what an editor can do in the face of these changes. Today, editors are caught between the increased demands of clients and the increased competition among editors for work. The one thing there is no shortage of is the number of people who call themselves editors; the number of "editors" rises daily and, as that number increases, there is a downward pressure applied to compensation and an upward pressure applied to the number of tasks expected to be performed by the editor—too many editors are competing for that shrinking pot of available work.

Little by little, the face of editing is changing. Whether it is really for the better for anyone—author, publisher, or editor—is questionable. Editing is a hands-on task that requires sufficient time and expertise to do competently, let alone well, yet all parties are losing sight of this, as the growing requirements with reduced time allocations attest.

6

The Blurring of Roles and the Downward Pressure on Price

When hired to "edit," are you hired to be a developmental editor? A copyeditor? A proofreader? A compositor? Is what you are being paid commensurate with what you are being asked to do?

Today, many clients are using the term *proofreading* as an all-inclusive term, one that incorporates the "whatever is needed" concept. The problem with not clearly separating and defining the various tasks, and clarifying with the client precisely what they want, is that most publishers pay a lesser fee for proofreading than for editing. By not establishing the parameters, you give away your skills. Clients expect it, but I am not yet prepared to do that.

What is happening in our editorial world is that globalization has combined with the quartet of recession, consolidation, rapid growth in freelance editor ranks, and lack of in-house jobs to put downward pressure on pricing. Consequently, instead of price rising with skill level and experience, we see it flattening or declining as a result of our need to compete with colleagues around the world. This is a significant change from when I first entered this world of editing 27 years ago.

More importantly, this globalization + quartet of downward pressure on pricing has also led to the blurring of roles. I have found that the younger and less experienced the in-house editor I deal with is, the more blurry the demarcation. Sadly, as the number of freelance editors grows, which happens on a daily basis, so grows the competition for editorial work. With that growth in competition, we see a "class" division between older, more-experienced editors and younger, less-experienced editors, with the former trying to unblur the roles and distinguish via price the different skills required for the different roles, and the latter accepting the blurring of roles and the accompanying lower price in exchange for work.

This downward pressure, however, has moved editorial work into the technological age, something that was actively and vociferously opposed in my early years by many of my colleagues. Now, to make a good living from editorial work, we must incorporate things into our work efficiencies that can make parts of our work less labor-intensive, such as macros, using multiple monitors, and other labor-saving devices.

Yet even increased efficiencies and greater use of technology can only go so far. The real battle, the one that needs to be waged but isn't, is establishing a minimum worth for each of the different roles and insisting that the meaning of "edit" be clearly defined and appropriately compensated. Unfortunately, this is not a war that an individual editor can fight and win; it requires a group effort, and an organized group that speaks for freelance editors regarding work issues doesn't exist.

The difficulty is that the people doing the hiring do not understand the different roles and their parameters. They do not understand the differences in skills required or the value of experience. They are bound by imposed financial limits that compete with project needs; for example, they have a $1,000 budget even though it is clear that the project requires $3,000 worth of skilled labor. In the end, they compromise by hiring less-skilled editors who are willing to work for the budgeted price, knowing that they will not get all of the needed work done at the needed level of expertise. These same editors are willing to do editing work—sometimes substantive work—at proofreading prices, just to get any work or pay at all.

Unfortunately, the ramifications of this "dumbing/pricing down" extend far beyond the borders of traditional publishing and into nontraditional publishing. Editors who work in traditional publishing become acclimatized to this blurring and price pressure and begin to accept it as "normal" or "standard." This acceptance then does become the standard and so is extended to all facets of publishing, cheapening the end product. All that everyone is interested in is the financial bottom line; lost is the idea of product quality or any differentiation in skills between editing/levels of editing and proofreading.

Editorial work, like authorial work, is labor intensive. Labor-intensive products, unlike mass-production products, see a degradation in quality as price lowers (interestingly, it does not necessarily see an increase in quality as price rises; it appears that quality and price are only linked in the downward spiral). The acceptance of the financial bottom line as the paramount concern, however, means that quality has little to no role to play.

I think it will be interesting to see how low the editorial bottom line will go in future years and how we will react to that lowering. I'm certain of one thing: Were I to be starting my career path today, I would think long and hard about choosing this path.

7

A Rose by Another Name Is Still Copyediting

I recently received an e-mail from a long-ago client who lost my services when they lowered their payscale to substarvation rates and began off-shore outsourcing nearly 100% of their production process, the exception supposedly being proofreading, for which they paid sub-substarvation prices. Their e-mail stated:

> We are a new team with a new process, but still need qualified readers for our books, so I hope you don't mind that we are contacting you at this time.
>
> We now do all of our composition and copyediting in India. However, we do put all of our books through a cold read using US-based freelancers. Our readers work on first proofs (PDFs) . . .
>
> The assignment involves checking grammar, style (APA 6th Edition), punctuation, consistency, and poor phrasing. Rework awkward sentences only if confusing or very awkward. Feel free to query the Editor or Author. We realize there will be a lot of questions with this test and perhaps the first few assignments. When in doubt—make the change and add a query. We want to see your "stuff."

Needless to say, the rate of pay is very, very low. They attached a PDF "test," which they would pay me to take at the lowest rate they offer. The former client deserves a few kudos for at least offering to pay for the test-taking.

This is an interesting ploy for obtaining copyediting from American-based editors. Calling it a rose doesn't make it any less copyediting. It is worth noting that, by requiring it be done using a PDF rather than in Microsoft Word, the client is implying to most editors that it is *not* copyediting but proofreading, because experienced editors will tell you that the trend is to do proofreading in PDFs. Very few publishers, especially when dealing with book-length projects, will ask for copyediting to be done using PDFs. It is much more difficult to edit a PDF than it is to edit a Word document, as many of the tools that editors use in the editing process are simply unavailable, including specialty spell-checking and the myriad macros that editors use.

The attached "test" was a PDF of composed pages. But *if* it was already satisfactorily edited (which I would assume, because why would a publisher knowingly send a manuscript out for editing to incompetent editors?), the "cold reader"—also known as a proofreader—should not be checking "poor phrasing" or "rework[ing] awkward sentences." Those are editing tasks; they require decision-making skills, knowledge of grammar, and specialized subject-matter language, all of which are why the editor creates a stylesheet that is supposed to accompany the manuscript when it is sent for proofreading.

But call it what you want—rose, stinkweed, proofreading, cold reading—it doesn't matter: The service they want is copyediting and they want it at substarvation pay.

The e-mail follows a recent trend among publishers. The trend is to offshore outsource copyediting and then ask the local people whom the publisher previously hired to do the editing, to "proofread" at a rate that matches what the publisher is paying its offshore editors while simultaneously demanding that the "proofreader" correct all of the errors introduced or not fixed by the offshore editors. Publishers are squeezing local editors by taking away the work and then trying to get the same work after the fact under another guise, one that has always commanded a lesser fee.

In an attempt to lower costs, proofreading is now the new copyediting and copyediting is now the new typesetting/composition. Yes, I know that traditionally typesetting/composition meant simply putting the tendered manuscript into a WYSIWYG form that was called pages and, for the most part, that is what is happening with outsourced offshored copyediting. Publishers are banking on local proofreaders to do the copyediting.

Not only is this sneaky, but it is also difficult to do well. Traditional proofreading meant comparing the typeset pages to the edited and coded manuscript that had already been copyedited, developmental edited, reviewed by in-house production staff, and reviewed and approved by the author to make sure that the typesetter didn't introduce new errors.

Much of this changed when publishers switched to electronic editing, as electronic editing reduced the likelihood of typesetting errors. Such errors weren't eliminated, merely exponentially reduced. With today's bean counters unwilling to assign much value to editorial skills, publishers are trying to squeeze more editorial work out of freelancers for less pay. As many authors have complained in recent years, this is a recipe for editorial disaster.

Copyediting (along with other forms of editing) is a skill set that becomes honed over the course of years. One doesn't simply hang out a shingle calling oneself an editor and suddenly become a highly competent editor. As with other skills, copyediting is a collection of myriad skills learned and honed over years of work and learning. It is not a wholly mechanical process; rather, it requires educated judgment calls.

It is this loss of perspective and experience that causes books that have been edited to seem as if they have never met the eyes of an editor. It is this loss that distinguishes a professionally edited, well-edited book from the amateur editor who is doing the editing for a neighbor as a favor.

It is this loss of perspective and experience that publishers seek to regain at a cheaper price by renaming the service they want as "cold reading" rather than copyediting. You can call a rose by another name, but it is still copyediting. It is this ploy that editors need to be aware of and need to say thanks, but no thanks to the "opportunity" being offered—especially if the opportunity is to do the editing in a software program that is really not designed for the task, such as editing in PDF format/software.

As the competition wars heat up, by which I mean as the ebook world with its lower profit margins overtakes the pbook world with its relatively higher profit margins, this ruse by publishers will gain momentum. The result will be increasing numbers of published books that make the literate reader grimace, with yet further squeezing of profit margins as readers rebel at paying high prices for poorly edited books.

Although bean counters have yet to grasp the notion, the long-term survival of publishers will depend as much on quality editing as on changing strategies to deal with ebooks. Editors do provide value, but need to receive value in exchange. Smart editors will just say no to opportunities disguised as roses that are really stinkweed.

8

LIGHT, MEDIUM, OR HEAVY?

One of the things I have never understood about my business is the concept of a client wanting a *light, medium,* or *heavy* edit. I've never understood it because these are words that really have no meaning when spoken in conjunction with *edit.*

(It is probably worth noting that these terms are used by publishers, not by authors. In the past, a manuscript was reviewed by in-house production editors for general problems and for anticipated difficulty of editing. The terms were then used to justify a lesser or higher fee to the copyeditor. Today, most publishers have a single fee and only skim the manuscripts in-house. No author has ever used those terms when describing what is wanted from me when hiring me to edit his or her manuscript.)

A professional editor gives a manuscript the edit it requires within the parameters of the job for which the editor was hired. If a client says to ignore references, I may ignore references, but if a client says a manuscript needs a heavy edit, I haven't got a clue of how my editing would—or should—differ from what I would do had the client asked for a light edit.

The three terms, instead, are signals to me as to how problematic the client believes a manuscript is. When a client asks for a light edit, I understand it to mean that the client believes the manuscript is in pretty good shape with no structural flaws and minimal grammar and spelling errors. Conversely, a heavy edit indicates to me that there are likely to be numerous structural flaws and lots of grammar and spelling errors, with medium edit falling somewhere between the two extremes.

Yet, there's the catch. Nearly all clients make the same mistake of confusing copyediting with developmental editing. In some cases, it is a mistake made out of ignorance; in other instances, it is a deliberate mistake made in hopes (perhaps even in expectation) that the editor will provide a developmental edit at the price of a copyedit.

This comes about because, for an editor, there really is no difference between light, medium, and heavy editing. A manuscript gets the edit it needs—except that edit is limited by whether the editor is hired to do a copyedit or a developmental edit. There are boundaries between the two that a professional editor will not cross in the absence of compensation.

Structural problems are a good example. The developmental edit is intended to deal with structural problems but not to focus much on grammar and spelling problems. In contrast, the copyedit is focused on grammar and spelling, and, except to note that there are structural problems, ignores structural problems. This is as it should be because the skills required and the time needed vary greatly. It is not uncommon to find that a developmental edit has a speed of one to two pages an hour, whereas a copyedit runs at six to 10 pages an hour.

The use of the terms *light, medium*, and *heavy* is problematic because clients and copyeditors are talking past each other when the terms are used. There is no common definition of what they mean and the client's use is usually based on a false assumption: that the copyeditor will do something different as part of the editing process based on the term chosen.

The assumption is false for many reasons, but the most fundamental reason is that, no matter how a client describes the edit, the copyeditor still needs to read and evaluate every word and all punctuation with the goal of ensuring that the manuscript communicates to readers. (Note that I have changed from the broader *editor* to the narrower *copyeditor*. This is because the problem particularly arises and is particularly acute when an editor is hired as a copyeditor rather than as a developmental editor.)

In my nearly 29 years of professional editing, I have not changed a single thing that I do as a copyeditor based on whether the client asks for a light, medium, or heavy edit. Copyediting is what it is; it doesn't change based on light, medium, or heavy.

But those terms do mean something to me as a copyeditor—or at least did in the past; perhaps not so much today. They are flags for the difficulties I can expect to encounter, which means they affect my estimation of the time it will take to edit a manuscript. In past years, I found the terms to be excellent indicators of what to expect; today, I find that they are rarely an accurate indicator. Instead, today, I find that the terms are used as substitutes for whether the manuscript is for a first edition or a revision; for whether the authors are known to be difficult or not difficult to work with; or for when a client wants an edit for a proofreading fee.

Invariably, when a publisher hires me to work on a first edition, I am told that the manuscript requires a heavy edit. When I am hired to work on the revision that will be the eighth edition of the book, I am invariably told it requires a light or medium edit, or I am told nothing at all, with the client assuming I understand that only a light or medium edit is required. So, as relatively meaningless as the terms were in the past, they have become even more irrelevant and meaningless today.

Except that I use those terms as a guide to negotiate schedule. For example, I was recently hired to edit a manuscript that was estimated to be 380 pages and to require a heavy edit. The schedule was two weeks. I immediately negotiated a longer schedule based on the client's claim that a heavy edit was required (the sample chapters the client sent didn't show any unusual problems, but there were a lot more chapters yet to come, so it was a guessing game). I subsequently renegotiated the newly negotiated schedule because, when I received the complete manuscript, the page count was 490—the combination of a heavy edit and more pages warranted a longer, just-in-case, schedule.

I think editors need to clearly separate what tasks they will do based on the *type of edit*—copyedit or developmental edit—that a client asks for and ignore requests for a light, medium, or heavy edit except insofar as such terms are viewed as descriptors of the number and type of problems anticipated and how they might affect the editing schedule. After all, how would you edit any differently a manuscript that was to be lightly edited from one that was to receive a medium or heavy edit? Wouldn't you (don't you) do all the same things regardless of the characterization of the edit?

One last note: Some clients do, in fact, pay more for a heavy edit and less for a light or medium edit. The number of publishers doing so is rapidly declining as the squeeze on editorial costs increases. But if you do have such a client, then the characterization is also important for setting the fee. Where this is the case, a more thorough evaluation of the manuscript is necessary to ensure that it has been properly characterized—especially as copyeditors do all the same things, regardless of the characterization of the edit.

9

THE ELUSIVE EDITORIAL HIGGS BOSON

Physicists believe that they have discovered the subatomic parti-cle—Higgs boson or "God particle"—that will help explain what gives all matter in the universe size and shape. For us editors, that "God particle" of editing remains elusive.

Editing is much more than looking at *Chicago* section 8.18 and apply-ing the "rule" that *president* is lowercase unless the president is named, as in "The president boasted versus "Boasting about his tenure, President Smith So, just as physicists search for the Higgs boson of life, I search for the Higgs boson of editing. What is the essence of editing that gives it life? That gives a well-edited manuscript style? That makes editing a great and learned profession? That sets editors apart from other users of the same language?

It is true that, these days, a goodly portion of an editor's time is spent on mechanical work. There is little genius in play when we manipulate a reference to make it conform to a set style. The genius is not in fixing those references, but in helping authors communicate their intent and meaning to readers, which is done by word choice and sentence structure.

It is true that today, for example, the meanings of *since* and *because* have so blurred and merged that they are nearly synonymous. Conse-quently, authors and editors often don't choose between them—each is viewed as a 100% substitute for the other. (And I also admit that there are only a handful of us editors, like me, who still insist on the difference and who are reluctant to embrace the "new" English. The dinosaurs, perhaps, of editing.)

Yet isn't there a subtle, oh so slight, yet meaningful difference between the two words? Doesn't *since* still cast off an aura of time passing? Doesn't *because* still conjure up its root in causation?

I raise the *since/because* issue because I see it as a good representation of the subtleties of the editorial God particle and the difficult search for that element. Just as we have a whisper of difference in today's meanings of *since* and *because,* so we have just a whisper of the existence of the editorial Higgs boson.

I asked a colleague whether she ever thought about the philosophical underpinnings of editing. She looked at me as if I was from another planet and said: "No, and I don't know of any editor who has done so." To be truthful, neither do I know any editor who has spent even a fleeting moment thinking about the philosophy of editing. Instead, we tend to focus on the job at hand; after all, thinking about philosophy (or philosophically) pays no bills.

But, as the years have passed, I have been increasingly thinking about the philosophy of editing. I know what good editing does (and perhaps why I am a good editor), which is this: Good editing enhances the communication between an author and a reader, making sure that the author says precisely what the author intends to say and that the reader understands what the author says as what the author intends it to say. Diagrammatically, the editor sits between the author and reader as the "translator," ensuring that communication flows unerringly. But that is only what makes for good editing; it doesn't address the loftier philosophy of editing.

The philosophy of editing seeks to answer the *why* questions, rather than the *what* or *how* questions—the philosophy, rather than the mechanics. Why do we choose particular structures? Why do we resist the singular *their*? Why does English lack Why is "to go boldly" not the same, or as understandable, as "to boldly go"? Why is the editor's role more like that of a librettist than a composer (and why is it that the composer gets all the credit)? Why is it that, in editing, there are only guides and not written-in-stone rules as in other learned professions?

And on and on go the questions—the questions for which there are no style guides to provide answers or to point the searcher in a search direction. But perhaps the overarching question—the question that truly embraces the philosophy of editing concept—is this: Why does editing lack a universally accepted and applied moral and ethical code of conduct; that is, one that is universally understood and accepted by all parties to the editorial transaction and to which all parties subject themselves?

Sure, there are rogue scientists and rogue soldiers and rogue priests and rogue politicians and rogue whatevers—but there are no rogue editors, because there are no ethical and moral expectations, outside the standard, run-of-the-mill, societal expectations, that are applicable to and bind the parties of an editorial transaction. And that is because there are no editors hunting for the editorial Higgs boson.

Editing should be a serious profession. Yes, I know that we editors claim we are a serious profession, but then we act otherwise. We do little to no deep thinking about our profession. (Consider this: Nearly all professions have a "think tank"—except editing. Nearly all professions have a lobbying group to promote their ideas and goals among policy makers and the public—except editing.) Individual writers may do little deep thinking about the philosophy of writing, but that gauntlet is picked up by those whose focus is on "literary criticism"—the H.L. Menckens and George Bernard Shaws and Michel Foucaults and Harold Blooms and Noam Chomskys, who are both writers and literary critics.

Literary criticism is based on the philosophical discussion of literature's methods and goals. The editorial Higgs boson could be defined as being "the philosophical discussion of editing's methods and goals." Where are the editors who focus on the philosophy of editing? Where are "the philosophical discussion of editing's methods and goals"?

Increasingly I am thinking about the philosophy of editing and I am searching for that editorial God particle—that wisp of truth that will change the profession of editing at its core, that will ultimately lead to the "laws" of editing. Just as physics and chemistry and language and business have their immutable laws (Murphy's being the most commonly invoked one that crosses all professional boundaries), so does editing—they just wait to be discovered.

Think about how a pursuit of the editorial Higgs boson could reshape the conversations that editors have amongst themselves. Instead of "What does *Chicago* say about *xyz*?" the question would become, "Why does *Chicago* say this about *xyz*?" and the discussion would be less about a supposed "this is the way it must be" to more like "should this be the way it is done?"

Such discussions might eventually lead to the creation—or perhaps more accurately, the recognition—of the 10 Editorial Commandments, which might govern all parties to the editorial transaction. At that moment in time, editing will be able to take its place in the pantheon of the great professions; the editorial Higgs boson will have been found.

What do you think? More importantly, if you were asked to contribute to the creation of the 10 Editorial Commandments, what would your contribution be?

10

EXPECTATIONS

The clash between client and editor often is caused by unmet expectations—the client's expectations as to what services the editor will provide within what timeframe and for what price.

In the negotiations between client and editor, the client wants more for less and the editor wants more for less: The client wants more work for less money, the editor wants more money for less work. This is just like every other business negotiation, except for one thing: Client and editor expectations are rarely expressed; the parties act as if the other side already knows what the other expects.

The clash arises because clients expect an editor to do whatever it takes to make the client's manuscript near-perfect, regardless of the balance between the expectation and the rate of pay/time given to do the work, and editors feel pressure to do whatever is needed to make a manuscript near-perfect, even if the pay, the time given to do the work, or both are inadequate. Both parties are wrong.

The most difficult thing to impress upon colleagues, something I have repeated over the years, is that compensation (which includes the time allotted to do the work) and work *must* correlate. If you are being paid a copyedit wage, then you copyedit, not developmental edit. If the manuscript needs a developmental edit, alert the client, explain why it is needed, and explain, for what should be at least the second time, why you are not doing it. And, clearly, if you are expected to do a developmental edit within a copyedit timeframe, explain—multiple times, if necessary—why you cannot.

Recently, an editor lamented that a client had an unrealistic expectation as regards how many pages an hour the editor should churn on a particular project. (I use *churn* to mean move through, to edit. Although technically this is not a correct use of the word, I find that the number of pages to edit in an hour has much in common with the idea of the frequent buying and selling of securities, which is a meaning of *churn*. *Churn out*, the transitive verb form, is perhaps closer in meaning to my use as editorial churn, in that it refers to producing mechanically or copiously, to which I would add nearly robotically.) The manuscript needed a developmental edit and the client expected not only the developmental edit but a churn rate of 10 to 12 pages an hour. The editor, however, was not being paid for such an edit.

The editor's obligation is to provide the best editing the editor can within the parameters set by the client. If the client's parameters include a churn of 10 to 12 pages an hour, then the editor should strive to meet that churn goal and do the best editing job that the editor can at that rate on that manuscript. If the editing level decreases because of the churn and the complexity of the manuscript, the editor also has an obligation to alert the client to the editing limitations that result because of the churn rate required. It is then the client's obligation to determine what balance is desirable.

But the immutable law, as far as I am concerned, is this: An editor does not owe a client a near-perfect edit of a manuscript; the editor owes the client the best edit that balances against the fiscal and time constraints imposed by the client—nothing more, nothing less. It is unreasonable to give a Mercedes performance when you are given a Yugo to drive. It is unreasonable to provide a Yugo when you want a Mercedes performance. Give a Yugo, receive a Yugo; give a Mercedes, receive a Mercedes.

I make it very clear to clients the difference between a copyedit and a developmental edit. I also make it clear that the faster the churn rate, the less careful the editing will be. Some clients expect not only a high churn rate but a multi-pass edit. Perhaps if the churn expectation is five pages an hour, it is reasonable to expect at least a two-pass edit, which makes the effective churn rate 10 pages an hour, but that is certainly not true when the churn expectation is 10 pages an hour, which would make the effective rate 20 pages an hour with a second pass.

However, there are two problems that must be addressed. Both stem from how the editor is paid. If an editor is on an hourly rate, the client often sets a budget based on the expected churn rate (i.e., manuscript size ÷ churn rate = number of hours; number of hours × hourly rate = budget). However, an editor may not be aware of the budget and thus expect that every hour spent editing will be compensated. If there is an upper limit, a budget amount, the editor needs to determine the maximum number of hours for which the client will pay and scale the editorial services accordingly. If the client is not forthcoming about the compensation limitations, then the editor needs to make it clear upfront that the editor expects to be paid for the time spent, regardless of whether it exceeds the client's budget (subject, of course, to ethical constraints).

If the editor is paid on a per-page or project basis, the total fee does not change, regardless of the number of hours. Consequently, if the editor spends 20 hours or 100 hours editing, the fee remains the same. As in the hourly situation, the editor needs to balance the fee the editor will receive against the client's editorial expectations—*before* beginning editing or by the time the first pages are edited. Exactly what services the editor will provide for the fee to be earned needs to be spelled out so that there is no confusion on the part of either party. However, should the editor not take this step and discuss any editing limitations, then, in the circumstance of the per-page or project basis for compensation, the client is entitled to Mercedes performance even if the editor is paid a Yugo fee—as long as the client has made the Mercedes expectation clear before the compensation was agreed to.

Sometimes there can be no meeting of the minds: The client is unwilling to lower expectations or raise the fee or do both. In this instance, the editor should bail from the project, assuming that this discussion is taking place at the beginning of the project and not in the middle. If in the middle of the project, the editor should offer the client the option to either pay for work done and find another editor to complete the project or to accept a defined level of editing that meets the client's churn expectations, even if it doesn't meet the client's editorial expectations, that would balance against the fee being paid.

The more clarity the editor brings to the project, by which I mean the more the editor explains the balance, the more likely it is that the editor and the client will work together amicably. It is important to remember that it is the editor who is initially dissatisfied with the lack of balance between expectations and pay; thus, it is the editor's obligation to educate the client as to the need for the balance and as to what will meet that need. The client's obligation is to listen, understand, and correct the imbalance in a way that is satisfactory to both the client and the editor.

But under no circumstance should the editor voluntarily (especially not while grumbling about it) accept the imbalance between expectation and compensation. Ultimately, the editor must say, "This is what I will do for this compensation—nothing more, nothing less—and I will do it expertly and professionally, but I will not provide [*fill in the blank, e.g., developmental edit*] for the price of [*e.g., a copyedit*]." Editors must educate their clients about editing, and not assume that clients are already educated about it.

Most importantly, editors must realize that this is a business relationship and must be treated as one. I understand the need of editors to do the near-perfect edit on every job. Unfortunately, our creditors are unwilling to accept a near-perfect edit as payment. An editor who feels she cannot compromise on the edit to be delivered, such as doing a one-pass edit when she would normally do a two-pass edit, should decline jobs that require compromised editing; happiness in what we do should be our number-one motivation.

11

THE COMMANDMENTS:
THOU SHALT USE A PROFESSIONAL EDITOR

My first commandment for authors is this: *Thou shalt use a professional editor!* I know I've said this before—many times—and I know that some of you will respond that you are capable of doing your own editing, or that crowd editing works just fine, or that your neighbor's nephew's sister-in-law, who taught fourth graders English, does a fantastic job. Yet, haven't you bought a book or two whose author you wanted to strangle because it was pretty obvious that a professional editor wasn't used (or the editor's advice wasn't followed)?

This is a topic that never dies.

Consider this statement: "Lobbyists fighting spending cuts find an ally in group that usually backs them" (*New York Times*, April 10, 2013, page A12). What is wrong with this statement? (It was an article headline, which accounts for its brusqueness.) Does your neighbor's nephew's sister-in-law know? I would guess that, if it passed muster at the *New York Times*, it would pass her muster and that of the crowd editors, too.

I read this statement several times because I couldn't quite figure out what was meant. Reading the article clarified the headline, but suppose I hadn't read the article? Or suppose this was a sentence in your book, albeit written with the missing prepositions as: "The lobbyists fighting spending cuts find an ally in a group that usually backs them." The question that needs to be asked is: "Does 'them' mean 'spending cuts' or 'lobbyists'?" Should the sentence be: "The lobbyists fighting spending cuts find an ally in a group that usually backs spending cuts" or "The lobbyists fighting spending cuts find an ally in a group that usually backs the lobbyists"?

Two distinct meanings are possible, yet most readers would not catch that possibility. And this is the problem with having your book "edited" by someone other than a professional editor. Experienced, professional editors are trained to catch these types of errors; they have spent years mastering the art of *not* reading what they expect but of reading what is actually before them.

As the example illustrates, not catching this error can lead to misunderstanding. It makes a difference whether "them" means "spending cuts" or "lobbyists." Readers will generally give more credence to the former than to the latter. After all, it has become clear in recent years, particularly with the intransigence of the Gun Owners of America and the National Rifle Association over the issue of background checks, that lobbyists are not among the favored species.

There is a second aspect to this commandment, which is the professional editor's fee. Think about how you work. Would you not agree that the less you are paid (or anticipate being paid), the less diligent you are in your work? What I mean is this: If you are currently paid $20 an hour and are satisfied with that sum for your current job, you perform your work diligently. If your employer comes to you and says that, although your job will remain the same, your pay henceforth will be $10 an hour, are you likely to be as diligent? Or will you consider cutting corners? Most people would be less diligent and would cut corners.

Editors—professional and amateur alike—are no different. If you have a 50,000-word manuscript (approximately 200 manuscript pages), do you honestly think that the editor who is being paid $300 will be as thorough and professional as the editor who is being paid $1,500? How fast will the editor need to go through your manuscript to earn a living wage? Do you expect that an editor who has to work faster will be as accurate as the editor who can take more time?

Most editors do multiple passes; this is especially true when the project is fiction and it is important to first grasp the whole story and get a feel for the characters. How many passes do you think that editor who is paid $300 will do? And, if the editor is doing the project at their own expense (i.e., as part of a crowd edit or as a friend for free), how thorough an edit and how many passes is it reasonable to expect? How many passes would you do if it meant giving up your leisure time?

Again, we all know people who would sacrifice their first-born to do a good job because they volunteered to do so, but that is the gamble you take. And the gamble can be devastating if it is lost. For an author, how many bad reviews can your book withstand? How many two- and three-star reviews that complain about the grammar would it take to sink your ability to sell your book, even at $2.99? (For an editor, how many times can you afford to do developmental editing for proofreading fees before you can't pay your bills? How many such projects will it take to kill your love for the craft of editing or the freedom of freelancing?)

Professional editors are word doctors for authors. Just as you (or I) would not undertake to self-treat for cancer, we should not self-treat our books, which are significant parts of our lives. Just as we would go to the doctor about our cancer, so we should go to the professional editor about our manuscript.

One reason we go to the doctor to have our cancer treated is because the doctor has experience in dealing with cancer. We rely on the doctor's accumulated knowledge to tell us how serious a problem we have and for suggestions about courses of treatment. We know doctors are not perfect, but we expect them to be better than our neighbor's nephew's sister-in-law who taught health sciences at the high school.

All we need do is substitute professional editor for doctor and the argument is made: One reason we go to the professional editor to have our manuscript edited is because the professional editor has experience in dealing with manuscripts. We rely on the professional editor's accumulated knowledge to tell us about any manuscript problems and for suggestions about how to correct them. We know professional editors are not perfect, but we expect the professional editor to be better than our neighbor's nephew's sister-in-law who taught English to fourth graders (or even at the local college).

When an author hires a professional editor, the author is hiring experience with manuscripts and the knowledge that the editor has accumulated about how to structure and tell a story (*all* manuscripts tell a story) so that the author's message is communicated and received. You spent months, if not years, of your life putting together a story that you want more than a handful of friends to read and understand. Should you not, then, hire a professional editor and pay an appropriate fee for that editor's services to ensure that your manuscript is ready and is the best it can be?

Thus, the first commandment for authors: **Thou shalt use a professional editor!**

12

THE COMMANDMENTS:
THOU SHALT TREAT EDITORS AS PARTNERS

We recently edited a new book that was badly written. Not only was it badly written, but we were financially and time-wise constrained. So, as we typically do, we did the best we could within the limitations imposed.

The usual process is for us to receive a manuscript that an author has already gone through a few times and often has had crowd-edited by friends and colleagues. In addition, it has received whatever developmental editing it will receive. We are hired to copyedit the manuscript. After we have copyedited the manuscript, it goes back to the author to approve or reject any changes we have made, to answer/address any author queries we have inserted, and to give it yet another read in case we missed something.

This last step is important. Like authors, we editors are human and we make mistakes and we do miss things that seem very obvious. In this particular editing job, the editor missed a very obvious error. The author had written "Jack and Jill is a married couple" and the editor failed to change the *is* to *are*. Out of more than 100 changes the editor made to this particular chapter, the editor missed this change, but that was enough. The author latched onto this error and wrote: "I suggest you review the edited pages I sent in and develop a list for you to use when speaking with the editor of this project. As I am not compensated to help you do your job, I will offer the most blatant example and then let you do your due diligence on your end."

This author ignored the commandment: *Thou shalt treat the editor as a partner, not as an adversary.*

I looked at the "edited" pages the author had returned and found only one change the author had made (added a description), which was clearly not a change because of an editing error. Aside from that one change and a comment that praised a rewording done by the editor, the author noted no other "errors." So I went through the particular chapter and a couple of others to see if I could figure out what the author's complaint was, but I couldn't find anything.

The author failed to treat the editor as a partner; instead, the editor was treated as an adversary. First, by not listing or identifying what the author perceived as errors. It is difficult to address unidentified "errors." Second, the author made a general, broad-brush complaint. This is not helpful to anyone. The author failed to understand that the editing of his book is a collaborative process between the editor and the author, not an adversarial process. The professional editors I know are willing to correct errors they have made, but they are not willing to keep reediting a manuscript simply because an author proclaims dissatisfaction (and especially if the author is rude).

The third error this author (and many authors) made is refusing to understand and accept the parameters of the editing process for which the editor was hired. For example, this author also complained about the layout (not an editor's job at all) and about the failure of the copyeditor to provide both a copyedit and a developmental edit.

The fourth and most important error the author made is to believe that to point out errors is doing the editor's job and that the author has no role in doing so because the author is "uncompensated." The author is the one who has everything at stake, not the editor. The book will be published in the author's name, not the editor's name. Any error that remains will be attributable to the author, not to the anonymous editor. As the largest stakeholder in the final manuscript, the author does have a responsibility to identify perceived errors.

I find it troubling that an author would look at 100 errors, find 99 of them corrected, but ignore the 99 and rant about the one that was missed (the author should point out the error, but not go on a rant about the editing). I also find it troubling that an author willingly ignores the sorry state of the delivered manuscript and the time and financial constraints under which the editor is working, and focuses on the one error, which error was introduced by the author.

Authors need to look at the manuscript broadly and not focus on one or two errors that slip past the editor. Authors need to remember that editors are human and suffer from the same problem as do authors: They sometimes see what they expect to see. We are not immune just because we are editors. Authors also need to recognize that the editor could have as easily caught the error about which the author is now complaining, but missed one of the other 99 errors.

Authors need to recognize that the editorial process is a collaborative process. If an author is reviewing an edited manuscript, the author should at least point out the missed error. The author could also correct it.

In this case, the author was uninterested in the constraints under which the editor worked. When publishers and authors demand a short editing schedule, they have to expect errors to remain. Something has to give to meet the schedule; the most obvious thing to give is a second pass. This is especially true when the client demands that material be submitted in batches.

As many of us have experienced, publishers and authors are also putting pressure on pricing. For many authors and publishers, the paramount consideration is price, followed by meeting a short schedule. Quality takes a backseat to those requirements. Low price and fast schedule cannot equate to a perfect edit. A perfect edit takes time.

Authors *do* have responsibilities when it comes to their manuscripts. To think otherwise is to end in the publication of a poorly prepared manuscript. Authors need to think of editors as their partners, not as their adversaries. Authors also need to get away from the false demarcations of who is responsible for what when it comes to their manuscripts.

Thus the commandment for authors: **Thou shalt treat your editor as a partner, not as an adversary!**

13

Relationships and the Unwritten Rules

Every relationship is governed by rules. It doesn't matter whether the relationship is between spouses, parent and child, government and citizen, rock and hard place, or authors and editors. If there is a relationship, there are rules that govern it.

Some of the rules are written. The relationship between spouses is partially governed by the rules (laws) enacted by their place of domicile or even by a prenuptial agreement. Similarly, sometimes some of the rules that govern the relationship between author and editor are written, such as when there is a contract between them.

But the majority of the rules that govern relationships are unwritten. They come about as a result of the values we have absorbed each day that we live. We begin as a blank slate and, with each day that passes, we gain a little bit more of our moral compass. It is these unwritten rules that are the more important rules.

In the author-editor relationship, it is the unwritten rules that are most important. I do not disagree with the notion that a written agreement that says author shall pay editor $x on y date is not important; rather, I believe that the moral compulsion for the author to actually make the payment is the more important part of the relationship. As I used to tell clients when I practiced law, an honest handshake was much more valuable than a dishonest signature on a contract.

One unwritten rule (really, a group of rules) in the author-editor relationship addresses responsibilities. Who is responsible for what. Left unsaid, just like the rule is left unsaid, are the reasons why the author has certain responsibilities and the editor has others. But these unwritten rules, which are often the basis for controversy between the author and editor, are the rules that form the foundation of the relationship. In their absence, chaos reigns; in their presence, a foundation for dispute resolution is available.

What brings this to mind is a recent experience I had with an author. Let me be clear about several things. First, I did not have a direct relationship with the author; my direct client was a third party who hired and paid me. Second, the parameters of the work I was to perform were negotiated between my client and the author. My client relayed the decisions made between the author and them to me.

Even though there was no direct relationship between the author and me, the unwritten rules of responsibility were still applicable.

The parameters of the job were to copyedit the author's 400-page manuscript on specialized financing within eight workdays. The edit was specified as "light," a term that really has no meaning but indicates that neither the author nor the client thought there were major problems with the manuscript.

It is important to note that my company was hired to perform a copyedit, not a developmental edit, and that there was a rush schedule. The normal process, and the one I expected to be followed, was copyediting, return to author to accept or reject copyediting, proofreading, publication.

After the book was printed, reviewers began panning it. Complaints about content, editing, and proofreading arose, with some complaints about comprehensibility. The author was incensed and decided that all the fault was with the third party. The author demanded that my client, the third party, insert author corrections into the manuscript and reprint the book. The author provided a PDF of the book with author corrections added. Needless to say, my client was not happy.

I was asked to review the author's complaints and the editing, and advise my client. My client provided me with the reviewer's comments, the printer file, and the author-corrected files; I had my own copies of the edited manuscript that I had submitted to my client. (I make it a point to keep copies of what I submit to clients for years.) Let me say upfront that I have an excellent relationship with my client and have edited numerous books for them. This kerfuffle has no effect on our relationship; the question is how to respond to the author.

I spent some time going through the author's complaints. Two of the author's complaints regarding mistakes in spelling that we missed were justified. We probably shouldn't have missed them. On the other hand, there were more than a dozen errors surrounding those missed spellings that we did catch, including one that resulted in an AQ (author query) regarding the word immediately adjacent to one of the missed spelling errors.

The reviewer specifically quoted a sentence that the reviewer found incomprehensible. The reviewer was certainly correct, but the evolution of that sentence is what intrigues me. It turns out that the copyedited version that we submitted differs from the version that was printed. The author rejected one of the editor's suggested changes to the sentence and made a couple of additional changes that we knew nothing about.

Another complaint was that a theory name was misspelled (the name began *Sho* when it should have been *Scho*) and the editor didn't catch the misspelling. I searched the entire book and discovered that the name appeared twice in the book, both times spelled the same way by the author (i.e., spelled incorrectly), with more than 200 pages separating the two appearances.

I think you are getting the idea.

I then looked at the author's corrected files to see what corrections were being proposed as necessary because of editing errors. This was revelatory. Some of the corrections were rewrites that added additional information that could not be gleaned from any of the surrounding material. There was nothing particularly wrong with the sentences before the additions, but the additions did add clarification. The question is, "How would the editor know to add the clarifying material?"

Other corrections made incomprehensible what began as poor writing; that is, the corrections would do more harm than good. Importantly, a large number of them were simply wrong, such as adding commas where no comma belongs, deleting a word or two so that a sentence went from poorly written to incomprehensible, adding a misspelled word or the wrong word to an otherwise difficult sentence, and so on.

Bottom line is that most of the author's proposed corrections would make things worse, not better. And that the author was demanding rewrites, not pinpointing editing errors or oversights.

One other thing I noted is that some of the errors the author complained of should have been caught by a proofreader. Whether the manuscript was proofread or not, I do not know, but I do know that if it was proofread, the proofreader was not a professional, or at least not one I would consider professional. More importantly, the author should have caught these errors during the author review.

The author also refuses to accept that there is a difference between a developmental edit and a copyedit, that separate fees are charged for each service, and that the author paid only for a copyedit.

The question is the unwritten relationship rules: who has responsibility for what. It is not that there weren't some editor errors; there were. However, all of the editor errors could have been and should have been caught by the proofreader and the author during their review. It is one reason why there are proofreading and author reviews.

More important, however, is that the responsibility for a manuscript is a shared responsibility. This author insists that the responsibility lies solely with the editor. The author refuses to accept the idea that the author-editor relationship is a partnership and that the editor's responsibilities are limited by the parameters imposed, ultimately, by the author; the author denies the commandment we discussed in *The Commandments: Thou Shalt Treat Editors as Partners*.

Ultimately, my client has to make a political decision: Should they appease the author or stand their ground? I think they have a solid basis for standing their ground. The book desperately needed a developmental edit, but no one wanted to spend the money to have it done. The author did not determine in advance what was needed and expected by way of a copyedit. For example, the author assumed that fact checking was automatically included, yet did not specify that as one of the tasks, did not pay for it, and did not allot sufficient time for it to be done (remember that the editing schedule was eight workdays).

Realistic—and knowledgeable—division of responsibility is important in the author-editor relationship. As an unwritten rule, however, division of responsibility is so fluid that it is easy for one party to attempt to shift what should be their responsibility to the other party. Both the author and the editor should give careful thought to the division of responsibility before they begin the relationship and should recognize that such division is governed by the parameters set for the project.

More importantly, authors should clearly state, in writing, their expectations and the services they want an editor to perform, and be prepared to pay for those services.

14

THE MISSING INGREDIENT: GRAMMAR SKILLS

Over the past several weeks, I have had opportunities to speak with the heads of production at several of my clients. After our direct business discussions, we sort of wandered off-topic to discuss the current state of copyediting and copyeditors.

What I found interesting was that each of the people I spoke with had the same lament: There is a dearth of copyeditors with good grammar skills. What they have noticed is the wide gap in skill level between those who are nearing retirement (high on the skill scale) and those now entering the field or who have been in the field for only a few years (low on the skill scale).

Grammar and spelling skills appear to be declining among editors, or so I was told. These clients believe that editors increasingly are relying on software programs to tell them when there is a grammar or spelling error, and taking the software's suggested correction without exercising the independent judgment that is required to determine whether the software is correct.

What brought this up was my mentioning that I occasionally speak at gatherings of freelancers about the business of freelance editing. In each instance, the client suggested that it would be significantly more beneficial—for both the client and the copyeditors seeking business—if grammar were addressed. One client said that, of 100 editing tests administered, they were lucky if one got a passing grade and that it was rare for testees to get very high passing grades.

Another problem they all cited was the obvious reliance on spell-checker. One client wondered if the editors even owned printed dictionaries and usage guides or, if they did, whether the editors knew how to use them. Two examples were cited: The first was *there* and *their*. The client remarked that it was not unusual, anymore, to receive a copyedited manuscript with the incorrect term left as presented by the author. The second was *that* and *who*. Apparently people have become objects and many copyeditors do not correct a sentence such as "The students and teachers that became" or "The patients that were tested." Other examples given were *that* and *which* and *since* and *because*.

I don't know if the full cause of the problem can be laid at the feet of the education system, but certainly a significant portion of it can. I know that, when my children were in school, grammar was barely touched on as a subject; it was far less emphasized than during my school days. I also know that, when I look at the writing of many educators, there is a clear lack of facility with grammar. This is not to say that the best of us don't make grammar mistakes; rather, the problem is that what was once occasional error has become commonplace.

Yet, the question is this: How many copyeditors recognize that their grammar skills are less than stellar and would be willing to pay to attend a conference devoted to improving grammar skills? I suspect, based on conversations that I have had with colleagues, that most think the problem is not their problem but is that of someone else. It is the state of humanness that lets us readily perceive the faults of others but not our own.

I expect the problem to get worse long before it gets better. Unless how teachers are taught/educated undergoes significant reform and a new emphasis is placed on communication skills that include grammar, spelling, and writing, I do not think improvement will occur. As the transmitters of knowledge, teachers have to be the first to gain it.

It also may symptomatic of today's culture. In my youth, one way grammar skills were picked up was by osmosis—reading well-edited books, magazines, and newspapers could only lead to absorption of some of the "rules." But today, reading overall is in decline. Interestingly, what is on the incline are those tasks that reward brevity and substitution—all that matters is that the general message be sent and understood; the Twittering of grammar.

It doesn't help that we are in an age of anyone who wants can publish. It means that a lot of grammatically and spelling-poor material is available for reading, which only acts to reinforce poor habits. Is there an easy solution? No. But based on the discussions I had with clients, there is a definite need for copyeditors to recognize their limitations and voluntarily undertake the effort to improve their skills.

What do you think? Would you pay for a grammar-focused class or do you think you already have a high skill level?

15

PROFESSIONAL EDITORS:
PUBLISHERS AND AUTHORS NEED THEM—PART I

One way to distinguish between a professional editor and your neighbor who poses as one is by their resource library. The professional editor knows that, to do a quality job, one needs to have good resources and to be familiar with them. The Internet is not a substitute for a professional editor's library (would you trust your doctor's drug guide to Wikipedia?). Professional editing *does* equate with a quality book.

Professional editors are familiar with and use style guides, for example, *The Chicago Manual of Style; Scientific Style and Format; AMA Manual of Style;* and *Publication Manual of the American Psychological Association.* There are more—lots more. It seems that every professional and academic discipline has its own style. Professional editors also own and use language usage guides, which are discussed in Part II of this essay.

Style guides are important because a good author is a storyteller but not necessarily a good writer. Good writing includes logical organization and making sure that there is a flow and consistency to a story. It does no good, for example, to begin a chapter in the year 1861 and suddenly, three paragraphs later, the year is 1965, unless the paragraphs between transition the reader from 1861 to 1965.

Think of the chaos there would be if a book's references were formatted willy-nilly, or capitalization shifted all over the place, or spelling changed page by page, or compound adjectives (the hyphenated kind) were sometimes hyphenated and sometimes not. How would meaning be transferred from author to reader?

English was a language with no rules until a few hundred years ago. Then authors began to realize that they could no longer read and understand writings from 100 years earlier, and wondered whether their work would be readable 100 years later. Thus began the quest to standardize English. English is still an unruly language, thus the need for style guides—style guides bring order to chaos. Style guides help ensure consistency so that authors can write and know that how their book uses language will convey the author's meaning—today and tomorrow—because everyone is on the same page.

True, the average reader doesn't read with the *Chicago Manual of Style* next to them. Most readers don't know it exists. It is the publisher and the editor who need to know and need to apply the rules—as arbitrary as they may be—to the author's manuscript. Why? So that a diverse population with diverse linguistic skills can join together and understand the author's work. The style guides provide a common meeting ground and act as arbiters of language, broadening the ability of the audience to read and understand the author's words. More importantly, by bringing order to chaos, the rules heighten quality—something publishers need to do in the age of ebooks.

The professional editor is a master of the relevant style guides and knows the rules of grammar, syntax, spelling, and other language conventions. Professional editors continuously invest in the tools of their profession and tend to read widely. Professional editors know that their primary responsibilities are to ensure consistency, accuracy, and universality, by which I mean that the author's work meets and embraces language conventions that ensure the widest possible audience can read and understand the author's work: The professional editor is a communication enhancer who firms up the link between the author and the reader.

Alas, publishers and authors often look for the least expensive way to produce a book, which means that professional editors with skills, experience, and knowledge are often not hired. Why? Because the professional editor's work is not readily discernible. A professional editor's work is like polishing silver—adding shine and luster, not replacing the silver.

A smart author will insist on the publisher hiring a professional editor; a smart publisher will insist on hiring a professional editor and pay a professional price, recognizing that poor editorial work tarnishes the author's—and publisher's—silver. A professional editor's sure hand can make the difference between an also-ran and a bestseller.

Both authors and publishers should recognize that there is more to being a professional editor than simply calling oneself an editor.

16

PROFESSIONAL EDITORS:
PUBLISHERS AND AUTHORS NEED THEM—PART II

As noted in Part I, one way to distinguish between a professional editor and your neighbor who poses as one is by their style guide library. The professional knows that, to do a good job, one needs to have good resources and to be familiar with them. The Internet is not a substitute for a professional editor's library.

In addition to style manuals, a professional editor's library includes usage books, that is, books that discuss and provide guidance on correct usage of language. For example, my library includes *Garner's Modern American Usage; Merriam Webster's Dictionary of English Usage; Mathews' Dictionary of Americanisms; The American Heritage Guide to Contemporary Usage and Style; Brown's Composition of Scientific Words; The BBI Dictionary of English Word Combinations; The New Fowler's Modern English Usage;* H.L. Mencken's multivolume work *The American Language: An Inquiry into the Development of English in the United States;* and *Sheehan's Word Parts Dictionary,* among other language resources.

We haven't even gotten to the dictionaries and grammar guides, or the books about language cognition and origins, all of which form a part of a professional editor's library. The editor's resource library is an important facet of what distinguishes the professional from the casual editor. Another facet is the professional editor's skill with and knowledge of these resources.

Authors and publishers who care about the quality of their books care about the professionalism of their editors. They recognize that a professional editor is skilled and knowledgeable and brings something important to the book: the firming of the communication link between the author and the reader.

It is this communication link to which the usage guides are inextricably connected. Usage guides help an editor choose the right word. Is it *Arkansan, Arkansawyer,* or *Arkie*? How about *aren't I* vs. *amn't I* vs. *an't I*? Given the choice, which of the following is the superior phrase: *catch fire* or *catch on fire*? Or *cater-corner* vs. *catter-corner* vs. *kitty-corner*?

A professional editor considers who is the intended audience for the book. If a book is being written for a local audience, then localisms may be excellent word choices, although not so fine for a national audience. But what about a term that has been broadly heard but little understood?

Recently, I read a news article that used the term *mugwump*. How many readers understood the term or its origins? A professional editor would look at the context and apply the correct definition. Before the 1880s, mugwump meant an important person, the high-muck-a-muck. In the 1880s, it became transformed to refer to Republicans who supported the Democrats' presidential candidate. Today it means an independent. Is this important? If you are writing a book whose events take place in 1884, don't you want your readers to understand what the term meant in 1884, not what it means today or meant in 1801?

So we return to the question of book quality. It is these skills and knowledge that professional editors bring to a manuscript. But publishers are increasingly less interested in those skills and knowledge because their accountants see no financial gain in emphasizing editorial quality. And authors too often believe that their manuscripts as given to the publisher are "perfect"; they see no gain in paying for a professional editor, much less any editing at all.

A book's quality is amalgam of multiple endeavors, not least of which is the author's original creativity. Equally important, however, is editing by a professional who respects his or her profession enough to invest time and money in continuously acquiring and fine-tuning the skills, knowledge, and resources that distinguish the professional editor from all other claimants to the editorial mantle. Publishers and authors who fail to recognize that distinction—between professional and nonprofessional editing—embark on the road to mediocre quality at best.

This mediocrity brings with it a backlash from consumers who are unwilling to pay the wanted price, who do not buy future books written by the author, and who give negative reviews. This backlash is increasingly evident in the ebookers' revolt over pricing and quality in ebooks.

Publishers need to recognize that they cannot continue to pay slave wages and expect professional editing—the two simply *do not* go hand-in-hand. Professional editing and quality *do*, however, go hand-in-hand.

Part II

TOOLS

"As efficient as your process is, it is not efficient enough!"

—*Richard H. Adin, An American Editor*

A skilled, professional editor relies on a variety of tools to do the job well, as well as efficiently and economically. This section looks at hardware, software, online, bookshelf, and other tools that can make the difference between a professional and an amateur editor, and even between a successful and a struggling one.

17

THE PROFESSIONAL EDITOR'S BOOKSHELF

I have been a professional editor for more than 25 years and, during those years, I have purchased, read, and used numerous references. Even now, I look for additional language reference books to buy.

There is no list of must-have reference books that *every* professional editor must own or have immediate access to, with the possible exception of standard dictionaries; which books should be part of an editor's reference library depends a great deal on the types of manuscripts the editor works on and the type of editing performed (by which I mean whether one does developmental editing, copyediting, or both).

One book every editor should have (in addition to dictionaries) is the appropriate style manual. There are many style manuals available; even news organizations like the New York Times and Associated Press have their own style manuals. Sometimes the required style manual is nothing more than the grammar and style rules created by the client, but usually it is one of the standard manuals, such as the *Publication Manual of the American Psychological Association, The Chicago Manual of Style*, the *MLA (Modern Language Association) Style Manual and Guide to Scholarly Publishing*, the *AMA (American Medical Association) Manual of Style*, and the Council of Science Editors' *Scientific Style and Format*, to name but a few. It is the style manual that is the arbiter of the rules to be applied to a manuscript; for example, how a reference is to be styled, how a quotation is to be delineated, whether serial commas should be used, whether prefixes should be hyphenated or closed up, whether a phrase should be hyphenated, etc.

In addition to the appropriate style manual, an editor's bookshelf must contain at least one dictionary, although many editors will have several.

Two of my favorite dictionaries are *The American Heritage Dictionary of the English Language* and *Merriam-Webster's Collegiate Dictionary*. Although one would think that all dictionaries are the same, they are not, and clients often have a preference. Along with a standard language dictionary, specialized dictionaries often are needed. For example, medical editors often own several medical specialty dictionaries, such as *Stedman's Medical Dictionary*, *Dorland's Illustrated Medical Dictionary*, and the *APA Dictionary of Psychology*, in addition to the standard English language dictionaries.

My bookshelf also includes "word" books; that is, books that are lists of accepted words and their spelling for a particular specialty subject area. Because I do a lot of medical editing, I have numerous medical word books. Specialty areas, like medicine, also require specialty reference books. My medical library, for example, includes several drug reference manuals, drug interaction guides, and medical test guides. And because a lot of my specialty work also includes chemical compounds, my library also includes chemical reference books like *The Merck Index*.

But my bookshelf also includes books devoted to language usage, such as *Garner's Modern American Usage*, *The American Heritage Guide to Contemporary Usage and Style,* and *Merriam Webster's Dictionary of English Usage*. These are the books that go into detailed explanation of when, for example, *which* is correct rather than *that*, and the difference between *farther* and *further* in usage.

Usage books only tell part of the story. Another part is told in a word's or phrase's history (etymology). Some of this information is available in the standard dictionary, especially the *Oxford English Dictionary* and the *American Heritage Dictionary of the English Language*, as well as from specialty books like *A Dictionary of Americanisms, Chambers Dictionary of Etymology,* and *The Oxford Dictionary of Word Histories*. These resources are valuable in determining whether a word or phrase is being used appropriately.

Also useful are texts that help an editor analyze the roots and origins of a word, especially when an author uses a wholly unfamiliar word, including one not found in the standard language references, or creates a new word. *Composition of Scientific Words* is particularly helpful with science words and the *Word Parts Dictionary* is useful with standard English words.

In addition to books about words, a professional editor's bookshelf includes books about grammar. Grammar books also address the correct word issue, but the focus is more on correct sentence structure; for example, the restrictive versus the nonrestrictive clause, use of commas, passive versus active voice, and the like. I suspect many editors make use of *The Gregg Reference Manual* when grammar questions arise.

Some editors rely on online resources in this Internet Age. I find that troublesome to the extent that there is no assurance of reliability or accuracy. I know the source of my *Merriam-Webster's Collegiate Dictionary*, but have no idea of the source for or accuracy of a Wikipedia article. Having grown up in the print age, I am not comfortable relying on the Internet as the source of my information. But making use of online resources is also an important part of an editor's job; the key is knowing which resources to accept and which to reject. A professional editor can knowledgeably make that decision.

Why is the editor's bookshelf important? Because it helps separate the professional editor from the amateur. The professional editor has a deep interest in language and how language is used. The professional editor wants to improve communication between the author and the reader. The professional editor devotes significant time and resources to mastering language so that, when a manuscript leaves the editor's hands, it is better communicates the author's message. Nonprofessional editors do not make the investment nor work to master the language skills that are needed.

The difference between a professional and a nonprofessional editor can be the difference between clear communication and miscommunication of an author's message. The comprehensiveness of the editor's bookshelf, the editor's resources, is a clue to the editor's professionalism, and something that every author should be interested in.

18

ON MY BOOKSHELF

One of the things that editors don't often discuss is what's on their editorial bookshelves. If someone asks for a recommendation, say for a grammar book, editors chime in with their favorites, but the overall bookshelf—the tomes they rely on in their daily work—are rarely discussed.

Knowing what's on an editor's bookshelf is like having a window into the editor's "soul." Okay, perhaps a bit of hyperbole, but only a bit.

I remember hiring a freelance editor years ago and, when I received back some edited chapters for a medical project, I was concerned by the spelling errors that remained. I inquired whether the editor used medical spellcheck software as an initial screening tool, and was surprised to learn the editor did not. This was an experienced medical editor who had a related medical background before becoming a freelance editor. The editor told me that he/she did not use medical spellcheck software because he/she didn't trust it and believed his/her background was sufficient and he/she could do much better without it. Alas, the fruits of the editor's efforts didn't support that belief.

I know I am limited in what I can require freelance editors I hire to use and own. It is a fine line between freelancer and employee, and it is a line that cannot be crossed without financial penalty. I can recommend but not require. However, I do inquire before hiring.

(Just as having the right resource materials handy is important, so is it important to have the right tools handy. Although I cannot require the freelance editor I hire to own and use EditTools or Editor's Toolkit Plus, or PerfectIt, or any other piece of software—Microsoft Word being the sole exception—owning and using these tools, and others, would improve the editor's accuracy, consistency, and efficiency, and increase their effective hourly rate. It seems to me that it is to the freelancer's own benefit to buy and use these tools.)

Knowing what resources an editor uses other than the Internet gives an insight into the quality of the editing I am likely to receive. It is no guarantee, just an insight. Too many editors today, I believe, rely too much on Internet sources, and do so to the exclusion of local resources. I know of editors who do not own a dictionary, for example, because they can use the Internet. I suspect that, in another decade or so, online-only resources will be the accepted norm. My problem with it (well, I really have several problems with online-only resources, not least of which is reliability) is that, when an editor tells me that they rely on online-only resources, I cannot get a feel for how competent an editor they may be. The Internet is so vast and the quality of the resources so variable that it doesn't give me confidence. Consequently, I want to know about local (as opposed to Internet) resources that the editor owns and uses.

It is not that the local resources need to be exhaustive; rather, they should reflect the editor's sense of professionalism and be geared toward the focus of the editor's work. For example, if a medical editor tells me that they use only *Stedman's Medical Dictionary*, I wonder why they do not also have and use *Dorland's Illustrated Medical Dictionary*, which is the other leading medical dictionary in the United States. And I also wonder about them when they tell me that they are using *Stedman's* 26th edition instead of the current 28th edition, or *Dorland's* 31st edition when the current edition is 32. (In my library, I have the current editions of both dictionaries as well as the past three—or more—editions. Sometimes it is important to check past usage as well as current usage. And sometimes words get dropped from dictionaries.)

Specialty dictionaries are important but are insufficient by themselves. We deal with languages that are ever-changing and no single dictionary or usage guide is always and forever sufficient. So, I also like to know what primary language resource books the editor uses. I find that I often have to go to more than one dictionary to determine whether a word is used correctly (for example, *Merriam-Webster's Collegiate Dictionary* 11th edition did not have the sense of *ultramontane* that fit an author's usage, but *The American Heritage Dictionary* 5th edition did).

And as the fact of specialty dictionaries implies, the more general dictionaries, such as *The American Heritage Dictionary*, often lack field-specific terms, or, more importantly, do not accurately reflect what is the standard in a particular field. So additional supplemental dictionaries are important, such as the *APA Dictionary of Psychology*. And authors love to use popular phrases, which makes resources like the *Oxford Dictionary of Phrase, Saying, and Quotation*; the *Oxford Dictionary of Phrase and Fable*; the *Dictionary of Modern Slang*; and *The Macmillan Dictionary of Contemporary Phrase and Fable*; as well as thesauruses, valuable.

What do you do when faced with a word that you cannot locate? Authors love to "create" a word by combining forms. This is not an unusual occurrence in medical writing (which is why I prefer character count to word count for determining the manuscript page count). Do you immediately reject the combination? Resolution of the problem is not always easy, but I have found Brown's *Composition of Scientific Words*, *The BBI Dictionary of English Word Combinations*, and Sheehan's *Word Parts Dictionary* to be invaluable. Also useful, albeit for a different purpose, is Bothamley's *Dictionary of Theories*. It provides a capsule way to determine if the author's use of, for example, "paradoxical cold" or "paralanguage" is appropriate.

Which brings us to the base issues of editing—usage and grammar. I like to know what usage sources an editor owns and uses. It is not enough to make a decision about grammar; an editor must be able to defend it and to be able to defend it, so an editor must have some sources to consult. Many editors have a single source; some rely solely on the grammar sections found in various style manuals. But usage changes over time and I think a professional editor has to follow those trends and have the local sources to do so. I, for example, use H.L. Mencken's *The American Language* (4th ed., revised with supplements), *Garner's Modern American Usage* (as well as its two predecessor editions), *Merriam Webster's Dictionary of English Usage*, *The American Heritage Guide to Contemporary Usage and Style*, Good's *Who's (. . . Oops!) Whose Grammar Book Is This Anyway?*, *The Gregg Reference Manual*, and Burchfield's *Fowler's Modern English Usage*, as well as several other usage and grammar guides, in addition to the sections on usage and grammar that appear in various editions of *The Chicago Manual of Style*, the Council of Science Editors' *Scientific Style and Format*, and the APA's *Publication Manual*.

It is not unusual for me to have several of my resources open on my desk as I compare and contrast the views of each before making a decision. The books I named above are only a small portion of my local resources. As an editor, I believe it is important to also be able to trace the etymology of a word or phrase, so I have numerous etymological books handy.

The point is that a professional editor relies on much more than just a single dictionary and a single style manual. A professional editor has and uses a library of resources because language is constantly changing and because no single source covers it all. I grant that the Internet has made more resources available and accessible, but it is not always easy to determine the reliability and accuracy of online information. Print publications rely on reputations earned over decades. When I hire a freelance editor, I want to know that the editor has and uses resources in which I have faith.

Do you agree? What's in your professional library?

19

It's the Little Things: Hardware

Although most of the editing tools I use are software, we do need to begin with hardware. I don't plan to discuss the innards of a computer or whether one should buy a laptop or a desktop computer, although my experience with both indicates that editing on a desktop is more efficient *for me*. But there are a couple of pieces of hardware that are worthy of note: monitors and XKeys.

Monitors

When I first began electronic editing, more than 20 years ago, color monitors were not available. The monitors were black and white (or green or amber), were small, and were heavy CRTs (cathode ray tubes). Using a single monitor at a "large" screen size of 12 inches meant investing a ton of money into a single piece of hardware. How times have changed.

The advent of LCD monitors with large screens has been a boon to editing. Instead of seeing a few lines of text, one can see a page, and thus get a better feel for context. LCDs have two other bonuses: small size (compared to the equivalent CRT) and, today, a low price.

As I have noted in other essays, I read a lot of "stuff" and I read, years ago, the results of a productivity study that showed that using two monitors nearly doubled productivity and using three monitors increased productivity by another 20% or so (the third-monitor stat is from memory and may be off, but the study did show an increase in productivity over two monitors), and there was yet still another increase with four monitors but it was a less dramatic increase than the third-monitor increase.

I can attest at least to the three-monitor productivity increase (I wanted four monitors but just couldn't find room for #4). I have used a three-monitor setup in my work for years and would not consider returning to anything less. I need to mention, however, that I do not think just any monitor will do. I have found that the best monitors for my work are those that pivot between portrait and landscape modes.

My setup uses three 24-inch pivoting LCD monitors (I happen to like Samsung monitors and the three monitors are the Samsung SyncMaster 2443BWT model). The left monitor is almost always in portrait mode, as is the center monitor; the right monitor is usually in landscape. But should I need all in portrait or a second in landscape, I just have to rotate them.

The three-monitor setup lets me logically divide my work. Here is how I usually have my work setup. On the left monitor is the manuscript I am editing. Portrait mode lets me see a page (or close to it) at a time. The center monitor is where my Internet access is located. I use an online collaborative stylesheet system that operates through my website, so this gives me access to the stylesheet (always up) and to Internet resources if I need to check things. On the right monitor, I put my local resources, such as an electronic specialty dictionary or word book, and the manuscript references or bibliography. Just by moving my head or my mouse, I have instant access to all the editing resources I need.

Compare this to editing on a single monitor. Think about how much time has to be spent going between screens. If you use the landscape orientation so that you can "split" the screen and have, say, a manuscript and the stylesheet visible at all times, what you are seeing is less than what I can see and requires more scrolling time.

So that little thing of having at least two monitors boosts productivity and efficiency greatly.

XKeys

Xkeys is equally as valuable, perhaps even more so, as the three-monitor setup. I use, and have used for at least 10 years, the 58-key professional PS2 model. When I originally bought my XKeys, only the

PS2 model would retain its programming in a power failure. This appears to no longer be the case. (One other important note: XKeys sells its own macro software. I have never used it or bought it, so I have no opinion about it. I use macro software called Macro Express with my XKeys, which I will discuss when I discuss software.)

XKeys sits to the left of my keyboard in a place of honor. It has increased my productivity many times over (I'll say by 1,000%, but I really have no idea of the percentage). I have programmed the XKeys for "odd" key combinations, such as Ctrl+Alt+Shift+F1, as well as for familiar combinations such as F1.

XKeys increases the number of key combinations available for macros by 58 because you can add hard-to-press combinations to a single key. (Actually, if I wanted, my XKeys Pro can handle 114 key combinations. It really is a two-layer device, but to access the second layer and return to the first layer requires additional key presses, so I have never bothered.) When I discuss software, I will go into more detail about the advantage of XKeys, but suffice it to say that I can now, with the press of a single button, run a macro or apply a style. It is much quicker than using a keyboard combination or the mouse.

But here is the most important part of XKeys—I can create a custom "keyboard" for each client or project type or project without reprogramming the XKeys! I have certain macros that I use for every client and every project, such as my Toggle macro, which is part of my EditTools software, so I have permanently assigned a particular XKey button to that macro. I don't even have to divert my eyes from the manuscript to press the key. Habit takes over. The point is that every "custom keyboard" I create has certain macros pre-assigned to it, and only the remaining buttons need to be assigned.

And because XKeys is just running the programmed key combination, I can assign to that key combination either a macro from within a program such as Microsoft Word or via Macro Express. XKeys is also program-neutral; that is, I have custom keyboards not only for clients and projects, but also for programs, such as InDesign.

XKeys and a three-monitor setup are important allies for me in my never-ending quest to improve my accuracy and efficiency, which will translate to an improved bottom line.

In the original version of this essay, I forgot to mention my Logitech programmable mouse. It's another piece of hardware that enhances my efficiency and productivity. I wouldn't work without it.

20

IT'S THE LITTLE THINGS: SOFTWARE

Here, I explore (albeit very cursorily) some of the software I use—in conjunction with the XKeys—to increase my efficiency and productivity as part of my striving to be the best editor I can be and provide my clients with the best editing available. All of the software involves using Microsoft Word macros and center on being able to use XKeys for one-button access to them.

The software programs are from a variety of vendors, including myself (wordsnSync) and include the following:

- Microsoft Word add-ins created by Jack Lyon of the Editorium

- PerfectIt from Intelligent Editing

- EditTools from wordsnSync, which is my software and company

- Macro Express from Insight

Each of the software applications provides its own productivity benefits, but all, except Macro Express, are based on Microsoft VBA (Visual Basic for Applications). Not included in the list is Microsoft Word's built-in VBA programming language. It is well worth every editor's time to learn at least the basics of VBA, particularly how to do wildcard searches.

The Editorium macros work with all versions of Word for Windows and all versions of Word for Mac through 2004.

PerfectIt is PC only. It works on a Mac that is running Windows and Word for Windows.

EditTools is PC only. It works on a Mac that is running Windows and Word for Windows.

Macro Express is PC only. However, similar programs are available for Macs.

Macro Express

Macro Express (ME) is simultaneously a simple and a complex macro writing program. For most editors, nothing more than the simple aspects are required. In fact, I rarely use ME for long, complex macros, preferring to use VBA. But ME does have a singular advantage over all of the other options: It is program-agnostic. Consequently, I can write procedures that I can use in multiple programs or for a specific program. Here's a simple sample: Think about how many times during a manuscript edit you need to delete a space and replace it with a hyphen. How do you currently do it? Press Delete, press hyphen? I press the + key on the number keypad at the right of my keyboard. It is a simple macro that I have assigned to that particular key and that I have made available for use in all my programs via Macro Express. It means that I can keep my hand on my mouse and simply extend my thumb to press the single key, saving perhaps a couple of seconds with each use.

On the other hand, ME lets me take advantage of some of Word's features in combination. Back when I wrote this procedure in ME, I wasn't up to speed with VBA, so ME made life easy. The procedure lets me insert a local bookmark where I am currently at and go immediately to another bookmark. When I begin prepping a file for editing, the first thing I do is insert special bookmarks where the references, figures, tables, and any other special features are. The ME routine lets me travel, for example, from the text table callout to the table and, when I'm done editing the table, to return to the callout in the text.

ME lets me create custom "keyboards" for clients and/or projects. These custom keyboards contain macros for the client/project that make life easy. They also contain some universal macros, that is, macros that I know I will use in every project. And ME lets me assign the key combination of my choice to each macro.

When used in conjunction with XKeys, all I need to do is press a single button to run a macro.

Editorium Macros

Jack Lyon, founder of the Editorium, has written several macro programs designed to help speed certain editorial tasks. I have tried many of his macros and they all are excellent. You really can't go wrong with any of them if they fit your needs. And when I started using macros to increase productivity, I used more of his programs than I do now. I still use, on a regular basis, ListFixer and NoteStripper. For the editing that I do, these are the most useful and valuable of the Editorium macros. Colleagues swear by—and rightfully so—his other programs, particularly FileCleaner and MegaReplacer. I suggest that, if you haven't tried the Editorium macros, you do so and find the ones that are most beneficial for you.

PerfectIt

PerfectIt is a relatively recent addition to my armamentarium of editing tools. PerfectIt is a series of auto-running macros that looks for common mistakes *after* the manuscript is edited. For example, the manuscripts I work on often are riddled with acronyms. One of the things I try to do is be sure that, after an acronym has been defined, future spellouts are converted to the acronym form. That's one of the things that PerfectIt checks. It also looks for missing punctuation in lists, acronyms that are defined multiple ways, and numerous other of the little things that can get past even the most diligent editor. It is a valuable program and well worth its price.

EditTools

EditTools is my favorite (I am the author and seller of EditTools), probably because the macros were created to meet my specific editing needs. However, they would be a great boon to any editor.

Among the many macros in EditTools, my favorites are Toggle, Journals, and Search Count Replace.

My Toggle database includes more than 1,200 entries and Toggle lets me make corrections with a single XKeys button press. For example, I have a medical dataset for Toggle so that, when I come across and acronym that hasn't been spelled out yet, such as CHF, I press a single key and CHF becomes congestive heart failure (CHF). And some clients prefer that in-sentence lists be numbered in parentheses rather than lettered followed by a period [i.e., (1) rather than a.], and Toggle lets me make the change with a single button press. The key is what is in my dataset, and I am the sole master of that—I can add as I wish.

Journals is another major timesaver for me. It isn't unusual for me to have a chapter with 300+ references. Journals is a macro that searches for journal (or book) names and, if they are correct, highlights them in green; if they are incorrect, it corrects them and highlights them in cyan. Like Toggle, Journals uses a dataset that I created to meet my needs; my current dataset has nearly 5,000 journal names. The highlighting gives me visual confirmation that I do not need to worry about whether a journal name is correct.

Search Count Replace (SCR) solves another common editing problem. As I said earlier, many of the manuscripts I work on are riddled with acronyms. SCR lets me determine how many times an acronym is used in the manuscript and, if it doesn't meet the client's minimum number requirement, I can tell it to replace subsequent instances of the acronym with something else; if the number does meet the client's requirements, I can tell it to highlight the acronym throughout the document, which tells me later that the acronym has already been spelled out.

EditTools also makes custom dictionaries accessible and usable. There also are several other macros included, including one that corrects page ranges in references.

All of these software programs and macros increase my speed, accuracy, and efficiency and better the final product that I deliver to my clients. Most have trial periods; I suggest you try them. With trial periods, you have nothing to lose—and everything to gain—by doing so.

As noted earlier, the named programs have limitations in that they do not work on Apple products in the absence of simulation of Windows and use of Word for Windows. This has been a major reason why I choose to buy PCs rather than Macs for my business. In today's state of publishing, it is imperative that I do as much as possible to make my business efficient and myself more productive. This is not a reflection on the quality of the Macs; it is strictly a business decision. It is the same reason that I do not buy PCs "off-the-shelf" but have them custom built locally. (Customization is another reason why I do not buy Apple computers; Apple offers very limited customization and what customization is offered does not meet what I have decided I need to make myself more productive and efficient.)

21

It's the Little Things: Software Redux

Not discussed in my previous essays was Microsoft Word's built-in macro language, Visual Basic for Applications (VBA). But this resource is exceedingly valuable to an editor. Every editor should at least master using wild cards and should try to learn the fundamentals of writing "simple" VBA macros.

I edit a lot of very long manuscripts—2,000 to 10,000+ manuscript pages—in the STM (science, technical, and medical) fields. It is not unusual for these manuscripts to have chapters with 300 to 1,500 references, and the one thing I can almost universally rely on is that the references are not in proper form, and are even inconsistent among themselves.

For example, a manuscript had a citation style that looks like this for a journal article:

Surname Initials, Surname Initials. Article title. Journal vol;page-page, year.

In one chapter with nearly 500 references, not a single reference was in that form. The style was all over the place and it was my job to fix it.

Fixing the problems means I can do each reference individually or I can identify patterns and write a macro or use wildcards with Find and Replace (F&R). For most editors, the easier solution is to use wildcards with F&R. Using F&R means breaking down the references into their parts. It isn't possible—at least as far as I have been able to determine—to create a single macro or F&R routine to take care of all of the variations that the authors provide. Consequently, I try to address parts of the problem.

For example, if the authors have put some of the citations in this form:

26, 1988, 1101-1105.

and I want to change it to this form:

26:1101-1105, 1988.

I make use of wildcards as follows:

Find: ([0-9]@)(,)([0-9]{4})(,)([0-9]@)(-)([0-9]@)(.)
Replace: \1:\5\6\7\4\3\8

Similarly, if the authors have really made it complex by using the citation form:

2005, Dec;24(12):2037-042.

which I need to become:

24(12):2037-042, 2005.

I use a two-step wildcard F&R as follows:

1st Find: ([0-9]{4})(, [A-z]@;)
1st Replace: \1; 2nd Find: ([0-9]{4})(; @)([0-9]@[(][0-9]@[)]:[0-9]@-[0-9]@)(.)
2nd Replace: \3, \1\4

Every time I figure out the wildcard F&R, I copy the parameters to a word document that I keep handy for the next chapter. This way I only have to copy and paste, and click Replace All. I do have to go through several F&Rs, which will correct most—but not all—of the variations; but it is better to have 90% corrected automatically than to have to do them all manually.

And to address problems where, for example, the authors give the reference author names as AW Smith instead of Smith AW, I write a simple macro that I assign to my keyboard (and my XKeys) to make that reversal:

```
Sub ReverseAuthorName1()
'
'ReverseAuthorName1 Macro
'Macro created 4/7/2010 by Freelance Editorial Services
'
    Selection.MoveRight    Unit:=wdWord,    Count:=1,    Extend:=wdExtend
    Selection.Cut
    Selection.MoveRight Unit:=wdWord, Count:=1
    Selection.PasteAndFormat (wdPasteDefault)
End Sub
```

As you can see, even a simple macro can make life easier and editing more productive. What do you do when an author has added punctuation following the journal name and there isn't supposed to be any? For example, the author gives you:

N Engl J Med. 1998;2:200-210

and the correct form for your client is

N Engl J Med 2:200-210, 1998?

We know how to move the year to the end globally but that doesn't solve the problem of the punctuation following the journal name. You could modify your wildcard F&R, but that won't remove the punctuation where the rest of the cite doesn't match the Find parameter. The answer is to write a macro.

Here is the macro I use. It works so I haven't improved it as I've grown more knowledgeable about VBA. This macro can be much more simply and efficiently written; it was one of my earliest attempts at macro writing.

```
Sub RefsRemovePuncAfterJournalName()
'
' Remove Punctuation After Journal Name in References Macro
' Macro created 10/7/2004 by Freelance Editorial Services
'
Selection.Find.ClearFormatting
Selection.Find.Replacement.ClearFormatting
With Selection.Find
.Text = "/, "
.Replacement.Text = "/,Œ‰"
.Forward = True
.Wrap = wdFindContinue
.Format = False
.MatchCase = True
.MatchWholeWord = False
.MatchWildCards = False
.MatchSoundsLike = False
.MatchAllWordForms = False
End With
Selection.Find.Execute Replace:=wdReplaceAll
' Replace [number],[space] with [number],[smiley]‰
Selection.Find.ClearFormatting
Selection.Find.Replacement.ClearFormatting
With Selection.Find
.Text = "([0-9])[, ]"
.Replacement.Text = "\1," & ChrW(9786) & "‰"
.Forward = True
.Wrap = wdFindContinue
.Format = False
.MatchCase = False
.MatchWholeWord = False
.MatchWildCards = True
.MatchSoundsLike = False
.MatchAllWordForms = False
End With
Selection.Find.Execute Replace:=wdReplaceAll
' Replace [space][number] with ¿‰[number]
```

```
Selection.Find.ClearFormatting
Selection.Find.Replacement.ClearFormatting
With Selection.Find
.Text = " ([0-9]{4})(;)"
.Replacement.Text = "¿‰\1\2''
.Forward = True
.Wrap = wdFindContinue
.Format = True
.MatchCase = False
.MatchWholeWord = False
.MatchWildCards = True
.MatchSoundsLike = False
.MatchAllWordForms = False
End With
Selection.Find.Execute Replace:=wdReplaceAll
' Replace ,¿ with [space]
Selection.Find.ClearFormatting
Selection.Find.Replacement.ClearFormatting
With Selection.Find
.Text = ",¿"
.Replacement.Text = " "
.Forward = True
.Wrap = wdFindContinue
.Format = False
.MatchCase = True
.MatchWholeWord = False
.MatchWildCards = False
.MatchSoundsLike = False
.MatchAllWordForms = False
End With
Selection.Find.Execute Replace:=wdReplaceAll
' Replace .¿ with [space]
Selection.Find.ClearFormatting
Selection.Find.Replacement.ClearFormatting
With Selection.Find
.Text = ".¿"
.Replacement.Text = " "
```

```
.Forward = True
.Wrap = wdFindContinue
.Format = False
.MatchCase = True
.MatchWholeWord = False
.MatchWildCards = False
.MatchSoundsLike = False
.MatchAllWordForms = False
End With
Selection.Find.Execute Replace:=wdReplaceAll
' Replace [smiley] with [space]
Selection.Find.ClearFormatting
Selection.Find.Replacement.ClearFormatting
With Selection.Find
.Text = ChrW(9786)
.Replacement.Text = " "
.Forward = True
.Wrap = wdFindContinue
.Format = False
.MatchCase = True
.MatchWholeWord = False
.MatchWildCards = False
.MatchSoundsLike = False
.MatchAllWordForms = False
End With
Selection.Find.Execute Replace:=wdReplaceAll
' Replace ¿, Œ, and ‰ with [space]
Selection.Find.ClearFormatting
Selection.Find.Replacement.ClearFormatting
With Selection.Find
.Text = "[¿Œ‰]"
.Replacement.Text = " "
.Forward = True
.Wrap = wdFindContinue
.Format = False
.MatchCase = False
.MatchWholeWord = False
```

```
.MatchWildCards = True
.MatchSoundsLike = False
.MatchAllWordForms = False
End With
Selection.Find.Execute Replace:=wdReplaceAll
Selection.Find.ClearFormatting
Selection.Find.Replacement.ClearFormatting
With Selection.Find
.Text = "([A-z]@)(.)(^32)([0-9]@{4})(;)"
.Replacement.Text = "\1\3\4\5"
.Forward = True
.Wrap = wdFindContinue
.Format = False
.MatchCase = False
.MatchWholeWord = False
.MatchWildCards = True
.MatchSoundsLike = False
.MatchAllWordForms = False
End With
Selection.Find.Execute Replace:=wdReplaceAll
' This section resets the wildcards to off
Selection.Find.ClearFormatting
Selection.Find.Replacement.ClearFormatting
With Selection.Find
.Text = ""
.Replacement.Text = ""
.Forward = True
.Wrap = wdFindContinue
.Format = False
.MatchCase = True
.MatchWholeWord = False
.MatchWildCards = False
.MatchSoundsLike = False
.MatchAllWordForms = False
End With
Selection.Find.Execute
Replace:=wdReplaceAll
```

```
Selection.Find.ClearFormatting
Selection.Find.Replacement.ClearFormatting
With Selection.Find
.Text = ""
.Replacement.Text = ""
.Forward = True
.Wrap = wdFindContinue
.Format = False
.MatchCase = True
.MatchWholeWord = False
.MatchWildCards = False
.MatchSoundsLike = False
.MatchAllWordForms = False
End With
Selection.Find.Execute
Replace:=wdReplaceAll
End Sub
```

The macro looks more complex than it really is. The point is that you, too, can write these macros for your own needs if you make the effort to learn a little VBA. But even if you don't want to go that far, you need to learn how to use wildcards. The time that wildcards and macros can save you puts money in your pocket. More importantly, it prevents the frustration you encounter when you face a lengthy reference list and discover that not one author-provided reference is in correct form.

I suggest picking up a book on VBA programming and also checking out the information on macros and wildcards found in *Microsoft Word for Publishing Professionals* by Jack Lyon (ISBN 9781434102362; available at www.editorium.com and through bookstores). Jack's book is one of the best sources for introductory information on macro writing available. His new *Macro Cookbook for Microsoft Word* (ISBN 9781434103321) is equally useful and highlights just the macro aspects of using Word for publishing projects.

Live, learn, and prosper!

22

EDITORS AND "PROFESSIONAL" RESOURCES: A QUESTIONABLE RELIANCE

Editors rely on lots of "professional" resources to guide their editorial decisions when working on manuscripts. In addition to dictionaries and word books, we rely on language usage guides and style manuals, among other tools.

But it isn't unusual for an author (or publisher) to have a different view of what is appropriate and desirable from the "professional" resources. And many editors will fight tooth and nail to make the client conform to the rules laid down in a style manual. As between language usage guides like *Garner's Modern American Usage* and style manuals like *The Chicago Manual of Style*, I believe that editors should adhere to the rules of the former but take the rules of the latter with a lot of salt.

The distinction between the two types of manuals is important. A language manual is a guide to the proper use of language such as word choice; for example, when *comprise* is appropriate and when *compose* is appropriate. A style manual, although it will discuss in passing similar issues, is really more focused on structural issues such as capitalization: Should it be president of the United States or President of the United States? Here's the question: How much does it matter whether it is president or President?

When an author insists that a particular structural form be followed that I think is wrong, I will tell the author why I believe the author is wrong and I will cite, where appropriate, the professional sources. *But,* and I think this is something professional editors lose sight of, those professional sources—such as *The Chicago Manual of Style* (*CMOS*) and the *Publication Manual of the American Psychological Association*—are merely books of opinion. Granted, we give them great weight, but they are just opinion. And it has never been particularly clear to me why the *consensus opinion* of the "panel of experts" of *CMOS* is any better than my client's opinion. After all, isn't the key clarity and consistency, not conformity to some arbitrary consensus.

If these style manuals were *the* authoritative source, there would only be one of them to which we would all adhere; the fact that there is disagreement among them indicates that we are dealing with opinion to which we give credence and different amounts of weight. (I should mention that, if an author is looking to be published by a particular publisher whose style is to follow the rules in one of the standard style manuals, then it is incumbent on the editor to advise the author of the necessity of adhering to those rules and even insist that the author do so. But where the author is self-publishing or the author's target press doesn't adhere to a standard, then the world is more open.)

It seems to me that, if there is such a divergence of opinion as to warrant the publication of so many different style manuals, then adding another opinion to the mix and giving that opinion greater credence is acceptable. I am not convinced that my opinion, or the opinion of *CMOS*, is so much better than that of the author that the author's opinion should be resisted until the author concedes defeat. In the end, I think but one criterion is the standard to be applied: Will the reader be able to follow and understand what the author is trying to convey? (However, I would also say that there is one other immutable rule: that the author be consistent.) If the answer is yes, then even if what the author wants assaults *my* sense of good taste or violates the traditional style manual canon, the author wins—and should win.

The battles that are not concedeable by an editor are those that make the author's work difficult to understand and those of incorrect word choice (e.g., using *comprise* when *compose* is the correct word).

A professional editor is hired to give advice. Whether to accept or reject that advice is up to the person doing the hiring. Although we like to think we are the gods of grammar, syntax, spelling, and style, the truth is we are simply more knowledgeable (usually) than those who hire us—we are qualified to give an opinion, perhaps even a forceful or "expert" opinion, but still just an opinion. We are advisors giving advice based on experience and knowledge, but we are not the final decision makers—and this is a lesson that many of us forget. We may be frustrated because we really do know better, but we must not forget that our "bibles" are just collections of consensus-made opinion, not rules cast in stone.

If they were rules cast in stone, there would be no changes, only additions, to the rules, and new editions of the guides would appear with much less frequency than they currently do. More importantly, there would be only one style manual to which all editors would adhere—after all, whether it is president or President isn't truly dependent on whether the manuscript is for a medical journal, a psychology journal, a chemistry journal, a sociology journal, or a history journal.

Style manuals serve a purpose, giving us a base from which to proceed and some support for our decisions, but we should not put them on the pedestal of inerrancy, just on a higher rung of credibility.

23

Working Effectively Online I—The Books

I am celebrating the start of my 28th year as a professional editor. Over the course of those years, I have watched the world of editing change. Sadly, many of my colleagues have not changed with it.

In my beginning years, nearly all editing work was done on paper. I hated working on paper! I hated it because of the types of editing projects I undertake—generally the books I work on are several thousand manuscript pages and often, when published, are either a very large single volume (very-large-width spine) or are multivolume. Imagine realizing that you made a mistake in the first 500 manuscript pages and trying to find each mistake when editing on paper. Difficult at best, impossible realistically. More importantly, think of the money it cost me—after all, it was my mistake and the client shouldn't be penalized for my mistake—and the time I spent trying to find those errors. Online editing has definitely eased that task; now correcting a mistake is significantly less expensive and less time-consuming.

Those years were also the time when computers were being introduced into the workplace for everyone, rather than for a select few. Remember XyWrite? It was the software program that many publishers adopted when it first became available. Lippincott, before it was Lippincott-Raven, then Lippincott Williams and Wilkins, went so far as to create a customized version of XyWrite and would only hire editors who took, at the editor's own expense, a day-long class in New York City on using the customized template. Alas, XyWrite was soon swept away by WordPerfect, which was ultimately swept away by Microsoft Word.

Yet in those beginning years, I saw both the future of editing and an opportunity. The future clearly was online editing and the opportunity was to be among the very few who could and would offer solely online editing of manuscripts. And that was how I promoted myself. I would send out "cost comparisons" demonstrating how much money I could save a publisher by electronically editing and coding their manuscripts instead of working on paper. And in the beginning, those savings were huge.

Today it is the rare manuscript that is edited on paper. Nearly all manuscripts are edited electronically and almost never does paper move hand to hand—the Internet has changed how professional editors work. Yet one thing hasn't changed in all these years: There is still a sizable number of editors who have not mastered the basic tools of their profession. Their knowledge of the tools they use daily is minimal—just enough to get by. Ask them to use a feature that they have not used before and they get flustered.

Succeeding as a professional editor in the 21st century requires more than knowledge of language, spelling, and grammar—it also requires mastery of the tools we use daily. It requires learning new skills, particularly how to harness the built-in power of the software we use, and finding and using complementary software that enhances the already great power of our basic editing software. For example, it is not enough to master Microsoft Word; one needs also to be familiar with programs like MacroExpress, PerfectIt, the Editorium macros, and EditTools.

Even though we need to enhance our skills with ancillary programs, we also need to enhance our skills regarding what Microsoft Word can do that makes our workflow increasingly efficient. Thus, three books that should be in every professional editor's library, and regularly consulted, are these:

- *Microsoft Word for Publishing Professionals: Power-Packed Tips for Editors, Typesetters, Proofreaders, and Indexers* by Jack Lyon

- *Macro Cookbook for Microsoft Word* by Jack Lyon

- *Effective Onscreen Editing: New Tools for an Old Profession*, 2nd ed., by Geoff Hart

Each of these books can be considered, from the editor's perspective, a bible for working with Microsoft Word. They both educate and help to solve problems. Most importantly, if you take the time to work through the books, they will give you mastery over the one bit of software that is simultaneously an editor's bane and savior: Microsoft Word.

Although there are many editors who resist delving deeply into the tools of our trade, and who even loathe having to rely on these tools, the reality is that working in Word is a fundamental requirement of professional editing. If one software program is used nearly universally in the publishing industry for editorial matters, that program is Word. And I do not see Word's role changing in the near future; rather, I see that mastery of Word will become part of the testing process that publishers will use when choosing editors to hire.

More importantly for the professional editor, mastery of Microsoft Word is the avenue by which we can become more efficient and proficient. Increased efficiency and proficiency means our earning more money and making ourselves more saleable in an ever-more-competitive market.

One good reason to master Word is to clean up author files. One constant over the many years that I have been editing electronically is that authors continue to amaze me with how they prepare their manuscripts for editing. If it is a feature in Word, they feel obligated to use it in their manuscript, albeit usually incorrectly. It is the rare file I receive that can be cleaned and readied for editing within a few minutes. Authors are uncannily creative with how they misuse Word. These three books—*Microsoft Word for Publishing Professionals*, *Macro Cookbook for Microsoft Word*, and *Effective Onscreen Editing*—can help you deal with author creativity, as well as with whatever other problems we encounter just because we use Microsoft Word.

Mastering Word means less time spent on noneditorial matters. As our primary focus is (or should be) on language, grammar, and spelling, mastering Word reduces the time we need to spend on ancillary problems. These are the key three books to mastering Word for editors.

24

WORKING EFFECTIVELY ONLINE II—THE MACROS

There is a reason why macros are a topic in all three books— *Microsoft Word for Publishing Professionals, Macro Cookbook for Microsoft Word,* and *Effective Onscreen Editing*—that I discussed earlier:

Macros are the power tool that editors need to master but are afraid to tackle!

No tool in the Microsoft Word armamentarium is more powerful, more useful, yet more challenging than macros. Macros have their own truncated language and require a type of thinking that is contrary to the type of thought process that editors apply to editorial tasks. Mastering macros requires a change in direction; however, the rewards one can reap by mastering macros can increase an editor's efficiency many fold.

We need to begin with this truism:

The more efficiently an editor works, the more money an editor earns.

We also need to accept that it makes no sense to keep reinventing the macro. If someone has already created a macro that does what you need, don't reinvent it—buy it. It will take you more time to write the macro from scratch than to earn back the money spent (and that's without considering the return on investment you will get from repeated use).

Macros are efficient tools for performing repetitive and/or cumbersome tasks in Microsoft Word. Every second you save by using a macro is money in your pocket.

Something else to keep in mind: Many times macros are part of a package. This is true of Editorium macros and EditTools. Colleagues have told me that they could really use xyz macro but don't need the rest of the package and so won't buy the package, thinking it a waste of money. This is faulty thinking. If you will get repeated use of a single macro in a package, it will earn back the cost quickly. Plus, even though you think you cannot use other included macros, having them around will encourage you to experiment and discover new ways to use previously unusable macros.

A good example is my EditTools collection of macros. I have been told numerous times that, for example, if the Search, Count, and Replace macro were available as a standalone macro, the editor would buy it because it really would be useful in their work, unlike the other macros in the package. Perhaps this is true, but the editor is not thinking through how they work and what tasks they perform when they edit. How many times, for example, do you have to take an author-used acronym and spell it out? If you use the Toggle macro, you only need to press a key (or key combination) to change *WHO* to *World Health Organization (WHO)*. My Toggle macro dataset has more than 1,300 items in it, every one an item that I can change from one thing to another by pressing a single key. Think about how much time I save using this macro, which means both more money in my pocket and no chance of mistyping. (If you are like me, accurate typing is not a high skill. I'm good, but too many times, I will type something only to discover I typed it incorrectly and have to fix it. That uses up more precious time and lowers my earning power. The Toggle macro eliminates that problem for those items in the Toggle dataset. Once entered into the dataset correctly, it will be typed correctly forever after.)

My point is that editors tend to be resistant to spending money to make money, which is something I consider a major mistake for a professional editor. One should always weigh the outlay against the return on investment—but the return has to be looked at over the long-term, not the short-term.

Yet this is also a reason why learning to write Word macros is important to the professional editor: The editor who masters macro creation can devise macros that will conform to how the editor works and save the editor time while making the editor money.

You begin simply, by recording a simple macro; for example, a macro that replaces two spaces with one space. As you master the steps to record simple macros, you can move on to more complex macros or to combining macros, and the three books mentioned above will help, especially *Macro Cookbook*.

Consider this: I have a client that uses a template for all its projects. Editors are required to use the template and to apply styles to the manuscript. To ensure that head structure is correct, before sending the file to the editor either the in-house production editor or the author labels each head using something like <1>, <2>, etc. to designate the level. That is very useful to me because I no longer have to try to guess head relationships. But it is also an opportunity for me to make a bit more money from the project. Why? Because I charge by the page, so everything I can do to save time earns me a higher effective hourly rate (i.e., if I can do a project in 30 hours rather than 40 hours, my effective hourly rate is greater, which is another reason why the Toggle macro is so useful).

The opportunity comes about because I can macroize the task, which is what I did. I wrote a series of macros that search for specific codes (e.g., <1>), delete the code, apply the appropriate style, then automatically search for the next instance and keeps going until no more of the code can be found. Not only could I macroize the task for each code individually, but I could also create a macro that would serially run all of these individual macros, giving me the option of running each macro individually or together as a single macro. With some chapters running more than 300 manuscript pages, and a typical chapter running 50+ manuscript pages, think about how quickly—and accurately—I can code the chapter, all because I have gained a level of mastery over macros.

Similarly, many of the chapters I work on have reference lists that run from a few hundred references to more than 1,000 references. I wish I could automate everything about references, but I can't because macros are dumb and rely on patterns. But what I can and did do is create a Journals macro that compares the author-provided journal title with the correct form of journal title in a journal dataset. The macro highlights correct names in green and, with tracking on, changes incorrect forms to correct forms. (My dataset of journal names has more than 7,400 journals in it.) Think about how much time I save not having to check journal titles and not having to correct incorrect journal titles. (There are still some journal titles that I have to check because they are not yet in the dataset, but I add these to the dataset as I come across them so that next time I won't have to check them.)

If you want to be a more successful professional editor, you need to think in terms of macros. Think about how you can macroize an otherwise repetitive task, whether that task is unique to a specific project or is the type of task that needs to be done on many different projects. Not only do you need to think in terms of macros, but you need to master macros. The best time to start mastering macros is now.

25

Working Effectively Online III— Mastering Word

Recall that Part I (The Professional Editor: Working Effectively Online I—The Books) of this series called for professional editors to master the tools of their trade, particularly Microsoft Word if they edit using Word. There are good reasons to do so.

A few weeks ago, I was working on a book chapter that ran 453 manuscript pages, 49 pages of which were reference citations. (Yes, the number is correct; one chapter in this project I am editing ran 453 manuscript pages. Most of the chapters run 30 to 50 manuscript pages, but several are 200+-page chapters.) The project was for a client who uses a custom template and part of my job is to apply the template to the manuscript, styling every paragraph plus applying particular styles to items that need special styling in addition to the basic paragraph style, such as applying a special "overstyle" to a word that should be in a san serif typeface.

I used the macros I had written (and mentioned in The Professional Editor: Working Effectively Online II—The Macros) to style the heads and then I had to manually style the text paragraphs as I couldn't decipher a pattern that I could capture in a macro. It took a while to get the whole document styled and ready for editing (I like to do the master styling before I edit because that lets me determine, as I read the material, whether something needs to be styled differently), but I did finish—and because of the macros, I finished in much less time—and was prepared to begin editing.

That is when I realized I had made a mistake: I forgot to turn off Track Changes when I did the styling (I'll prevent that from happening again by adding some code to my macros to turn Tracking off if it is on then, when the macro is done, turning it back on if it was on when the macro started). As all of us Word users know, that means a gazillion annoying balloon popups telling me when I had styled the text and the style I applied—there was no safe place for me to put my cursor! (Yes, I could have turned off show formatting in tracking, but the client wants to see certain formatting changes, so that was not a viable solution.)

It would have been an easy enough fix to just accept all changes in the document, except that I had already run my Never Spell Word and Journals macros and I did not want those changes accepted—I hadn't edited the chapter yet and so I hadn't approved the changes the macros made.

Here is where having some mastery of Word helps. What I needed was to have Word accept just the formatting changes and retain everything else. Because I have made an effort to learn something new about Word regularly, I knew how to solve my problem. The following steps are what I did in Word 2010 (I know this will work in Word 2007 and there should be a similar method in Word 2003 and in Mac versions of Word, but you will have to do your own exploring in those versions).

1. I switched to the *Review Tab* and clicked on the tiny down arrow-head in *Show Markup*.

2. I deselected everything but *Formatting*.

3. I clicked on the tiny arrow in Accept and then clicked *Accept all changes shown*.

4. I returned to the *Show Markup* dropdown and reselected everything I had deselected.

With this simple four-step process, I was able to solve my problem—only the formatting changes were accepted; all the rest of the changes that I had made using my macros remained for me to accept or reject.

This doesn't seem like a big deal at first glance, but it was to me. If I couldn't find a way to accept just the formatting changes, my choices would have been to (a) live with the annoyance (and I really do find it annoying) or (b) start over with the chapter and eat the time I had already spent styling this massive chapter (I charge a per-page rate, not an hourly rate, so I would have had to eat the time regardless, but even had I been charging an hourly rate I wouldn't have charged the client—the fault was mine and it was for my convenience). Neither option was particularly welcome.

Perhaps you would have chosen to just live with the balloons. That's okay as long as you know that there was an option to fix the problem quickly and easily. That is the essence of my clarion call to master the tools we use: knowing what our options are and not having a decision thrust upon us simply because we don't know enough about how our tools work. Would you hire a carpenter who owned and used only a single saw blade because the carpenter didn't know that different saw blades are used for different purposes and give different types of cuts?

We expect those we hire to perform services for us—whether they be a carpenter, a doctor, an auto mechanic, or some other tradesperson or professional—to have mastery of the tools of their profession so that they can give us knowledgeable advice. Shouldn't we similarly be masters of the tools of our own profession?

I discussed the value of learning to write macros in "Working Effectively Online II—The Macros." Absent mastery of Word, absent knowing what functions Word can perform and can't perform, how can we learn to write macros to ease performance of those functions? A macro is merely a method to accomplish a task more quickly, efficiently, and uniformly; it is not a method to perform a function that otherwise cannot be done. Macros call upon the same commands that you do when using Word. Consequently, mastering Word, which is, for many editors, a fundamental tool, is a step toward conquering macros. Neither mastery of Word nor creation of macros lives in isolation of the other. They are interdependent and should provide an impetus for editors to master the tools they use.

(Although I focus on Word and VBA [Visual Basic for Applications] as the tools to master, I know that some of you use tools other than Word and its macro language. For example, your focus may well be InDesign or some other text program. But what applies to Word applies to the programs you use as well. The point is less learning to master Word than it is to master whatever tool you use. InDesign, as an example, also has a scripting language that can be learned and it has its own text editor, InCopy, that also warrants learning and mastering.)

26

WORKING EFFECTIVELY ONLINE IV— MASTERING MACROS

Mastering macros has been discussed before, but it is worth repeating that they can save you time, enhance your productivity and efficiency, and thus make you money. This time, let's consider how macros can do that—especially if you charge by the page or by the project. (If you charge by the hour, using macros can make your job easier, but they won't necessarily make you money; in fact, using macros might cost you money by reducing the number of hours you work on a project and, thus, the amount you can bill.)

I mentioned in an earlier essay that I often work on exceedingly large projects and chapters. Recently, I worked on one chapter that had 78 pages of references—801 references in total. To see the original reference file as provided by the authors, go here:

http://americaneditor.files.wordpress.com/2011/11/refs-original.pdf

In the usual course of editing, I have to read all of the references to make sure that all of the required information is present and that they are in the proper style. Included in the criteria, because I was working on a medical textbook, was the requirement that journal names conform to National Library of Medicine's (NLM's) abbreviations. For those of you who are unfamiliar with the NLM database, it contains more than 10,000 journals from a variety of science and medical disciplines. Although the database is readily accessible, over the years, the one truism about manuscripts I receive for editing is this: Authors use their own abbreviations for journal titles.

Before I created my Journals macro, I had to look up every journal name that I didn't know and I had to manually make necessary corrections. A very time-consuming process; not so bad when you have 50 references, but a nightmare when you have hundreds. Although I could remember a lot of journal names, I couldn't remember the vast majority, especially those rarely cited.

Because I charge a per-page rate for my editing services, time is of the essence. It doesn't take the loss of a great deal of time to drag an effective hourly rate down to minimum wage and lower. Consequently, I decided I had to steel myself to learn to write macros.

The key to a macro is this: seeing a pattern that you can explain to the macro. If you cannot decipher a pattern for the problem area, then it is unlikely that you will be able to draft a macro to solve the problem. Remember this: macros are dumb! They will look for only what you tell them to find—nothing more, nothing less. Consequently, if you tell a macro to search for **N. Engl J. Med** (note the periods), it will not find **N Engl J Med** (same text but no periods). (It is possible to write a wildcard find that will find both variations, but it is still finding only what you have designated.)

Not only do you need to decipher a "find" pattern, but you also need to determine what you want the macro to do when it finds a match. This can be as simple as a replace or something more complex, such as applying various colored highlighting.

Ultimately, the Journals macro was created. My PubMed Journals dataset contains more than 7,700 entries. What that means is that when I run the macro against the submitted reference list, the macro will highlight in green journal names that found in the dataset that are correct as provided by the author. Seeing a name in green lets me skim over the journal title because I know—visually—that it is correct. Running the Journals macro on the references file took 4.5 minutes to complete and resulted in the file you can see by clicking here: REFS after Journals macro.

But if the name is incorrect, it either corrects the name or ignores it; which it does depends on whether the incorrect variation is in the dataset. The corrections are not only done with Tracking on, but corrected journal names are highlighted in cyan, which tells me that the name had to be corrected but is now correct.

An even more telling example, using the same original references file, is shown in REFS to AMA style. In this case, the journals had to conform to American Medical Association (AMA) style, which is the abbreviated journal name in italic and followed by period (e.g., *N Engl J Med.*). If you look at the original reference file, you will see that none of the journal names are in italics and only a handful have the correct abbreviation followed by a period. Yet, I was able to make the change to most of the journals in the reference list by using my Journals macro along with my AMA style dataset, which contains more than 11,400 entries, in less than five minutes.

What this all means is that, when working on the references, only a handful require me to check the journal name or to manually make corrections. Every cyan- and green-highlighted journal name means money in my pocket because I do not have to spend time verifying those journal names. Unfortunately, running the journals macro doesn't mean that the reference as a whole is in proper form. Nor does the macro catch every instance of a journal. As noted earlier, macros are dumb and will only find exact matches that meet all of the find criteria that form the pattern, which is more than just the journal name.

Yet the point I want to make remains unchanged: It took less than five minutes to run the macro and to relieve myself of most of the work otherwise necessary and that I would have to do manually. Think about how long it would take just to type the correct journal names even if you could recall every one without having to look them up, or to manually italicize each journal name, or even to manually add a period after each journal name.

In the end, it comes down to this: Mastering the world of macros is a time- and effort-saver for editors, as well as a money maker.

Sometimes the macro we need is too complex for us to write; after all, few of us are programmers and that is what macro writing is—programming. My advice is to learn macro writing beginning with simple macros and progressing to increasingly difficult macros, and to learn to program as complex a macro as you can—but do not spend so much time at it that you are taken away from what should be your main focus: editing. If you can use a macro now to help with multiple projects that have the same or very similar problems, consider hiring a programmer to write the macro for you. Hiring isn't inexpensive, but it doesn't take long to earn back the cost, plus it can give you a model that you can learn to adapt to other needs. If someone has already written the macro you need, don't reinvent the macro—buy it.

Whether you write the macro yourself, buy it, or hire someone to write it for you, the process is the same. First, you need to describe a pattern and variations on that pattern. Second, you need to be able to describe the action you want taken. In other words, you need a communicable plan of action or a checklist of criteria against which you can assess the macro as it is developed.

The more you can macroize, the more efficient and profitable your editing will be. The place to get started is with Jack Lyon's *Macro Cookbook for Microsoft Word*.

27

WORKING EFFECTIVELY ONLINE V—STYLESHEETS

When professional editors work on projects, they create a stylesheet for each one, a central form that details the editing decisions they have made. For example, in the medical world, *distension* and *distention* are correct spellings of the same word. An editor would decide which spelling is to be used for a project and note it on the stylesheet. Some may be handwritten, some may be online. I (and those who work for me) use an online version.

The stylesheet serves multiple purposes, the two most prominent ones being a guide to the editor as the editing project moves over days, weeks, even months, and a guide to the proofreader. In my editing world, our online stylesheet serves additional important purposes. First, it is designed to enable two or more editors to work together on a project, yet use the same stylesheet and see decisions made by other editors in real time. In my system, there is virtually no limit to the number of editors who can access and use the same online stylesheet.

Second, it lets me make a project's stylesheet available to my client 24 hours a day, seven days a week. In my system, the client is given access to the online stylesheet to view it and to print it, but the client cannot make any changes to the stylesheet. Because this is where all editorial decisions regarding the project are stored, the client can review the decisions and alert us to any of which the client disapproves. That allows us to make changes before the "mistake" becomes very costly to correct. Client access also means that, when the client sends material from the project to the proofreader, the client can also provide the proofreader with a current-to-the-minute stylesheet.

Beyond these vital functions, I can give the book author(s) client-type access (i.e., view and print but not change) so the author can give us guidance. (It should be noted that just as editors need to create a stylesheet, so should authors. The smoothest editing projects I have encountered in 28 years of editing have been those in which the authors created stylesheets and provided them before I began editing.)

I realize that much of what is, in my eyes, wonderful about my online stylesheet is because of the type and size of projects on which I work. The projects are often medical, with thousands of pages of manuscript, and require two to four editors. My system helps reduce inconsistencies that would otherwise occur when multiple editors work on a project. (What is wonderful for my work may be inappropriate for most editors who work on much smaller projects by themselves.)

Yet every editor needs to use a stylesheet to reduce inconsistencies and to alert, ultimately, the client to the decisions made. Many editors still do stylesheets on paper, which works when stylesheets are kept small, but leads to the question of how large should a stylesheet be?

Editors are in disagreement about this. I believe a stylesheet should be comprehensive. Many of my stylesheets run 40 to 50 pages. Again, my view is colored by the types of projects I do. Most of the books I do will have subsequent editions—a comprehensive stylesheet can clarify decisions made in earlier editions.

Many editors think short and sweet is better. After all, who can remember what is contained in 40 pages of style information? I think that misses the purpose of a stylesheet, which is to answer a question when it arises. No one has to read and remember everything in a stylesheet; an editor needs to concentrate on certain information, such as what form to follow for references, and then use the stylesheet to answer questions as they arise.

Regardless of how you use a stylesheet, I think editors universally agree that one must be created and kept. And this is another instance of when a mastery of your tools, especially macros, can be timesaving. Even if not timesaving, it can make using a stylesheet easier.

In the years before I created my current online stylesheet, which is based on my website, I used a local online stylesheet with macros. The macros let me select text in the main text and then process it. The selected text would be copied, the macro would then shift focus from the main text to the stylesheet and would put the cursor in the correct alphabetical box on the stylesheet. Then the macro would paste the selected text into the box, select all entries in the box, sort the entries alphabetically, save the stylesheet, and return focus to the main text. Seems complicated and difficult, but it was (is) neither, and adding to and using the stylesheet was quick and accurate.

I am an advocate of using multiple monitors when editing. My current setup uses three 24-inch pivoting monitors—usually two in portrait orientation and one in landscape, although occasionally two are in landscape. (I am thinking about adding a fourth.) I think editors should use at least two monitors, keeping the text they are editing on one and the stylesheet open on the second. With this system, macros won't be needed as it is easy enough to select, copy, and paste and occasionally alphabetize.

The ultimate point is that, to be an effective editor, you must use stylesheets. To be an efficient editor, you should use a readily available electronic stylesheet. A stylesheet is intended to promote consistency; consequently, an editor should not only keep it handy, but should note all editorial decisions on it.

28

Working Effectively Online VI—The Books

One thing I have noticed when discussing resources with my colleagues nowadays is that they often rely on online resources rather than printed books for everything they can. For example, rather than opening *The American Heritage Dictionary of the English Language,* now in its just-released fifth edition, to check a spelling or a definition, they will go to Dictionary.com or Merriam-Webster online.

The good about doing so is that (presumably) the online sources are not only accurate, but are updated regularly and thus more current, than a print book can be, at least if the supplementation is in print form. Even the venerated *Oxford English Dictionary* has turned to online, offering a year's subscription for the (relatively) paltry sum of $295.

I don't disapprove of using online resources—as long as one is choosy about the resource. What is good about the Internet is also what is bad about the Internet. It is easy to post information; anyone can do it. I make use of online resources that are specific to the type of editing I do and that are no longer available in print form or I don't use often enough to warrant purchase of a print version. Three good examples for me are the National Library of Medicine (NLM)'s *Catalog,* which provides access to NLM bibliographic data for journals and books; NLM's *PubMed,* which comprises more than 21 million citations for biomedical literature from MEDLINE, life science journals, and online books; and Integrated Taxonomic Information System (ITIS)'s *Catalogue of Life: 2011 Annual Checklist,* a comprehensive catalogue of all known species of organisms on Earth that contains 1,347,224 species, which is probably just slightly over two-thirds of the world's known species.

But when it comes chemical compounds, spelling, definitions, grammar, and usage, I prefer the printed book.

I was thinking about this anomaly—doing 100% of my editing work online yet still using print resources to check things—and wondering whether my continued reliance on print books as resources lessens the effectiveness of my online editing. Alas, I can come to no definitive conclusion.

The answer is, at best, "maybe or maybe not." For example, in experimenting with using *Dorland's Illustrated Medical Dictionary* (31st ed.) online versus the print version, I discovered that the online version is ill-designed and requires multiple steps to get to what may be a dead end. Generally, I found using the print version easier and quicker. The same was true when I experimented with *Stedman's Medical Dictionary* (28th edition).

I also have a habit of liking to look in multiple sources. As a result, I have built up a good library that is focused on my subject areas. I also like to check history. For example, while *Dorland's 31st* likes eponyms to be nonpossessive, the possessive was preferred for years and many editions past. When a client insists that, for a particular book, the possessive needs to be used except in those instances that were specifically noted to be nonpossessive (I always loved that about *Dorland's*—there was no rhyme nor reason to when an eponym was possessive or not; they were just possessive or not—before the 31st edition), I simply whip out a copy of an earlier edition, something I cannot do with online sources.

Let's not forget the expense. A lot of colleagues use only free resources. I've always been leery of free sources. After all, it takes time and money to put this material together, to check it for accuracy, and to update it. I know I struggle just to find time to update the list of books I've edited, to the point that I have neglected to do the updating for a couple of years. I've viewed this like the free antivirus programs—they are great until the first time they aren't great. We all know that the free antivirus program cannot be as good as the paid version of the same program for the logical reason that, if it were as good, the company would be out of business.

The online sources that I would rely on in many areas are not inexpensive. And the cost grows as one renews each year. In contrast, I buy a print book and its cost amortizes over the years of use; it is a one-time payment, which appeals to the frugal in me.

Regardless of whether we use print or online resources, the bottom line is whether we use a sufficient number and variety of resources to ensure that we are providing the best quality of editing or information that we can to our clients. I once asked at a seminar, "How many editors present regularly check word usage and, if you do, in how many sources?" I was surprised to discover how few check usage and wasn't surprised that those who do usually check one source. When I probed further, I discovered that usage was checked by Binging or Googling.

I admit that I had never thought to Bing or Google a usage question; I have always turned to the various usage books I have sitting next to my desk. Interestingly, the most important usage guide for American English, *Garner's Modern American Usage* (3rd edition) by Bryan Garner, isn't available online except as part of Oxford University Press' Dictionary Pro package, which must be expensive because they don't post a price—you have to request it.

I guess this is one area where one has to compromise. Some things are readily and reliably researched online; some things are better researched in print. Whatever your editorial field is, you need to keep handy both online and print resources. The biggest advantage that print has is the ability to go back to earlier editions if necessary—online resources tend to always go forward without preserving the previous. Yet, as I have discovered on several occasions, there are times when the answer to a question cannot be found in the current edition, but can be found in a previous edition, which is why I keep past editions of all my resource books.

I suspect that, in future years, fewer print resources will be used by editors and a greater reliance will be placed on online resources, especially as those of us who grew up using print resources retire and those who grew up on the Internet take over.

29

WORKING EFFECTIVELY ONLINE VII— MACROS AGAIN

In prior essays, I talked about how effective online editing includes mastering macros. What wasn't discussed is how to plan a macro.

For the simple macro, the macro that, for example, replaces two spaces with one space, not much planning is required; what is needed is fairly obvious. As a macro grows more complex, however, the difference between success and failure is often how much effort was placed in the planning of the macro. A well-planned macro nearly writes itself.

Consider most of the macros in the EditTools collection. These are complex macros that require multiple routines to accomplish designated goals and tasks. Because of their complexity, it is easy to get lost in the programming and thus not produce a usable macro.

Consequently, when planning a macro, I use a decision-tree process. I also use Storyboard paper that I buy from Levenger because it helps me visualize what I need to do. More importantly, it breaks what I need to do down into manageable chunks.

I begin at the end of the process: I define what I want the macro to accomplish. I then try to define each step that will take me to that endpoint. I use the *If . . . Then . . .* process: **If** *abc* is found, **Then** do *xyz*, but **If** *abc* is not found, **Then** do *pqr*.

Using the storyboard, I make each *If . . . Then . . .* its own entry. In the blank box on the left, I write the *If . . . Then . . .* ; on the lines to the right, I write the code, line by line to make the *If . . . Then . . .* happen. It takes at least a pair of boxes to make a single whole *If . . . Then . . .* phrase because the first is the found and the second is the not found.

Sometimes more than one not found is required so a single *If . . . Then . . .* process may need more than a pair of boxes.

Note, however, that I am using the *If . . . Then . . .* concept as a substitute for a lot of possibilities. It should not be taken literally as an *If . . . Then . . .* in coding terms. It is simply a way of breaking the process down into manageable chunks.

Making these small blocks of code serves many purposes. To make them reusable, I also number them. The numbers are not used except as a way to cross-reference. If I have already written a chunk of code that will do what I need done in the next step, I simply refer to the block of code by number for later copy and paste.

The small chunks also serve a much more important purpose: They make it easier to figure out why something is not occurring as I intend. Plus, they can be reused in other future macros—no sense reinventing the macro. And they make it much easier to rearrange a macro's coding when I subsequently think of a better or more efficient way to accomplish a task.

Yet I can hear the question now: Why do on paper what you need to do online? Yes, it can be repetitive work to first do the coding on paper and then transfer the coding to online, but the process allows me to think twice about what I am doing and—definitely of more importance—coding online takes away the storyboard decision-making tree, thus making it harder to visualize the entire process or even how a small portion fits into the scheme of the macro. A little extra work now often saves a lot of extra work later.

If you look at the Storyboard paper, you see the box at the left in which I place my decision-tree information. That information serves much the same purpose as inserting a comment into a macro. But on the Storyboard, I can readily see what comes before and what comes after the block on which I am working, which can be difficult to do onscreen.

No matter what method you ultimately choose, you need to have a decision-tree method at hand to avoid missing important steps in the macro process or leaving out things you want the macro to do depending on what is found or not found. If you use or have available Microsoft PowerPoint (or a similar program), you can use it to create an onscreen storyboard. I have tried it, but found it too cumbersome for me; at heart, for these kinds of tasks, I'm still a creature of habit and my generation, and paper and pencil seem to work best.

The key is, however, to plan your macro. Even if the coding is beyond your capabilities and you intend to hire someone to code the macro for you, having a decision tree that can be given to the coder will reduce your costs and ensure that the coder understands what you want. The coder may have suggestions for improvement, but the decision tree ensures that everyone is on the same page.

The decision tree can also make your learning to code complex macros easier and quicker. Combine it with Jack Lyon's *Macro Cookbook for Microsoft Word,* and you will discover that, as you learn to code a small portion of a macro, you are mastering macros. You will also find a greater sense of accomplishment as one coding success follows another in logical sequence.

The combination of the decision-tree process and the *Macro Cookbook* is a sure way to master the macro process a professional editor needs. Remember that the more efficiently you can edit the more money you can make over the long-term. The biggest failing professional editors have is the inability to get beyond the short-term outlook. Taking on the challenge of mastering macros will help you extend your outlook to the longer term.

30

ARE EDITORS TO LINKEDIN AS OIL IS TO WATER?

This guest essay is by Ruth E. Thaler-Carter. Ruth is a freelance writer and editor and is the owner of Communication Central, which sponsors each year a fall multiday conference for freelancers.

I spend a lot of time—some colleagues would say too much time—participating in more than a dozen LinkedIn discussion groups, as well as several e-mail discussion lists: the Copy Editing List (CEL), a Google Group for freelancers that I manage, a Yahoo Group list for DC-area publishing professionals that I co-own, the Editorial Freelancers Association (EFA) members-only list, all of which are pretty active, and a few others that are more sporadic or occasional in nature. Not to mention Facebook!

I'm not sure that the relationship between an editor and such online activity is the same as that of oil and water, but they do mix, even as they also can separate.

I could easily spend entire days doing nothing but reading and responding to online discussions. I've joked with my husband that these groups make it much too easy to stay glued to the computer, even when my better instincts and extrovert nature say to get off my duff and out in the real world, or at least get a little exercise.

In some ways, social media are like reading the newspaper, both in (some) content and how they become part of a daily routine. My husband is retired and gets up later than I do, so checking e-mail and social media sites is my first-thing-in-the-morning routine these days; I read the newspaper with my second cup of coffee, when he's up, and the rest of it still later in the day, when we have dinner together; anything I haven't finished by then, I read in the evenings.

From a business perspective, my online activity has two sides. The negative is that it can be a timewaster or distraction—it takes time away from consciously and organizedly prospecting for new clients; it could take time away from doing work; and it could be considered economically foolish, because I'm giving advice or answering questions without getting paid for doing so.

The positive side is that I'm increasing my level of visibility and status as an expert in writing, editing, proofreading, and freelancing in general; I've gotten some new, well-paying clients through my activity in most of these environments; I've made wonderful friends and gained valuable colleagues; I've learned a lot, especially from CEL; I'm usually up to date on breaking news, both in my profession and in the world at large; and I like to think I'm helping people do things better and more professionally than they might otherwise. That's a mitzvah—a good deed, a service to other people—and I do believe in networking from a helping perspective, not just for promoting or getting something for oneself.

The important thing is that I don't let this activity interfere with actually getting my work done, no matter how much fun, and occasionally how rewarding, it is to participate in these online communities. Work comes first.

I do get frustrated at some LinkedIn discussions. So many of the people in these groups aren't at a level of expertise, experience, skill, or professionalism for me to consider them as equals, but that can make someone with actual editorial experience and knowledge an important member of a group. And it can be annoying to see the same questions and comments come up again and again and again. It is incredibly frustrating to see accurate information be argued against by people with no training who have no idea what "professional" means in terms of writing, editing, proofreading, or other aspects of the editorial business, much less what it means to be a professional freelancer.

A recent LinkedIn discussion, for instance, started out by posing this question: "Would I be burned as a witch if I were to posit that all style guides are worthless?" and added: "Especially since I'm not a professional in the field of publishing?"

For one thing, you get burned at the stake for fiercely upholding a conviction, and somehow this scenario doesn't fit (I can't quite pin down why the image doesn't work; I just know it's off somehow). For another, and more importantly, why is someone who isn't even in publishing pontificating about whether style guides are worthwhile? And—perhaps even more importantly—why should those of us who are in publishing care what someone like that thinks or says?

It seemed worth responding if only because style manuals are so basic to our work as editors that their role and value should be defended whenever and wherever possible. The asker might be one of the thousands (millions?) of people who want to publish their precious ideas these days and considering whether to hire an editor, so it could be worth trying to make him understand why a professional editor would use a style guide. Most of the other participants in the discussion agreed that style guides and manuals are important to professional-level writing and publishing, especially in nonfiction work. It became clear that the original poster really didn't want to be convinced or educated, though, and I finally left the discussion in annoyance at myself for spending more than five minutes' time and one answer on it.

In a LinkedIn group for self-professed "grammar geeks," some discussions answer grammar and usage questions accurately and interestingly, but many of the responses are from people who know even less than those asking the questions. It's especially funny—albeit a little aggravating—to see non-native speakers of English present themselves as experts and give erroneous answers to fairly basic grammar questions. I chime in to make sure no one takes such answers as gospel. Someone has to provide accurate information.

One LinkedIn irony of the past week was seeing someone called a "top influencer" and knowing that was because she was unusually active over several days with increasingly incoherent and inflammatory posts complaining about being moderated (censored, in her words) in several groups.

Answering questions in various online forums often does help me fine-tune my own thinking about a topic, and has given me ideas for essays to write and conversations to have with my real peers—colleagues at CEL and my Google Group e-mail and Yahoo e-mail lists, and members of the EFA, American Copy Editors Society, Society for Professional Journalists, Society for Technical Communication, etc. I much prefer e-mail lists for discussions of the editorial profession and the freelance life, but LinkedIn adds a different dimension—and can be a good way to reach and educate people who need either editors or insights on how to be better ones.

The trick to making smart use of these online forums is to use some discipline. I have colleagues who are also active in discussion lists and online groups, and many of them find the volume of messages overwhelming. Online lists and discussions are time-takers, even when they provide useful information.

Some people set aside certain times of the day to participate in online conversations—first thing in the morning, last thing in the evening; I like to start the day by clearing out the overnight accumulation of forum and list messages, but will post responses only if I'm not on deadline for a current assignment.

I have a sorting process: First to be read in e-mail are messages from real people—clients, colleagues, and friends; then my various discussion lists; then, and only then, LinkedIn; Facebook usually once in the morning and then at the end of the day or in the evening.

Some colleagues only check on e-mail at certain points during the day; I keep my e-mail program open throughout the day in case some of my on-call clients want to reach me for fast-turnaround assignments, but I've trained myself to take a quick glimpse at incoming messages and not respond to them if I'm in the middle of a writing, editing, or proofreading project, because work comes first. If I'm immersed in a project and need a short brain-break, though, I'll stop and respond to a couple of list messages or group posts as a way of refreshing my brain—after I've gotten up and jogged around the apartment for a few minutes, that is.

It's tempting to receive discussion lists as individual messages, because then you get to be the first person to answer someone's question. However, constant individual messages from a busy list are overwhelming, so I receive my lists in what's called digest mode—batches of messages that arrive together a few times a day, instead of dozens or a couple hundred that flow in individually throughout the day. That's a good way to manage the influx of information and messages.

As long as I can enforce some discipline on myself, I'll stay involved with my online groups and lists with the goals of adding to my client list and making the world a better place for freelancers and those who use us. For this freelance writer/editor, LinkedIn, other online activity, and editing do mix like oil and water—in a good way!

31

WHAT HAPPENS WHEN
THE CLOUD ISN'T AVAILABLE?

I invest in my business. When a new version of a tool that I use becomes available, I buy it. I want to make my job easier for me and better for my clients. But the current emphasis on cloud computing worries me.

I recently received notice from Lippincott, Williams and Wilkins of the release of a new version of medical abbreviation software. I have been using this software since version 1. In previous years, I would simply order the new release and, a few days later, I would receive a CD to use to install the software on my computer. Sometimes, rather than a CD, I would receive a download link. Either method worked fine because both let me install the database locally.

The new release changes the system. Now, the only thing I can do is buy a one-year online subscription. This is problematic in several ways, with the two most prominent problems being that it now becomes a yearly expense and I have to rely on both Lippincott's servers and my Internet connection to be working correctly to access the abbreviations database.

This trend is but the tip of the iceberg when it comes to cloud computing. Amazon, Microsoft, Google, Adobe, and other megagiants of the technology world are all trying to move users of their products to the cloud. They all promise little to no downtime and, of course, more security than I have on my local computer. But all of these are unproven promises and rely on too many other factors that they do not control. What happens, for example, if Google's servers are working just fine but my gateway-to-the-Internet provider, that is, my local ISP, is down?

I don't know about you, but I have never been hacked and have never had a virus infection on my local computer. I am careful and make sure I use high-quality security software that I keep current. Every week, however, I read about how some megacorporation's secure computers have been hacked.

And what about backup? I haven't figured out how I would back up the cloud to protect myself. I would have to rely on Amazon or Microsoft or whoever having a good plan in place, one that works, and one that fulfills my needs, not the needs of the average netizen. I have multiple backup systems in play constantly, all designed to keep me running in case I let my finger hit the delete button too quickly or a hard drive gets corrupted.

Cloud computing is generally reliable. The key word is *generally*. As we all know, it is very easy for Internet service to be down and for servers to be down. Even Amazon's servers haven't been fail-proof.

As a small business, I am reluctant to place the fate of my business in the hands of cloud computing. I rely on dictionaries and word databases in my editing. I rely on being able to access my files so that I can edit them when I want to edit them. Currently, if my Internet service disappears for a few days, I may not be able to search PubMed online to make sure a citation is correct, but I can edit the substance of a manuscript with all of the tools I generally use because they are all local to my computer.

In addition, because I designed my own computer, I have removable hard drives. I can "hot swap" them as needed. What this means is that I can keep a mirror image of my entire computer at hand and, if my primary drives fail for some reason, I simply pull them out and replace them with the backup drives—all done in a matter of seconds, not hours or days.

Cloud computing has another disadvantage. I have no doubt that there are many of you who are still using older versions of Microsoft Word; after all, what real improvements has Microsoft made to Word that fundamentally affect its primary function—word processing? There have been a few innovations, but nothing earth-shattering that says you must upgrade from Word 2003 to Word 2010. You bought Word 2003 once and continue to use it happily. But with cloud computing, that will no longer be possible. Cloud computing means you renew your license yearly and always work with the most current version of a software program, whether you want it or not. Cloud computing is really just a way to increase a company's profits by forcing those who don't buy the "latest and greatest software" to buy it.

I see no advantage to the independent editor to cloud computing. The proponents of cloud computing tout how easy it is to collaborate in the cloud. OK, I admit it is easier for two (or more) people to work simultaneously on the same document via the cloud than if the document resides on their local computers. But (a) how many of us really work that way and (b) how productive would such a method be for an author and editor? In my view, I think it would add to the cost of editing and increase the difficulty significantly. Most editors I know make changes in an initial pass and then review the changes one or more times before passing the work on to the author. How disruptive to the editing process would it be for an author to see preliminary/temporary changes or queries or editor "notes to self" because of the collaborative features?

I suspect that ultimately cloud computing will be a failure except for games. If I buy an ebook, I want to know (believe) that I can access it 10 years from now, and the only way I can do so is by downloading it to my local computer. When I accept editorial work from a client, I want to be free to do my job, mull over the changes I have made, and send the client what I think is the best I can do, but I do not want the client to become resistive because the client was able to watch the process from the start.

Perhaps most importantly, I want to have my own style of working, not an imposed style that forces me to sit idle when I can't access the cloud, regardless of the reason. As part of my style, I want to be able to establish safeguards for my clients' manuscripts and I want to be able to access them as I wish. In addition, I want to be able to decide when and what tools I will buy; I do not want to be caught in the never-ending leasing cycle.

I have made it a point to notify companies that are trying to force me to buy their product in the cloud that I won't. I'll find an alternative or do without rather than encourage further inroads into my working independence.

Is cloud computing for you?

32

REMOVABLE DRIVES AND WINDOWS 8

When I first began my career as a professional editor three decades ago, I bought a computer that was "off-the-shelf." It was a Gateway (remember the cows?). Gateway let me "customize" the computer by giving me a few options in each of several categories, but, like buying a car, some options were available only if you also bought another option—even if you didn't want that other option.

Over those early years, I bought several computers—it was my practice to buy a new computer every 12 to 18 months—because technology was rapidly changing and I increasingly was selling my services as an online editor rather than a hard-copy editor. In fact, after the first couple of years, I refused to accept editing projects that weren't done online. At that time, doing so separated me from most of my colleagues who were resistant to giving up hard-copy editing.

Every computer I bought was a problem in the sense that I wasn't getting what I wanted. They all worked fine in a general sense, but they didn't contain the components I wanted in the configurations I wanted. This problem of the computer manufacturer knowing better than me what I wanted and needed was even worse with Apple, which not only limited my options with the hardware, but did the same with the software, and wanted to charge me more for the "privilege."

After my first three computer purchases, I decided I'd had enough. I either would have to learn to build a computer myself or I would have to find someone to do it for me. I chose the latter path because I wanted someone to take responsibility and action when things went wrong. That began my buying only custom-built computers, a practice I continue today (the sole exception being my very rarely used laptop, which I would have had custom-built had I had more time before I needed it).

Having your computer custom built is more expensive than buying a preconfigured computer, but not by much. Buying the closest preconfigured computer to what I currently use would have saved me about $275, but it would not have come close to what I got by custom-building. For example, two things that always drove me nuts were the noise and internal heat the computer generated from fans and hard drives and other components. By custom-building the computer, I was able to choose a high-end case that virtually muffles all computer-related noise and gives it oversized, silent fans to reduce internal heat. Now I don't hear even a whisper of noise and internal-heat-related problems have been virtually eliminated.

But the most important feature of my computers are the hot-swappable hard drives (*hot-swappable* means I can remove a drive and insert a different drive within seconds and without rebooting my computer—just like changing one music CD for another). I have mentioned these before, but I cannot emphasize enough how important these are to me. I rely on my computers for my livelihood. If my computers are down or data is lost, I'm in trouble—I do not earn any money when my computers are not working correctly (which is one of the reasons I also avoid free antivirus/antimalware software). Having removable hard drives helps prevent downtime and lost data (I also take other precautions).

I should note that my computers are built with three hard drives. One is the operating system and programs drive (C:), one is my standard work drive (D:), and the third is my miscellaneous drive (E:). The E drive gets most of the swapping these days because it is the drive that I use to image my other two drives and thus use as a portable backup.

The removable drives were particularly useful to me with the arrival of Windows 8. I wanted to upgrade to it, but I was not sure how much I will like it. It is a wholly different experience from previous versions of Windows and, from what I am reading, may not be suitable for the way I work. Yet it offers me something that I want: cross-device compatibility.

I have been a holdout as regards going from the telephone-only cell phone to a smart phone. I'm still using a cell phone from eight years ago. But I made the smart phone upgrade with Windows 8. I wanted a Windows 8 cell phone with a Windows 8 computer. My hope is that the experiences will be so similar that I won't have to master multiple methods of doing things. That remains to be seen, but that is my hope and plan.

Which brings me back to my computer. Windows 7 has been by far the best Windows operating system. It works well, never crashes as a system, only occasionally does MS Word crash in it (but the recovery is quick and excellent in terms of saved data), and has been easy to use. I am somewhat reluctant to give up what clearly is working well. This is where the removable hard drives come to the rescue.

My plan was to duplicate my C: drive on another hard drive, stick it in the slot, and upgrade that drive to Windows 8. That would give me both a Windows 7 drive and a Windows 8 drive. I will be able to "play" with and familiarize myself with Windows 8 without losing any valuable work time. When I'm ready to play with Windows 8, I'll simply pop out the Windows 7 drive, pop in the Windows 8 drive, and play. When I need to get back to work, I'll repeat the process in reverse. Each swap will take me a few seconds. Even if I will need to reboot the computer because I am swapping out the operating system, the total procedure time will take me less than two minutes.

Should I decide that I do not like Windows 8 for my work operating system, it will be no problem. I just will stop swapping the hard drives—no need to uninstall, reinstall, and reconfigure operating systems and other programs.

I know that many people do not want the hassle of trying to figure out what components they want in a computer, do not want to pay 10¢ more than necessary for a computer, and prefer the comfort of having limited options and buying from a reputable company. Yet designing your own computer isn't difficult and there usually is a local computer shop that will build and warrant the computer. (My local shop warrants the computers for three years—parts and labor—and so makes sure that he installs only high-quality components.)

If nothing else, having removable hard drives should be enough incentive to having your computer custom built. What do you do now when you travel to protect your business from disaster? With my removable drives, I do several things. First, I image my C: and D: drives onto other hard drives. I then store one set of hard drives in a safe deposit box and a second set with my neighbor. If disaster should strike while I'm gone, I can be back in business, everything in proper working order with no program or data loss, as quickly as I can get a new computer shell built—a couple of days at most. More importantly, in case of theft, the thief gets nothing but a computer shell—no data at all.

Removable hard drives give me the best of the computing world for my business's future. Custom-building my computers ensures that they serve my needs for computing power. Custom-building also ensures that I have high-quality components that are less likely to fail and disrupt my business (and thus my income flow). Removable hard drives let me try new programs without disrupting what already works.

Buying a limited-option, preconfigured computer means conforming my work style to what someone else thinks it should be, not to what is best and most efficient for me. I prefer to make my own business decisions.

33

AUTHOR QUERIES

What is the role of an editor? Aside from the usual things like correcting grammar and misspellings and making sure that sentences have ending punctuation, it is to query the author about unclear sentences, text that doesn't flow, missing material, and myriad other nitpicky things that can change a so-so manuscript into next year's Pulitzer Prize winner.

I've been editing professionally for 29 years. What I have noticed over those years is that certain author queries repeat themselves ad nauseum. I bet I've written "AQ: Please provide complete cite. Need to add/provide" a gazillion times over those years and I expect to continue writing that query in the years to come.

I have also found that clients want queries done differently. Most want them inserted as Word comments, but some want them placed inline (i.e., in the text) and in bold. What I want is to do what the client wants but as quickly and painlessly as possible. After all, the longer it takes me to write and place a query, the less money I make. Thus, I use EditTools' Insert Query macro.

I don't often use the inline method of querying but when I do, the Insert Query macro makes it look like this:

> ... and according to Jones and Smith (1999), {[AQ: Reference not in reference list. Please add this reference to the list or delete it here.]} the experiment

As I noted earlier, I find that there are a lot of queries that get repeated; they are not project-specific. For example, I find that I need to use this query often:

AQ: Recur/recurrence mean to happen again repeatedly; reoccur/reoccurrence mean to happen again but only once. Which do you mean here?

I also often need to use this one:

AQ: Do you mean e.g. rather than i.e.? When the items are only examples and the list is not all inclusive, e.g. is used. If the listed items are all the possibilities, then i.e. is used. If i.e. is correct, consider removing material from parens and making it a proper part of the sentence.

Imagine having to write these queries each time you want to ask the author about usage. It will take time, plus you may have to correct a typing error. It is much easier to have a query saved as a standard query and to call it up when needed.

My queries dataset currently has 84 "standard" queries. I don't use all of them in every project, but these are queries that I have found that I use repeatedly over the course of time.

Authors often will write something like "Within the past decade" I usually question such statements because most of the books I work on have a long shelf-life and the chapters themselves were written months before I see them. Thus the timeframe is uncertain. So I ask:

AQ: Using this type of time reference allows the time to shift. The shift occurs because the reference was made when you were writing the text but doesn't allow for either editing and production time until publication or for the book's expected several-year shelf-life. It would be better to write, for example, "since 2000" (substitute the appropriate year), so that the time reference always remains static.

As you can see, it would cost me a lot of time, and thus money, to write these types of queries with any frequency. Besides, isn't it better to do it once? Don't we prefer to copy and paste than to constantly rewrite?

With the Insert Query macro, I not only have the query in my dataset, but before inserting it into the document, I can modify it specifically for the matter at hand. I can either save the modified version to my dataset for future use or just use it the one time without losing the pre-modified version.

I'm sure you are wondering how I can quickly sort through 84 queries to find the one I want for the particular project. It isn't as difficult as you think. First, the queries are spread over five tabs in the macro, so if I need a query that relates to a reference, I go to the Reference tab. Second, I can reorder the queries in a tab so the ones I make most use of in a particular project are always at or near the top. Third, if I do not need to modify a query, all I need to do is click on it and then click Insert—a fairly fast method for inserting a query. I do not need to first open a comment dialog box; the macro does it for me when it inserts the query into the document.

Everything has to be weighed in terms of time and keystrokes. The more time and keystrokes that are involved in querying an author, the less money I make. Also important is that, if I have to manually write a query like one of those above just three or four times in a manuscript, I will become frustrated. They are long, they are detailed, and they are prone to mistyping. By "standardizing" them with the Insert Query macro, I get it right every time I use the query. And it takes me no longer to create the original query than if I were opening a comment dialog box in Word and entering it there. All of the time and effort savings occur with subsequent use.

Here are a few more of my standardized author (and compositor) queries:

AQ: This is a single-author chapter. Please identify to whom "our" refers.

AQ: Please identify where by section title if within the chapter, by chapter if in another chapter.

AQ: Acronyms that are deleted from the text are either used fewer than 3 times in the text and are now spelled out in the text or do not appear in the text.

AQ: This is chapter _____. If you are referring the reader to a specific section in this chapter, please identify where by section title and whether above or below, and delete the chapter number. If you intend a different chapter, please correct the chapter number.

COMP: Please make the letter J in J-shaped sans serif.

In today's competitive editing world, it is important to find ways to increase efficiency and productivity. Tools like the Insert Query macro are an important part of the process for increasing efficiency and productivity. EditTools is designed to increase my speed, efficiency, and accuracy, thereby increasing my effective hourly rate for editing.

34

DOMAINS AND E-MAIL

In other essays, I discussed invoices and the importance of a professional look for them. A professional-looking invoice that establishes you as a business is only part of the solution to being perceived as a business, rather than as someone who is just looking for "vacation money." Your e-mail address is another facet of the "look."

When I see an e-mail from *yourname@gmail.com*, I wonder how well the sender is doing. Why would I buy a product from a gmail address? Having your own domain name is neither expensive nor difficult these days. Editors who write me seeking work from addresses such as gmail.com, aol.com, and yahoo.com give an initial first impression that editing is part-time work for them. I do understand that this may well (and often is) a misperception, but we are talking about first impressions—not true impressions, just first impressions. Such addresses make me wonder whether the editor is in the business as a business or just looking for occasional work more as a hobby.

Unlike some of my colleagues, I do not think an editor needs to have a website. I think having one can be beneficial, but, depending on how you run your business and who your clients are, a website may be unnecessary. But having your own domain is an absolute *must*. If you buy goods over the Internet, as most of us do, do you prefer to buy from what appears to be a company or from an unknown person with a generic address?

You use your invoice to convey the image of a business. Why would you tarnish that image by not having a business domain name and an e-mail address based on your domain?

129

One argument I have heard is that it costs too much money. The reality is that it doesn't. 1and1, for example, which hosts my websites and is the registrar of all my domain names (37 of them), offers the first-year registration of a .com domain for $7.99 ($10.99 for subsequent years). Website hosting for the first year is as low as 99¢ a month ($4.99/month in subsequent years). Other ISPs offer similarly low prices. Even if this did cost more, it's an investment in your business and is still worth doing.

Another argument I've heard is that "it doesn't matter; my clients don't care." I'm sure there is some truth to this sentiment, but it fails to address the underlying concern: How do current and *prospective* clients view you? Do they view as a "real business" or as someone looking for extra income to pay for two weeks at Disneyworld? Perhaps your clients don't care, but they can not care just as easily if you have your own domain name. You really have no way of knowing whether prospective clients care or not, unless you keep track of the ones who never respond to your queries. For all you know, an unprofessional e-mail address is why.

Years ago, when I taught a marketing class for editors, I said that whatever you do and however you do it reflects on whether you are viewed as a professional and a business or as someone who is doing editing work just to earn extra play money. In those days, impressions were generated largely by telephone, snail mail, and letterhead; today, that impression is given by websites and e-mail addresses.

Ultimately, looking like a professional business is like a three-legged stool. The stool requires all three legs to be stable; editors today require more than topnotch skills and a good-looking invoice to give and rein-force the impression that they are a business. In today's Internet world, we have to give an impression of ourselves using somewhat anonymous tools, of which invoices and e-mail are two such tools.

Not only should an editor have their own domain (I advise against domain names that are simply your name, such as *janesmith.com*) but, once the editor has established a business-like-sounding domain name, the editor needs to create an appropriate signature for e-mails.

The signature should reflect that you are a business. It should include your name, business name, mailing address, website URL, e-mail address, and blog information if you blog. Here is the text of my signature:

Richard H. Adin
Direct Line: 845-471-3566
rhadin@freelance-editorial-services.com
rhadin@wordsnSync.com

Blog: www.americaneditor.wordpress.com

Freelance Editorial Services
52 Oakwood Blvd.
Poughkeepsie, NY 12603-4112
www.freelance-editorial-services.com
www.wordsnSync.com

It is a little fancier than it appears here (but not much), but the point is that every e-mail includes this signature and, with every e-mail, I reinforce the idea that I am a company by repeating the company name, Freelance Editorial Services.

My invoices include the company logo, company name, physical address, and telephone number (and, of course, my Employer Identification Number—*not* my Social Security number). They do not include my name. Many years ago, my invoices did include my name; in fact, the head on the invoice was almost a replica of my e-mail signature. But clients wrote checks to me or looked to make a direct deposit into an account that bore my name, neither of which did I want. I want payment made to Freelance Editorial Services because that is my company name and I want to be viewed as a company, not as an individual.

(Here's a tip regarding invoices: For many years, my invoices included both a telephone number and an e-mail address. About seven years ago, I found that a couple of clients were using the e-mail as a means to create a payment delay—it was so easy to not receive e-mail replies! I stopped including my e-mail address on my invoices and now only include a telephone number and physical address. If there is a question about an invoice from accounts payable, accounts payable calls me, which enables me to resolve all problems immediately without back-and-forthing. I can do this because of the types of clients I serve; you may not be able to do so.)

I'm sure you are asking, why does it matter? Why do I want to be viewed as a company rather than as an individual? Because companies get taken seriously, paid promptly, and treated as business partners. A domain-based e-mail address makes you look more like a company and a business.

35

EDITING TOOLS:
MULTIFILE F&R AND SEARCH, COUNT, REPLACE

As regular readers of this blog know, I occasionally discuss macros that are included in the EditTools package. I created EditTools to enhance my editing skills, and to increase my productivity and efficiency, and thus increase my effective hourly rate.

In this essay, I tackle two more of the macros in EditTools: MultiFile Find and Replace and Enhanced Search, Count, and Replace.

MultiFile Find and Replace

On occasion, while editing a chapter, I discover that I made an error in previous chapters or that a style decision I made in earlier chapters has met its nemesis in the current chapter and needs to be changed. In the olden days, this meant that I had to reopen each chapter I had previously edited and do a find-and-replace. This was time-consuming and, because I work on a per-page basis, potentially costly. Thus was born MultiFile Find and Replace (MFR).

When I have finished editing a chapter (document), I place it in a different directory than the directory that contains chapters yet to be edited and the chapter I am currently editing. Edited chapters that I have not yet sent to the client are placed in an MFR directory; once they are sent to the client and thus no longer subject to my revision, they are moved to the Done directory.

(My directory structure for a project is as follows: The parent directory is the name of the client [e.g., XYZ Publishers] and each project from this client has its own subdirectory, which is the name of the project or its author(s). The subdirectories within the project directory are Original, CE, Figures, Count, MFR, and Done. Original contains all of the files I receive from the client for the project. This assures me that I always have access to the base files. The files in Original are then sorted, with figure files copied [*not* moved] to the Figures directory and the text files to be edited copied to the Count directory. I next count the manuscript pages contained in the files in the Count directory. [I often do not receive all of the files for a project at the same time, which is why there is a Count directory.] Once a file has been counted, it is moved [*not* copied] to the CE directory for editing. After editing, the edited file is moved to the MFR directory, where it remains until it is added to a batch of files for shipping to the client. When sent to the client, the file is moved to the Done directory.)

MFR works just like the normal find-and-replace except that it works on every file in a directory and it automatically tracks changes. The same caution that you would exercise with Word's find-and-replace, you need to exercise with MFR. MFR opens a file, does a search, replaces where appropriate, and then saves the newly revised file.

Before I created EditTools, I used MFR in a prospective fashion. I used it to make changes to files that are waiting to be edited. However, I rarely do this anymore, preferring to make use of EditTool's Never Spell Word macro for prospective changes.

Enhanced Search, Count, and Replace

Enhanced Search, Count, and Replace (ESCR) is a workhorse macro for me. It is one of my most often used macros; perhaps the only macro I use more frequently is the Toggle macro.

As I have said in prior essays, I work on a lot of professional books. The one commonality to every professional book—regardless of subject matter—is that acronyms are used extensively. Acronyms are the short-hand language to which "insiders" of a profession are generally privy. Yet not all acronyms are commonly understood even by "insiders." I daresay that most people know what is meant by AIDS, even if they cannot give the definition of the acronym, but do not know either the meaning or definition of CREST as used in CREST syndrome (for the curious, CREST means "calcinosis cutis, Raynaud phenomenon, esophageal motility disorder, sclerodactyly, and telangiectasis").

Consequently, my clients generally have a rule that they want applied: Every acronym—except the most commonly understood acronyms—has to be spelled out at first use in a chapter (sometimes a book); to be kept as an acronym, it must be used at least three times in the chapter (otherwise spell it out); and subsequent spell-outs of the acronym need to be changed to the acronym for consistency.

In olden days, this was a problem. It was a nightmare when editing was done on paper; it downgraded to a headache (albeit a severe one) with the advent of computers and increasingly sophisticated word-processing search functions. Yet even today this is a major headache in the absence of ESCR.

ESCR is not perfect by any means, but it is a significant improvement over other methods of searching for an acronym and its spelled-out version, counting the number of times each appears, and replacing the miscreant versions. With ESCR, my process is greatly simplified and the time it takes to search, count, and replace is reduced to seconds.

By the way, although I am always talking about using ESCR for acronyms, the macro is not limited to acronyms. That is just how I primarily use it. ESCR will work on any word or phrase that you can select, so if you want to know whether the author excessively uses the phrase *in order to*, ESCR will do the job—and it will let you change the phrase to something else.

At the first appearance of an acronym, I ascertain whether it is spelled out; for example, does it appear as *acquired immunodeficiency syndrome (AIDS)* or just *AIDS*? If it doesn't appear both spelled out and in acronym form, I add the spelled-out version so that both appear. I then select both the spelled-out phrase and the acronym, including the parens or brackets, and run ESCR. (How do I know that it hasn't been spelled out previously? Because if it had been, it would have been highlighted, which is the signal to tell me that I already have checked this acronym and it has already been verified and spelled out.)

ESCR generates a report that tells me how many times, for example, each of *AIDS, AIDs, Acquired immunodeficiency syndrome, acquired immunodeficiency syndrome,* and *Acquired Immunodeficiency Syndrome* appears in the remainder of the open document. It excludes from the count the selected text; it only counts subsequent instances. I then have, for each item it reports, the option to have ESCR replace the existing text with different text or to highlight the existing text. So, if ESCR reports the following (the number following the text indicating the number of times the text appears subsequently in the document):

AIDS 15
AIDs 2
Acquired immunodeficiency syndrome 5
acquired immunodeficiency syndrome 10
Acquired Immunodeficiency Syndrome 1

I can tell ESCR to highlight every instance of items 1 and 5, indicating they are OK as they are, and to change the text of items 2, 3, and 4 from what they currently are to *AIDS*. ESCR will then go through the document—and with track changes on—will highlight every instance of *AIDS* and *Acquired Immunodeficiency Syndrome*, but will change every instance of *AIDs, Acquired immunodeficiency syndrome,* and *acquired immunodeficiency syndrome* to *AIDS*. (The highlighting serves two purposes: it tells me that, [a] as already noted, the acronym was spelled out earlier in the document, and [b] the highlighted material is correct.)

What could be easier or more efficient? ESCR and MFR make my editing more productive, more efficient, and more accurate.

36

Preparing for Disaster

I run a business; I am a professional editor; I work full-time as an editor. In addition, I have several professional editors who work for me. All of us rely on my ability to obtain work and keep clients happy and returning. Fortunately, I have been successful at this for many years.

Yet always in the back of my mind is a worry. I worry about what will happen should my computer be struck by a virus, by malware, or by equipment failure. I worry because my business depends on my equipment.

My worrying was much greater in my early years than it is today. The years have seen significant improvements in both hardware and software. Additionally, over the years, I have learned how best to prepare myself for an emergency.

Let me begin with hardware. As I have said, over the years, it was my practice to replace our computers every 18 to 24 months. Technology was making great strides and I wanted to stay abreast—not cutting edge but just one step behind. In the very beginning, I bought, as most people do, off-the-shelf computers. I learned very quickly that I was throwing away my money.

I have never owned an Apple product. I do understand why people swear by Apple computers, but I look at Apple computers and see a high price for mediocre equipment. I do not mean that negatively. Apple's mediocre components can be much better than many of the off-the-shelf computers' components. What I do mean is that, for the same or a little more money (or even a little less money), I can have a custom-built computer that uses the best-quality individual components. Apple's mediocre quality is in comparison to high-quality custom-built computers. The other problem with Apples has been the behind-the-times support for Word's macro language. I rely on macros but Microsoft's Apple support has always been half-hearted, and Apple itself hasn't shown much interest in supporting Microsoft VBA on its computers. The combination of inability to customize my computer and lack of robust macro support led me to the Windows world, where I have remained.

What I want are computers that meet my future needs, not my current needs. I also want computers that work with me to prevent a disaster from destroying my business. Thus, I have our computers custom-built. Our current computers are now about five years old and still going strong (although I am thinking about a couple of upgrades, even though the upgrades will make no visible difference in my work).

There are two things that are absolute must-haves for my computers: (1) an Antec (or similar) case and (2) hot-swappable hard drives. The Antec case is required because I like quiet and want superior component cooling. Although expensive, the Antec cases are very quiet and offer superior cooling. If I unplugged my NAS (network-attached storage) box, you would be able to hear a pin drop in my office because my computer is so quiet, and I've never had to worry about hardware failure from overheating. This is purely a luxury must-have as the case doesn't enhance performance; it just eliminates annoying sounds and minimizes the risk of component overheating.

But the hot-swappable hard drives are very important. These are drives that can be easily and quickly (in a couple of seconds) be removed from the computer and replaced with other drives. It isn't so much the being-replaced-with-another-drive that is important as that I have duplicate drives, one in safe storage, the other in the computer, which minimizes the risk of downtime and lost work. And when I travel, I can remove all of the hard drives and put them in a safe deposit box and not worry about something happening in my absence that would put me out of business (or let thieves get hold of my data). (Removable hard drives are available aftermarket for Macs.)

The removable drives also let me take weekly images of my hard drives on a dedicated drive as a way to protect against a disaster that would require all new drives or a new computer. The image would let me recreate my computer in minutes. Combined with Carbonite's remote backup, which occurs automatically every time I modify a file, I can recreate my current computer in a few hours. (Carbonite is available for Macs.)

Also important hardware-wise are my triple-monitor setup and the NAS box. The NAS box has four hard drives (two paired sets) in it and is responsible for storing my daily backups. I like easy and automatic backups, so I use Backup4All, which backs up the files into standard zip files. The NAS box lets me store several months worth of backups. (NAS boxes are available for use with Macs.)

Software also plays an important role in my disaster preparations. I have already mentioned two, Carbonite and Backup4All, and I use the built-in imaging software that comes with Windows 7 to do the disk imaging. But a very important program is PC Tools' Registry Mechanic. I have been using the program for a number of years and it has come to the rescue a couple of times. I have it run every day after bootup. What I especially like about Registry Mechanic is that it creates a restore point so that I can restore a problem Registry to an earlier one that was problem-free. To do the restore takes a few seconds—a couple of mouse clicks and a reboot.

Being able to go back in time and replace my Registry is an important tool in fighting malware. Malware often changes entries in the Registry and sometimes it is very difficult to remove the malware from the Registry. Restoring an older version of the Registry, from before the malware invasion, often can solve the problem. In all my years of using a computer, I have never had to completely erase my boot drive and reinstall all my software to remove a virus or malware or to fix a problem Registry.

I also use BitDefender Internet Security for antivirus and firewall protection. Over the years, I have used various antivirus and firewall software programs, including free ones, but for the past five years, my choice has been BitDefender. I am not a fan of free antivirus software. It is not that such software cannot be good, but I know from my own business that I cannot give away my services and survive. So there has to be something that is held back or that doesn't work as well with the free versions; otherwise, what would induce you to upgrade to a paid version? And if there is limited income coming in to an antivirus/antimalware company, how does the company generate enough income to constantly update the virus and malware signatures? (One exception may be Microsoft's AV software because Microsoft generates a lot of revenue from other products.)

As I've said before, if my computer is not working, I'm not working. If I'm not working, I'm not earning any money and I'm not meeting my clients' needs. It is not uncommon to read about an editor whose computer got infected with a virus and now is having problems. I can say that, in all my years of editing on computer—and I started back in the late 1980s—I have never been down because of virus or malware invasion. I attribute this to using the right tools in the right combinations.

Passwords also concern me. I worry about password theft. I don't care if someone steals my password to *Consumers Report*, but I do care if they steal my banking passwords or the passwords to my websites and e-mail. Consequently, I use RoboForm to store and input my passwords. I have been using it for many years, since version 1. Letting RoboForm enter the information avoids the problem of keyloggers grabbing my password as I type.

Finally, as discussed in previous essays, I use an online stylesheet. This stylesheet is at my website. If my website goes down, I'm in trouble. Over the years, I have tried several different website hosts. About nine years ago, I moved to 1and1, where I have remained. In the past five years, my website has been unavailable a total of two hours (approximately), with one exception, which was my fault, when it was down nearly four hours while 1and1 restored my website. (In doing a programming upgrade, I accidentally erased all of the coding of the live site rather than of a sandbox site. I called 1and1 tech support—they always answer with a live person within two or two minutes, and usually less—and it took them a few hours, but they did fully restore my websites.)

Although some of the programs may not be available for Apple computers, I suspect that equivalent programs are. We rely on our computers to earn our livings, which means we should be taking those steps necessary to ensure that any downtime is minimal—and that all our data is safe.

What special steps do you take?

(*Disclosure:* I have no financial interest in any of the products mentioned. They are products that I have purchased and use.)

37

LIABILITY INSURANCE—NYET

One problem with working as an editor for large organizations is the contract that the organization wants you to sign. Some of the clauses have validity, others I wouldn't sign regardless of the promised fee. Recent discussions on various lists have focused on another requirement: to carry liability insurance (an errors and omissions policy) for such things as defamation and other events that have nothing to do with editing.

These contracts are boilerplate and prepared by attorneys who rarely have a clue about what an editor does, for the express purpose of covering all of the possible arcane matters that can affect a publisher. As editors, we need to say "Nyet!" to these inapplicable clauses.

When I am faced with a demand for errors and omissions insurance, I ask the client to specify clearly and precisely against what risks I need to insure myself and against which the client will seek indemnification. I point out, for example, that defamation is not something an editor does; it is something a writer does. I make it a point to educate the client as to what precisely an editor does and does not do, after which I ask the client whether I am being hired as an editor or to perform some other function, one that has the potential to make me wish I were insured.

If the client expects me to undertake tasks that *could* make me liable for such things as would be covered by an errors and omissions policy, I know I need to decline the job—because it is not an editing job. Copyeditors don't decide dosages or medicines, don't determine whether a beam's angle is correct, do not determine whether a street is a dead end or a highway on-ramp, or decide whether a named person is properly described.

I also ask the client whether the client truly believes that anyone would issue an errors and omissions insurance policy that protects against subjective decisions. What I mean is this: What insurance company will insure against my choosing to refer to people as "that" instead of "who" (as in "the patients that" vs. "the patients who") or will reimburse the client for my use of "followup" (which the *American Heritage Dictionary 5e* says is OK, along with "follow-up") as opposed to "follow-up" (which is the only form accepted by *Merriam-Webster Collegiate 11e*)?

"And what," I ask clients, "if I use *recur* when it should be *reoccur?*" (In case you are wondering, recur usually means to occur repeatedly whereas reoccur means to occur again once, but in medicine, recur is used for both meanings.) "Do you really think an insurance company is going to pay a claim for my using one over the other?" What if I don't use serial (Oxford) commas or if I do use them and the nonuse/use changes meaning (as in the infamous "eats, shoots and leaves")?

Every editor knows that issues of language and grammar are rarely right-wrong matters; rather, they are matters of opinion in the sense that both sides of a language and grammar question can be, and often are, correct. How do you insure against making a decision that can be correct but just doesn't tickle a client's fancy? Perhaps spelling is in a separate category most of the time, but as *followup* versus *follow-up* illustrates, spelling is not in a separate category all of the time.

Clients are intelligent; what clients are not is omniscient. Consequently, when I am faced with a contract clause that requires me to obtain errors and omissions insurance, I endeavor to educate the client. First, I ascertain what the client thinks my job is. Then I educate the client as to what my job really is. If we cannot come to agreement on the parameters of the job I am being hired to do, I say thank you and walk away. To do otherwise is to bring me trouble.

A fundamental rule of editing is that client and editor must agree on the parameters of the job or the client needs to find someone else to do the job. Any editor who fails to grasp and embrace this rule is bound to have unsuccessful client relationships.

After I educate the client about what my job is, I undertake to educate the client as to why the insurance clause should be stricken. The usual response by a client is that, if the clause has no relevance to my work, then we'll leave it in and ignore it. Alas, to agree to leave in and ignore is to invite danger (for me) into the client-editor relationship. Meaningless clauses need to be struck, not ignored, because once a contract is signed, the unstruck clause is no longer meaningless. It may be that I cannot be held liable for defamatory text written by the author, but I still need to buy the insurance or be in breach of the contract. And do I really want to incur the expense of defending against a client's attempt to make me liable for not catching that the dose should be 12 mg, not 120 mg?

If the client insists on retaining the clause, I send a revised estimate for the project. I take my original price and add to it a price for the purchase *and* administration (i.e., my administration) of the insurance. I submit that revised price to the client and explain that my other clients do not require such insurance and that it will be a special purchase just for this client, thus the additional charge. In addition, because the purpose of the insurance is not to protect me but to protect and indemnify the client, the only beneficiary of the insurance is the client, so it is only fair that the client pay the cost.

My experience has been that, at this point, the client is willing to strike the clause. But I am prepared for when the client simply says sign or go. I always will (and have occasionally had to do so) choose go and refuse to sign.

The only insurance I carry specifically for the benefit of clients is Worker's Compensation. I maintain such a policy because it proves to the IRS that I am an independent contractor and clients who worry about proving that I am not an employee accept the certificate of insurance in lieu of all other items of proof, such as copies of tax returns or lists of clients, that they would otherwise require (and which I do not wish to divulge).

Part of being a businessperson is drawing lines that I will not permit clients to cross. Those lines are important. They form the basis of the relationship between me and my clients. One of my lines is that I will not sign contracts that contain terms that are not applicable to what I am hired to do, especially if those terms will cost me money.

What do you when faced for a demand for an errors and omissions insurance policy for your copyediting work?

38

THE EDITOR'S INTEREST: COPYRIGHT OR NOT

A question that sometimes arises, usually when an editor has difficulty getting paid for his or her work, is: What can the editor do to collect payment? I've been a long-time advocate of the position that the editor has a copyright interest in the *edited version* of the manuscript, a card that the editor should play in payment disputes.

We need to step back a little. First, if you are an editor and have a written contract governing the relationship between you and the client, unless the contract specifically provides for your copyright interest, you don't have one—your relationship is governed by the four corners of the written contract.

Second, the law is unsettled, not clear, or whatever other description you want (muddy, perhaps?), as regards an editor's interest in the edited manuscript.

Third, the editor's interest I advocate extends *only* to the edited version. The author and/or publisher has an unencumbered copyright interest in the original manuscript the editor received; it is only the editor's edited version in which the editor has an interest—and that interest is wholly extinguished upon being paid in full (i.e., the check has cleared, not the check has been received).

As you can see, I am talking about a narrow interest, not the broader interest that an author has in the manuscript. This narrower interest can readily be extinguished in two ways: (1) payment for service in full or (2) wholesale rejection of the edited manuscript. Acceptance of even a single comma, or corrected spelling—that is, of any single edit—is, in my view, sufficient to retain the editor's interest.

Here is where opinions begin to scatter. I have been told by lawyers for one major publisher that I do not have such an interest. It was a great thrust to the heart by the publisher but, alas, it missed. If lawyers scare you, then this isn't the position to take. But if you have some titanium backbone, the response is (and the one I made):

"I am willing to find out in a court of law. Are you willing to take the chance that the court sides with me, because if you are and if you lose, you will make life exceedingly difficult for your publisher client. Isn't it smarter to simply pay my bill?"

The reality is that it is smarter to pay my bill and not hire me again. It is unlikely that what is owed me is such a large amount of money that the risk of losing in court is worth taking.

Of course, there are steps that should be taken when using this collection method. You should send both an e-mail and a certified-mail return-receipt letter to the client notifying the client of your interest and demanding that they either pay your invoice in full immediately (be sure to give a specific payment date) or

- not publish the edited manuscript;

- if they publish the manuscript, that they not sell any copies or distribute any copies;

- if they sell or distribute any copies, that they place 100% of all receipts in a trust fund pending outcome of litigation;

- and that they notify the author(s) in writing that you are claiming a copyright interest in the edited version of the manuscript because of the client's failure to pay for your services, which payment would extinguish your copyright interest.

You'd be surprised at how much influence a screaming author can have, especially if the author liked your work! If you know how to contact the author, you should send a copy of the e-mail and letter directly to the author as well as to the publisher.

All right, I admit we haven't yet determined how valid the editor's claimed copyright interest is, but I'm not sure it is possible to determine its validity in the absence of a major court's definitive decision (lower court decisions have little precedential value; just witness the five decisions on Obamacare). Because it is an open question, I see no problem in making the claim. Personally, I see no problem in defending the claim, either.

A court decision adverse to a publisher and in favor of an editor on this could have significant ramifications for publishers. It would add pressure to pay on time because an editor could prevent release of the manuscript in its edited form. Of course, it could also encourage publishers to add editing to the list of items to be bypassed in the book production process, but doing so would remove one of the few remaining justifications for traditional publishing.

The most likely result would be the influx of contracts. Today, most publishers still work on the handshake basis; that is, they contact an editor and ask if the editor is available, tell the editor what is wanted, and send the manuscript for editing. Sometimes a purchase order is included. In return, the editor edits the manuscript, returns it with an invoice, and receives timely payment. Welcome to the world of 99% of publishers and editors.

The problem is the 1% with whom a handshake is like striking a bargain with the devil who has its fingers crossed behind its back. They promise payment in 30 days and then, when the work is done, tell you it will be six months. Or they tell you how much they love your work until the invoice arrives, at which point they tell you how bad your work is and want you to reduce the invoice. Or they tell you the manuscript is 250 pages and only requires a very light edit when the reality is it is a 400-page manuscript that requires a very heavy edit because the author's English language skills are virtually nonexistent.

With the 99% of clients, a contract or a handshake means the same thing and either will work. With these clients, the issue of the editor's copyright interest never arises. Even if they hate your work, they will pay your invoice on time and just not call again. Paying your invoice costs less than two hours of attorney time, so business sense dictates payment.

With the 1% of clients, neither a contract nor a handshake has any meaning. It is with these clients that one must be prepared to use the complete arsenal available to collect for work done. Unfortunately, we often don't discover that a client is part of the 1% until the work is done (perhaps a particularly good reason to bill and get paid in installments), at which time the 1-percenter thinks we are over the barrel. It is with these clients that the copyright claim is most effective and should be invoked.

Do editors have a copyright interest in the edited version of the manuscript? Maybe, maybe not, but it is a weapon in the editor's collection arsenal that should not be ignored.

39

EDITORS AND CONTRACTS: EDITOR BEWARE!

My editing world is, admittedly, fairly narrow. Years ago, I decided that I would only do a certain type of work (subject-matter–wise) and only for select clients (i.e., publishers, not authors). Consequently, the following discussion is shaped by 28 years of that narrow world and is focused on contracts between freelancer and publisher/vendor.

Over my editing career, I have been asked to sign a contract fewer than six times; I have never asked a client to sign one. Until recently, the last contract I was asked to sign happened a decade or more ago. I'm not sure why this is the case, except that I think my clients view the situation as I do—a contract isn't necessary between companies.

Also until recently, the purpose of the contract wasn't really to detail the relationship's obligations but to establish that I am not an employee and cannot be construed to be an employee of the client. In other words, it was to protect the client from my claiming that I was an employee of the client and entitled to employee benefits. The contract was designed to establish my relationship with the client should the Internal Revenue Service come knocking on the client's door.

For the most part, once a client realized it was issuing payment to a company rather than to an individual, and once the client realized that I have payroll obligations, something employees of the client wouldn't have, I think the necessity for a contract disappeared.

But recently I was asked to sign a contract.

The story begins with a publisher who asked me to edit a book that will run between 7,000 and 9,000 manuscript pages. The book has a "fussy" author (that's fussy in the good sense of being both knowledgeable about and caring of the use of language, not in the negative sense of being troublesome) and a short deadline of 12 weeks. Manuscripts of this size are what I commonly deal with and the short deadline just raises a challenge, not an obstacle that can't be overcome. (And it is projects and deadlines like these that make investing in macros invaluable!)

Although I was asked by the publisher to take on the project, the work and payment would come through a third-party vendor. The publisher would simply tell the vendor that I was to be hired to do the editing and that the rate had been agreed on. I was to work with the vendor and not the publisher.

That arrangement is not unusual in today's publishing world. It is more common, perhaps, at least in my niches, for my name to be on a list of preapproved editors from among which the vendor can choose and negotiate a rate. I admit that I rarely find that to be good for me.

So the project is agreed to and the procedure agreed to and the work starts. Nothing more occurs until I submit the first batch of edited chapters and an invoice. That is when the vendor tells me that there is a contract that the vendor requires every freelancer to sign. The purpose, I'm told, is to ensure confidentiality. (I wonder who would want to see the edited manuscript for one of these books other than the author, but I also have no problem with agreeing to confidentiality.)

So the standard agreement was sent for my signature.

Let's start with a few questions to set the stage: How many editors read such agreements? How many understand the agreement? How many editors are willing to say no and refuse to sign absent significant changes? How many editors are fearful that, if they do not sign the agreement, an avenue of work will dry up and leave them in dire straits? How many editors would say to themselves, "Although I don't want to sign, I'd better, because I've already completed x% of the work and I want to get paid"?

Okay, you have the idea as to the stage-setting questions and undoubtedly can add more to the list, yet it is the answers that matter.

The contract I was offered was wholly one-sided. I had all of the obligations and none of the benefits. I wasn't even assured of receiving the project I had been hired for if I signed the contract. In addition, the contract was riddled with grammar and spelling errors, which would leave the terms of the contract in a state of flux. But the worst clause of all—and there were many candidates for this honor, not least of which was the clause that required editing perfection and set the vendor up as the sole judge of whether the editing was perfect—was that any dispute arising from the relationship between myself and the vendor had to be resolved in a court in *India*! The contract even mentioned Indian labor laws, as if I would have any idea of what Indian labor laws permit, do not permit, or require. Interestingly, the contract was open-ended; no work was promised and no specific project named—the contract remained in force until explicitly terminated by the vendor. Does indenture sound familiar?

I have nothing against India but I have never visited the country, I have never worked in the country, I have no plans to either visit it or work there, and I know nothing about Indian labor laws. Why would I sign such a contract? More importantly, why would any non-India–based editor sign such a contract (perhaps it shouldn't even be signed by an India-based editor)?

And consider the perfection clause I mentioned earlier. Professional editors know that there is no such thing as perfect editing. There are very few rigid rules in editing that apply universally and never change, which is why we have, for example, 16 editions of *The Chicago Manual of Style* and 11 editions of *Merriam-Webster's Collegiate Dictionary* and three editions of *Garner's Modern American Usage*.

I offered to sign a modified contract, but that was rejected. A colleague, Ruth Thaler-Carter, suggested to me that, at the very least, I should insist on a clause that reads along these lines (with additional modifications by me): "Freelancer cannot be held responsible for changes made by the Vendor once Freelancer has submitted his/her/its editorial work to Vendor and, should Vendor make changes that result in any form of liability to Freelancer, Vendor agrees to indemnify and hold harmless Freelancer at Vendor's expense."

Editors face a dilemma. They want and need the work that comes to them via third-party vendors, yet they really shouldn't sign open-ended, one-sided contracts, especially ones that require them to use a foreign court system to resolve disputes. What editor could afford to go from the United States to India to enforce a claim for $500?

There is no easy solution to this problem. In my case, it was resolved to my satisfaction, but that was because of the intervention of the publisher, not because the vendor wanted to be reasonable. The vendor's position was that you either sign the agreement as presented or you get no work. The vendor is really in the catbird seat because there are thousands of editors from which it can choose, but there are, by comparison, few vendors.

Could you walk away from such a job? Most editors cannot, which brings me back to a topic I've mentioned before: Professional editors really need a professional guild, at least a national one but preferably a worldwide one, whose focus is on protecting the member editors and finding the member editors work. We also should do our best to have enough work in hand or in the pipeline, as well as a savings cushion, to be able to say no to draconian or unreasonable contracts.

Even if you believe you have no choice but to sign on the dotted line, you should take the time to carefully read and evaluate any proffered contract. In addition, you should try to negotiate the more onerous clauses. Under no circumstance should you sign a contract like this that is open-ended. If you must sign such a contract, limit it to the project at hand. You never know when an open-ended contract will come back to bite you.

40

CONTRACTS—A SLIPPERY SLOPE

When I first began editing as a freelancer, I never was offered a contract by a client. I was hired to copyedit or developmental edit, and it was understood that I would do my best and the client would pay me for my work. Even the structure for payment was understood to be what constituted a billable (i.e., hourly or a page, which consisted of x). It was a "handshake" agreement.

For the most part, even today, this is how I conduct much of my work. Yet, increasingly, I am being asked to sign a contract. This has occurred since the last time I addressed this issue, when I talked about a contract from India. Today, I am talking about a contract from the United States.

Because this is the "client's" standard contract, I have to wonder how many editors either read the contract that is proffered or, if they do read it, understand it; or if they simply sign it and consider doing so a necessity to have any business. I also wonder how many, if any, editors simply reject a burdensome contract.

As some of you know, my background is as a lawyer. Before becoming a professional editor, I practiced law for a number of years and learned early on in that career that business-to-business contracts really do need to be read and understood, and not just blindly signed.

The latest contract that I received simply reinforced that learning. It would almost be impossible to write a more one-sided and unfair contract short of one that says I would be responsible for the other party's financial losses should the stock market decline for the next 100 years.

Good editors are language-smart, but sometimes not business-smart. Sometimes the need or desire to have work outweighs the common sense that dictates "do not sign the proffered contract." But it shouldn't, because some contracts are so exploitative that you have to wonder about the company that is proffering it. Would you trust the dog that bites the hand that feeds it?

Essentially that is what a contract is—an expression of distrust. The question is how much distrust is tolerable. I find that, the more onerous the contract, which indicates that the offeror really distrusts the people with whom it "wants to work," the less worthy the profferor is of being trusted. And thus I prefer not to sign.

Consider statements that say you will be paid "for satisfactorily rendered services." What exactly does that mean? Who decides? How long do they have to decide? Is it satisfactory to leave "due to" in a manuscript? Is it satisfactory to not distinguish between "since" and "because"? Suppose you think a series of items should be a bulleted list rather than a run-on sentence. Is that okay?

What about a clause that says the client can audit your books? Are you an independent contractor or an employee?

Or consider the attorney-in-fact clause, which says that you appoint the client as attorney in fact to sign your name to any necessary applications for intellectual property protection for any reason. The only thing missed is taking possession of the bathtub.

One of the strongest methods to ensure payment is the availability of the lawsuit remedy. Yet contracts insist that any claims be arbitrated and that doing so be at *your* expense. Back in the beginning of time, arbitrators had a reputation for lack of bias and for fairness; that reputation is long gone. I would be hard-pressed to voluntarily give up my right to sue.

The contract I was most recently offered also stated that my work product was a work for hire and that I waive any claim to ownership in my work product. Period. End of story. The waiver doesn't come about because I have been paid or even because the client is obligated to pay me. No, it comes about because I unconditionally waive all my rights (which I'll do immediately after the cheese the moon is made of is placed for sale in my local supermarket).

When you receive a contract to sign, do you look at the limitation of liability clause? You should. Invariably, the client has no liability. There is no mention of your not having any liability, which means that you might have some.

My favorite clause is the one that reads similar to this: "This agreement shall be interpreted as written and negotiated jointly by the parties." Rarely is a client willing to negotiate any term of the proffered contract; it is a take-it-or-leave-it proposition. But this clause has a great deal of legal significance should a dispute arise.

Finally, I love when I get a contract that incorporates the material in an attached exhibit and the attached exhibit is not filled out. An early learned rule is never to sign a contract with blanks. Good luck proving it was incorrectly filled out after you signed, not before.

The list of objectionable clauses and why they are objectionable can go on, but simply listing them doesn't answer the fundamental question: What can I, the editor who is offered such a contract, do about it? What *should* I do about it?

I usually send a note back saying I cannot agree to the contract as submitted and give reasons paragraph by paragraph. Usually there are a couple of unobjectionable paragraphs, but, for the most part, the more wrapped in legalese the contract is, the less likely I am to sign it.

I usually begin by noting that the contract has little relevancy to the services for which I am being hired. What relevance does a clause about patents have to copyediting? I suggest that, if a contract is necessary, we should discuss realistic terms that are relevant to what I am expected to do as an editor. I also make it clear that, contrary to the assertion in a contract, there are no universal, objective standards to which either party can look as measures of quality for editing, so it is necessary that the client define precisely what standards the client will apply to my work product.

I go through this exercise knowing that it is futile; with rare exception, these contracts are nonnegotiable. But I want the client to understand that I do pay attention to detail, and this is a subtle way of enforcing that message.

In the end, it usually comes down to either signing the contract as submitted by the client or passing on the work. Given that choice, I decide how trustworthy I think the client is. If I think I can trust the client, I will sign the contract; if I have any doubts at all, I will not. There is little sense in inviting trouble. Usually—but not always—my refusing to sign the contract means no work from the client. Several times in recent months, however, the client has simply worked with me as if nothing about a contract had ever been discussed. In these cases, the work with the client has been ongoing, not just a single project and then no more.

Regardless, editors need to be careful about the contracts they sign. It is better to not sign and lose the work than to work for a client whom you can't trust. Just as you have a minimum acceptable fee for taking on work, so you should have a standard for contracts below which you will not descend. At the very least, never sign one before reading it carefully and assessing its potential impact on you and your business.

41

NONDISCLOSURE AGREEMENTS

Have you been asked to sign a nondisclosure agreement (NDA)? In recent months, I have been asked three times to sign such an agreement, and three times I have declined to sign the agreement as provided.

If you have been asked to sign such an agreement, how carefully have you considered its terms, what those terms mean, and what effect those terms might have on your business? Based on conversations with colleagues, I suspect that most of the time the agreement is just signed and considered a requirement of doing business. For the most part, I would think the agreement is meaningless—after all, exactly what trade secrets are editors being made privy to?—but because such agreements could return to haunt me years down the road, I am careful about what contracts I sign.

These agreements are particularly problematic when they are with an offshore company. Citations to foreign laws and provisions to litigate in foreign (to me) courts are red flags—these are two things that I simply cannot agree to. I imagine having a dispute with a client whose NDA requires me to litigate in Indian courts. I have no doubt that Indian courts will fairly apply Indian law, but what do I know about either Indian law or the Indian court system? And based on what I read about how long litigation takes in India, I'd likely be buried before any dispute was resolved, after having spent many thousands of dollars prosecuting or defending an action.

It is bad enough when I am asked to sign agreements that are governed by U.S. law and courts. My pocketbook isn't unlimited; it is paltry compared to that of the company that wants me to sign the NDA.

Interestingly, none of the NDAs I have been presented with have ever really defined what I am not supposed to disclose. They use terms like "trade secrets" but they never clarify what that means. I make it a point—before signing—to ask for an *exhaustive* list of what constitutes a trade secret. I want to make sure that (a) it is information to which I am privy and (b) that I agree that it is a trade secret. More importantly, I don't want to be ambushed. How can I know what not to disclose if you don't tell me specifically that the information is a trade secret?

The NDAs also usually include a very broad clause that is a mother clause to another, somewhat subsidiary, broad clause. The first says that anything you invent or improve upon becomes the company's intellectual property. The child clause says that you give the company permission to execute your name to any paperwork it deems necessary to lay claim to your inventions. Together, both clauses cover everything you have done from the day you were born and everything you will do to the day you die (when read in conjunction with the clause that says the NDA will continue in force even after your relationship with the company ends).

I suspect that no reasonable court would uphold such clauses, at least based on my knowledge of American courts, but the truth is, I have no idea what a court in India or Germany or Spain or Tunisia or Brazil or anywhere but America is likely to do—and even with American courts, all I'm doing is "educated" guessing. To find out what a court would in fact do, I would have to initiate a lawsuit—an expensive proposition.

Also missing from the NDA is any benefit to me. There is no guarantee of work; there is no payment in exchange for my signature; there is no reciprocal agreement that the company will not disclose my trade secrets. What is usually said is that they cannot hire me without the NDA, but that is not the same as saying they will hire me if I sign the NDA. And there is certainly nothing in the NDA that says that, should they hire me, they will pay what I consider a reasonable rate. The NDAs are decidedly one-sided.

I have certain rules by which I conduct my business. First, any disputes have to be settled in the American judicial system under American law. I am an American editor with an office in America.

Second, I will not sign any agreement that gives the company the right to execute documents of any type in my name. I have no idea who these people are. My signature is one of the most valuable things I own; giving it away seems to me not to be a smart idea.

Third, I will not sign broad agreements. Agreements must be specific and limited. All of the NDAs are written for consultants who are going to come to the company and examine its books and procedures and make recommendations and improvements, or who are being hired to create something specific to improve the company's workflow. I'm not doing anything even remotely close to that. I edit books. I have no idea what the contract terms are between the companies I work for and their company or author clients. I make sure sentences end with punctuation and that *flippant* is spelled correctly. I don't determine whether a book is worthy of publication or how many units to print or how large the marketing budget should be or whether the book should be digitized or anything else that remotely could be called a trade secret by a reasonable person. Thus, the danger of these broad clauses and why extraneous/inappropriate clauses must be stripped from the agreement.

Fourth, I will not sign a contract that is so one-sided that it should be titled "Certificate of Indenture." I must get something in return, something much more than a future promise of possibly some work. I will offer to sign an NDA for a specific project with the NDA limited to the specific project.

Fifth, I will not sign an agreement that gives a company the right to lay claim to things I create, invent, or improve upon that facilitate my doing my work. I have spent, for example, many thousands of dollars developing EditTools and my (patent-pending online) Max Stylesheet. EditTools makes my work go more smoothly and quicker; the Max Stylesheet makes it easy both for multiple editors to work closely on a project and clients to access a book's stylesheet years after I edited it. Both are tools for my business and marketing points. Yet, under the presented NDAs, the companies could lay claim to these items and could execute documents to take title to them without compensating me.

I understand the need for NDAs. After all, no company would like to give a consultant access to its databases only to find that the consultant is selling the data to the company's competitors. But companies need to look at who they are asking to sign NDAs and not simply have a blanket rule that requires everyone to sign one. An editor like me who has no access to company information is not really a candidate for an NDA.

More importantly, I need to carefully read and consider any agreement presented to me. What are its implications? What if something does go wrong? What if nothing goes wrong but the company sues me anyway? How important is this company's business to me?

The bottom line is this: The company doesn't trust me enough to give me work without signing an Orwellian NDA but expects me to trust it to do what is correct and honorable when it deals with me. A handshake will serve me, but not the company. Doesn't sound like a very promising relationship to me.

What do you think?

Part III

PROCESS

"If *you* don't believe you are the greatest, who will?"

—*Richard H. Adin, An American Editor*

To succeed in the business of editing, you have to understand the process that takes a manuscript from computer screen to published work, not just in terms of editing and proofreading, but also in terms of how the editor and author work together. This section goes into detail on how the process works (and sometimes doesn't).

42

The 3 Stages of Copyediting:
I—The Processing Stage

Mechanically, the copyediting process can be divided into three stages:

- the *processing stage,* where the manuscript is prepared for the copyediting process;

- the *copyediting stage,* in which the manuscript is actually copy-edited; and

- the *proofing stage,* where the manuscript is checked for the misses or new errors that may have occurred during the copyediting stage.

Each stage has its own methods and focus, but all three stages are performed (usually) by the same editor, and a professional editor has an arsenal of tools at hand to make the work of each stage more accurate and efficient. As with most things, every professional editor has his or her favorite tools. Unfortunately, some still use what I call the hit-or-miss method, which is dealing with each thing as they stumble upon it rather than having a coordinated routine that is applied to all projects.

It is true that every project is unique unto itself, but there are still universalities that fit neatly under a planned approach. For example, today it is well-established that only a single space follows punctuation, not the double space that was the convention when we were using typewriters to prepare manuscripts. Converting double spaces to single spaces is one of those universalities—and there are numerous others.

Today, most editorial work is done in Microsoft Word; it has become the de facto standard software for publishing—but only for the manuscript preparation stages. Typesetting is done in professional page makeup programs like InDesign, and one of the jobs of a professional editor is to prepare the author's manuscript—mechanically—for smooth transition from Word to InDesign (or whatever page makeup program is being used). Consequently, what is discussed in the following paragraphs assumes that the underlying program is Word.

Stage I: The Processing Stage

This stage is a mechanical stage. This is where the manuscript is cleaned up, and author excesses are laid to rest. Most of this work can be done by macro; it is the work that doesn't require constant decision making. In this stage, the editor changes, for example, double spaces to single spaces, changes double hyphens to em-dashes and hyphens between numbers to en-dashes, changes underline to italics, removes extra paragraph returns, puts punctuation inside quotation marks, superscripts reference numbers, and so forth.

The processing stage is an ideal stage for macros. To make the task easy, many editors use FileCleaner from the Editorium. This set of macros was developed specifically to address the common cleanup problems copyeditors deal with routinely. The Editorium also offers other macro programs to help automate the routine processing tasks. Two of my favorites—and two I could not do without—are Notestripper, which fixes the problems of embedded footnotes and endnotes that otherwise are not easily editable, and ListFixer, which takes Word's autogenerated lists and converts them to fixed text so they can be edited.

Another set of processing-stage macros is found in EditTools by wordsnSync. Two particularly useful macros in the EditTools collection for the processing stage are Superscript Me and Page Number Format. In-text reference numbering is often supposed to be superscripted, but authors tend to either place them in parens or brackets (i.e., (1) or [1]), and sometimes they use both methods. I regularly deal with chapters that have more than 500 reference callouts (I recall once editing a book-length chapter that had more than 2,800 reference callouts in it—not one of which was superscripted as required!). Think about how long it would take to manually delete the parens or brackets and to superscript the callout number—and then compare that to using Superscript Me, which does the task in seconds. Page Number Format addresses another typical problem: conforming the reference page range style the author used to the publisher's style. Again, in seconds, this problem can be fixed with EditTools.

EditTools and the Editorium macros are two commercially available programs of sophisticated macros to preprocess a manuscript and get it ready for editing. The idea is to take the drudgery out of the mechanical tasks that need to be done, and get those tasks done quickly, efficiently, and accurately.

Editors who do not use commercial programs to do these tasks either have to create their own macros to address their own needs, manually undertake the cleanup using Word's Find and Replace, or address each item as they come to it during the copyediting stage. Using Find and Replace to do one item at a time is a slow process and requires a checklist to ensure that none of the standard tasks is omitted. It also requires knowledge of and comfort with using Word's wildcard capabilities. Editors who prefer to create their own macros or use the Find and Replace approach would do well to invest some time and effort in learning VBA (Visual Basic for Applications), Word's macro language.

The least satisfactory method is to address each problem as you encounter it during the copyediting stage. Not only is this time-consuming, but it is distracting. During the copyediting stage, the focus should be on the substance, not the mechanics, although there will always be some overlap. Editors who do not already use macros from the Editorium or wordsnSync in the processing stage should consider trying them to see if the macros make their editing more efficient and less time-consuming.

Part II addresses the copyediting stage and some of the EditTools macros for this stage of the editing process.

(*Disclosure*: I have no financial connection to or other interest in either Intelligent Editing or the Editorium. I have purchased their macros and use them in my own editing business. I am the creator of EditTools and an owner of wordsnSync Ltd.)

43

THE 3 STAGES OF COPYEDITING:
II—THE COPYEDITING STAGE

Authors love to "help" their publishers (or even themselves if they are self-publishing) by formatting the document to make it look like they think it should look when published. As most editors will tell an author, doing so really adds to the cost of the editing because a good editor needs to clean out all these extraneous features and properly tag the content.

The simpler the formatting/styling done by an author, the less costly and time-consuming the copyediting will be, because it will free the copyeditor to do what the copyeditor is supposed to do.

Again, the mechanical aspects of preparing the file are addressed by various macros from the Editorium and some of the macros in EditTools. But it is here, in the second stage of copyediting—the true copyediting stage—where EditTools becomes a key component of the process.

Stage II: The Copyediting Stage

EditTools is a group of macros designed to improve accuracy in the editing process while increasing efficiency. Not all of the macros are usable in all projects, but each serves a purpose that, when combined, enhances the quality of the editing.

Consider, for example, Toggle, which is particularly useful in nonfiction books and articles but is equally usable for fiction. One of the things that a copyeditor has to do is make sure that there is consistency in a book. If the style is for all numbers 100 and lower to be written out except when used as a measure, the copyeditor has to convert 99 to ninety-nine but only where appropriate. And this is where Toggle comes into play. Think about how long it takes you to press a single key versus to type ninety-nine; and add up all of the single key press times versus the typing times (and the retyping because you mistyped!).

My current Toggle list has more than 1,300 entries in it, which means that, with the press of a single key (I assign my primary macros that I use repeatedly as I edit to single key presses such as to F4) I can change any of 1300+ items; for example,

- *which* to *that*

- *about* to *approximately*

- *since* to *because*

- *US* to *United States*

- *Marvin* to *Martha*

- *CFO* to *treasurer*

- *HIV* to *human immunodeficiency virus*

- *100* to *one hundred*

- *x* to the correct *times sign*

- *hyphen* to the correct *minus sign*

- and hundreds of other things

and whatever else I put in the list through the Toggle Manager (no need to understand programming or to open and close lists; the Toggle list is dealt with through the easy-to-use Toggle Manager)—all by the press of a single key. Creation of the list is wholly up to me and my needs; it is not prepackaged or limited.

Most books have multiple chapters and it is the rare author who creates a single file when writing. Thus the need for MultiFile Find and Replace. Should I discover that the character name Mariah is suddenly to be spelled Marya, I can now look for Mariah in all of the files the author submitted and replace it with Marya (with Track Changes on) immediately. This avoids the problem of missing a fundamental correction in a subsequent chapter.

One of the things I try to learn from a client before I begin editing is if the client has particular preferences, especially for spelling. This is particularly important when a book is being written by teams of authors, a common occurrence in medical books. When I learn of these preferences, or if as the editor I make a decision to accept one spelling over another, I enter the information in the Never Spell Word macro via the Never Spell Word Manager. For example, in medical terminology, there are two accepted spellings for distension: distension and distention. Once one form is chosen, I use NSW to ensure that it is used consistently. I could use either MultiFile Find and Replace or Word's own Find and Replace, but that would mean I have to go through a list of words repeatedly and manually. NSW lets me create a standard list as I edit—I can always add to it.

More importantly, perhaps, NSW—through its color-coding system—tells me that certain terms are OK as they are. For example, if the author decrees that WHO never needs to be spelled out as World Health Organization because everyone knows what it means, I can enter WHO in NSW, choose "no spell/OK as is," and every instance of WHO will be appropriately highlighted, reminding me that I do not need to spell it out.

As part of the NSW macro, there are several other tabs. There are some default names, but with the current release, you can customize the tab names and the data files they call upon. But these tabs serve a purpose, too. For example, because I do a lot of medical editing, drug names are important. But I admit I can't remember all of the drugs that are available, used to be available, and will be available, so I enter drug names as I come across them into the drug tab list and, next time I run the NSW macro for a medical project, every correct drug name in the manuscript that matches a drug name in my data list will be highlighted in green, telling me that the entry is correct—one less thing I need to verify because I have already done so. NSW builds on experience: Once I have verified something and entered it into a portion of the NSW macro, I no longer need to re-verify it.

One last example of how valuable EditTools is to a copyeditor: I do a lot of nonfiction books and most of them are replete with citations. If there is a subject you can think of, there is probably more than one journal that is published that addresses it. Thus the Journals macro and its Journals Manager.

The task of editing reference material is complicated and time-consuming. There are a lot of elements that the editor has to address and authors tend to complicate the editing of references by not being either consistent or accurate in their typing. It isn't unusual, for example, to find in the same reference list New Engl J of Medicine, N Engl J Med, N England Journal Med, and other variations of New England Journal of Medicine. In fact, in the PubMed database that is used for medical journal names and abbreviations, there are more than 10,000 named journals—and that isn't a complete list.

To the rescue comes the Journals macro. My medical journals dataset currently has more than 5,700 entries in it. Not all are unique journal names; there are also the author variations. But I run this macro over a reference list and, if the author has correctly cited the journal name, it is highlighted in green; if the cite is incorrect and the incorrect-to-correct form is in my data list, the incorrect form gets corrected automatically. If it isn't in my list, it will be—I will add it as I come to it during the editing process, thereby growing my list.

I recently had to edit a reference list of 732 entries—a whole lot of cites that would take a whole lot of time to do. Fortunately, every journal cited by the authors—and every variation they used—already was in my data list. Within seconds, I knew which journals were correct and those that were incorrect were automatically corrected.

The Journals macro also solves another problem: Like drugs, there are thousands of journal names. Who can remember them all? (Would you remember, for example, that a cite to the *Chinese Journal of Radiology* should be a cite to *Zhonghua Fang She Xian Yi Xue Za Zhi*?)

Although I've only skimmed the surface of EditTools, it is important to know that its primary function is to work with the editor *during* the copyediting stage, not before and not after. A professional editor uses tools to make the editing process quicker, more efficient, and—above all—more accurate. In the not-so-long-ago days, we had to keep track of everything by hand, repeat tasks endlessly, and use pencil on a paper manuscript. Today, we can harness the power of computers and, using the tools described in the three parts of this essay—Editorium macros, EditTools, and PerfectIt—we can harness the power of Word macros to make editing quality and accuracy better than ever.

The least satisfactory method is to address each problem as you encounter it during the copyediting stage. Not only is this time-consuming, it is distracting. During the copyediting stage, the focus should be on the substance, not the mechanics, although there will always be some overlap. Editors who do not already use the EditTools in the copyediting stage should consider trying them to see if the macros make their editing more efficient and accurate and less time-consuming.

Part III addresses the proofing stage and using PerfectIt for this stage of the editing process.

(*Disclosure:* I have no financial connection to or other interest in either Intelligent Editing or the Editorium. I have purchased their macros and use them in my own editing business. I am the creator of EditTools and an owner of wordsnSync Ltd.)

44

THE 3 STAGES OF COPYEDITING:
III—THE PROOFING STAGE

Now that the manuscript has been prepped and copyedited, it is time to take one last look through the manuscript to catch some things that may have been missed and to do a final cleanup. This is the proofing stage—the third stage of copyediting—and the stage where PerfectIt is so valuable.

Stage III: The Proofing Stage

No matter how good an editor is, the editor will have missed something; the more complex the manuscript, the more somethings are likely to have gotten by the editor's eagle eye. For example, 18 times in the manuscript, the editor hyphenated *time-consuming*, but twice did not. Are the exceptions correct or just missed hyphens? That is the question—among many questions—that PerfectIt asks.

PerfectIt analyzes your document in detail, looking for certain types of "common" errors. For example, if the rule is that numbers 10 and below are to be spelled out, it will flag instances of the number 10 in digit form and ask you whether it should be corrected. And what about capitalization of heads? Was it correct to use sentence style in this head when all other heads use title case style?

PerfectIt comes with 27 built-in tests, that is, things to look for. The tests include:

- hyphenation and dashes, including phrases with hyphens and dashes, single words split by hyphens or dashes, and compound words

- spelling consistency, including spelling variations, numerical characters, common typographical errors, and contractions

- abbreviations, including abbreviations in two forms, defined two ways, used before being defined, defined the same way more than once, abbreviations without definitions, and abbreviations not used

- capitalization, including capitalization in phrases and heads

- list punctuation and capitalization

- tables, boxes, and figures, including capitalization, punctuation, consistency, and order

- comments and highlighting left in the text

- final cleanup tasks, such as removing double spaces and creating a table of acronyms

PerfectIt also lets the editor create his or her own custom word lists, which are the tests to be run and the parameters for the tests. For example, rather than being presented with having to choose each time whether *self esteem* or *self-esteem* is preferred, the editor can create a custom word list that tells PerfectIt to (a) never find self-esteem, (b) always prefer self-esteem and so find instances of self esteem, or (c) always prefer self esteem and so find instances of self-esteem. This customization also works with spelling (i.e., not just phrases and hyphenation) so, if the editor prefers distension over distention, the editor can make distension the always-preferred spelling and instances of distention only will be found.

If the editor chooses *self-esteem* as the preferred form, when PerfectIt finds *self esteem*, it tells the editor how many locations this form appears in and provides an opportunity to go to those locations if needed. If the editor is certain that it needs to be corrected, clicking the Fix or Fix All button makes the corrections (with tracking on). No need to manually fix each instance.

PerfectIt's display is divided into several informational panels. At the top, it tells you what test is being run and what percentage of the proofing process has been completed. Immediately below the test name, PerfectIt describes the error it has found and how many instances of it. For example, if the test is "Abbreviations in two forms," the error description may say "Error description (1 of 3)," indicating that three errors have been found and this is the first one.

This panel is followed by the "Choose preferred abbreviation" panel. If the error is that sometimes the abbreviation is USA and sometimes it is U.S.A., this panel will tell you, for example, "USA (found 5 times)" and "U.S.A. (found 2 times)." You click on your preference and then look below this panel to the final panel, which shows the locations of the nonpreferred form. You can then fix them one at a time or all at once—or you can decide that these are not errors based on the context and thus not change one or more of the "errors." The editor always has the option of leaving something as it is. PerfectIt is mechanically finding these errors so that the editor can apply his or her editorial judgment.

PerfectIt is a perfect way to do a final check of an edited manuscript. It can save an editor from embarrassment and can reduce the number of errors that clients find. Although not a panacea for all errors and missed items, PerfectIt does focus on the more commonly missed items.

Editors who do not already use PerfectIt in the proofing stage should consider trying it. I can tell you that, when I found PerfectIt, I downloaded the trial version, and within five minutes of running it on a chapter, I bought it. I immediately saw its value, and have been recommending it since.

The combination of Editorium programs, EditTools, and PerfectIt will enhance every editor's accuracy and efficiency. Improving efficiency is a sure way to improve any editor's bottom line; improving accuracy is a sure way to improve editor and client relations because better editing results in lower client costs.

(*Disclosure:* I have no financial connection to or other interest in either Intelligent Editing or the Editorium. I have purchased their macros and use them in my own editing business. I am the creator of EditTools and an owner of wordsnSync Ltd.)

45

CITING SOURCES IN THE AGE OF THE INTERNET AND EBOOKS

It has been an ongoing frustration of mine, dealing with bibliographic information that cites the Internet and ebooks.

In the olden days, way back when I was a student, the rule was that citing a source meant it really existed and was verifiable; one couldn't cite and have accepted "James, J. (2010, August 10). Private conversation." But today, I guess, anything goes—at least if you are in the role of author but not in the role of paper-grader; that is, I find these types of cites in academic papers knowing full well that, if a student of the author submitted such a cite, it would be unacceptable.

More important, however, is that cites to web pages that no longer exist—if they ever really existed—seem to be de rigueur, and no one complains. It used to be that it was not enough to cite a source, but the source had to be reputable and accepted in the field. It was pretty hard to cite *Portnoy's Complaint* as an authority on sexual mores, yet I suspect that would not be true today.

Recently, I edited a book that relied on the Internet for 85% of its authority. A spot-check of the cited URLs showed that 50% of those checked either no longer existed or led to articles that had nothing to do with the topic at hand. Interestingly, in another book, the URLs led to third-party summaries of the cited articles, not to the articles themselves.

This does not bode well for the quality of authorship of future work. The problem is compounded when ebooks are thrown into the mix. I'm currently reading a 1,200-page ebook. If I cited the ebook for some proposition, how would a reader verify it without reading the whole ebook? eBooks, unlike pbooks, are not paginated. eBooks in the ePub format come with page numbers, but do they correspond to the pbook pagination? Or are they even the same across devices?

What the Internet and ebooks have done is encourage scholarly sloppiness. Increasingly, the response to a query about a source cite is, "Well, it was at that URL on the date I noted. What has happened since, I don't know and it doesn't really matter." And publishers and academicians are buying into this view of source cites—publishers because it is too difficult to get authors to provide solid cites and academicians because it is easier than the more traditional citing procedure.

No one is addressing, however, what this does to the value of the "research." I find that, when I am reading a book I bought and the author has used an URL citation or referred to an ebook, I begin to doubt the accuracy of the book. If I find that a cited URL no longer exists, the value of the book as a scholarly work diminishes rapidly.

I'm not sure what the solution to the problem is. Supposedly there are Internet archives whose purpose is to take snapshots of the Internet daily to preserve information, but I've not been able to access such an archive.

I recognize that, as the face of information changes, so must the acceptable methods of citation. Yet there needs to be a method of ensuring that a cited source exists today, tomorrow, next year, and next decade, or scholarly value will decline along with the availability of the source material. In addition, there needs to be a way to vet online sources such as Wikipedia for accuracy.

It is not enough that an online citation format appears in the standard style manuals; somehow, the online sources need to be preserved, vetted, and accepted, especially as reliance on such sources grows. In addition, there needs to be a system adopted for universally being able to find cited information in an ebook, not just a broad citation to the ebook, and whatever that method is, it needs to be implemented by ebook device makers and publishers. Whatever method is designed, there needs to be a correspondence between the pbook and ebook versions of the same book; in addition, the method has to be device-independent.

There is still a long way to go to make the Internet and ebooks scholarly sources, but the day is coming when it must be accomplished.

46

Symbiosis: The Authorial and Editorial Process

Although not usually thought of in these terms, there is a symbiotic relationship between the authorial and the editorial processes. In many ways, it is like the relationship between a composer and librettist. How well the relationship works can determine how good the end product is.

A well-written book is analogous to Maurice Ravel's *Bolero*. It begins softly, builds to a crescendo, and adds new characters and plot twists and turns (i.e., new instruments and sounds) until that climactic moment.

To bring off a well-written book successfully, not only must the author have great skills, but the editor must be skilled. To use another music analogy, consider opera. The role of the author is that of the composer; the role of the editor is that of the librettist. In the case of opera, the person credited with the opera is the composer; the librettist, although noted in an acknowledgment, is publicly forgotten. Yet, what makes an opera great is the symbiotic relationship between the composer and the librettist.

Consider Léo Delibes's opera *Lakme*. It happens to be one of my favorite operas. I especially love the "The Flower Duet," sung as Lakme and her servant Mallika gather flowers, which was written by the librettists Edmond Gondinet and Philippe Gille, who are essentially unknown in the opera world. It is the combination of the music and the duet between Lakme and Mallika that makes "The Flower Duet" so extraordinary.

Just as this combination of the known (composer) and unknown (librettist) can combine to create great, memorable music, so the relationship between an author (visible) and editor (invisible) can combine to create a great book.

Unfortunately, with the changes that are occurring in publishing and with the rise of ebooks, this symbiosis between author and editor is being strained to the point of near-breaking. Publishers are trying to cut production costs as finely as they can, and too many see editorial work—in the sense of editing and proofreading—as being of ephemeral value. It is no longer uncommon to hear a publisher say that readers don't complain about poor editing, so they obviously must not notice when editing is missing.

Authors, who with the rise of ebooks are increasingly taking on the role of the publisher, take the same tack but more often emphasize the expense. One author boasted on the copyright page of his meganovel that the ebook hadn't been copyedited because no one cared and he wasn't going to spend the money. That might have been okay if the ebook were being given away for free, but the ebook was $8.99! (I read enough of the ebook via a sample to realize it was in desperate need of an editor, so I passed on buying it.)

The authorial and editorial processes are really a single process; different phases of a single process, but a single process nonetheless. We tend to divide the phases of manuscript preparation into separate stages and processes, but that is really more for convenience than a reflection of the reality of the process. The two processes are so intertwined that they should be inseparable and authors should not fear an editor's input. A manuscript doesn't become less the author's work because of editing, but it may become more of the author's vision as a result of editing.

Consider Ernest Hemingway and F. Scott Fitzgerald and their editor, Maxwell Perkins. Although Perkins is considered to be perhaps the greatest editor of the 20th century, it is not Perkins who is remembered and revered (except by a few of us editors who know of him), but Hemingway and Fitzgerald. Yet both acknowledged that their books would not have been the masterpieces they were if it hadn't been for Perkins's contributions.

Ultimately, my point is that, like great music, great books are collaborative enterprises and, when part of the collaborative team is missing, the book suffers, the author suffers, and the reader suffers. Authors need to rethink their stance when they decline to spend money to hire a professional editor. And there is a world of difference between a professional editor and a friend whose job is maintaining a computer network who thinks he/she can edit a book because they have read a lot of books. Because the author wants to be viewed as a skilled writer, the author needs the help of a professional editor whose skills transcend those of the neighbor who dabbles because he/she reads.

The authorial and editorial process can help a book follow the path of *Lakme*—from beginning to finale—in creating another memorable "Flower" duet.

47

ARTIFICIAL OR ARBITRARY SCHEDULES

As I've noted before, I am now in my 28th year as an editor and I like to think I am as professional an editor as any of my colleagues. Yet there is one thing that always sticks in my craw when it comes to dealing with clients: the artificial schedule.

I call it an *artificial schedule*, but it could as readily be called an *arbitrary schedule*; the problems arise when compliance with the artificial schedule is rigidly demanded by the client. Occasionally, I have such a client.

Generally, when I have been handed an artificial schedule by a client, I write back and thank them, but advise them that my goal is to meet the project end date, not the interim dates, and that, to meet the end date and keep a project flowing, I will return edited material on a weekly basis (with an invoice, of course). Whether the artificial interim dates are met as a result of such weekly returns will be a matter of luck and chance, not calculation.

I should note that the projects that I work on and which come with interim artificial schedules are large projects, thousands of manuscript pages (my projects generally run 2,500 to 12,000—or more—manuscript pages, often requiring more than one editor). Small projects—that is, projects of fewer than 1,000 manuscript pages—usually come to me with just an end date.

The problem with the artificial schedule is that it fails to consider: (a) the quality of the author's writing and how much work needs to be done to the writing; (b) the complexity of the manuscript coding that needs to be applied; (c) whether all or just some of the authors are native or fluent English speakers; (d) whether all of the manuscript has been supplied or there are outstanding chapters; (e) the number and type of charts, graphs, and figures; (f) that the first chapters go much slower than subsequent chapters as I try to "get a feel" for the project and learn what "common" errors are made across chapters; (g) the number and condition of the references; and (h) the myriad other problems that do not surface until a chapter is being edited. (This is where I thank heaven for the Microsoft Word macros I use: Editor's Toolkit Plus from the Editorium, EditTools from wordsnSync, and PerfectIt from Intelligent Editing.)

Consider just one of the named stumbling blocks, item g. I recently edited a chapter that had 504 references, of which only a handful were even close to being correct. Most had to be looked up because the author submitted, for example, author names like this: "Young, GM, YV AS, Trimble T, Excuse, R, al et," and journal names like this: "Joint Quality Comm - Safety." Not only did punctuation have to be fixed, but YV AS had to be deciphered and the journal name checked and corrected. Imagine my consternation when I discovered that not only were the author names mostly wrong, but the article title was incorrect, as was the journal name (thank goodness, however, for my Journal macro, which corrected many of the journal names before I began editing the references). Fixing the reference list took a considerable amount of time, yet an artificial schedule doesn't allow for this.

It is the nature of an artificial schedule that it is often difficult to meet. The schedule is often created mathematically—x number of chapters divided by y number of weeks = z, the number of chapters expected weekly (or, instead of number of chapters it may be number of pages [which generally excludes figures] or some other calculable item)—but without regard to the real content. And because the client is a corporation, it lives or dies by schedules; it can't live with the uncertainty that is inherent in a schedule-less world.

Another problem with the artificial schedule is that, if enforced, it may well require the editor to work long days and weekends to meet it. While the in-house person who sent the schedule relaxes on the weekend, the editor is working away just to meet the artificial deadline. I did not become self-employed to work 24 hours a day, 7 days a week, and I value my leisure time.

As I noted earlier, I try to dissuade clients from establishing interim schedules. I do understand, however, that these are often required. In those instances, I accept them with grace, yet make certain that my client understands that I consider the interim dates as very broad guidelines and that the only dates on which I fixate are the end date and the weekly submission dates. Alas, that does not get through to all of my clients.

One client wanted the first batch of 15 chapters by x date. I was able to complete 14 of the 15 by the set date, but that was not good enough. The client wanted to know how soon the 15th chapter would be completed, was I going to be able to meet future dates, should the client find another editor to work on this project? I think I would have been more sympathetic to the client had this not been the first batch of chapters and were I behind by some significant number of chapters as the end date loomed closer.

We got past this kerfuffle as it became clear, by the third or fourth weekly submission, that I really did have a handle on the project and as the client began reviewing submitted chapters and noting the author-created problems and the high quality of the editing. But there are two points I wish to make:

1. *To the editor:* Remember that you are a professional and you must take charge of the project and the schedule. You should not be intimidated into accepting a schedule whose only connection to reality is that it exists. You need to educate the client about problems encountered and why the schedule won't work, yet be ever mindful that you agreed to meet a certain end date. Be professional; take charge.

2. *To the client:* Remember that the date that ultimately matters is the end date. It is not possible to tell, at least on a large project, from a first or second submission by an editor whether an end date is in jeopardy. Consider all of the things that may be imperfect about the material and make allowances for those imperfections and the time it realistically takes to correct them. Keep in mind that you and the editor are really a team with the same goal in mind. And remember that later chapters often take less time to edit as the editor becomes familiar with the author's "style" and the kinds of problems that exist in the manuscript, some of which may lend themselves to, for example, the writing of a macro for use in

subsequent chapters. (In such an instance, a macro can change a problem from a major headache to a minor inconvenience.)

When all is said and done, the professional editor will meet the client's end date with a well-edited manuscript, which is the ultimate result wanted by everyone concerned with the project.

48

SCHEDULES AND CLIENT EXPECTATIONS

A couple of months ago, I was hired to edit a new medical text. The publisher estimated the manuscript to be 2,500 pages and wanted a four-week turnaround with a medium-level edit. When I received the files for the entire project, I did a page count; the client had greatly undercounted the manuscript size. Instead of 2,500 ms pages, the actual count was 5,300 pages. Why the disparity? Because, for example, in the original manuscript, figure legends were in 7-point type and chapters had 70+ legends; tables and references (of which there could be several hundred in a chapter) were in 8-point type; paragraphs were single spaced. In addition, it had to be conformed to AMA style; almost nothing conformed to AMA style as presented.

I advised the client and suggested that a 10-week schedule would be more appropriate. I was told to start the editing and the client would get back to me about the schedule.

In two weeks, I was able to edit nearly 1,400 ms pages, but even at that rate, an eight-week schedule would be needed and it assumes that the initial pace could be maintained.

At the two-week mark, I was told to stop work on the project. Instead of being edited locally, the manuscript would be shipped overseas (i.e., outside the United States to India) for editing because (a) the budget was based on 2,500 ms pages and (b) there is insufficient flexibility in the schedule to extend it to eight to 10 weeks or longer. The client was assured that both its budget and schedule could be met in India.

I was not overly concerned about the loss of this particular project; I had others waiting. But I was concerned about how realistic client (not just this particular client, but clients in general) expectations are when it comes to both price and schedule; more so schedule than price. I wonder how Indian copyeditors—let alone copyeditors from anywhere—will be able to do a medium edit on a very technical medical textbook in four weeks. I am not questioning the Indian editors' editing skills, as I do not think this is a question of skills. I do understand how the price can be met in India, but not the schedule or the required editing level.

More importantly, it worries me what is becoming of the publishing industry. The upheaval caused by ebooks is not being well dealt with by anyone yet. One of the outstanding negatives to ebooks is the ease with which poor-quality books can saturate the marketplace. Too many ebook authors are writing as if they were Georges Simenon, an author who once stated that he was able to turn out a new novel every 21 days. (Simenon was prolific and I particularly enjoyed his Inspector Maigret novels.) But, unlike Simenon's novels, which were well-written and well-edited, many ebooks are neither.

At one time, readers could feel assured that the pbooks they were buying that were published by a traditional publisher also were well-edited. Publishers devoted the time and the money to ensure a minimum quality.

Yet that seems to be changing today. In the case of the books I work on, which are medical texts written by doctors for doctors, I am concerned that unrealistic expectations will cause a decline in quality in books that can have serious implications for the well-being of consumers. If a novel tells you that the Taj Mahal is in Tibet, no harm is done to the reader, only to the author's reputation. But if a medical text tells you to remove the left lung when it should be the right lung, the potential for harm is present; you have to hope someone catches this error before you are operated on.

Again, the question is not so much that of competency of the editors as it is the compression of the schedule. Editing a 200-page novel in four weeks is not wholly unreasonable; errors that slip by are not likely to be catastrophic, except possibly to the author's reputation. But to edit a 5,300-page medical text in four weeks strikes me as unreasonable, even if the editorial work is divided among numerous editors. I suppose the question boils down to how many editors are used, but as the number of editors used increases, the greater the likelihood of inconsistency and the greater the variation in skill level among the editors.

I know that publishers are increasingly being run by the "bean counters" who take steps to reduce editorial costs because there is no readily visible-to-the-consumer effect of an editor's work. Editors are the invisible people who can make a good manuscript better. Publishers are increasingly competing with the self-publishers and so must mimic the self-publishing way to final version, which is little to no editing and/or the least expensive editing possible, combined with a compressed production schedule in order to get the finished product to market more quickly.

I wonder if, in the end, this will be good for the industry as a whole; that is, not just for the traditional publisher, but for the self-publisher, too. In the attempt to get to market sooner and to publish as quickly and as often as possible, are publishers of all stripes sacrificing too much? Will the result be a changed literary landscape that would not be recognizable to a reader who grew up reading the Hemingways and Steinbecks of an earlier era?

Perhaps more importantly, in the case of nonfiction, is this compulsion to reduce costs and speed up production dangerous for the reader and consumer? Is our insatiable appetite for instant gratification and cheap pricing going to boomerang?

How do you give a high-quality edit to a highly technical manuscript of 5,300 pages in four weeks without making any significant editorial sacrifice? Are client expectations becoming increasingly unreasonable? Something to ponder, I think, and perhaps even to worry about.

49

CONSISTENCY

One of the directives I regularly get from clients is that they want consistency. For example, they do not want a word spelled out sometimes and an acronym used in place of the word at other times. In books, they want consistency across chapters whenever possible.

Years ago, when I edited journal articles, each journal had a style to be applied consistently across articles, regardless of whether I edited one article or 100 articles.

This drive for consistency is likely to have been the mother of the editor's stylesheet. The stylesheet serves multiple purposes, two being to let the editor check treatment of a term in hopes that treatment is consistent across a manuscript and for a proofreader to see what decisions the editor made (e.g., is it non-negotiable or nonnegotiable; distention or distension?) and apply those decisions where the editor may have been inconsistent.

We know as readers that consistency is important, even in fiction. I find it distracting and annoying when the heroine is "nearly six-foot tall with strawberry-blond hair and jade-colored eyes" in chapter 1 but has become "five-and-a-half feet tall with dirty-blond hair and hazel eyes that change color" in chapter 3. Going from Amazonian to ordinary in three chapters can alter a plotline significantly.

Knowing that consistency is important, what steps do editors take to ensure it? In my olden days of editing, I relied on the stylesheet; I had no other tool in my arsenal that was as facile for the purpose, especially not with the size of projects on which I generally work. The stylesheet worked well when it was small (relatively speaking), but, as it grew in length, it became a cumbersome tool for ensuring consistency. It became cumbersome because of the need to check it so often, and because, in the early days, the stylesheet was handwritten, which meant not alphabetized, making finding things difficult.

So I began experimenting and found ways to automate the stylesheet using programs like Macro Express, a program I still use (but not for my stylesheet). Ultimately, I designed an online stylesheet, which remains open in my web browser and gives me quick and easy access. Yet, I discovered that, as much of an improvement as the online stylesheet is, it was not enough. Consequently, I created two of the macros that appear in EditTools: Never Spell Word and Toggle. Using these two macros means there are fewer inconsistencies across long manuscripts.

When I get a project from client Y, I usually know that the client wants certain things to appear in its publications, or, if not across its publications, within the particular project I am working on. For example, the client may tell me that every time I see the head REFER, it should be changed to REFERRAL, or that a common acronym such as WHO never needs to be spelled out. (Usually the directive is that "common acronyms need not be spelled out at first use" without providing a list of those common acronyms; it is part of my job as an experienced editor to recognize which acronyms will be readily understood by readers of the book.)

Never Spell Word (NSW) lets me add words and phrases to a project-specific list and apply a specific color highlight to those words and phrases so I can be consistent across chapters. For example, if I enter WHO and assign it the highlight color magenta, and run NSW on the manuscript, I know each time that I see WHO in magenta that it does not need to be spelled out. If I come across "World Health Organization (WHO)" in the text, I'll see WHO in magenta and I'll know to delete "World Health Organization" and the parens around WHO.

Similarly, I can enter into the list to change World Health Organization to WHO. When I run the NSW macro, not only will the change be made (with tracking on), but WHO will be highlighted to indicate to me visually that this is correct.

The advantages of NSW over similar macros are basically twofold: (a) the highlighting, which gives a visual clue; and (b) the ease with which new items can be added to the list while editing. This second point is important; it means that the list is not static and it can grow as I find things to add to it.

NSW is only a part of the consistency equation, however. Toggle is another important tool. NSW is run on a file *after* basic file cleanup but *before* editing. It is run only once on a file, although I may add to its list as I edit a file. Toggle, in contrast, is not run on a file. Instead, it is used to change a word or phrase while editing. My current Toggle list has more than 1,500 entries in it. These are the things that I do not want to change universally (i.e., correct using the NSW macro); instead, I want to decide whether to make a change as I come to the item.

Using the WHO example, again, if I need to spell out WHO the first time it is used in a chapter but not on subsequent uses, then I want the information in my Toggle macro, not in my NSW macro because NSW will change it every time and I'll have to undo some instances, whereas Toggle will make the change only when I tell it to do so. Like NSW, Toggle can have and access multiple lists. There is a primary (or universal) main list and then there are supplemental project-specific lists that can be accessed simultaneously with the primary list.

In a Toggle list, I would enter "WHO" and ask that it be changed to "World Health Organization (WHO)"; it would appear in the Toggle list like this:

WHO | World Health Organization (WHO)

Now, when I come to WHO in the manuscript, if I want to spell it out, I place my cursor in WHO and run Toggle; it deletes WHO and enters World Health Organization (WHO). This is done with Track Changes on.

I've used a simple example, but Toggle can be used for both complex and simple changes. For example, an entry in my primary Toggle list is as follows:

1-methyl-4-phenyl-1,2,3,6-tetrahydropyridine | methylphenylte-trahydropyridine (MPTP)

Toggle promotes consistency in two ways: (a) it reduces spelling errors that occur when typing a replacement and (b) it is easy to use and fast.

If you know that a client wants to avoid "due to," it is difficult to create a universally applicable substitute. Toggle gives you as many options as you create. If a client always wants World Health Organization referred to as WHO, NSW can make that happen. It is easy to remember what a client wants when there are only a few things, but the more things a client wants and the more inconsistent an author is, the less valuable the stylesheet is to an editor and the more valuable macros like NSW and Toggle are—they increase consistency and reduce the time required to be consistent.

Postscript (*added after essay was published*): Last night, I finished a novel published by a major publisher in which, within three lines, a character's name appeared three times and each appearance was a different spelling. If the editor had used Never Spell Word, this would not have occurred. The editor would have entered the character's name at its first appearance into the NSW list (or, better yet in the case of fiction, the author should have supplied a list of characters with correct name spellings and all the names would be entered into the list before any editing began) and then, as the editor ran NSW on each chapter, if the character's name was not highlighted in green, the editor would know immediately that the name's spelling needed to be checked. Granted that the errors occurring in such close proximity should have been caught regardless of the use of NSW, but it does point out how such things can slip by and how the proper tools can help improve consistency.

50

WHAT AN AUTHOR SHOULD GIVE AN EDITOR

This topic has been swirling around my thoughts for several days, and I'm finally getting time to write about the topic.

The hardest job an editor has, I think, is determining what the author wants the final product to be like. The editor's role is to help the author mold the manuscript so that it ends up meeting the author's wants, not the editor's belief as to what the author wants.

The problem is that few authors provide the information necessary to accomplish the task. In the books I currently work on, any guidance comes from the publisher, not the author, which is not how it should be. Years ago, when I edited fiction and worked directly with authors, a lot of time and effort were wasted with back-and-forth communications in an attempt to land the author and me on the same page. It is one of the reasons why I stopped working directly with authors (although in the past year, I have had many requests from authors to edit their fiction, and I am contemplating doing so).

In the case of fiction, I think an author should provide an editor with the following information:

- a one-page summary of the story;

- a complete list of characters, including the desired name spelling, any relationships between characters (e.g., spouse of, sister of, granddaughter of), and a physical description of each character;

- a complete list of geographical locations, indicating whether each is real or made up, and with correct spelling;

- a list of special terms or made-up words;

- a timeline of major events; and

- an indication whether this is part of a series (e.g., book one of a trilogy).

Depending on the story and the author's plans, I would also ask the author to provide additional information.

It is true that an editor can gather all of the above information from a first read of the manuscript. But leaving the task to the editor means that there is no assurance that something important will not be missed or misinterpreted. More importantly, it wastes valuable (and costly) time that could be better spent actually editing.

With nonfiction, the list changes based on the type of book and the intended audience. As I have mentioned in other essays, most of my work is in medical textbooks written by doctors for doctors. What I would like to know in advance are such things as:

- which acronyms can be always used as acronyms and not spelled out because they are commonly understood by the intended audience;

- how certain terms should be approached (e.g.: Is ultrasound acceptable/preferred when talking about the procedure, which is more correctly called ultrasonography? Should it be x-ray or radiography?);

- preferred spelling where there is more than one spelling option (e.g., distension or distention?); and

- any other author preferences that I should be aware of.

The point is to make the editing and the review of the editing go smoothly and not end up being focused on something that is minor because it is a pet peeve of the author.

This review focus is really at the core of why an author should provide an editor with as much information as possible. Over the course of 28 years of editing, more times than not, when an author has complained about the editing, the complaint has been because no one passed on information about what the author wanted or expected. The author became focused on the tree rather than the forest.

An often-heard complaint from disgruntled fiction authors is that the editor screwed up the book. I don't doubt that the editor made mistakes, but my first thought goes to the information that the author provided. Was the editor just handed the manuscript or was the editor given sufficient information so that the editor's mistakes are really the sign of an incompetent editor and not of a lazy author?

Unfortunately, there are authors who believe that the only role an editor should play is that of spellchecker, because whatever the author wrote is perfect as is, with the exception of the occasional misspelling. I remember editing a novel early in my career where I correct the misuse of *their, there, where, were, your,* and *you're* only to receive a nasty note from the author telling me how I had taken a well-written manuscript and made it a poorly written one, and that I had been hired just to check spelling, not to change words or meaning. I scratched my head vigorously because I would have thought that changing *where* to *were* was correcting a misspelling and not changing meaning, but I clearly was missing something. As it turns out, the author believed that using the wrong words reinforced the character's illiteracy. The author may have intended that but missed the connection because the character used polysyllabic words that indicated a good command of language except for these words. More important, however, was that the author's failure to communicate to me that the character was intended to be illiterate meant that I didn't catch the characterization error that resulted from other word choices. The book was a disaster from the author's intended perspective and I didn't help matters because of the lack of pre-editing information.

Authors and editors should collaborate, not fight each other. The goal of each is to make the book the best it can be. Authors need to take a more proactive role in the collaborative effort by providing basic information—without waiting to be asked for the information—before the editor begins work. Together, the author and editor can make the author's voice heard.

51

LOSING MONEY THE PAPER WAY

A reader of An American Editor asked: "Can you comment on copyediting on paper vs. MS track changes? What do most clients expect and is there a difference in your opinion on the quality of the editing?" I had thought these were matters long resolved, but apparently not.

I began my freelance career in 1984, which was the dawn of the computer age as regards online editing. This was before Microsoft Windows and was in the days when WordPerfect ruled what world there was to rule in word processing. This was still the age of editing on paper.

By 1985, I was refusing to accept freelance editing work that was on paper. In fact, I advertised—including with graphs and charts—that I could save clients money by editing online rather than on paper and that I could improve consistency, reducing EAs (editor alterations), the correction of which the client would be charged by the compositor a handsome sum (each EA and AA [author alteration] bore a charge).

Within a year, I had convinced several clients that online editing was the way to go and I was one of the very few editors who had that capability or—more importantly—who was willing to edit online rather than on paper. And so my business boomed.

It was many years, however, before paper editing was truly abandoned by publishers. In fact, I recall taking an Editorial Freelancers Association class on editing with several of the people who worked for me (my hope was that I would learn something I didn't already know about the editorial process) and being shocked when, in response to a question, the instructor said it wasn't necessary to learn how to edit online because few authors provided digital files and few publishers were encouraging the move away from paper. The instructor claimed online editing was a fad that would pass. And so no time at all was spent on electronic editing.

Needless to say, the instructor and those who shared the instructor's thinking were wrong and were rapidly being left behind as the technological revolution hit even staid publishing houses.

I tell you this history because there is a reason why authors and publishers migrated from a paper-based world to a digital world: Technology really was everyone's friend when it came to publishing.

I made the transition early because I quickly recognized that paper-based editing was a way to lose money, not make it. In paper-based editing, how would you find, for example, every instance of the phrase ", and on days" in both the chapter you are working on and in the 10 preceding chapters that you have already edited? Or how about ascertaining whether an acronym is repeated in a chapter, how many times it is repeated, whether the spelled-out version also exists, and how many times it exists?

With the computer, it is easy, but on paper, it is unlikely you will find every instance and to do so would require an excessive amount of time. If you have to do such searches frequently in paper-based editing, you would rapidly exhaust your client's budget and thus your prospects of earning a decent return for your efforts.

Of course, searching for items that need correcting is just one facet of editing that a computer can do better than paper-based editing. Let us not forget the "what-you-expect-is-what-you-see" phenomenon. It is not unusual for an editor to see the correctly spelled word because it is expected, when what is actually written is misspelled. In paper-based editing, too often, the error remained and was picked up by the proofreader, which resulted in an EA. Online editing doesn't cure the problem, but does help minimize it with spell checking.

(Another phenomenon of the EA/AA allocations in paper-based editing was that, if there were too many, the publisher reserved the right to charge the editor or the author for the excess, thereby, in the editor's case, reducing the editor's earnings. The usual penalty for the editor was, however, simply to not be hired again and not told why.)

No matter how you cut it, paper-based editing is time-consuming, subject to more errors not being caught, and likely a money-losing proposition for the editor unless the client has an unlimited budget and is willing to spend it. Because paper-based editing is slower, schedules have to be longer, but in my experience, few clients consider that need.

As between paper-based editing and online editing, I do not think there is much of a contest. I wouldn't accept a paper-based editing project nor would I recommend someone else accept one. Yet, there is a caveat to this: If the paper-based project is, for example, a five-page journal article, then some of the benefits of online editing are not so overwhelmingly beneficial. Most of the benefits of online editing as compared to paper-based editing are evident with long documents such as books and reports. This is not to imply that there aren't benefits for short documents as well; just that the benefit-to-nonbenefit ratio comes closer to 1:1 the shorter the document to be edited. In my case, I would not accept a paper-based project regardless of length.

As for what most clients expect, I think today that most expect an editor to edit online, not on paper. Considering that few authors submit paper manuscripts as opposed to digital manuscripts, client expectations would seem to me to follow; that is, digital file equals online editing. Publishers today generally will not accept a paper manuscript, except in very exceptional cases.

Tracking an editor's changes in Microsoft Word seems to be the standard today. Publishers give authors the option to accept or reject changes, and tracking makes it easier to know what changes have been made. I know that, in my business, we always edit with tracking on.

The final question was addressed to the quality of the editing. This is a very complex question. No matter whether a project is paper-based or online, in the first instance, the quality of the editing depends on the skill of the editor—the more skilled the editor, the better the quality of the editing.

I think the real question is addressed less to quality than to consistency and accuracy, which are part of quality but also separate. I think that consistency and accuracy are much greater in online editing than in paper-based editing because there are so many tools available to help increase consistency and accuracy, tools that are not available for paper-based editing.

What are your thoughts regarding paper-based versus online editing?

52

THE LOGISTICS OF LARGE PROJECTS

As I wrote recently, I have been hired to help edit a portion of a very large project. My portion runs to 5,000 manuscript pages, which have to be edited within six weeks.

After having written about the ethical issues of having undertaken a project that was bigger than the original editors could handle, I thought it would be worthwhile to discuss some of the logistical problems of massive projects. Let's begin at the beginning: This project, before editing of any chapters, ran approximately 8,000 manuscript pages. (I use approximately deliberately as this was the in-house editor's estimate; I only know with certainty the page count for the chapters I have actually received.)

Projects of that size are the types of project that I often receive and, over the years, I have developed a system for working with such massive amounts of manuscript. In fact, it was because of my receiving projects of that size that I developed EditTools. As you can imagine, with such projects, consistency becomes a problem, and the stylesheet seems to grow on its own.

The first logistical problem I address is that of editors: How many editors will be needed to edit the manuscript within the time allotted by the schedule? I built my business, Freelance Editorial Services, around the idea that a team of editors can do better financially than a solo editor. Although this notion has been disputed many times over the years, I still believe it to be true, based on discussions that I have with solo colleagues. It is this team concept that enables me to undertake such large projects with confidence, knowing that I will have a sufficient number of well-qualified editors to do the work.

The second logical problem I address is the online stylesheet and giving access to it to the editors who will be working on the project. When several editors work collaboratively on a project, this online stylesheet enables all of the editors to see what decisions have been made, and to conform their decisions with the decisions that have been made by coeditors. Consequently, if an editor makes a new editorial decision (i.e., it has not been previously decided by an editor and inserted on the stylesheet) to use *distension* rather than *distention*, or to use *coworker* rather than *co-worker*, all of the other editors can immediately see that decision—within seconds of its being entered into the stylesheet—and can conform their editing to that decision or dispute it. It also means that errors can be caught and corrected. For example, if an editor enters adriamycin, another editor can correct it to Adriamycin (it is a brand name, not a generic drug) and immediately notify all editors of the original error and correction.

In addition, my client also has access to the stylesheet. The client can view and print it, but not modify it. This serves two purposes: (a) The client can provide proofreaders with up-to-the-minute copies of the stylesheet and (b) the client can look at our editorial decisions and decide that he would prefer, for example, *distention* rather than *distension*, and notify an editor of the preference, and the editor can then make the change and notify all of the coeditors, who can then make any necessary corrections in chapters not already submitted to the client.

The third logistical problem I address is the creation of a starter NSW (Never Spell Word) file for the project. The NSW module of EditTools is where known client preferences are stored. For example, if I know that the client prefers *distention* to *distension*, I enter into the NSW file the information to change instances of *distension* to *distention*. Also into this file go editorial decisions, such as marking *DNA* as an acronym that does not ever need to be spelled out but that the acronym *US* (for *ultrasound*) should always be spelled out as *ultrasound*. The NSW file also serves to remind editors of other editorial-decision–related information. I provide each editor with a starter NSW file and each editor will add to their NSW file as they edit.

The NSW macro is run before beginning editing a chapter. Its purpose is to promote consistency across chapters and to make it easier for an editor to visually see editorial decisions that have been made. The NSW macro includes several components. For example, my basic NSW for medical editing also includes a dataset for drugs and organisms. Its use helps speed editing by providing visual clues, such as an indication that a drug name is correct even though the spell checker is flagging it as erroneous—it becomes one less thing that I need to verify.

The fourth logistical problem I tackle is references. These projects often have *lots* of references. One chapter of the project that I just received, for example, runs 305 manuscript pages, of which there are 61 pages of references—a total of 652 references (most of the chapters have more than 300 references).

Dealing with references can be time-consuming. My approach is to separate the references from the main chapter, putting them in their own file. This serves four purposes: (a) Microsoft, in its wisdom, has determined that, if spell check determines there are more than some number of errors in a document, it will display a message that there are too many errors for Word to display and turn off spell check. Although spell check is not perfect, it is a tool that I do use when editing. I would prefer it to flag a correctly spelled word as misspelled, giving me an alert, than my possibly missing something. Spell check is a tool, not a solution. (However, it does help that EditTools helps me create custom dictionaries so that correct words that are currently flagged as errors by spell check can easily be added to a custom dictionary and not flagged in the future.) By moving the references to their own file, I eliminate this problem of Word turning off spell check for "too many" errors.

(b) It provides me with an opportunity to run my Journals macro. Every time I come across a new variation of a spelling of a journal name, I add it to one of my journal datasets. My PubMed (medical) journals dataset currently has more 14,675 entries. With the references in a separate file, I can run that dataset against the reference list and have my macro correct those journal names that are incorrect (assuming the information is in my dataset) and mark as correct those that are correct. What this means is that, rather than having to check journal names for 652 references in a chapter, I have to do so for at most a handful. It also means that I can concentrate on the other reference errors, if any, such as missing author names. Instead of spending several hours on the references alone, I can edit the references in a much shorter amount of time. (It took 26 minutes for the Journals macro to check the 652 references against the 14,675 entries in the dataset.)

(c) The third purpose is that separating the references from the main text lets me run the Page Number Format macro. In less than a minute, I had changed the page numbers in the 652 references from the 1607-10 to 1607-1610 format. How long would it take to do this manually? Having the references in their own file means I do not have to worry about the macro making unwanted changes in the main text, especially as this macro runs without tracking.

(d) The fourth purpose of separating the references from the main body of the chapter is that it lets me run my Wildcard Find and Replace macro just on the references. There is no chance that I will use the macro and make unwanted changes to the main text. WFR is efficient because it lets me create a macro that works, such as one to close up the year-volume-pages cite, and save it for future reuse. WFR even lets me combine several of the macros into a single script (that also can be saved for repeat use) so that the macros run sequentially in my designated order. As an example: I have created macros to change author names from the format *Author, F. H.,* to *Author FH,*. If you have to do this manually for several thousand author names, you begin to appreciate the power and usefulness of WFR and how much time it can save. (I also will use WFR on the main text when appropriate. What I avoid by separating out the references is the possibility of something happening to either the main text or the references that shouldn't.)

These steps are among those I take that make handling of large projects easier and more profitable. There are additional things that I do for each chapter, but the point is that, by dealing with manuscripts in a logical way, projects become manageable. In addition, by using the right tools, editing is more accurate, consistent, and faster, which leads to a happy client, more work, and increased profitability.

Do you have any thoughts on how to handle large amounts of manuscript? Do you take any special steps for preparing a manuscript for editing or while editing?

Part IV

PROFITS

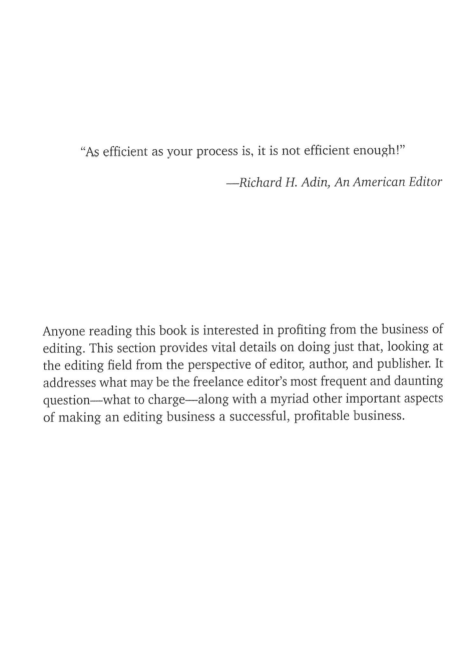

"As efficient as your process is, it is not efficient enough!"

—*Richard H. Adin, An American Editor*

Anyone reading this book is interested in profiting from the business of editing. This section provides vital details on doing just that, looking at the editing field from the perspective of editor, author, and publisher. It addresses what may be the freelance editor's most frequent and daunting question—what to charge—along with a myriad other important aspects of making an editing business a successful, profitable business.

53

GREAT EXPECTATIONS:
A RECIPE FOR DISAPPOINTMENT

I once had a client who would take my copyedited manuscript and re-copyedit it, send it back to me with marginal notes about "mistakes and errors," and demand that I re-re-copyedit the manuscript. Back then—which was a very, very long time ago, when I was in my editing infancy and didn't know better—I did as I was asked (which was expected by the client to be at no charge) only to have the client send me another missive, complaining about my "corrections" to the client's "errors and misses."

I learned very quickly that this was a client meant for someone else, not for me; perhaps for an editor with a masochistic streak. The problem was that the client had great expectations, a tiny budget, and an inability to clone—a clear recipe for disappointment. In addition, the client assumed, and incorrectly in this instance, a superior knowledge of the rules of grammar and spelling. It also didn't help that many of the "errors" about which the client complained were either judgment calls or problems of development that a developmental editor should resolve, not a copyeditor.

The issue comes to the fore again because of a recent discussion I had with a colleague about editing quality. My colleague's view is that, regardless of how little one is paid and regardless of the parameters of the job one is hired to do, it is the editor's responsibility to provide as near to perfection an edit as possible—doesn't matter if you are hired to copyedit; if the manuscript requires a developmental edit, then that is what you are supposed to give it. My colleague's clients have come to expect this extraordinary level of work from him, and thus, when he submitted an edited manuscript that hadn't reached that level, he received a negative missive from his client. Yet, if you looked at his work in light of the pay he received and the parameters of the job for which he was hired, he actually gave them better than the client should have received.

There is a disconnect between clients and editors that seems to be growing. Client staff are often less-experienced and less-well trained as editors than the editors they hire. Their roles, too, are often significantly different, with the in-house person being primarily responsible for project management, not for actual editorial work. But expectations of in-house staff are often unrelated to the editor's business realities. (I should note that the client could just as easily be an author rather than a publisher and my comments should be viewed as applying equally to both.)

Everyone involved needs to sit back and rethink their expectations. Everyone needs to recognize that there is no such thing as "perfection" in the editing world. Each person who reads a manuscript will read it differently and find different errors. Every hand that touches a manuscript will fix some errors and risks introducing new errors. It's all because we are human and come to these tasks from different perspectives. It is also because of phenomena like the WYSIWYG conundrum and differences in how completely an editor adheres to rigid rules of style.

To say that the rate of pay isn't an influence is to view the world through blinders. The editorial product is really no different from any other commodity in the sense that the more you pay, the better quality you get. How can one realistically expect "perfection" at a less-than-minimum-wage rate?

Pay is a real problem in the editing world. Because no one ever remarks (except an editor) after reading a well-written, well-edited book, "The editor must have been fantastic" (instead, the comment usually is "What a great author!"), but does remark after reading a poorly written/edited book, "Didn't they hire an editor" or "What a lousy editing job," clients tend to pay little respect to the editing process, which lack of respect is reflected in the race to the pay bottom.

Freelance editors are in business to make a living (read "profit") and so must balance client expectations against real-world realities. Clients, on the other hand, are focused on their own profits, which can be affected by poor craftsmanship, and thus want the most bang they can get for their buck. And that is where the disconnect is: the editor's balance versus the client's bang for the buck—they are not in equilibrium.

This disequilibrium is now beginning to hit the publishing world in great force. eBooks have become a great leveler. eBooks make authors' work more quickly and readily accessible to a larger audience, which makes editorial errors more glaring and noticed by an ever-increasing number of readers. Books that might have sold 100 copies in print can easily sell thousands as low-cost ebooks. Where the audience of 100 may have been forgiving of error, if not oblivious to it, within the audience of thousands, there will be some who are less forgiving and more vocal about errors.

Somehow the disequilibrium between the editor's balance and the client's expectations must come into balance, and it needs to be done sooner rather than later. Clients need to recognize that, to get better editing, they need to hire better editors and that better editors, as is true in all professions, command higher prices. Clients need to rethink the idea that one price fits all, and learn to balance their expectations against what they are willing to pay. Otherwise, their great expectations will continue to be a sure recipe for disaster. And freelance editors need to realize that they need to balance their drive for perfection with fairness in compensation. If they want to do time-consuming, painstakingly "perfect" work, they need to at least try to negotiate commensurate pay.

54

GETTING PAID:
THINGS FOR A FREELANCER TO THINK ABOUT

Recently, freelancers have been discussing, yet again, being stiffed by clients and how to deal with it. Along with expressions of sympathy from colleagues, several concrete suggestions were given. It isn't necessary to repeat those suggestions, which were largely based on having a contract, here; rather, I think we should explore more fundamental concepts.

Some editors require a contract for every project; others do not. The primary distinction between the two groups is who is the client—that is, the former group tends to work directly with authors and individuals, the latter group tends to work with established publishers.

Editors see the contract as a guarantor of payment, until they learn otherwise. Written contracts are useful only if you are prepared to enforce them; otherwise, a handshake is equally as good as a written contract. In truth, the handshake may be even better because the person who will honor the handshake is the person who wouldn't breach the contract.

But let's accept that a written contract is a panacea to the ill of having a client try to evade payment (or an editor not do what was he/she was hired for). The question becomes, what should be in the contract?

Usually what is missing is what I consider to be the most important clause of all: the clause that determines the dispute resolution venue; that is, where any dispute that arises must be settled and how it must be settled.

Ever look at the terms and conditions of your credit cards? How about of your mortgage or auto finance loan? Every lender includes these "venue" clauses, and we should learn from the specialists. Your contract can include arbitration terms or straight-to-court terms. If arbitration terms are included, think about who you want to do the arbitrating. Remember that, for it to be enforceable, the arbitrator must be independent—it can't be your best friend, your business partner, your personal attorney.

I prefer the straight-to-court approach, but I don't want to travel, so I make the venue—on those rare occasions when I use a contract—my local court, in my county, and specifically not the small claims court. In addition, I make sure that the contract states that it is being entered into in my hometown and that my sole place of business is my hometown. This is important for establishing the court's jurisdiction.

The clause might read something like this:

> This contract is entered into in Poughkeepsie, Dutchess County, New York, which is the sole place of business of Freelance Editorial Services, the "editor."
>
> Any legal action brought to enforce or terminate this contract or any term of this contract must be brought in the Supreme Court of the State of New York located in Poughkeepsie, Dutchess County, New York, which the parties to this contract agree is the proper venue and the court that has jurisdiction over any dispute regarding this contract.

I also include a clause that requires the other party to be responsible for my legal fees and costs should I prevail in any action brought by any party to the agreement to enforce or break the agreement. Importantly, I also include a clause that makes my state law the law that governs the contract. Imagine having to defend your contract based on the laws of another state or country.

Another important clause is the one that sets up service of process for any action brought under the contract. This is especially important for those who deal with nonresidents. No contract is worth anything if it can't be enforced and it can't be enforced if a court can't get jurisdiction over the person. Consequently, I include a clause that says that service of process will be effective if it is served by the usual court-ordered process on the party at the address below the party's signature and, in the event that such service is unsuccessful, on the secretary of state for the State of New York as agent for the party.

OK, that covers getting us to court. But is there something else that should be done? Definitely. No matter how you slice it or dice it, the best clause to have in your contract is the copyright clause.

The copyright clause says that the parties agree that you own a copyright interest in the edited version of the manuscript until you are paid in full for your work. Once you are paid in full, your interest automatically expires but, until that time, the author agrees that his work cannot be published in any form that includes any of your work and that, should it be published, you must be listed as coauthor and are entitled to 100% of any revenues generated, as well as damages of not less than $x,xxx for publishing without your consent.

This clause can be your most potent clause, whether in negotiation with the author for payment or in a lawsuit.

These are things to think about. Adding these clauses can protect you, but can also make it difficult to get clients. I am still a firm believer that a written contract is only good for the honest; the dishonest won't abide by it no matter what. But balm for the soul, which is what a contract is, is sometimes more important than whether it will be effective.

PS: Don't just write this contract yourself. Hire an attorney to draft a form contract for you. Your specialty is editing, not law; hire the specialist to do the specialist's work. Just tell the attorney what you want.

PPS: Don't be surprised if an attorney says, for example, the copyright law doesn't say you have an interest. The reality is a contract can contain any terms the parties agree to; whether a court will enforce those terms can only be determined by a court when challenged, so put the clause in anyway. Until the U.S. Supreme Court rules definitively and clearly on a matter, all else is conjecture.

55

THINKING ABOUT MONEY:
WHAT FREELANCERS NEED TO UNDERSTAND

Every freelance editor I know thinks about money, especially in these tough economic times. It isn't that money is the uppermost concern, but it is pretty darn close. Yet few freelance editors really understand the financial end of our business.

Editors tend to look at the money they receive or bill for as the amount they are earning, not realizing that they are actually earning less than they think (or possibly more than they think). For example, someone who charges $25 an hour thinks they are earning $25 an hour. They really aren't; they are earning less. Why? Because they aren't thinking in terms of the effective workday hourly rate, which is, in the end, for a business like ours, the only true indicator of what we are earning. This was the meat of what I discussed at Communication Central's *Finding Your Niche* conference, but it really needs to be taken one step further than the workday effective hourly rate: it needs to be determined over a longer period of time, even as long as the fiscal year.

Here is how to calculate your workday effective hourly rate (EHR):

Calculating the Workday Effective Hourly Rate (EHR)

The formula is essentially the same if you charge by the page or by the project. Here is the formula for a per-page rate:

Calculating the EHR

- If you charge a per-page rate, then your workday EHR is calculated as follows:

$$EHR\,workday = \frac{(PB \times PPR)}{TWH}$$

- PB = total # of pages billed
- PPR = per-page rate
- TWH = total workday hours

What this requires is that you keep track of your time—both working and non-work–related (e.g., time spent on administrative tasks, as well as on making tea or walking the dog)—during your set business hours. Here is an example of a calculation made using an hourly rate:

Calculating the EHR

- If you charge an hourly rate, then your workday EHR is calculated as follows:

$$EHR\,workday = \frac{(HB \times HR)}{TWH}$$

- HB = total # of hours billed
- HR = hourly rate
- TWH = total workday hours

Note how what was once $30 an hour has become significantly less. To have a true picture of what you are earning, you need to calculate your EHR over longer periods—1 month, 3 months, 6 months, 1 year. Only with that calculation in hand will you know what you are really earning. It is nice to think that we are earning $30 an hour, but we need to recognize that the $30-hour unit represents billable time and doesn't include all of the non-billable time we spend each day, week, and month doing such things as prospecting for new work, filing, billing, replacing office supplies . . . and chatting with friends on Facebook, searching for a better source for pet food, and the like.

Why is this information important? Because knowing what you are truly earning can help you put your business in proper order. It can be the impetus to seeking more work or to spending less time doing nonproductive things.

Freelancers tend to kid themselves about their earnings. Even if we earn a decent income by the end of the year, we may have had to work much too hard to earn it, or perhaps we could have increased it significantly had we only worked smarter. Everything about our business flows out of knowing what our true EHR is over an extended period of time.

LIVING IN A DREAM WORLD:
THE PROFESSIONAL EDITOR'S FEE

I'm wondering if there is a psychedelic resurgence going on. No, I'm not planning on taking another trip back to the 1960s and their various hallucinogenic crazes. There really is no need to resurrect the past. To relive the psychedelic past, all I need do is review the applications for employment I have been receiving in the past few months.

I admit that there are few jobs that are as glamorous, legendary, and desirable as that of a freelance editor. Perhaps the life of a Hollywood superstar comes close, but I suspect that even that life pales in comparison to the life that wannabe editors believe freelance editors live.

I can sense your confusion. You are wondering what I'm talking about, so let me lay it out clearly and concisely: Of the two dozen most recent job applications I have received, 21 (87.5%) have stated that the minimum acceptable pay for copyediting is $25 per page. (Applicants are required to tell me their minimum acceptable pay level because I don't want to waste my time—or their time—knowing that we shall never meet on common ground when it comes to pay.) Somewhere someone must be paying these rates, because too many applicants are setting them as the floor. I'm just wondering who is paying these rates; I'd like to apply to work with them.

In addition to the pay limitations, 17 (70.8%) have written to tell me that they see no need to complete a copyediting test. All I need do is look at their résumé, especially their education, because it amply demonstrates their qualifications. That not one of the submitted résumés conforms to the explicit instructions regarding how the résumé is to be presented seems not to matter. Nor, apparently, does it matter that it is made clear that, without the completed copyediting test, the job application will not be considered at all.

I wish I could say that it gets better, but it doesn't. Of those who actually do attempt the copyediting test, many, when returning the test, include a note saying that, although they completed the test, they have neither medical editing experience nor any interest in pursuing medical editing, which is 90% of what I do and which I make clear in my hiring information. They assume that I would be able to keep them supplied with work in their preferred subject areas, which they occasionally name.

Then comes the copyediting test itself. It isn't that hard, the instructions are pretty clear, and a sample of the coding is provided—yet, barely 1% of the test-takers do a decent job of editing, or even code properly.

But none of this matters much when it comes to the expected pay. Occasionally, I will choose one applicant who completes the test but didn't pass it (and didn't submit a résumé in the correct form) and ask if they would be interested in working for me at $x per page. I make it clear that there are certain resources that they would need to purchase if they didn't already own them (which I know, based on the test). The contacted applicant is never interested; the applicant makes it clear that $25 per page is the minimum acceptable fee and that they aren't budging.

What does this tell us about how people view the editorial world? It tells me that people have an unrealistic sense of it, that they have done no investigation, that they see being a freelance editor as the golden path to fame and fortune—a profession with low entry requirements but high, immediate rewards. (It is worth noting that some of these applicants actually have full-time jobs in publishing, so you would think they would have a more realistic view.)

The problem with this mythical view is that, because so many people have it and believe it, it frightens away those who need our services. When I've asked indie authors why they aren't hiring professional editors, in most cases, the response is that the cost is too high. If I follow up by asking if they got price quotes from professional editors, the answer almost always is "no," because they already "know" that professional editors are too expensive.

How do they know this? Somewhere, somehow, a misperception occurred. Equating the fees charged by all professional editors is as wrong as equating the cost of every painting with that of a Rembrandt. But then I look at the minimum fees job applicants demand compared to what the real-world editorial market actually pays and I wonder how that disconnect came about.

Combating this misperception is difficult, yet it is a task that editors need to undertake if we hope to survive as a profession the shift in the publishing industry from traditional publishing to self-publishing. What are your suggestions for combating this misperception that professional editors are too expensive?

57

THE PUBLISHER'S SEARCH FOR SAVINGS

A current issue of *The Atlantic* had a very interesting article, "Making It in America," which asks a very difficult question: The article explores manufacturing jobs and wonders what will be the future for the un-skilled laborer. The article is well worth reading and thinking about, even though the professional editor is skilled labor, because just as manufacturers seek cost savings, so do publishers, especially in the Internet Age.

One problem with publisher attempts to save costs is that, much too often, the effort is focused on editorial costs, the so-called hidden costs, which generally means reducing the compensation paid to freelance editors. I would be less concerned about taking a cut in my compensation if my compensation had risen over the course of years. However, it hasn't; the rate being offered by many publishers today is the same rate publishers were offering in 1995. Another way of saying it is that publishers have been the beneficiaries of editorial cost savings since 1995 because they haven't increased the rate of pay in the past 17 years commensurate with the increases in costs of living.

But advocating that is beating one's head against a reinforced brick wall. Why? Because editorial costs are hidden costs in the sense that, unlike a book cover that buyers see immediately and that can either improve or lessen chances of a sale, editorial matters are not noted until after the book is already purchased, usually weeks after purchase, when the return period has already expired. We may curse the publisher of a book riddled with editorial errors, but whereas we might "blacklist" an author, we don't "blacklist" a publisher. Consumers simply do not shop for books by publisher; publisher brands are weak brands. When was the last time you asked a bookseller for the latest book published by Harper & Row?

Regardless, recently, I received a communication from a major publisher with its latest idea for lowering costs. I applaud the publisher for thinking about ways to save costs and for experimenting; this is something that too few publishers do, yet need to do in the ebook age. But I'm not convinced that the approach being taken will result in any significant savings.

The underpinning of the approach is that there is a difference between editing and reading: The former is time-consuming, the latter less so. I have been thinking about this division and have asked colleagues for their view of whether the reading effort while editing differs from the reading effort when looking only for errors such as misspelling and homonym misuse, but not "copyediting."

The colleagues I spoke with regarding whether the "copyediting read" differed significantly (or at all) from the "error read," were similarly minded—amongst themselves and with me. Their was universal agreement that the reading effort remained the same and was equally time- and effort-intensive. Asking an editor to read for errors but not copyedit is like asking a fish to swim in air—the editorial skills are not so easily shunted aside.

In my case, there could be no cost savings even if there was a difference, because I charge by the page, not the hour. Fifty pages are still 50 pages, whether thoroughly read or not. Consequently, while I think the publisher has the right idea—look for cost savings—this attempt is unlikely to result in significant savings. The publisher would likely save more by simply switching from an hourly based fee for editing to a per-page rate. Such a move, although many editors cannot see it, also would greatly benefit editors.

Let's begin with human nature. If I am paid by the hour, I have no incentive to do a job either faster or more efficiently. (I assume that the quality of the editing would not differ, regardless of how the editor is paid.) If I am happy earning $21/hour, I am as happy earning it for 40 hours as I am earning it for 50 hours; after all, what I am happy with is the $21/hour, which is constant, and having the work in an increasingly competitive environment.

But think about if I am paid by the page. If I am paid $3.50 a page, I can earn my comfortable $21/hour by editing at a rate of 6 pages an hour. Imagine how luxurious it would feel if I could edit at the same level of quality but at 10 pages an hour—I would then earn $35/hour. There is now an incentive for me to increase my efficiency and speed without sacrificing quality.

For the publisher, the per-page rate sets a maximum fee for a project. There is no more budget speculation about what a project will cost because hours are no longer part of the formula; instead, the focus is on saving time by getting the project completed sooner—a shorter turnaround. The costs are controlled because an editor can't dally over the manuscript in the belief that the longer it takes to edit, the greater the editor's income.

It also gives the publisher an opportunity to weed out from its stable of editors those who are inefficient and more costly because of their inefficiency. Remember that savings are not only gotten by reducing payout to an editor; even greater and more important savings can be had by shortening the time from manuscript to published book, especially in the eBook Age, when faster-than-instant gratification is demanded.

Shifting to a per-page payment also frees a publisher to evaluate ways to increase accuracy, efficiency, and productivity. A colleague who was discussing EditTools with me (trying to find out what enhancements are coming in the near future) told me that, as a result of using tools like EditTools, she has been able to increase the number of pages she can edit in an hour by as much as 50%, with an even higher level of quality than previously, both of which have resulted in increased work opportunities. Whereas many publishers and editors currently have little incentive to experiment with these types of tools, switching to a per-page rate from an hourly rate would provide that incentive. The ultimate results would be cost savings for the publisher and increased income for the editor.

Unfortunately, in the cost savings game, win-win situations are rare. Neither publishers nor editors are willing to break from the traditional path. One of my clients told me that they are unwilling to insist that editors accept a per-page rate; in fact, the client expressed reluctance to use editors who want to work on a per-page rate, saying that they fear editors would make less money and thus exacerbate the problem of finding quality editors. The client went on to say that, even after 15 years of my working for them on a per-page rate, they consider me an exception and the per-page rate experimental; additionally, few editors have asked for a per-page rather than an hourly rate. Similarly, no matter how many presentations I have made over the years demonstrating why the per-page rate is better for editors as a general rule (as with anything, whether it is better depends on what you do; there is no universal rule that applies in every circumstance), many editors refuse to try it and, of those who do, a goodly number have told me that "they lost their shirt" on project X on a per-page rate and thus refuse to use it ever again.

I am at a loss for how to convince publishers of the benefits of the per-page rate for their bottom lines; corporate thinking runs in hourly segments, and, as one client noted, there are too many "approvals" required. But those publishers I have talked with who have moved many of their freelance editors to the per-page rate tell me that they can see overall cost savings.

As for the editors who "lost their shirts" on a project, the answer is this: First, you cannot evaluate the profitability of a client based on a single project. Similarly, you cannot evaluate the profitability of a payment method on a single project. You must evaluate both on the basis of at least three completed projects. There are lots of reasons why the shirt could have been lost on the single project, not least of which was the editor's continuing to approach the project as if it was hourly paying. I can tell you from my own experience that it takes time to learn how to efficiently address a manuscript and that, even today, I occasionally get a project on which I lose my shirt. But if I lose my shirt on one out of 100 projects, the other 99 more than make up for the one's loss.

Perhaps a discussion of the factors that can cause you to lose your shirt should be another day's topic. Until then, do you stick with hourly-only projects, do a mix, or per-page/project fee only? Why and what is your experience? Why are you reluctant to move from an hourly fee to a per-page fee? Are you really satisfied with the hourly rate publishers pay?

58

THE RULE OF THREE

My 28 years of experience as editor were preceded by 14 years in the business world in various capacities, which gives me a more diverse perspective than you might otherwise expect. However, my experience as an editor is perhaps more limited than yours in that I only work on long-form nonfiction for publishers; that is, I do not work on, for example, journal articles and similar short-form material, and I do not work directly with authors.

On the other hand, one lesson I learned early in my career as a freelance editor is this: *Business is business*. There are certain fundamentals to running a business that remain true across all business types, just as there are things that are unique to the editing business. When the discussion centers on something that seems inappropriate to your editorial business, don't dismiss it. Think about it and think about how it can be made to apply to your business. A good example of this is today's topic—what I call "The Rule of Three."

My Rule of Three applies generally to two things in my business: whether I should keep or fire a client and whether a client is profitable for me. The two are intertwined. My Rule of Three is one factor in the answer to whether I should keep or fire a client, but it is the determinant in whether a client is profitable for me. If a client is not profitable for me, the client is fired; if the client is profitable for me, I may keep or fire the client based on other factors that I consider.

So what is the Rule of Three?

The Rule of Three is this: I never make a decision about a client, especially about the profitability to me of a client, until I have edited three manuscripts from that client. Experience has taught me that one or two manuscripts are not necessarily indicative of the types of manuscripts I can expect to receive from a client. The first manuscript may be so problematic that I am lucky if I earn minimum wage, let alone my desired effective hourly rate. Or it may be so deceptively easy that I surpass my goal easily. Or it may fall somewhere between the two extremes, which is what usually happens.

But wherever the first project falls on the continuum, I need to look at additional projects to determine how typical/atypical this first project was.

When I first started my editing career, I was advised that I needed to review the manuscript from any job offered before I accepted the job and, if I accepted a job that turned out to be much more complicated than I expected, I needed to be wary of taking on more projects from that client. I was given this advice by several experienced colleagues and I followed it for a few months—until I realized (a) how much time I was wasting on attempting to evaluate the difficulties of manuscripts and (b) how many clients I was considering firing because their manuscripts were not as "advertised."

It was at this point that I implemented my trusty Rule of Three, and I have never looked back. I stopped trying to evaluate manuscripts in advance. I discovered that the bits and pieces of what I previewed were not necessarily representative of the manuscript as a whole. Look at it this way: I typically work on multi-author books, where each chapter is written by a different author or group of authors, that run 3,000-plus manuscript pages. When I was sent sample chapters to evaluate, sometimes I got chapters that were well-written, sometimes I got chapters that were problematic because English was not the author(s) native language, and sometimes I got a little bit of both. But what did three chapters out of 130 chapters really tell me? Nothing very useful.

So I took the path of the Rule of Three and now I simply say I'll do the project. By keeping careful records, especially of the time I spent editing, I found that I could make a reliable general conclusion about a client by evaluating my records *after* having edited three manuscripts. Three manuscripts seem to give a good balance of what I can expect to receive from a client over the course of time.

This is not to say that I do not occasionally "lose my shirt" on a project or run into a manuscript that is so troublesome I would like to make the authors and the in-house production editor run with the bulls, but I can look back over my 28 years and say that the clients with whom I have stayed (and who have stayed with me) are profitable for me and let me exceed my goal effective hourly rate over the course of the year.

Like most businesses, editing has a rhythm. Once you find the rhythm with a client, it can be made to work for the editor rather than against the editor. Regular readers of this column know of my praise for macros. Macros let you take advantage of the rhythm. The Rule of Three lets you find a rhythm and macros let you take advantage of having found that rhythm.

When you think about the Rule of Three, also think about this: Just as you are evaluating a client, a client evaluates you. Clients continuously evaluate editors. Similarly, I apply the Rule of Three on a continuing basis; after all, clients and manuscripts do change. The key is keeping careful and accurate records, and not being misled by one manuscript (or part of a manuscript). You need to look at and for patterns and trends. You need to stay ahead of the curve, and when a good client becomes a bad client, you need to be willing to cut your losses.

Similarly, just because a client was unacceptable three years ago doesn't mean the client isn't acceptable this year. Try again and apply the Rule of Three again before automatically declining work.

59

REDUCING FEES

One of the hardest subjects to address in the editing world is that of fees: How much should I charge? The variables that go into the answer make a pat answer difficult.

Perhaps equally vexing is the included-but-unasked question: Should I ever reduce my fee? It is this question that I attempt to tackle here. (The final answer has to lie in your individual circumstances; there is no always-true answer.)

If I were to survey colleagues and ask the question, I have no doubt that very few, if any, would respond that yes, there are times when fees should be reduced. I expect most would say that fees should be raised and, if that is not possible, at least held steady. Of course, in an ideal world, this would be 100% sound advice, but few of us edit in an ideal world.

When considering the answer to the question, you should consider what kind of work you do and for whom do you work. I think the answer may be different, for example, if you work only for publishers than if you work directly with authors. It also may depend on whether you work alone or as part of a group; whether volume is important; and myriad other variables.

Regardless, however, every editor should be asking and considering the question, especially if they have unwanted downtime.

I recently had to address this question in my own business. I admit that I didn't struggle too long with the pros and cons.

I was offered the opportunity to have enough volume to keep myself and several editors very busy for many months. In exchange, the client wanted a lower per-page editing rate. Although it is very rare for me to have any downtime, it is not that it never happens. During the height of the recession, we did well, but I was still unable to keep all of my editors busy all of the time.

So, faced with the prospect of a large volume of work that conceivably could keep all of us busy year-round, I had to decide whether to lower my per-page rate. In the end, I did, because the economics were such that the exchange would be well worth accepting. So far, this has been true.

But I work in a narrow area (medicine) and for publishers and pack-agers only. I do not work directly with authors. Because of what my editors and I do, we are able to use techniques to increase efficiency and speed, and we are always searching for new ways to increase both without decreasing accuracy.

A willingness to consider reducing fees requires an understanding of your marketplace. When it comes to editing a book that is being translated from Chinese to English, an editor who is fluent in Chinese can probably charge more than an editor who knows no Chinese. Conse-quently, simply knowing what the Chinese-fluent editor is able to charge is not an indication of what you can or should charge if you are the non-Chinese-language editor.

On the other hand, if you are a Chinese-fluent editor with time on your hands and you know that you are competing with other similarly fluent editors, it may be in your interests to negotiate a volume contract at reduced prices. There is no medal for stubbornness when it comes to fees.

Colleagues will often argue that low-price editing lowers the price for all editors and, thus, we need to stick together at the higher price level. I know that they want me to take this argument seriously, but that is not possible.

First, the entry to editing is easy and the bar so low that virtually anyone can hang out a shingle that says "professional editor." Every day, hundreds more "professional" editors appear, and these new editors have prices all over the rainbow. Granted that, once hired, their lack of skill may become apparent, but they still get hired first because a key factor in the hiring process is price.

Second, colleagues who ask you to hold the price may not themselves be doing so. When faced with the prospect of no work and thus no money to pay bills, they often work for less. The reality is that our business is not a cooperative business; we compete all the time with each other and, in doing so, we tend to look out for our own best interests.

Finally, we face the problem of establishing what should be a base price for all editors. In my 28+ years as an editor, although numbers have been tossed about, no one has been able to come up with a universal minimum price—or universal method for calculating the same—that is good for all editors and all situations.

Which brings me back to the question of whether lowering fees should be considered. The answer is so dependent on so many variables that there is no correct, universal answer. In my case, the resolution of the question was easy. Because of how I charge (per-page), how I work (i.e., the use of macros and other efficiencies), and what I want (to know that I will have no downtime and that I will not have to constantly market), and because the amount in question was nominal on a per-page basis (although it would add up to a significant sum over the long term), coming to the answer that I should agree to lower my rate was easy.

For you, the answer may be much more difficult or may be *no*, but it is a question that should be addressed and analyzed, not simply shunted aside with *no* as the foregone conclusion. This question is one that every business has to face regularly, and our business is no different.

60

KILLING ME SOFTLY

I recently reviewed the various groups I am a member of on LinkedIn and was astounded to find a U.S.-based editor soliciting editing work and offering to do that work for $1 per page in all genres. Some further searching led me to discover that this person was not alone in her/his pricing.

What astounds me is less that someone is offering to do editorial work for such a low fee than that people actually believe that is a fair price to pay for professional editing. I recently spoke with an author whose ebooks are badly edited—yes, *edited* is the correct word—who told me that he/she had paid a professional editor $200 to edit the novel in question and so was surprised at all the errors the novel contained.

I've written about the publisher who wants copyediting but calls it proofreading in an attempt to pay a lower price. In my own business, I have been under pressure to reduce my fee or see the work offshored.

I am being killed softly.

Unfortunately, so is my profession for the past quarter-century being killed softly.

I write "being killed softly" because that is exactly what is happening. There are no trumpets blaring; clients aren't shouting and ordering me to work for starvation wages. Instead, what they are doing is saying that they can get the services I provide for significantly less money because the competition is so keen, driving pricing downward.

There is no discussion about whether the services clients get for less money are valuable services. The base assumption is that any editor will do and any editor will do a competent, quality job. Alas, there is little to disprove the assumption in the absence of post-editing proofreading, but that work is being driven by the same dynamic and so clients set a mouse to catch a mouse, rather than a cat to catch a mouse. If the proofreader's skills match the skills of the editor, little by way of error will be caught. We see this every day when we pick up a book and discover errors that should have been caught by a professional editor and/or proofreader.

When passing out the blame for this situation, we can look elsewhere—to the international conglomerate bean counters, to the Internet that has brought globalization to the editing profession, to the death of locally owned publishing companies that count quality higher than cost—or we can look to ourselves—to our insistence on being wholly independent and our resistance to banding together to form a strong lobbying group, to our willingness to provide stellar service for suboptimal wages, to the ease with which we permit entrance to a skilled profession. Looking at ourselves is where we should start.

Individually, we may strike gnat-like blows against this professional decline, but these will continue to prove of little avail. The profession of editing used to be a highly respected profession. It always was an underpaying profession, but it was a prestigious profession. All that has changed in recent decades. Our bohemian attitude toward our profession has worked to hurry its decline. It is now one of those work-at-home-and-earn-big-bucks professions that draws anyone in need of supplementary income.

It has become this way because we have let it become so.

I wondered if anyone was going to challenge the $1/page person, but no one did. There was no challenge of the price or of skills or of services. The idea that, at this price, level superior services can be provided is rapidly becoming the norm. That a good editor can often only edit five or six pages an hour—and, in many instances, even fewer pages an hour—does not seem to be a concern to either clients or to the editors advertising inexpensive services.

It is increasingly difficult to compete for business in the editorial marketplace. There are still pockets of clients who pay reasonable fees, but I expect those pockets to diminish and eventually disappear, and to do so in the not-too-distant future. Those of us with specialty skills are beginning to see the encroachment of downward pricing pressure.

What I find most interesting is that so many people do not even notice poor editing. There is a cadre of people who care about precision communication, but that cadre grows smaller with each passing year. A rigorous language education is now passé. The result is that there are fewer individuals who can recognize good editing from bad/no editing, and even fewer who care, being more concerned with cost.

I have no surefire solution to the problem. My hope is that someday someone in charge will see the light and decide that quality is at least of equal importance to cost control and recognize that it is not possible for an editor to provide a quality job at $1/page. Unfortunately, I do not see that day arriving any time soon.

What solutions do you propose?

61

BEST-PRICE "BIDS"

I was recently asked to give my best price on a possibly large project. My client was soliciting my bid for my editorial services on a project coming from one of its clients. In other words, I would not be directly working for the ultimate client.

It was an STM (Science, Technology, Math) project and supposedly would run 3,000 to 4,000 manuscript pages a month. My client wanted a price for both the original editing and for a review of the editing. A lot of detail was missing, so before I would give a price, I asked some questions.

Over my 29 years of editing, I have been asked many times to bid against myself with the client promising a large amount of work. What I learned was that there is a difference between what is promised/proposed in terms of quantity and what actually is delivered, which means that, in the past, I lowered my price expecting lots of work only to do much less work than "promised" for that lower price. Consequently, I no longer simply bid against myself; I attach conditions.

Make no mistake. When you are asked to give a price in such a situation, you are being asked to bid against yourself (as well as against others). You should not bid against yourself without assurances that the work will really materialize in the quantities and on the schedule given in the solicitation.

The first question I ask is how many pages are expected for the entire project. To me, it makes a difference if I am pricing for 3,000 pages or 18,000 pages of manuscript. The closer the count is to 3,000, the less inclined I am to lower my price, because 3,000 to 5,000 manuscript pages is a normal-size project for me. Conversely, the closer it is to 18,000 or more manuscript pages, the more inclined I am to discount my price.

But then I ask what often turns out to be the stickler question: What is the minimum guaranteed manuscript page count? That is, what is the minimum amount of pages for which I will be paid *regardless of whether the client sends me that amount of pages*? The answer to this question tells me a lot of things about a project.

First, it tells me whether the original request's numbers are puffery or real. If the original request spoke of 3,000 pages a month for six months but the minimum guarantee is just 3,000 pages, it is likely that the project is no more than 6,000 pages. The more the client is willing to guarantee, the more likely it is that the project is as claimed.

Second, it tells me whether the client simply is trying to get me to commit to a lower price. This is a major problem. Even if the project turns out as advertised, I run the risk of establishing a price that the client will expect for all future projects, regardless of size. This is no different from consumer expectations in a host of areas, but that doesn't mean it is a desirable result when it comes to my pricing.

Third, it tells me I need to be wary and make sure that I know a lot more about the project than I currently do *before* pricing it. The very worst thing I can do when being asked to bid is to not know as much as I can about the project and the likelihood of it really being as described *before* I make a bid. Once I make my bid, I am stuck, and I am the culprit who sticks me with what turns out to be an untenable bid.

Of major concern is how difficult the editing will be. The more difficult the editing, the less inclined I am to lower my price. Consequently, I need to see several samples, something I do not ordinarily ask for.

In the instant case, one of the things that was supplied to me were a couple of samples showing the type of editing expected and a copy of the ultimate client's guidelines for editors. When I saw the guidelines, I knew there would be trouble. It was a list of more than 60 items that the editor was expected to do—many of which are not normally done by a copyeditor, and certainly not done without an extra fee.

Editing is a labor-intensive business, which complicates the matter of bidding. How little are my services really worth? If I ask my clients, they don't respond with a value of my services; rather, they respond that they can hire an editor for $x less than they pay me. There is never a discussion about quality or speed or knowledge; the only discussion is about market availability of editors who will work for less than I charge, and it is this single dynamic that has brought about the request for bidding for editorial services.

Sometimes there is little that one can do except participate in the auction. When I am in such a position, as with this recent request, I condition my bid on three things: (a) There has to be a minimum guaranteed number of manuscript pages within a certain period of time for which I will be paid regardless; (b) the quoted price is the price only for this project and not transferable to any other project; and (c) after x number of manuscript pages have been edited, the bid price will be revisited to be certain that there were no "hidden" complications that should have been included in the solicitation or that there are no problems that arise that are out of my control that warrant a higher price than the bid price.

A major problem of bidding against oneself is that it is difficult to protect oneself and still get the job. But experience has taught me to be suspicious of jobs that have no flexibility and I would prefer to not get the work than to get work on which I cannot make any money.

Which raises another matter about bidding. When I bid on a project, I have a firm grasp of exactly what services I am willing to perform for what price. Consequently, when I am asked to bid on a project that wants more services, I start my evaluation from the price point that I would normally charge for providing the requested services. It is a bad idea to have a single price for copyediting because that doesn't consider the various services that can be provided, even, if 99% of the time, that single price is the price you charge or bid.

In this case, I bid much higher than my normal copyediting rate, but lower than the rate I would normally charge for editing performed with all of the required services. As I know who the ultimate client is, I do not expect to "win" this bid based on the price and conditions I submitted. I assure you, I will not shed a single tear should my bid be rejected.

62

WILDCARD MACROS AND MONEY

I thought the mention of money might catch your interest. But macros—especially wildcard macros—and money do go hand in hand. Consider the following two scenarios I recently experienced in the references of a project (same project, different chapters).

In the first scenario, there were, over two chapters, nearly 500 references that the authors had formatted like this:

Agarwal, S., Loh, Y. H., Mcloughlin, E. M., Huang, J., Park, I. H., Miller, J. D., Huo, H., Okuka, M., Dos Reis, R. M., Loewer, S., Ng, H. H., Keefe, D. L., Goldman, F. D., Klingelhutz, A. J., Liu, L. and Daley, G. Q. (2011) Telomere elongation in induced pluripotent stem cells from dyskeratosis congenita patients. *Nature,* 464, 292-6.

In the second scenario, the references were formatted like this:

Adhami F, G Liao, YM Morozov, et al: "Cerebral ischemia-hypoxia induces intravascular coagulation and autophagy." *Am J Pathol* 2006; 169(2): 566-583.

What they needed to look like is this:

Airley R, Loncaster J, Davidson S, et al. Glucose transporter glut-1 expression correlates with tumor hypoxia and predicts metastasis-free survival in advanced carcinoma of the cervix. *Clin Cancer Res* 2001;7(4):928-934.

The money question is, how to I get the references from where they are to where they need to be quickly and efficiently so that I make money and not lose money? The answer lies in wildcard macros.

For most editors, this kind of project is a daunting task that needs to be tackled manually. In the first scenario, the editor will manually remove each extraneous period, manually move the year to precede the volume number, and manually correct the punctuation problems in the citation. In other words, most editors will spend a good two or three minutes—if not longer—correcting *each* reference entry. I, on the other hand, spent less than 30 minutes cleaning up these references and verifying the journal names.

It is not that I am a brilliant macro writer—I am not. A skilled macro writer is someone like Jack Lyon, the creator of the Editorium macros that so many of us use. Instead, what I am is a smart user of the tools that will help me accomplish what needs to be done. In this case, I am a smart user of EditTools' Wildcard Find and Replace (WFR) macro tool.

WFR has been designed to make creating and using wildcard macros easy. You do not need to know how to write the macros—the tool will do it for you; instead, you need to know how to tackle a problem, how to break it down into its component parts.

The first step is to find a pattern. Remember that macros are dumb and work on patterns. I began by analyzing the patterns in the author names: Agarwal, S., Loh, Y. H., Mcloughlin, E. M. I realized that, for example, each of the first names was represented by an initial followed by a period and a space except that the final initial was followed by both a period and a comma (e.g., Y. H.,). Thus each group was separated by a period-comma combination. I also noticed that some authors had a single initial and some had two initials (and I recalled from other reference lists that some authors had three initials).

Beginning with the single initial name, I used WFR to create the first macro. WFR lets me select from menus what I want (e.g., the Character menu gives me several options, including Exact Characters, Exclude Characters, lower case, UPPER CASE, Mixed Case) and based on my selection, WFR creates the entry for me (e.g., choosing UPPER CASE in the first field inserts an unlimited [A-Z]@ into the field, which WFR turns into ([A-Z]@), the correct form for a wildcard). I do not need to know how to write the entry, I need only give the correct instruction. Thus, the first thing I wanted the macro to find was the surname, which is mixed case. So, from the menu of options, I chose Mixed Case and unlimited (unlimited because some surnames are short and others are long and I need to cover all of them) and WFR created ([A-Za-z]@) for me.

I continued to make my selections by filling in the fields in the WFR form so that in the end the fields were filled in for me like this (the @ indicates any number of the find criterion; the {1,1} indicates a minimum of 1 and a maximum of 1 of the find criterion; and in #3 and #7, preceding the { is a space):

Field # Find Replace
1 [A-Za-z]@ \1
2 , \3
3 {1,1} \4
4 [A-Z]{1,1} \6
5 . \7
6 ,
7 {1,1}

The Replace fields are where I tell the macro what to replace the find with. Again, this can be achieved by making selections from a menu. The \4, for example, indicates that what I want is found in field #4. So the Replace information tells the macro that I want the found criteria replaced with Surname (#1), a space (#3), the initial (#4), a comma (#6), and a space (#7). WFR creates a wildcard find string that looks like this:

([A-Za-z]@)(,)({1,1})([A-Z]{1,1})(.)(,)({1,1})

and a replace string that looks like this:

\1\3\4\6\7

and when the macro is run, every author name that looks like

Agarwal, S.,

becomes

Agarwal S,

Clearly, this one macro is not enough to clean up all the variations. In fact, for the first scenario, it took 11 macros just for the name cleanup. But this is another feature of WFR. After I create a macro, I can save it, with a lengthy description, in a file with similar macros, so I can use the macro again without having to create it again. But to have to run 11 macros individually is time-consuming, so WFR will let me create a script that will run all 11 macros in whatever order I want them to run.

A script is easy to create—you just double-click on the macros you want to add to a script and then save them. The script can be added to or subtracted from at any time.

Ultimately, I created another set of four macros to deal with the author names in the second scenario. All of these macros—those for scenario 1 and those for scenario 2—can be modified to deal with different patterns as the need arises. I will not have to keep reinventing the macros.

Another feature of WFR is that the macros are editable. If you discover that you should have included or omitted something, you do not need to recreate the entire macro; just choose to edit it.

And WFR lets you test the macro to make sure it works as you expect. (One note of caution when working with wildcard macros: It is best to turn tracking off. With tracking on, wildcard macros often produce bizarre results. Run the same macro with tracking off and everything works fine.)

It took me about 30 minutes to write all of the macros for both scenarios. Once I wrote them, however, when I came to the next chapter that needed the cleanup, the cleanup was done in less than a minute. Compare a less-than-a-minute cleanup time to the time it would take to do the cleanup manually. The wildcard macros make me money by making my work easy, quick, and efficient.

The beauty of EditTools' Wildcard Find and Replace macro is that you do not need to be a macro guru to create these macros. You simply need to break the tasks down into steps and use WFR to create the macros for you. One important point that is worth repeating: Macros are dumb. They will do what you tell them to do even if they shouldn't. It is still your responsibility as an editor to check the items. Macros do make mistakes.

If you haven't tried WFR, you should. It is an easy way to delve into the world of wildcard macros. And unlike using the wildcard feature of Word's Find and Replace, WFR lets you save the macros for future use and gives you a way to run several wildcard macros sequentially without having to create them.

63

ONE PRICE DOESN'T FIT ALL

Questions have risen, yet again, regarding pricing. Not how much, but whether to post prices on websites and whether to accept a "long-term" contract that sets a standard price for all editing services.

Of course, there is disagreement among editors on both questions.

I think it is a bad idea to post prices. The primary reason is that no two people agree as to what services are included under the rubric of, for example, copyediting, and what services are excluded. There are nearly as many definitions of copyediting as there are copyeditors, or so it seems.

Just as each manuscript is unique, so are the services that each manuscript needs different. By posting a price, you may turn away business that you might otherwise get if you had the opportunity to discuss what services are wanted and that you provide.

Not posting prices gives you an opportunity to interact with a prospective client. What editors do is personal; that is, we are not selling widgets but selling a very personalized service on a one-to-one basis. Consequently, price is only one element in the decision of whether to hire or fire an editor (or client); a significant element is how well personalities mesh—are the editor and the client on the same wavelength?

Posted prices lock you into a set scheme. If you post that you charge $30 an hour for copyediting services, it doesn't matter that the price includes; for example, fact-checking. All the prospective client sees is the price you posted and that a competitor editor has posted copyediting services for $20 an hour. You lose the opportunity to demonstrate to the prospect the superiority or comprehensiveness of your services or your experience.

It also means that, if you do take on the client and the project really should have been priced at $40 an hour, you are locked into the $30-an-hour price. Yes, I know you can include a clause in your contract that allows for adjusting the price. But is that really the reputation you want—one of a bait-and-switcher?

Accepting a "long-term" contract that sets a standard rate for all editing services is, I think, a different matter. I have had this debate with myself in the past and have consistently ended up on the side of accepting the contract in exchange for steady work.

Perhaps the worst feeling I have had in 29 years of freelance editing occurred in slack times—those periods between jobs when I would wonder whether more work would be forthcoming. After experiencing slack times a couple of times in my early years, I decided it was better to earn less money when working and be always busy than to earn more money when working but not always be working.

Consequently, I did two things. First, I made an effort to figure out how to be more efficient and productive so that I could accept a lower payscale yet earn the hourly rate I wanted. Second, I resolved to try to find clients who were interested in long-term relationships in which they would keep me busy and I would accept the work for a fixed rate. I have been successful at both these endeavors.

But I did learn early on the important lesson that one price doesn't fit all clients. Even though I may offer a client a single set price for all the work they send my way, I do not offer every client that same price. The reason is the same as for why I do not post prices at my website: The work that each client wants is different and the complexity—on average—of their projects differs, sometimes greatly.

For example, some clients do not want editors to check or style references; they just want the editor to make sure that all the pertinent information is present. Other clients want the editor to not only style the references but to check the references, and to find and supply any missing material. Reference work for the former group of clients might take minutes whereas for the latter group, it could take hours.

I know that some editors are thinking that setting a single price for a client can be dangerous because some projects are more difficult than others. (This is also the argument that some editors use to justify sticking with an hourly rate rather than going to a per-page or project rate.) Yes, that is true, which is why I apply my Rule of Three. My experience has been that few projects over the course of time are money-losers; most are money-makers if handled properly.

The keys are pretty simple: First, don't box yourself in by posting prices on your website *unless* you intend to minutely detail exactly what services are included and excluded for that price. Second, consider, if you are working with publishers and packagers, trying to work out a long-term deal in which you offer set services for a lower price in exchange for a steady stream of work. Third, spend time trying to figure out how to streamline your editing and implementing the procedures you discover. Remember that the more you can automate, the more you can earn, especially if you work on a per-page or project fee basis.

One last thing. I have been asked whether my advice not to post prices still holds if one posted a minimum price, for example, "copyediting from $30 an hour." My answer is yes. If someone had a very simple project but is only willing to pay $25 an hour, posting your minimum price would eliminate you from consideration, even though you would jump at the opportunity to take on the project were it offered.

An editor's mantra must be that, just as each author's book differs from books in the same genre written by other authors, so do editing services differ based on the editor and the project, which means that pricing differs—one price doesn't fit all!

64

NEW YEAR, NEW BOOKS

It's a new year and one of the first tasks I undertook as the calendar changed from 2012 to 2013 was to create the "books" I will use during 2013 to track how my business is doing. It doesn't take me long to create the new books (less than an hour), but it is—aside from obtaining business to keep track of—the most important task I will undertake in the new year.

I know that there are many ways of keeping track of how well one's business is doing. Over my 30 years as a freelancer, I have modified not only what information I keep, but how I keep it. About 10 years ago, I settled on my current system, which has been holding up well for me.

But before deciding how to keep the records, the decision as to what records to keep must be made. Once I decided on the information I needed, I then decided on how I was going to keep and use the information.

Basically, in addition to the usual chores of tracking income and expenses, there is certain information I want to know about each project I work on. Item #1 in the must-know column is how much time I am spending working on a project. Even the editors who subcontract to me are required to include on their invoices the number of hours worked.

Don't misunderstand: I do not care if a subcontractor takes 10 hours or 30 hours to complete a project; I care that the effective hourly rate I am receiving from a client is sufficient to warrant continuing to do work for the client and I care that the subcontractor is making a reasonable effective hourly rate. As part of the effective hourly rate discussion, I also keep in mind my *Rule of Three*, which is a critical determinant of whether I keep or fire a client. (Note, however, that this rule does not apply to one-shot projects such as are often encountered when working directly with authors.)

Keeping track of hours and my effective hourly rate also serves as a clue as to whether I am working as efficiently as I can. The data give me information so that I can determine that, over the course of time, my effective hourly rate for a project should be at least $x; that is, the average of all my projects over that period. If that number is $75 an hour and I find that my most recent projects came in at $35 to $50 an hour, I know I need to do some investigating. So, accurate hours are important—even though I charge a per-page or project rate rather than an hourly rate, my thinking is geared toward the effective hourly rate (EHR) statistic.

Another bit of information that I want to know is how projects break down by individual publishers and, within individual publishers, by in-house editor. Am I getting a balanced workload from a publisher/editor or are the projects skewed in one direction? If skewed, are they skewed toward a low EHR or a high EHR?

Along with that information, I also want to know how problematic a project was. For example, was the project loaded with incomplete references that were almost uniformly in the wrong style and thus required an excessive amount of time to edit? Consequently, I also rate a completed project on a scale of 1 to 10 (1 being easy, 5 being average or "balanced," 10 being excessively difficult). If I find that a particular in-house editor sends me only projects that rate 8 or 9, I think about whether I want to continue to accept projects from that editor.

There are a lot of factors that go into my rating a project, including how much information I *did not* receive about a project that I needed and how extensive the client's style exceptions are (e.g., it raises the difficulty number if the client tells me to adhere to AMA 10th ed. style, but then sends me a list of 100 exceptions). This is the most subjective of the data I keep, but it is important because the last thing I want is to find that nearly all my projects are in the 8 to 10 range, but are without compensation that matches the difficulty level.

Of course, I also track page count, but do so for more than calculating the EHR: I want to track ratings along with manuscript length. This ratio is one reason I prefer very large projects (i.e., thousands of manuscript pages)—such projects allow me to get a rhythm going and make more effective use of editing tools such as EditTools. Page count also tells me how busy I am and whether or not I should consider doing more books in a particular series.

There are other little bits of information I track, but the above are the keys. I use both QuickBooks Pro and Microsoft Excel to maintain my records. QuickBooks Pro makes it easy to compare performance over time; for example, I can easily compare income and expense information for the first month of 2013 against the first month of 2012, 2011, and as far back as my first use of QuickBooks Pro. QuickBook Pros also allows me to check on sources of revenue in detail. And tracking accounts receivable is a breeze. (It also makes it easy to generate the reports I need for my accountant for tax filings.)

Excel lets me easily keep duplicate information about billing (I like to know that, should one program fail for some reason, I have an alternative handy) and it allows me to track the bits of information I am interested in collecting and to manipulate them for analysis. QuickBooks Pro doesn't require a resetting of the forms each year—it is a continuous history; Excel, however, does require me to reset the forms each year. I'm sure that a more advanced user of Excel wouldn't have to reset the forms, but using Excel is not my job, editing is, and it is pretty easy to reset the forms for each new year. (I do retain, however, the prior years' forms for a comparative history. I have Excel information going back to my first days as a freelancer.)

At the beginning of a new year, you should think about what data you want to keep and how to keep it. The key is to make sure that you have enough data to make business-related decisions on facts and not on supposition. Keeping track of data is *not* time-consuming; it *is* necessary to maintaining a healthy and prosperous business.

65

THINKING ABOUT INVOICES

Have you given much thought to your invoice form and what it says about you?

It seems like an odd question, but it really is a basic business question. The ramifications of how your invoice presents you are several, not the least of which is how you are viewed by clients when it comes to payment terms.

Some companies require freelancers to fill out and sign an "invoice" form. They do this for several reasons. First, it ensures that the information the company needs to pay the freelancer is all there and easily accessible. Second, it acts as reinforcement for the idea that the invoicer really is a freelancer and not an employee in disguise in contravention of IRS rules. Third, and perhaps most importantly to a freelancer, it acts as a way to classify a freelancer and thus apply payment terms.

Have you ever noticed that companies often ignore your payment terms? Your invoice says payable on receipt, but you are paid in 30 or 45 days. Your invoice says payable in 30 days, yet payment may take 60 days. Good luck trying to impose a penalty for late payment. In the battle of wills between publisher and freelancer, it is the publisher who holds all the cards, except if the publisher doesn't pay at all.

(I have always found it interesting that a publisher feels free to ignore the payment terms and to ignore any late charges on invoices that a freelancer submits, but, should the freelancer order a book from the publisher and not pay on time, the publisher will hound the freelancer to death for both payment and any publisher-imposed late fees.)

What brings this to mind were recent discussions I had with colleagues who were complaining about how a publisher unilaterally extended the time to pay their invoices, yet that same publisher continues to pay me within the 15-day payment term my invoices set.

The primary reason for this difference in treatment is how the publisher views my business. I am viewed as business vendor, not as a freelancer.

This difference in view extends not just to how I am paid, but also to how clients treat me. For example, one client who insists that freelancers complete a publisher-provided invoice form and sign it, yet accepts my invoices as I print them and without my signature.

Another publisher sends files in which the figure and table callouts are highlighted and instructs freelancers to not delete the highlighting—but that does not apply to me. (In this instance, it doesn't apply for at least two reasons. First, the publisher doesn't view me the same as it views other freelancers. Second, I spent some time explaining to the publisher how I rely on EditTools while editing to increase consistency and accuracy, and sent a sample file showing the highlighting EditTools inserts in action. I then explained that I could either leave all the highlighting or remove all the highlighting, their choice. The publisher chose removal. What is important is that the publisher did not immediately dismiss me by telling me to do it the publisher's way or find work elsewhere. Instead, the publisher held a business-to-business discussion with me and saw and understood the value in the way I work.)

My point is that I have spent many years cultivating the view that I am a business, not a freelancer. Too many "clients" (both actual and prospective) view freelance editors as something other than "real" businesses or businesspeople. I used to hear clients refer to freelance editors as part-timers and as people for whom this is a "vacation income." I don't hear that anymore, but the attitude hasn't changed.

Colleagues have told me that they get calls from clients who see no reason why the freelancer can't do a job on a rush basis over the weekend at the same price as they would do it leisurely during the business week. Even when they try to explain that they are a business and that they can't just drop everything, especially without additional compensation, the message doesn't get through.

The solution to the problem is complex, not simple, but it begins with how we present ourselves and how we insist on being perceived. To my mind, it begins—but does not end—with the invoice. When your invoice asks that checks be made payable to Jane Doe and includes your Social Security number, you are feeding the image that this is a casual secondary source of income for you. Yes, I know and you know, and maybe even the in-house editor knows, this isn't true, but accounts payable and the company as a company doesn't see it that way.

If the invoice instead gives a business name, a name that makes it clear that the check will require depositing into a business checking account, and an employer identification number rather than a Social Security number, that anonymous accounts payable clerk is likely to begin to view you differently.

I think it also matters how the invoice is presented. I know that when I receive an invoice from someone that is just a Word or Excel document, I think "not very professional," especially if everything is in a bland Times New Roman font. Your invoice should be a "designed" form into which you enter data, and printed in PDF if sent electronically (color is *not* needed and even best avoided; it is layout that matters). I understand that the information will be the same, but information is not what we are talking about—presentation is important in establishing credentials as a business.

We've had these types of discussion before. For years, I noted that, to be treated as a business, you must act like a business. Years ago, that began with the way you answered your telephone, which either lent credence to your being a business or to your editing being "vacation income." Today, when so little is done by telephone, it is important that the material that a client sees conveys the image of a business. The image begins, I think, with the most important item we send a client—the invoice for our work (perhaps equally important are your e-mail address and e-mail signature: Not having your own business name domain sends the wrong message, which is a discussion for another day).

Remember that the people who make the decision on how fast you will be paid are not the people who evaluate your editing skill. They are far removed from the editing process and make decisions about you based on things they see that are unrelated to your editing skills. Consequently, you need to create a professional image on paper, beginning—but not ending—with your invoice.

66

THE ETHICS OF BILLING

Consider this scenario:

You are asked to edit a manuscript that, according to the client, will require a "heavy" edit. The prospective client asks how much you will charge. You have three choices: (a) Charge by the page; (b) charge by the project; or (c) charge by the hour. You've looked at a sample of the manuscript, and tell the client that you will charge $35 per hour to edit the manuscript. The client accepts and tells you that the budget for the project is $3,500. When you receive the complete manuscript, you find that the page count is 550 manuscript pages.

As you edit the manuscript, you discover that some chapters require more time to edit than others but that, on average, you are able to edit 12 pages an hour. Finally, the day has arrived when you have finished editing the manuscript. On finish, you have spent 46 hours editing.

Based on your hourly rate, your bill to the client should be $1,610 (46 hours × $35/hour), but you know that the client is prepared to pay $3,500, which is the budget for the project and represents the equivalent of 100 hours of work at the agreed-upon hourly rate. How much do you bill the client?

To me, this is an open-and-shut case: You bill for the 46 hours you spent, not a penny more. But what I have discovered is that many editors disagree with me, and believe that it is okay to bill for the budgeted $3,500.

These editors take the position that the client expects the editing to take 100 hours, expects to pay $3,500, and should not reap the benefit of having hired a more efficient editor who was able to complete the job in less-than-expected time. These editors go further and say that it is the editor who should reap the benefit of the editor's efficiency.

Yet that is not quite the end of the discussion. What happens, I have asked, if, instead of the editing taking 46 hours, it takes 120 hours? Who absorbs the 20 hours over the expressly stated budget? Here the position shifts and the usual—although not always—response is that the additional hours are billed to the client as well because the agreement is an hourly fee. To be fair, a small minority of the editors who believe it is okay to bill for the budget amount also believe that the budget amount is the upper limit and that, if an edit takes longer, it is the editor who absorbs the overage. At least some of the editors who think billing for the budget amount is okay also believe that any hours over the expressed budget should be absorbed by the editor.

Another group of editors thinks that, if it looks like the budget will be exceeded, at the moment of that revelation, the editor needs to contact the client and come to an agreement with the client about how to proceed. To me, this latter group belongs with the group who will bill for the overage because a client will be hard-pressed to say "stop" in the middle of editing.

The question of what to bill is a matter of ethics. Ethics are the rules and standards that govern the conduct of a person or a member of a profession. At least in the latter aspect (member of a profession), editing is not governed by standards of conduct; as a result, ethics decisions (yes, *ethics* is both singular and plural) are based on one's personal standards.

Consequently, there is no ethical standard to which one can point and say that billing in the described scenario needs to follow a particular rule or standard of conduct. Regardless of that universal absence, I think there is a fundamental, universally agreed-upon, understood, and expected standard that applies: the keeping of one's bargain or word; in other words, avoiding deceptive practices.

I think that standard (or expectation) should govern the question of how much to bill in the scenario described. The agreement was for $35/hour of editing with the understanding that the client had $3,500 at most to spend. If the editor could not fulfill that agreement, then the editor should decline the contract or choose an alternate method of billing in which the sum is fixed and not correlated to the number of hours, such as a project fee or a per-page rate.

Yet, as I noted earlier, many editors disagree with me. I recall having this discussion 20 years ago on an editorial forum, and 20 years later, the discussion still arises.

I hesitate to call the "bill-for-all-you-can" approach dishonest, but that is what it seems like to me. To my mind, the idea of a bargain between two parties is that each should be a winner, not that one be a winner and the other a loser. In the case of the scenario described, the editor is the winner in at least two aspects: (a) The $35/hour fee the editor desired has been agreed to, and (b) the editor has been awarded the job at the fee the editor desires. The client is the winner in at least two aspects: (a) In the event that the editor finds the project easier to deal with than the client expects and can do the job in fewer hours, the client expects to pay less money for the editing and save on its budget, and (b) the client expects its potential out-of-pocket costs are limited to the budgeted amount.

Under the ethics standards proposed by the editors who believe they alone should reap the rewards, the editor is the winner (a) because the editor will be paid *more* than the agreed-upon hourly rate should the editor complete the project more quickly than the client anticipates, and (b) because the editor does not accept the client's budget as a ceiling, the editor is protected against a project taking longer and will bill for overage. For the reasons that the editor is a winner, only the client is a loser.

If in relationships there is supposed to be balance, there is no balance in the situation where the editor always wins and the client always loses. (It also raises the question of what the incentive is for the editor to edit efficiently as the editor will earn more by being as inefficient as possible.)

The argument I have not yet made against the unbalanced approach's inherent dishonesty, but which is an important argument, is this: The agreement between editor and client was for an hourly fee of $35, an amount that the editor proposed and the client accepted. If the editor finishes the project in 46 hours but charges the client's budget of $3,500, the editor is really charging $76/hour—more than double the agreed-upon fee, and not the amount that was the basis of the bargain. That another editor might have taken 75 or 90 or 100 or more hours to do the same work with the same level of competency as the editor provided in 46 hours is, to me, a specious justification. Just as I can imagine an editor taking 75 hours to do the editing, I can imagine an editor taking 28 hours, yet none of the "bill-for-all-you-can" editors suggest that the client should be billed for just 28 hours because it is quite possible that another editor would have been even more efficient.

In editing, ethics is a personal matter. However, I do not see any acceptable justification being proposed for abandoning the "golden rule"—do unto others as you would have done unto you—just because an opportunity to do so arises. An agreed-upon bargain is one that should be kept and honored. That is how I conduct my business and how I expect those who do business with me to act.

What do you think? With which view are you aligned? Do you think billing for the budget amount if you take fewer hours to perform the job is ethically justifiable? Do you think it justifiable, especially without the concurrence of the client, to ignore the client's expressed budget limit and bill for overage?

67

RAISING PRICES

It seems like there is no such thing as an easy topic when it comes to the business of editing. In reviewing past essays, it seems I have called nearly every topic a difficult topic for editors. And here I go again. The issues of *whether, when,* and *how/how much* to raise prices are three more difficult issues with which an editor has to grapple.

Whether to raise one's prices depends on a lot of factors. Who are your clients; what types of documents you edit; what services you provide; whether quantity of work is more important to you than receiving what you consider fair or adequate compensation; what both your direct and indirect competitors charge; how easily a client can move the work to a lower-priced editor; and myriad other considerations.

Each editor is different. For example, I prefer to have every day of the year loaded with work—enough to keep myself and several other editors busy—and so am willing to accept a price that is lower than I think my work is worth. Some colleagues with whom I have discussed this topic prefer to have less work, even with not knowing how much down time they will have, but receive higher compensation. Where you fit in this scheme, only you can decide, as there is no single correct answer.

However, regardless of where your preferences fit, you must be aware of market conditions and what your competition is charging. I know that there is a school of thought that says we need to move away from thinking in terms of hourly pay (with which I agree) and instead think in terms of the value we add to a product (with which I agree philosophically but recognize the impracticability of in real-world editing). The oft-used example is web design, where the designer, when asked by the client what the price will be, replies with her own question, "Why do you want your website redesigned?" The client responds that the redesign will generate $100,000 of new business, so the designer says, "Isn't it worth spending $20,000 to earn $100,000?" Needless to say, the client agrees, the designer charges what she values her work to be worth, and all is well. Alas, that doesn't work for editing.

That is not how negotiations go between editors and clients. Editors cannot identify anything in their work that will increase a client's sales by a sum certain or a definite quantity. No client says to an editor, "The value of your editing will increase my book's sales by 50%." Editing is more invisible than that. Additionally, editing protects the after-sale reputation of the client; it doesn't generate the initial sales.

So whether we should raise (or lower) our prices depends on a lot of factors that are outside our control but are important to consider. Once that hurdle is overcome, the timing of a price raise must be considered.

Some editors do a general announcement at the first of the year. A new year seems like a logical time to raise prices, especially if your clientele is individual authors rather than companies. If your clients are companies, however, you need to consider timing in several ways: How much lead time is necessary between the announcement and the implementation? Is there a better (or worse) time of the year to raise prices for a company client? Should you even raise current client prices or just use the new pricing for new clients?

When raising prices, I try to keep in mind the client's fiscal year. I recognize that my clients plan a budget far in advance and that trying to raise prices in the middle of a budget is asking the client to hire someone else. Consequently, if I raise prices, I try to give six to 12 months' notice. I also make it clear that any already scheduled project will not be affected by the price rise. So, at the same time that I announce a price increase, I encourage the client to pre-schedule as many projects as it can to lock in the old price.

The last piece of the puzzle is the how/how much. Some editors announce a single price increase (e.g., $1 for the year); others announce an overall amount but in increments (e.g., $1 for the year in 25¢ increments every 3 months); and still other editors simply go for small but more-frequent amounts (e.g., 25¢ every 3 months).

One thing that is important to consider in the how/how much contemplation is the percentage the increase represents. This has long been a trick of marketing. To say you will receive a $5 discount is not as effective as saying you will receive a 50% discount, even though that 50% equals $5. Similarly, it looks better and a client may more easily accept a small price increase represented in dollars than the same amount represented as a percentage if the percentage exceeds 5%. In my experience, 5% seems to be the magic percentage. However, what you need to do is make the raise look as minimal as possible; the more minimal it looks, the more palatable it will be to the client.

I am not a fan of incremental raises. Clients rapidly come to think you are nickel-and-diming them. I think it is best to do yearly increases of relatively nominal amounts.

Of course, all this assumes that you are able to raise your prices. Some editors are able to do so, but many editors, myself included in the past couple of years, have been able to only hold steady on our pricing and even have had to lower our pricing. This is a result of competition plus the lack of, in the United States, a true professional organization that separates professional from nonprofessional editors.

Ease of entry and the constant influx of people who claim to be editors has put significant downward pressure on editing prices. Combine this with the globalization of editing and trouble is brewing in raising-prices land. In addition, one's approach to editing is important.

I, for example, have decided that I would rather be busy and keep other editors busy than raise my prices. I prefer quantity. Consequently, I consciously decided that it is preferable to compete within my sphere than to have idle time, even though I would receive a higher price. (This does not mean, however, that I will accept work at a price that is below what I have determined to be my minimum acceptable price—my pricing floor.) My ultimate earnings would be about the same, but I prefer not to have the idle time. Consequently, to meet my goal of no idle time for myself and additional editors, I had to lower my pricing.

Did I make the smart move? Again, it depends on what you want. But I also look at it like a challenge. This is one of the reasons I created EditTools and keep modifying and adding to it: I needed and wanted to maximize my effective hourly rate while lowering my price so I could keep busy and still make an acceptable amount. In other words, I take steps that have the same ultimate effect as raising my price—steps that make the editing go faster, although with increased accuracy, which means my effective hourly rate rises.

Raising prices depends on so many factors that no one can give you one-size-fits-all advice. The most difficult part of the equation is the *whether* factor. Resolving that question—whether to raise, retain, or lower your price—is the most difficult and the most important consideration; once you resolve that, the *when* and *how/how much* will fall into place.

68

LOWER YOUR RATE?

I recently wrote about raising one's rates. Although the essay focused on raising rates, I did, somewhat off-handedly, mention *lowering* rates. No one commented on that possibility, and I suspect that very few readers even contemplated the wisdom of lowering one's rates.

I'm here to tell you that sometimes it is a smarter business move to lower one's rate than it is to either maintain or raise one's rate. I'm sure the resistance barriers are already rising.

Let's begin with the obvious. The decision of whether to lower or raise rates rests on many of the same factors, regardless of which way you lean. It makes no sense to charge $100 an hour when all your direct competition is charging $25 an hour. Similarly, it makes no sense to do the reverse, at least not with such a great spread; perhaps a smaller spread will work.

But what is not obvious is the reason why lowering one's rate can be a smart business move. Consider why businesses generally lower prices or charge membership fees or issue loyalty cards with rewards. Now recall that you, too, are a business. You want exactly what your credit card company or your grocery store wants: repeat and loyal business. It costs much less to work with repeat clients than to find new client. ♪.

When I think about my rates, I consider the types of clients I deal with and what I want from those clients. I want to "lock them in" to me; I want them to ask me first to undertake an assignment and I want them to be reluctant to hire another editor. When those projects that are worth $20,000 in fees come around, I want the very first reaction to be to call me.

I understand that quality of editing is important. I also understand that many, if not most, editors rely on the quality of their work to bring in repeat business. I know I certainly do not skimp on quality. Yet that is what all of my competition does as well.

As I have written previously, I want to keep myself and those editors who work for me busy all year-round, not just a few weeks or months a year. Thus quantity of work is important to me. The question becomes: How do I get the quantity at the least cost and effort? One important answer is that I offer a discounted price to clients who are willing to offer me assurances that I will be called first.

Does this always work? No, it doesn't. Some clients have corporate policies that prohibit such negotiations; others take the position that they cannot accurately forecast when and how much manuscript will arrive and thus cannot agree to "guarantee" an amount of work. Some clients have other reasons why such a proposition wouldn't work with them.

But there are clients for whom this does work and it works to both our benefits: I am assured a steady supply of work and they are assured some money savings, along with a high-quality edit. Not only does it not hurt anything to try to work out some arrangement for repeat business with a client, but even if it doesn't work out, the client recognizes you for what you are: a businessperson.

Of course, all of the above fits my business model and works with publishers. Such an approach is difficult to take with authors because most authors cannot generate enough work in the course of a year to make such negotiations worthwhile. An editor needs to evaluate his business and his wants and needs before considering fee reduction. But every editor should think about whether this is a concept that can be made to work for you in your business.

In a way, this hearkens back to the concept of effective hourly rate. What good does it do you as an editor to have an hourly rate of $50 if your EHR is really $20? High EHRs depend on not only the rate and expenses, but the number of hours you are actually editing. If you charge $50 an hour but only edit 20 hours a week, your EHR is $25, not $50—and that's before considering expenses. To my mind, I would rather work 40 hours a week at an hourly rate of $40. (And, no, I'm not advocating hourly rates; it is just that using an hourly rate makes the examples easier, less complex, more pointed, and much shorter.)

Lowering one's rate can have several advantages. Such a move can increase the quantity of work. It can also "lock-in" a client. And it can make a wholly new-to-you client willing to talk seriously to you about adding you to their list of editors.

Something else to keep in mind. Lowering your rate for client A does not mean you have to lower your rate for client B. Each client should be considered individually. I think an editor should have standardized base rates for certain types of work but then the rate should be adjusted based on the client and even on experience with a client. Editing services are unique to each client and sometimes to each project, and one's rate(s) should reflect that. However, some clients offer the possibility of a quantity of work over years, which work is of a similar nature and thus requires a set rate.

Also necessary to keep in mind when thinking about rates is whether it is possible to make use of economies of scale, which is something every business has to consider. In manufacturing, the concept is illustrated by the idea that the larger the quantity you buy, the lower the individual piece price. Although editors do not work like manufacturers, the basic concept can still apply.

I know that I can edit certain types of books more quickly than other types without loss of quality because I know that I have tools available to make the work go faster. Knowing that I have certain efficiencies in my business allows me to be flexible with rates for clients whose books are ones to which I can apply those efficiencies. Lacking the ability to apply those efficiencies would prevent me from lowering my rate and would induce me to raise it.

The bottom line is that, for the right client and for the right return, editors should consider whether to lower their rates and not reflexively dismiss the possibility. As with raising rates, lowering rates should not be approached willy-nilly. Doing either must be the result of careful evaluation of what benefit (and harm) will accrue to you. What editors must overcome is the reflexive response that one should never consider lowering one's rate, let alone actually do it.

Whether to lower or raise one's rate for a client is a business decision and must be approached like one—objectively, not emotionally.

69

The Demand for Perfection

In a LinkedIn group, there has been a discussion about errors that are missed by editors. The discussion is a great illustration of the disconnect between reasonable and unreasonable expectations in editing.

On the one hand, you have an author who admits his manuscript is far from perfect and who expects the editor to make it error-free or keep working on it at the editor's expense until the manuscript is error-free. On the other hand, you have editors who offer a broad range for what constitutes an acceptable number of errors. The discussion began with the question, "How many errors is it acceptable for an editor to miss in a 200-page manuscript?" The answers ranged from zero to (you pick a number).

Needless to say, there was a gap that could not be bridged. Authors (and some editors—usually editors who were also authors) remained steadfast in the belief that an error-free manuscript was not only a desirable goal but an achievable goal. Others, including myself, remained steadfast in the belief that, as long as editing is done by humans, there will be errors.

Fundamentally, however, the entire discussion missed the salient point. The discussion remained focused on coming up with a number, such as 5 errors in 1,000 pages, rather than on the core issue: What constitutes an error?

Editing has always been a profession of opinion. Unlike the physical sciences that are governed by strict "laws," editorial decisions are governed by informed opinion, nothing more. One person's error is another person's artistic breakthrough. Although we point to "authorities" such as dictionaries and manuals of style and usage to justify decisions we make, we really aren't pointing to immutable, unbreakable "laws" or "rules"—we are pointing to consensus opinion at best.

That the consensus opinion is formed by a group of people to whom we grant the power to be the diviners of what is and what should not be, the truth is that their opinion is rarely more informed or valuable than our opinion. Their opinion has an aura, a mystique, if you will, of authority, something our opinion lacks, but that doesn't change their opinion from opinion to gospel. It has the force and validity we give it.

Which brings me back to error. Is it error to be diametrically opposite consensus opinion? If it were, we would still be preaching that the sun revolves around the earth—or is that something different? Surely it is different because it is fact, immutable, provable, and today unquestionable (except by the fringe few)— it is nothing like an editorial opinion.

Is it *grey* or *gray*? *One* or *1*? Is *they* singular or only plural? Can we safely and correctly split the infinitive? Is *due to* acceptable or must it be replaced with the correct, precise phrase? Can *since* and *because* be used synonymously or is *since* only for expression of time passage?

At precisely what point in the journey do we pass from opinion to error? Who decides what is error?

Perhaps of all the questions, this last question is the most important, because once we assign the power to determine error, we assign the right to make editorial decisions and we determine whose opinion is superior. The fallacy in my argument is, of course, demonstrated by the three Ws (or is it W's?): *w8, weight, wait*. Is it an error to leave unchanged "I'll w8 for you" or "I'll *weight* for you"?

The immediate answer I expect from colleagues is, "Yes, it is clearly error to use *w8* or *weight* when you mean *wait*." But let us consider the response. First, it assumes that I intend *wait*. Based on the education we have received and our years of experience with interpreting language, it is very likely that *wait* is intended. It is a 99.9999999% safe bet. But it is not a 100% sure bet in the absence of surrounding information.

The second problem is that to declare the use of *w8* or *weight* for *wait* as an error is to declare that English is a static language; that meanings and spellings never change; that because it was linguistically true yesterday, it must be linguistically true today, and will be linguistically true tomorrow. Where, then, has the growth in dictionaries come from? How did *since* become an acceptable clone of *because*?

So we go round and round, with no beginning and no end, in resolving the question of what is an error. No matter how it is sliced and diced, what is an error in the editorial sense is a matter of opinion, not a matter of fact. We can turn it into a matter of fact by prefacing the editorial process with a declaration that these authorities—x, y, and z—shall govern matters of spelling, grammar, and usage, which is what we do in our daily work.

When dealing with publishers, such parameters are usually laid out in advance of the work. In my experience, few authors have enough familiarity with these editorial resources to make such a predetermination. I suspect that it is one novelist in 5,000 who says "Please follow the _____ style manual" when hiring an editor.

When an author demands perfection as the standard, predetermining who and what will be the arbiters of what constitutes an error is fundamental. However, there are other factors that need to come into play as well. Consider time.

Most novelists I have dealt with have said that they spent more than a year—often many years—on writing and rewriting and having their novel peer-reviewed and redrafted again to bring the manuscript to its current state of readiness for editing. Then they drop the bombshell of wanting an error-free edited manuscript in 30 (or fewer) days. After years of writing and rewriting and not producing an error-free manuscript, the expectation is that the editor can fix all problems quickly. Does anything more need to be said about the matter of time?

Consider money. I have yet to meet the publisher or author who says that neither time nor money is a problem. Editors are rarely, if ever, given unlimited time and an unlimited budget in which to produce an error-free edited manuscript. I also have not met a publisher or author who will agree to pay $150 an hour for as many hours as it takes to achieve an error-free manuscript. Usually what I hear, and what colleagues tell me they, too, hear, is that the edited manuscript is needed within 30 (or fewer) days and that the budget is capped at, say, 30 hours at $20 an hour.

It isn't clear to me how perfection is to be achieved on a limited budget with a limited amount of time. It took months or years to bring the manuscript to the more-perfect, but still imperfect, state it is in at the time it is presented for editing. Why is the expectation that it can be moved from its current state of imperfection to a state of perfection within days at very little cost? Why do some authors consider this a reasonable expectation?

An error-free manuscript should be the goal for which an editor should strive, but it should not become an albatross. It is unreasonable, I think, to demand perfection from someone else when you do not produce it yourself. But if you are going to demand editorial perfection, be prepared to define what constitutes an error in advance and who and what shall be the arbiters of right versus wrong (error vs. non-error), to accept an open-ended schedule, and to provide an unlimited budget at a reasonable (to the editor) rate of pay.

70

WHAT TO CHARGE—PART I

One problem with editing as a profession is that it is easy to set oneself up as an editor. The result is that every day brings new editors into competition with existing editors. And every day the question gets asked: "What should I charge?"

The first response to that question, at least in the United States, is to take a look at the EFA (Editorial Freelancers Association) list of editorial rates. It does no harm to look at the rate schedule, as long as you recognize the failings of the schedule and do not rely on it for setting your rates.

The EFA schedule of rates is based on surveys of EFA members. Consequently, the survey excludes data from the many thousands of nonmembers. More importantly, the portion of the membership that responds to the survey is just a small fraction of the EFA membership, which itself is but a miniscule fraction of the universe of editorial freelancers. There are other biases in the survey as well.

The EFA schedule is also problematic because it fails to define its terms. For example, what does "basic copyediting" include/exclude that distinguishes it from "heavy copyediting"? What justifies the range difference? Suppose the copyediting were "medium." How does that differ from "heavy" or "basic"?

Bottom line is that the EFA schedule of rates is a place to begin but not to stop. It should be reviewed, then discarded.

A problem with the query about what to charge is that the asker believes in a false assumption—that there is a "going rate." There really isn't a going rate in editing. It is true that many publishers pay similar fees for work, but if you look at what work is required, you will see that there is a great variance among publishers. In the case of authors, there is no rate similarity that is author-imposed. Authors deal with editors on a one-to-one basis, and negotiate rates one-to-one. Publishers, in contrast, deal with many editors simultaneously and thus have company-established pay guidelines that they impose.

Although there is no going rate per se, it could be argued that there is a de facto one because Publisher A will offer pretty much the same as Publisher B by way of compensation; only the amount of work demanded (i.e., services required for that pay) varies—and should be carefully looked at and incorporated into your determination of what to charge.

Ultimately, any "going rate" has little meaning in the absence of it meeting your needs, which is the crux of the issue of what to charge.

The most important factor in setting a rate is knowing what your effective hourly rate (EHR) has to be for you to make the income you need. We have discussed the EHR several times.

The EHR gives you a better picture of what you are really earning. For example, if you charge $30 an hour but are able to charge and receive payment for only 20 hours of a 40-hour workweek, your "gross" EHR is $15, not $30. You need to account for all of the hours in a workweek. The gross EHR isn't a "true" EHR because it accounts only for hours, but it is better than blindly choosing a number that sounds good or matches the rate of some other editor whose circumstances and needs are likely to be different than yours.

The true EHR also accounts for expenses incurred by your business. For example, if you work from your home and pay $500 a month in utilities, you might attribute $250 a month to your freelance work. That works out to $57.70 a week (or $1.44/hour) in utilities expense that you "would not otherwise incur" if you were working outside the home and for someone else who supplied the utilities during the workweek. (Even if your utilities bill would not be lowered by your working outside the home, some portion of the utility cost is attributable to your working from home.)

Utilities are but one of the expenses that are attributable to your freelance business. Health insurance is another, especially if you had employer-paid health insurance before pursuing your freelance career. The point is that you need to identify all your freelance-related expenses and add them to the mix to determine what to charge.

Let's pursue the example of a true EHR using an hourly rate of $30. If you charge $30/hour for copyediting (however you define copyediting) and have billable work for 20 hours, your gross EHR = $15 an hour, which is calculated this way:

$30 per hour × 20 billable hours in 1 week = $600
$600 ÷ 40 hours (standard workweek) = $15 EHR

Now that we know the gross EHR, we need to fine-tune it to determine the "true" EHR. Consequently, from the gross EHR subtract the cost of utilities, as follows:

$15 (gross EHR) − $1.44 (freelance portion of utilities per hour) = $13.56 ("true" EHR)

We are only using utilities as a cost here, but the deduction from the gross EHR would be the freelance portion of all expenses of maintaining your business, broken down into its hourly value, such as the appropriate portion of health insurance, other required insurance(s), telephone and Internet service, rent or mortgage, hardware and software, etc. In other words, the $13.56 in the example is still high.

Once you have figured out your EHR, you need to determine your target gross yearly income. In reality, you will pick a number that you would like to earn and see if it is feasible.

Let's assume that your target gross income for a year is $50,000. That equates to a gross of weekly income of $961.54 (based on a 52-week year), which equates to a minimum EHR of $24.04 (based on a standard 40-hour workweek). Is the $30/hour rate you charge sufficient to generate your desired annual gross income based on your EHR?

71

WHAT TO CHARGE—PART II

Is the $30/hour rate you charge sufficient to generate your desired annual gross income based on your EHR? The answer is "no."

Your current charge of $30/hour is not enough to generate the desired gross annual income of $50,000 because your *net* EHR is $13.56 (based on 20 billable hours in a 40-hour workweek), not the required minimum EHR of $24.04. Your EHR is $10.48 too little. Based on your EHR, your gross annual earnings will be approximately $28,200, or a little bit more than half of your desired annual gross income.

There are several options for curing this problem. First, you could increase the number of billable hours you work each week. At the hourly rate of $30, you need to generate at least enough work to bill for 34 hours every week for 52 weeks a year (or its equivalent). That will generate a *net* EHR of $24.06 ($30 × 34 hours = $1,020 ÷ 40-hour workweek = $24.06). That is not impossible to do, but if you haven't averaged at least 34 hours a week of billable-at-$30-an-hour-work over the course of a year in past years, you will have to devote some time, money, and effort to bring your workload to that level.

Second, you could lower the amount of your desired gross annual income. That would certainly change the calculation, but it would raise other questions, such as: Are you earning enough to meet your bills? Are you earning enough to warrant remaining a freelance editor? Is your annual income sufficient to support the lifestyle you want?

The third option is to raise your hourly rate to $51 an hour and continue to generate an average of 20 hours of work a week for 52 weeks, which would give you a net EHR of $24.06 and meet your income goals.

The fourth—and best—option is to calculate the *net* EHR you need to meet, which is, in this case, $25 (it really is $24.06, but rounded numbers are easier to deal with and so we round up). Then, instead of trying to charge and collect an hourly rate of $50, charge a per-page or project fee, and work to increase your efficiency so that you can generate your necessary EHR. It is more likely that clients will accept a per-page or project fee than an hourly fee that they view as too high or outside their budget.

Also very important to consider when deciding whether to charge by the hour or the page/project is this: If you charge $3 per manuscript page, you need to edit a little more than 8 pages an hour to meet the $25 EHR. If you can edit 10 pages an hour, your EHR will equal $30, which is $5 more than needed. As time passes and that extra $5 adds up, you build a cushion for those times when you have no work, a cushion that may still allow you to maintain the EHR of $25 over the course of the year.

And don't forget this: The $25 EHR is based on your generating enough work to bill for 20 hours a week on average. Thus, to meet your goal, you need to copyedit approximately 167 pages a week. (*A cautionary note:* Remember that all of these example calculations are based on our net EHR but that this net EHR is incomplete. You *must* do your own calculations based on your own business.)

Option 4 is, in my thinking, the best option because, as many free-lancers have noted, publishers generally do not offer rates above $25 an hour, and authors aren't knocking down doors in a scramble to pay editors $50 an hour. Most publishers offer a rate between $18 and $25 an hour; some publishers, to their discredit, I think, offer rates of $12 or less an hour. In addition, we are competing worldwide with editors who do not calculate their EHR needs and will accept work at any price offered. Consequently, the best way to charge is a per-page or project-fee rate because you can compete effectively yet increase your productivity and efficiency and thus raise your EHR to a sum much higher than the offered hourly rates—in other words, by becoming more efficient and speedy, you can make a $20 hourly rate (when converted from a per-page rate) into an EHR of $50.

Which brings us to the next matter: calculating a page. There are lots of ways to calculate a page. One of the most common formulas is

250 words = 1 page. But there are other formulas, such as counting characters. It really doesn't matter what you decide equals one page; what does matter is that you have a definition, that you make it known to clients, and that you apply it *before* quoting a price.

Regardless of how you ultimately decide to charge—whether by the hour, the page, the word, or the project—it is important to be able to calculate the number of pages because, for most people, the number of pages has meaning as a measure. In addition, editors think in terms of how many pages they can edit in an hour, not how many words they can edit in an hour.

In a recent online discussion, someone was looking for an editor to edit a 248,000-word manuscript that they said equaled 450 pages. Before bidding on such a project, you need to have a standard definition of what constitutes a page so that you can rationally determine what to bid. In this instance, the author calculated a page as 550 words, more than double the commonly used 250 words. Were I to bid on this project, I would bid as if the page count were 992 pages, not 450. One page equaling 550 words is not within my lexicon.

If I placed a bid based on the 992-page count, I would be prepared to explain what constitutes a page and how I calculated the manuscript's true (for editing) size. This count is important to me because I have a pretty good idea of how many pages I can edit in an hour. That number is a range that covers badly written manuscripts through well-written manuscripts. Knowing the correct number of pages by my definition of what constitutes a page and knowing how many of those pages I can edit, on average, in an hour, lets me knowledgeably decide if I can undertake the project and how much I need to charge.

If the author insists that the correct page count is 450, my response would be that it doesn't matter—this is my bid price for the manuscript as described, whether we call it 450 pages or 992 pages. What matters is that I have a definition for a page that I apply when calculating my fee.

This is important because I charge by the page, not by the hour. I have a high EHR that I want to meet and a key to knowing whether I can meet that EHR is knowing how many pages I can expect to edit in an hour. The more pages I can edit, the higher my EHR.

In contrast, if I charged by the hour, aside from the fact that my true EHR would be significantly lower than my hourly rate, it wouldn't matter how many pages I could edit in an hour. I am being paid by time, not by productivity—and I will not be rewarded for being efficient or productive; in fact, I will be punished if I am efficient and productive because I will earn less (in gross) on the project. When I charge by the page (or by the project), I am rewarded when I am efficient and productive.

Every time I exceed my required EHR, I am given a bonus. In contrast, if I charge by the hour, I can never exceed my required EHR (and usually cannot meet it), thus I can never receive a bonus.

I know the concept of EHR can be confusing, maybe even daunting, but combined with a firm definition of what constitutes one manuscript page, it is really the best way to determine what you should be charging.

In *What to Charge—Part III*, we will discuss tracking the EHR.

72

WHAT TO CHARGE—PART III

In parts I and II of *Business of Editing: What to Charge,* we discussed the effective hourly rate (EHR), how to calculate a true EHR, why it is important to have a definition of what constitutes a manuscript page, and why I think it is smarter to charge by the page or project rather than by the hour. But knowing your required EHR is not enough; you need to track it as well.

I use two programs to track my EHR: Timeless Time and Expense (TT&E) and Microsoft Excel. In the case of TT&E, I am using an older version because it does all that I need. TT&E is not freeware and it is a bit pricey if all you want is to track time, but I like that it makes it easy to track multiple projects. In any event, what you need is a good timing program that will track how much time you spend on a project and give you a total time.

Excel is a program that most of you are familiar with. However, as with TT&E, it is not necessary to use Excel; any quality spreadsheet program will do.

Tracking time is key. I round total time up to the nearest quarter hour. For example, if the total time I spent on a project is 25 hours and 1 minute (25:01), I enter that as 25.25 hours. I know that, somewhere along the line, I missed timing a few minutes of work, so this is a way to compensate.

Another thing I do is track the time based on billing cycles. If a project is to be billed only upon completion, then I track the time until the project is complete and being billed and use the single total time. If the project is being billed in batches, then I track the time for each batch and enter the time in Excel batch by batch.

As you can see from the following image, I use a simple form to track important data.

In the sample, I have given a spread of per-page price ranges. The key, of course, is to maximize price and minimize hours. (I know that some of you will point out the high pages-edited-per-hour rate that this illustration uses. The pages and hours shown are taken from a real project. Remember, however, that this is an illustration and your figures will differ.)

What is important is that, even at the lowest per-page price of $2 per page, the EHR exceeded the required EHR of $25 (based on editing 16 pages an hour; at a rate of 13 pages per hour, the EHR would still be exceeded but at 12 pages an hour, it would not be met. However, at $2.50 per page, where the illustration has a 19 pages-edited-per-hour rate, even at a rate of 12 pages per hour the EHR would be exceeded). This illustrates that it is possible to have a low rate and still meet and exceed the required EHR if you are efficient and productive. Do not, however, take this as an argument for a low per-page rate, nor an indication that you will always exceed the required EHR, nor an indication that one can always edit at such a high pages-per-hour rate—this is just an illustration of how to calculate and track the EHR.

Example of Workday EHR (Hourly)

- If —
  - Hours billed = 5
  - Hourly rate = $30
  - Total workday hours = 6.5
  - Then

$$\textbf{EHR workday} = \frac{(5 \times \$30)}{6.5} = \$23.08$$

If the per-page rate had been $2 for the whole project, the EHR would have been $38.45 based on the numbers. However, to achieve that EHR, the editor would have had to average, as indicated in the image, 19.23 pages an hour. Depending on the project and the parameters of the project, that may be doable.

But we stray off course.

The key to determining what to charge is determining your required EHR. But to determine that EHR, you have to have accumulated data. In the beginning, you guess, but as data accumulates, you can be more precise in your calculation. The important data are the EHR for each batch of submitted manuscript, as well as for the entire project, and your average number of pages edited per hour (shown in the image at the bottom far right).

Unfortunately, the image doesn't show the column labels. Column A is the Date; B is Batch #; C is Number of Pages; D is Per-page Rate; E is Number of Hours; F is EHR; G is Charge; H is Total; and K is the Average Pages/Hour. You need the column information for the following Excel formulas to make sense.

Although the information is important, columns A and B are not needed to calculate any of the other data in the table. The formula to calculate the EHR of column F is:

=IF(E11=0,"",(C11*D11)/E11)

where, for example, E11 represents the data in column E row 11. The
"" is an instruction to leave the cell in column F blank if the data in
E11 equals 0.

To calculate the Charge of column G, use the formula:

=SUM(C11*D11)

The Total column (H) needs two formulas. The first is only for the
very first row of data, which in this example is row 11:

=SUM(G11)

The formula is that simple because in this instance, the Charge and the
Total are identical. To calculate subsequent Totals by row, the formula is:

=SUM(G12+H11)

which means to add the new Charge found in this row (G12) to the Total
in the row immediately above (H11) so that the Total in this row is a
running total. Remember that the numbers (e.g., 12 in G12) represent
the row number; the letter represents the column.

All of the data is row-centric; that is, the calculations are for the row
only. The exception is the Total column, which is a running total.

The Profit/Loss Data row is where we get our overall information. The
formulas for the various entries are as follows:

Total Pages: =SUM(C11:C22)
Total Hours: =SUM(E11:E22)
Ave Effect Hrly Rate: =IF(E24=0,"",G24/E24)
Total Billed: =SUM(G11:G22)
Project Gross Profit: =SUM(G24-D24)

Finally, the formula for the Ave Pg/H is:

=IF(E24=0,"",C24/E24)

Because I hire other editors to work on projects, I need the IC Fee
and the Gross Profit percent (%) information. For those who never hire

someone else, these items can be omitted. For those who do hire, you manually enter the amount of total fee paid to the other editor under the IC fee and use this formula to calculate what percentage of the total fee you retained:

=IF(G24=0,"",H24/G24)

Although not shown in the illustration, you can also track your EHR over the course of time by adding up the total hours from each project and the total billed for each project and dividing the grand total billed by the grand total hours.

With this data at hand, you can determine whether you are charging enough for your services. Adjustments can be made as needed. This information will tell you the state of health of your business. If you see that you are not making your required EHR, you need to analyze why not. Are there things that you can do to improve your efficiency and productivity? Or is the only solution to raise your prices and find new clients?

Part IV adds some clarification and Part V concludes the series, tackling the question "Why bother?"

73

WHAT TO CHARGE—PART IV

Originally, part IV was scheduled to be the last part of this series, and was to tackle the question, "Why bother?" However, what was part IV is now part V. The change was made because I have received several requests for clarification on how to determine what to charge. The confusion seems to stem from two things:

1. The effective hourly rate (EHR) discussed in parts I, II, and III, is based on a 40-hour work week. The calculated EHR is what is needed to be earned each hour of that 40-hour work week. This does not mean that you must have 40 billable hours, just that this is the EHR that each hour has to earn even if the earning has to be compressed into 20 billable hours.

2. I did not take the calculation to the final step, which is determining the actual hourly rate. I assumed that readers would be able to make that final step themselves. I have been using the EHR for so many years that what to do seems obvious to me, but in reality, it is not so obvious—as readers have pointed out—and so that is the topic of this essay: *How do you calculate the actual hourly charge?*

For purposes of this example, let's change the dynamic a bit. Although we'll retain the $30 per hour charge, the 20 billable hours per week, and the 40-hour work week for purposes of calculating our current net EHR, let's make our expense number a more realistic $4.60 per hour (based on these monthly expenses allocated to the business: rent/mortgage = $500; heat, water, and electric = $200; telephone = $40; and maintenance = $50). This changes our net EHR to $10.40 ($15 gross EHR − $4.60 expenses) based on a 40-hour work week.

(If your work week is only 30 hours, the method of calculation is the same but the numbers change. For a 30-hour work week, your gross EHR would be $20 and the same expenses would equal $6.13 per hour, giving a net EHR of $13.87. The figures change because the number of hours over which the EHR has to be earned has changed. You need to calculate the EHR using your work week, expenses, and hourly charge.)

Although some readers think we only need to pay attention to billable hours, that is not true. It is true that, in a 40-hour work week, we do not actually edit or bill for 40 hours; we do have administrative matters and marketing, for example, that need to be addressed for which we cannot directly bill a client. But these are no different from the rent. They need to be paid for and every business calculates what it needs to charge customers by including time spent on non-billable matters. The same is true for sick days and vacation time. These items are part of the expense of doing business; we just cannot give them precise numbers like we can give rent.

Consequently, the hourly charge that we determine accounts for the facts that we have only so many billable hours in a week and we also have hours in the week that we have to devote to non-billable matters.

If we were to use the net EHR we calculated ($10.40), your average weekly earnings, after expenses, would be $416 or a yearly income after expenses of $21,632. But our goal is for that yearly income to be $50,000.

Here are the steps we need to take to obtain the EHR data and calculate how much we need to charge to reach our goal of $50,000 after expenses:

1. Calculate the EHR for $50,000:

   $50,000 ÷ 52 weeks = $961.54 per week
   $961.54 ÷ 40 hours = $24.04 EHR

2. Add the expenses to the EHR because the EHR currently only represents our net income (after expenses) goal:

   $24.04 EHR + $4.60 expenses per hour = $28.64 EHR
   (or an average gross weekly income of $1,145.60 which translates to gross yearly earnings of $59,571.20)

3. Calculate the number of billable hours in a year:

   20 billable hours per week × 52 weeks = 1,040 per year

4. To determine the hourly rate you have to charge, divide the gross annual income by the number of billable hours:

   $59,571.20 ÷ 1,040 billable hours = $57.28 per hour

Now you know what you have to bill per hour to have a net annual income of $50,000 while having only 20 billable hours a week.

Your question is: This number can be calculated without calculating the EHR, so why go through the trouble of calculating the EHR? Why not go to the heart of the matter directly?

The answer is that few of us can directly charge the hourly rate we need to earn. How many of your clients would *knowingly* pay you $60 an hour for copyediting? Most of us have difficulty transparently charging and collecting that amount, especially if we work for publishers. That is why we began this series with the hourly charge of $30.

We need to calculate the net EHR to see what we are really earning under our current charging scheme. Most of us see that this week we brought in $600 and the week before we brought in $900 and last year we had a gross income of $41,628. And we also see that, when it came time to pay the rent, we paid it, even if we struggled to do so—the same being true of our other bills. But few of us really know what we are really earning and, in the absence of knowing that, we have no foundation on which to evaluate the manner in which we run our businesses.

The hourly charge figure tells us that, if we want to continue our current way of doing business, we need to double our hourly charge (from $30 to $60). In other words, our current business methods are not sustainable at the level of our economic goals.

The $28.64 EHR, which is based on your economic goal, tells you what hourly rate you need to *average* over the 40-hour work week to meet your economic goal. This number is important because it is often a more-achievable number. It is also an argument for abandoning the hourly rate method for the per-page or project-fee method of billing, because, unlike the hourly method, these methods reward you for productivity and efficiency.

The result is that, with these three numbers in hand, you are in a position to evaluate your current business and can align your goals with your decision regarding what and how to charge. For example, if you know you need to charge $60 an hour for 20 billable hours to meet your goal, you can either find clients willing to pay that rate, increase the number of billable hours in your work week, or lower your economic goal. If you increase your billable hours from 20 to 30, the hourly charge drops by approximately one-third, from $57.28 to $38.19 (or from $60 to $40). (*Note:* The EHR does not change. The EHR changes only if the work week total hours change and/or the economic goal changes.)

In my experience, it has been impossible to charge the hourly rate I would need to meet my economic goals. On the other hand, by analyzing my work habits, increasing my productivity and efficiency, and using a per-page/project-fee method of charging, I have been able to meet, and almost always exceed, my required EHR. There are weeks when I do not meet the EHR over the course of the work-week hours, but those weeks are made up for by the weeks that I exceed my EHR.

The EHR also serves as the standard against which I judge my business. I evaluate clients and projects based on the EHR. Clients whose projects regularly do not meet or exceed my EHR become ex-clients, because I know they cannot be made profitable.

I am not in business to lose money or not meet my goals, which is why I rely on the EHR and review it constantly. Are you in business to lose money? Under your current setup, how do you know whether you are making or losing money and, if you are making money, how much you are really making?

Next is part V, which tackles the question, "Why bother?"

74

WHAT TO CHARGE—PART V

The previous four parts of this series (I, II, III, and IV) discussed the effective hourly rate, how to calculate it, and how track it. The remaining question, as several colleagues have noted to me, is: "Why bother?"

Professional editing is a business. If it were a hobby, it would not matter whether or not we made a profit because we would be pursuing editing purely for our love of editing. Yet, for most of us, editing is a business and, as a business, needs to be concerned with profit and loss. Even businesses that are organized as nonprofits need to be concerned with profit and loss. The difference between a for-profit and a nonprofit business arrangement is that the former distributes any profit to its "owners" whereas the latter uses any profit to further its goals (i.e., there is no distribution to owners because there are no "owners").

A business cannot make a profit if it does not generate income in excess of its costs of doing business. It's a simple concept but one that seems to be just outside the grasp of many business owners.

Knowing whether we are making a profit or suffering a loss is important to editors because we, just like all other businesses, need to constantly evaluate whether what we are doing is worth continuing to do. If we are not making a profit and if we cannot adjust what we are doing so that we do make a profit, perhaps we need to pursue a different career path or conduct our business differently.

Tracking one's effective hourly rate (EHR) is a way to determine the health of one's business. It is also an alert system to tell us if and when we need to make adjustments in how we operate our business.

If we know, for example, that no matter what we do, our current client base will not pay a rate higher than $20 an hour (or its equivalent) and, if we know that our EHR, as we are currently operating, needs to be higher than what our client base is willing to pay (the required EHR), then we know that we need to make adjustments in how we conduct our business.

This is the critical and most important reason to know and track the EHR. When we operate without knowledge of our EHR, we assume that, if we bring in $1,000, it represents mostly profit. This is the allure of the hourly rate: an hourly rate makes us believe that we are earning a decent income because we are assured that, for every hour we work, we earn that hourly rate. In real-world business, however, it is not so simple.

Editors, like all businesses, have a production line. I know we do not like to think in those terms, but the fact is that we do operate a production line. (A "production line" is not synonymous with "assembly line." Production line refers to the manner and order in which we do our work.) We receive a manuscript and we take certain steps in dealing with the manuscript, steps that we repeat with each project. For example, the first thing we may do is clean up the file to remove extraneous elements like extra spaces. Then we may break out reference lists from the main text, or put figure legends in a separate file, or insert bookmarks, or whatever. Ultimately, we get to the editing phase, but it is rarely the very first thing we do.

As part of our production line, we may do multiple passes. We may do a rough edit, then a second edit, then a cleanup, then a final pass to search for anything we may have missed. What exactly each of us does is not as important as that we recognize we have these steps and that we can articulate them. The articulation is important because part of what we need to do if we are not making a profit is determine what steps in the production line can be omitted or modified to make the step more efficient.

One publisher, for example, looks for the least-expensive editor who meets certain minimal qualifications and then provides a multi-page checklist of things it expects the editor to do. There are several interesting aspects to the list, one of which is the blurring of the roles of the developmental editor and the copyeditor. The publisher expects copyeditors to fulfill both functions for one very low price. In addition, the publisher has its own style, which differs from standard styles in small, subtle ways. However, failure to comply with the publisher's house style results in requests for the editor to repeatedly go over the manuscript to fix it for no additional fee.

Faced with not earning the EHR, an editor has to determine what changes can and must be made in the editor's production line to earn the EHR. Will, for example, eliminating a second or third pass over the manuscript reduce the hours sufficiently to raise the EHR? Will changing the production line to a single-pass process do the trick? What other adjustments can be made that will result in increasing the EHR? Or does the editor need to drop this particular client? Can the editor afford to drop this client (i.e., how easily can the revenue this client generates be replaced)?

The reason to bother with calculating and tracking the EHR is to create a foundation for making business decisions. Bringing in revenue of $50,000 a year is nice, but meaningless, if we do not know what our cost of doing business is or whether the procedures we follow are hampering, increasing, or having no effect on our profitability—or even how many hours we need to work to make that income. It is also meaningless if we do not know whether doing work for a particular client is profitable. If working for a particular publisher is not and cannot be profitable, should we not know this so we can decide whether or not to drop the publisher and find other clients?

Perhaps even more importantly, bothering with the EHR lets an editor determine how well the editor is doing over time. Is the editor's speed, efficiency, and productivity increasing, decreasing, or remaining stable—month to month, year to year?

The EHR also spreads the earning requirements over the full work week, thus accounting for the non-billable time we need to devote to business, such as for marketing. It also is (usually) a rate we can more realistically expect clients to accept. More importantly, unlike an hourly rate, the EHR forces us to think in terms of a business week and not just in terms of billable hours. Too many small-business owners think that only the hours that are part of the business calculation are the billable hours, which is incorrect.

Finally, the EHR, unlike an hourly rate, lets us fully measure productivity and efficiency. The more productive and efficient we are, the more often we exceed our EHR. When we charge by the hour, we can never exceed that hourly rate.

The EHR is foundational information that acts as a guide to business decision making. It is something against which a business can measure what the business is doing and determine whether the business is on the correct path or needs to alter its course—making calculating the EHR worthwhile.

Part V

THE CAREER OF EDITING

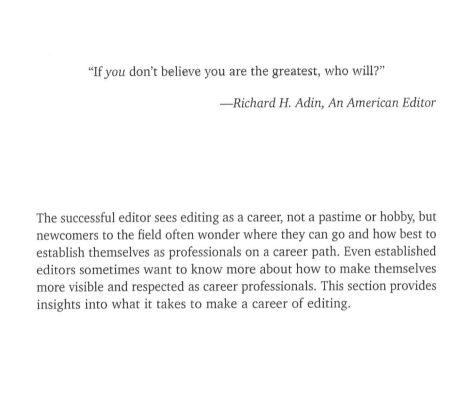

"If *you* don't believe you are the greatest, who will?"

—*Richard H. Adin, An American Editor*

The successful editor sees editing as a career, not a pastime or hobby, but newcomers to the field often wonder where they can go and how best to establish themselves as professionals on a career path. Even established editors sometimes want to know more about how to make themselves more visible and respected as career professionals. This section provides insights into what it takes to make a career of editing.

75

EDITING TESTS

A constant refrain over the years has been, "I've been editing for x years and they still want me to take a test!" Some editors routinely refuse to take editing tests, considering them an insult, whereas others take every test offered and wonder why they aren't getting work from the companies that tested them.

On my editor side, I understand the reluctance to take an editing test. After all, I've been a highly successful editor for 28 years and the person who is likely "grading" my test (should I take it) probably has no more than a few years' experience and maybe not even more than a few months. On my business side, however, I have learned—the hard way—the importance of requiring a test, regardless of the number of years of experience the editor claims.

Tests are a difficult proposition. For all the reasons that two editors will edit the same manuscript differently, so will editors complete a test differently. And taking a test means trying to figure out what the test-giver is really looking for.

I can't tell you how many times over the years I have taken a test and thought I did exceptionally well, only to never hear again from the test-giver. Clearly I missed something or what I did may have been correct but not what the test-giver wanted. The third possibility, which does occur with more frequency than it should, is that the test-giver lacks the experience to properly grade a completed test.

In the beginning, oh so many years ago, I thought there was a key to being successful with editing tests. Ultimately, I learned there is none—unless I could figure out what the test-giver was testing for. I have taken tests where the key was intricate knowledge of a particular style manual, others where it was how queries were framed, others where it was to determine my knowledge of the tools I was using, and yet others where it was a test of my knowledge of English usage. Needless to say, I suppose, is that there were also numerous tests where I had no clue as to what knowledge was being tested.

When I first began hiring editors, I looked at their résumés and hired them or not based on those. No test was given. My belief was that an experienced editor would be capable of handling the work. To my chagrin, I learned that, more often than not, it was not true and hiring the editor without a test was a major mistake, occasionally costing me clients. Consequently, I no longer will hire an editor who hasn't taken a test and passed it.

That experience also convinced me that, if I wanted new clients, I had to be willing to take their tests. And so I am. Passing or failing the test is a hit-or-miss proposition because the tests rarely give enough guidance and it is difficult to discern exactly what I am being tested for.

Often the tests are a hodgepodge of author manuscripts—a paragraph from this author, another from that author. The more hodgepodgy the test is, the more likely it is a test for developmental editing rather than copyediting. The less hodgepodgy the test is, the more likely it is a straight copyediting test and/or a test to demonstrate your knowledge of your editing tools.

When taking a test, a comprehensive stylesheet is important. The stylesheet gives you an opportunity to indicate just how fluent you are with the resources you would be expected to use should you be hired by the test-giver. I make it clear, for example, in the stylesheet exactly which dictionaries I used and that I am aware that, while dictionary A prefers xyz and dictionary B prefers xzy, I chose dictionary A to be the dominant dictionary.

I also use the stylesheet to explain my choices when it comes to English usage. I am not afraid to say that *Chicago Manual of Style* prefers abc over acb but *Garner's Modern American Usage* prefers to distinguish between the two, and to use each in specific circumstances. I also try to point out where style manuals differ. My objective is to demonstrate my mastery of the tools I will be expected to use.

My point is that I assume the test-giver needs to be educated and that I need to be the teacher. It may not win me the job, but I can at least believe I did all I could to get the job. Both test-givers and -takers need to remember that editing is often a matter of personal preference and, because that is so, more detailed explanation is often required.

I also include a cover statement that explains my approach to editing. It is important, I think, for the test-giver to understand the steps I take with every author manuscript and why I take these particular steps. Such understanding can help explain the editing choices I made on the test. My cover statement also includes a listing of the tools and resources I have and use. To say that I am a medical editor implies that I own at least one medical dictionary, but it is so much clearer when I say that I own and use both *Dorland's* and *Stedman's* medical dictionaries and that I have a subscription to the tri-monthly *Stedman's Medical Spell Checker* software.

The point is that I have a lot of competition for the work. The competition is both domestic and foreign in the Internet Age, so passing a test is insufficient by itself. I believe I need to do more to impress the test-giver that, of all the candidates for the work, I am the best choice and that the test-giver can back up any decision to choose me with all this additional information.

Does it always work? No. There are lots of reasons why I may not be chosen; reasons that fall outside the parameters of the test. The test is but one facet of a multifaceted decision tree. A number of times in recent years, I have been told that I was by far the best choice except for how I calculate a page or my minimum fee, or because I only work on a per-page basis and cannot accept an hourly rate, or that my payment terms are at odds with their terms, or whatever.

Test-taking is necessary. Unfortunately, there is no magic bullet to assure that one passes the test and fulfills every other consideration that enters the hiring decision. Like life itself, test-taking is a gamble and the odds are stacked.

76

Pricing Yourself out of the Market When Applying for Work

Part of my business involves having editors work for me on projects that I obtain from major publishers in the medical field. I constantly receive applications for work from editors. Every applicant receives my editing test, but I often never hear from them again, which is just as well, as their pay expectations are unrealistic.

One of the things that an editor who is looking to work for me has to state, when applying, is the minimum per-page fee the editor will accept. After all, why waste my time if I know that, no matter how good an editor the applicant may be, the minimum fee the applicant will accept is unrealistic and exponentially greater than the gross amount I will receive from my clients?

Of 10 applicants, nine will state a minimum acceptable fee that is stroking the stratosphere. It isn't that difficult to translate a per-page fee to an hourly fee to determine the "realness" of the asked-for amount. Most publishers expect editing of six to eight pages an hour and, when setting a budget for a project, base it on that rate of editing. So if you state your minimum acceptable fee is $25 per page, which I see often, you are asking for $150 to $200 an hour—a great fee if you can get it, but not based in the reality of the editing world.

There are four basic types of "employers" for editors: the publisher, the author, another editor, and a packager. ("Publisher" includes businesses and government agencies and anyone who ultimately will put their name on the document as the publisher.) In the case of the publisher and the author, the relationship between them and the editor is a direct one, so the editor can expect to receive the full amount of the fee the publisher or author is paying. And in the case of the author, the author may be expecting to pay a higher hourly rate than the publisher.

The latter two, however, are middlemen, and the job applicant should expect to receive less than what a middleman receives from the ultimate client. Middlemen are entitled to some return for their effort in finding the work (not to mention putting together and managing the team to produce it).

The finding of that ever-elusive work can be a costly endeavor. Plus, it is the middleman's reputation that is at stake when an editor is hired, not the editor's reputation. I know the difficulties of finding enough work to keep editors busy year-round and I know that my clients never ask who the editor is/was: If the job was done well, I get the kudos (which I then pass on to the editor who actually earned the kudos), but when something goes amiss, I'm the one who has to smooth ruffled feathers and I'm the one who spends hours doing so; I'm the one who stands to lose the client and future work. In addition, I'm the one who spends money promoting the group's services.

The middleman also acts as a buffer between a problematic client and the editor.

Perhaps more importantly from the editor's perspective, at least in my case as middleman, I'm the one who gambles on getting paid. Of course, I am speaking only for my own business in this regard, but I make it a habit to pay an editor for the editor's work within 24 hours, which is often before I bill the client and long before I actually receive payment. Should a client delay payment by weeks or months, or even never pay at all, the editor never knows as the editor was paid.

When applying for editorial work, the applicant needs to both keep in mind who the work is for and investigate what the going rate of pay is—and how it is calculated—for the type of work that the "employer" does. Of course, it would also help the applicant's chances if the applicant had the requisite skill and knowledge to edit the types of publications the employer works on or produces.

But a realistic financial expectation is a key to getting past the initial stages of review by the employer. No matter how good an editor you may be, no prospective employer will give you a second glance if you price yourself out of the market. You cannot assume that, if you pass a test but your fee request is above what the employer pays, you will have the opportunity to modify your request to bring it into line. That may occasionally happen, but it happens so rarely that an applicant should assume it never happens at all.

Again, it is the combination of realistic financial expectations and excellent editorial skills that wins work in today's very competitive editorial market. Applicants for editorial work need to know and understand the market in which they are seeking editorial work. Does your experience indicate otherwise?

77

How NOT to Get Work

When I originally wrote "Pricing Yourself out of the Market When Applying for Work," I thought that pricing mistakes were the leading cause of why one doesn't get work. Now I'm not so sure.

I recently received a job application in which the applicant wrote:

Minimum Acceptable Freelance Pay Price (Copyeditor): $25, per page
Minimum Acceptable Freelance Pay Price (Proofreader): $15, per page
Comments: I have no available work to show. Just give me any bullshit assignment, and let my work speak for itself. you will not be sorry. I am college student, looking to get into freelance writing/reporting. My only goal is to have articles published with my name on them and get payed (no matter how miniscule) for my words.

Aside from the obvious that the applicant never bothered to check out my website to see what we do, the comments provided would not induce me to consider this applicant at all. Nothing is right about the attempt other than it catches my attention in a negative manner. How many employers want to be told that their work is "bullshit"? And for those of us whose livelihood is word-based, does "payed" inspire confidence?

Although noting one's goal is laudatory, I would think that goal should be aligned with the prospective employer's goals.

Accepting at face value that the applicant really is a college student, I wonder what the applicant is being taught and what the applicant has been taught about how the job world works. Needless to say, this applicant won't be working for me.

78

THE MAKING OF A PROFESSIONAL EDITOR

On a list for professional editors in which I participate, a colleague posted about a post she recently read in an online forum from someone calling herself an editor. This "editor" related that she had been asked by a prospective client if she used the *Chicago Manual of Style*—and she had never heard of it! Her approach to editing and proofreading is not to "touch the style of the manuscript or document (but) simply proofread and correct any mistakes in grammar, spelling etc." The "editor" wondered whether her approach to editing was "odd." I think the real questions are not is her approach odd, but is her approach professional and is her approach the mark of an editor?

The issue is not one of using the *Chicago Manual of Style*—after all, the majority of the work I do does not use the *Chicago Manual of Style;* my work relies on other style manuals—but familiarity with the tools of professional editing and an understanding of the role that style manuals and other tools play in editing.

The quote raises multiple issues from a professional editor's perspective, not least of which is this: Does "simply proofread[ing] and correct[ing] any mistakes in grammar, spelling, etc." make someone *not* a professional editor? (And foundational to these questions are: What is proofreading? and What is copyediting?)

To answer the question, one must delve into what separates the professional editor from all those people who claim to be professional editors but really are, at best, amateurs. Most of us would accept that the idea that reading a novel and catching a few typographical errors doesn't change us from reader to professional editor, nor does it signal that "I should be an editor!"

On the surface, not knowing what are the dominant style manuals used by professional editors in your country is a sure sign that you are not a professional editor. (By the way, I do not know the country of the person being quoted, which could make a difference, but when read in context, I think it safe to assume that either the person or the prospective client or both are from the United States where the *Chicago Manual of Style* is prevalent.) Why? Because how can you know the correctness of a "grammar or spelling" decision in the absence of two things: an appropriate dictionary and an appropriate style manual?

Style manuals give you guidance on whether, for example, certain prefixes should be closed up rather than hyphenated; they give you guidance on whether it is proper to spell out 10 or leave it as a numeral; they give you rules to follow to ensure that the grammar decision made on page 1 is followed on page 23. Perhaps most importantly, they act as verification for the decisions being made. Style manuals promote consistency not only within a single document but across multiple documents. It is that consistency that prevents readers from getting bogged down in the wrong things when reading a book.

To say one does not correct style is the same as saying that one has chosen to accept a hodgepodge style. There is nothing wrong with deciding not to apply a particular style to a manuscript, regardless of how pedestrian or undisciplined such a decision makes a manuscript. What is wrong is not knowing that you are making such a decision because you have no idea what style, as applied to a manuscript, means.

Over my 28 years of editing, I like to think I have progressed from a novice with little knowledge to a professional with lots of knowledge, even though there are many professional editors with even greater knowledge about our profession. One of the paths to that growth is familiarizing oneself with the tools of our trade, namely, dictionaries, style manuals, usage manuals, and the like.

Also over those years, I have become savvier about discerning who is and is not a *professional* editor. I emphasize *professional* because I think that is the keystone. Our world does not lack for people whose shingles proclaim "Editor Inside." Our world does lack, however, for standards by which to judge just how professional that "Editor Inside" is. Thus, I have developed my own criteria against which I judge, in the absence of actually having the claimant edit manuscript for me, whether the claimant is a professional.

The first criterion is dictionaries. When I speak with an editor, one of the things I am interested in is the number and types of dictionaries the editor uses and has at his or her fingertips. Not all dictionaries are created equally; some have international reputations for quality, others have reputations for simply being. I do not put much stock in the skills of an editor who relies on the Free Dictionary and Wikipedia alone, or a medical editor who doesn't subscribe to Stedman's Electronic Spell Checker Pro.

The second criterion is style manuals. I expect a person who is an editor to have a broad interest in the things editors do and so I want to know what style manuals an editor uses and has at his or her fingertips. I know many editors who own one style manual, and that manual is often not even the latest edition. (One editor told me that the last good version of the *Chicago Manual of Style*, which is now in its 16th edition, was the 11th edition and that the 11th edition is the only manual the editor uses.) I have never had a project that uses the Council of Science Editor's *Scientific Style and Format* manual, but I own a copy of the current edition because sometimes I need to learn more about a subject area than I can find in the manual of style the client wants me to use.

The third criterion is usage guides. Language usage changes, sometimes rapidly, sometimes slowly, but the English we use today is not the English we used 50 years ago, let alone even 10 years ago. I think a professional editor is attuned to this changing and one way of keeping attuned is through the use of usage manuals. When an editor tells me that they rely on *Fowler's Modern English Usage,* I pause—American English has changed significantly since the release of the Burchfield edition. It is not that Fowler's shouldn't be on the editor's shelf and consulted; it is that an absence of *Garner's Modern American Usage* makes me question the editor's professionalism.

The fourth criterion is ancillary texts. Depending on the editor's areas of expertise, I expect a professional editor to make use of subject-matter-specific ancillary texts. For example, I would expect a medical editor to have resources about drugs available, or a resource like *The Merck Index* to verify chemical composition. An editor who works on contemporary novels may need to have access to resources on slang or quotations.

The fifth, and final, criterion is a basic one. I expect an editor to have resources devoted to grammar.

I think the difference between the amateur editor and the professional editor is witnessed by the above criteria, although not wholly determined by that criteria. To me, the criteria afford clues as to whether this editor is an editor I am willing to trust to do a professional editing job. Of course, a person could score perfectly on the foregoing criteria and still be a poor editor—it is almost impossible to know in the absence of the actual editing of a manuscript (be it project or test)—but an editor whose professional library is barren is an editor who edits by the seat of his or her pants. An editor who is unfamiliar with the leading texts in the profession and their field of editing is unlikely to produce a professional edit.

In the end, editing is a profession of decisions and many decisions to be made have more than a single answer. A professional editor is one who is aware of the alternative answers to a question and then makes a decision that is justifiable and supportable by more than "because I say so."

79

To Post or Not to Post Your Fee Schedule?

Recently, colleague Katharine O'Moore-Klopf gave a link to an article that appeared at *The Freelancery* blog, "Should you post your fees? Publish your pricing? Hit yourself with a stick?" Having read the article, I am not certain I agree with the author that there are only two reasons for posting a fee schedule: (1) "To make people quit calling" and (2) "When you sell mostly to first-time buyers, one-time clients."

I am not an advocate of posting a fee schedule, but then the type of work I do doesn't really warrant a fee schedule. Yet I can see situations in which posting a schedule can be valuable. After all, does it matter whether you tell a potential client that you charge $100 an hour through a posted schedule or in a live conversation? If the client is willing to pay that price and wants your services, either method should work; if they are unwilling to pay that price for your work, either method should turn them away, except that the latter method required your spending time to lose a client.

There are several issues to consider. First, you need to be knowledge-able about your clientele and about the clients you want to attract. Are these the types of people/clients who would expect to see a fee schedule?

Second, what is your reputation for the work you do? Is your reputation such that, if you charged a premium, the client would hire you anyway? Or is it such that your price will overcome your reputation?

Third, you need to be aware of what the "standard" price points are for your services. For example, if you charge $100 an hour for copyediting but most of your competition charges $20, in the absence of a reputation that provokes the feeling of must-have-at-any-price, posting a schedule is a sure way to not get a client, although, as noted above, the result would be the same face-to-face. The more your schedule is in line with what the market rate is, the less harm that can occur by posting your schedule. But posting such a schedule can tell clients that here is an editor with a stellar reputation whose fees are in line with what the client expects to pay (or is willing to pay).

I think the third point really is the key to the answer. If clients expect to pay $20 an hour and your schedule, whether posted or not, is $20 an hour, then posting the schedule may well draw in additional clients.

The more I think about it, the more I believe that the answer lies in first evaluating your fee schedule against the "norms" for what you do and then in light of the clients you wish to attract or retain. Another factor that needs to play a part in the decision-making process is how you calculate your fee.

We have been talking about a schedule in terms of dollars, but a schedule can be vaguer than that yet be equally informative. For example, in my case, if I were to post a schedule, I would say something like: "Freelance Editorial Services does not charge an hourly rate. We charge a per-page rate for copyediting with a page calculated as . . ." or "Freelance Editorial Services does not charge an hourly rate. We charge a project rate, which is calculated as follows: . . ."

However, posting a schedule by itself is not helpful to you or even to the client. There needs to be a justification for the schedule. For example, I might write something like this: "Over the 28 years of my editing career, my focus has been on medical books written by doctors for doctors. My specialty within that medical community is multi-thousand-page manuscripts and multi-author manuscripts that require the use of multiple Freelance Editorial Services editors to complete in a timely and accurate fashion." Perhaps I would write another sentence or two and then give my fee schedule.

The point is that combining a rationale with a fee schedule can be a fruitful way to generate additional business. Posting a schedule that stands alone, that isn't surrounded by reasons justifying the schedule, may do no harm but is unlikely to do much good either.

As with everything else we do, posting a fee schedule can be turned into a marketing tool. There are so many variables to be considered that it is not possible to blanketly say "never post a fee schedule" or "always post a fee schedule." The correct answer has to be: It depends on what you want to accomplish and whether posting a fee schedule can help you reach that goal.

A failing of myself and my colleagues is that we seek rigid answers to business questions and problems because we want to focus on what we do and like best: the editorial function. But to succeed, we really need to wear multiple hats and we really need to change hats depending on whether the question is an editorial question or a business question. Although both require analysis, the type of analysis process required is different for each.

What reasons do you have for either posting or not posting your fee schedule?

80

DO YOU WANT TO BE ACKNOWLEDGED?

On an editing forum, colleague Carolyn Haley asked a thought-provoking question about being acknowledged as a book's editor by the book's author if the editor is not satisfied with the quality of the to-be-published product. She wondered, "[H]ow big is the risk involved in allowing my name to be associated with low-quality books?"

Among the questions that are implicit in her question are these: (a) How much control over the final product does an editor really have? (b) Can an author credit an editor without the editor's approval? (c) What can an editor do to prevent or get acknowledgment by the author? (d) What harm or good can an acknowledgment do? (e) Who determines whether the final book is of low quality or high quality? (f) Does an acknowledgment really matter?

Alas, none of the questions—explicit or implicit—have easy, infallible answers. Although I gave Carolyn a short reply, I thought her question and dilemma was worth exploring among authors, publishers, and editors, not just the editors that frequent the original forum.

I think analysis has to begin with the baseline question: Does an acknowledgment, or lack of one, really matter? I tackled this question by informally surveying some colleagues, friends, and neighbors about their reading habits. Do they read the acknowledgments page in a book? If yes, do they read it in both fiction and nonfiction, or just fiction, or just nonfiction books? As I suspected, 5% of the sample read the acknowledgments, and of that 5%, 75% read it just in nonfiction.

I grant that my informal survey is far from scientific, but I'd guess it isn't far off the mark for the general reading public. Few readers care

304

that an author thanks her children for their patience and the many Hamburger Helper meals they tolerated during the authoring process, or the author's spouse or parents or first-grade teacher. We know none of these people and whether they were inspiring or not doesn't make much difference to our reading of fiction.

I was more surprised at the lack of interest in reading the acknowledgments in nonfiction. (Let me confess that I have the "habit" of reading every page—including copyright, dedication, acknowledgments, table of contents, preface, and foreword—in both fiction and nonfiction, a habit I frequently regret, especially in fiction.) Acknowledgments in nonfiction can be very revealing about the effort an author has put into his or her research and even can provide a clue as to the quality of that research.

Regardless, I think the informal survey justifies the conclusion that an acknowledgment probably doesn't matter. Even if it does matter, how does one judge whether a book is good or bad quality? I have been amazed over my 60+ reading years at how many books received awards for quality that I wouldn't consider quality at all. Consider James Joyce's *Ulysses*. This book is considered an important piece of English literature; I wouldn't give it a 2-dumpster rating, let alone a 2-star rating. I would never recommend anyone buy it or read it unless they wanted to commit mental suicide by reading. Yet, I can imagine that an acknowledged editor would be beaming. Book quality is in the eyes of the individual reader and I know few readers who would automatically say the editor must have been bad because the book is poor quality; readers are much more likely to blame the author, unless the book is riddled with basic spelling and grammar errors that even the least-competent editor should have picked up.

One also needs to consider what the average reader would make of an acknowledgment of the book's editor. How many readers really have a clue as to what an editor does? How many really care? The growth of self-published, editor-less ebooks demonstrates to me that readers are not equating good or bad quality with editor-no editor. I would be willing to venture that 99.9% of the positive or negative reactions to book "quality" by readers are aimed at the author and not at any editor. In fact, if the reader considers a book to be of poor quality, the reader is more likely to exclaim that the author should have hired an editor, and do so without having read the acknowledgments to see if an editor is listed.

In checking some of the ebooks I have in my to-be-read pile, I note that often the editor who is acknowledged is listed as "my wife," "my neighbor," "my beta reader"; in only one book was the listing such as to imply a professional editor. Consequently, I am not convinced that an author who is looking for an editor will suddenly start scanning acknowledgment pages to find an editor, not even of books that the author has read and liked. Nor is that author likely to recall who was named as editor of a book they liked but can no longer locate. Additionally, I suspect most authors are sophisticated enough to know that the final published form of a book does not necessarily reflect an editor's work because the author has the final say and can accept or reject an editor's work/suggestions.

So in the end, I come down on the side that says it doesn't matter. With more than 1.5 million books published each year in the United States alone, it doesn't even matter statistically. Unless the book garners a wide audience, in which case it would be a bestseller and the editor's belief that it is of low quality matters not at all, it is unlikely that more than a few people will read the book, some of whom will believe it is a 5-star contribution to literature and some of whom will view it as a 1-star insult.

This leads, then, to the question of whether an editor can prevent an author from acknowledging the editor. Absent a contractual term that gives the editor that right, I'd say no. The editor can ask and the author should be willing to do as asked, but there is little else that an editor can do. Yet, if it really doesn't matter, why make a mountain out of a molehill? An editor should always remember that one reader's great literature is another reader's trash.

The one caveat to all this is that I would be adamant about not being named if I had corrected misspellings and misuses of homonyms and language only to discover that the author rejected those corrections. Unlike the situation of the narrative—is it good, bad, or indifferent—the mechanics of spelling and word choice can reflect badly on an editor, *except* that I fall back to my original proposition, *to wit*, few people read acknowledgments or remember whether a book was edited and by whom it was edited. Ultimately, even in this scenario, I'm not sure it matters.

I'm curious as to what editors, authors, agents, and publishers who read *An American Editor* think of this "problem." What do you think?

81

BURNING BRIDGES

A few weeks ago, I watched a video of *The International* (2009), which stars Clive Owen and Naomi Watts. It was an okay movie, nothing great, but Clive Owen's character made a very profound statement:

"Sometimes in life, the hardest thing to know is which bridge to cross and which bridge to burn."

Sometimes in editing, the hardest thing to know is which bridge to cross and which to burn.

The issue comes up in at least three ways in editing: first is the non- or slow-paying client; the second is the client from at least one, if not more, level of hell; the third is in deciding whether to fight or pass on a contentious issue with an author. This essay discusses the first two issues and leaves the third for another day.

For those who deal directly with authors and expect to be paid directly by authors, I think the problem of burning the bridge is less traumatic. For the editor who works with publishers and packagers who send multiple titles to them for editing, the problem can be very traumatic. Yet, this is a problem that all small businesses have to face and deal with.

The first question an editor needs to ask is this: What are my lines in the sand—the things beyond which I will not ever tolerate? This is important because, if you do not have expressible lines in the sands, you will not know against what criteria to evaluate the errant client.

For example, if your invoices are payable within 30 days, how much past that 30-day due date are you comfortable waiting for payment? If you know that a client will pay promptly on day 45, is that acceptable or are you adamant that you must be paid within 30 days? If you know that a client will pay promptly on day 60, are you willing to wait 60 days for payment? What if you do not know on what day a client will promptly pay? How long are you willing to wait?

Every editor needs to establish those criteria, those lines in the sand that will trigger a reaction. You must know, just like all businesses must know, what is and is not acceptable behavior from a client.

The second question that needs to be asked is: What am I willing to do should that line in the sand be crossed? Are you willing to tell an author that you are claiming a copyright interest in the edits you made to the author's manuscript (not to the original, unedited manuscript)? Are you willing to tell publisher X that you claim a copyright interest that can be discharged upon payment in full of your outstanding invoices? And, if you are willing to make such a claim, are you willing to fight for that claim or is it just bluff and bluster?

You need to know exactly what you are willing to do to enforce your lines in the sand, because what you are willing to do by means of enforcement dictates what lines you are really willing to draw in the sand. If you are not willing to stand up for a copyright interest claim, why make the claim?

The third question that needs to be asked is this: If I enforce my claim, what will be the short-term and long-term consequences of doing so? This is important because it forces you to think about the consequences of any action you may take, which gives you the means to weigh your options and be sure that you are comfortable with them.

The fourth question that needs to be asked is this: If I fire client X, what effect will this have on my future income? I do not mean the very short-term future, but rather the long-term future. If I fire the individual author, will that cause me to lose the business of other authors? I know that, if I fire publisher X, I will no longer receive work from X, so in this instance, the effect is pretty easy to determine.

But the willingness to fire a client and live with the consequences is key to being a business. What good is it to be in a business that causes you heartburn on a daily basis? We all know that a client from hell can cause such distress that it affects both other business and personal time. How many times have you been grumpy with a spouse because you have been exasperated with a problem client?

Throughout the course of my 29 years of editing, I have run into authors I would like to shoot and publishers/packagers who had chips on their shoulder that were more like boulders than chips. I long ago decided that it was better to fire a client and lose the prospect of future work than to deal with constant problems and be curt with my family.

I recall a client who sent me a large volume of work every year (approximately $50,000 to $60,000 worth every year). In the beginning, they were a good client to work with, even though they were parsimonious with the fees. About my fourth or fifth year of working with them, they changed production directors. Previously, if they had a rush project, they would be willing to pay a premium fee (we are talking about editing projects of 1,500+ manuscript pages). The new director felt that I should consider myself blessed to have their work.

I finished a project, unhappy that I had undertaken the project but glad that it was over. A month later, I received an e-mail from the director saying a new chapter had arrived and they wanted me to edit it within two days. This was my line in the sand. I replied that I could not get to the chapter for two weeks as I was in the midst of a project for someone else. I could do it over the weekend, however, for a premium price, as I do not usually work on weekends. What I got back was an e-mail demanding that I set aside other work and tackle this chapter; what I replied was: "I write with great pleasure: You are fired! Please do not call me again."

Although I lost a lot of revenue, I felt greatly relieved to be rid of what had turned into a client from hell. My point is this: You must know and accept the limits of your tolerance of clients. And you must be willing to act on those limits. Firing/losing a client is not the end; it just means you need to take steps to replace the client with a better client, which is what being a business is about. Sometimes it is better to burn a bad bridge than to cross it!

82

DIFFICULT CLIENTS

Who is a difficult client? What does *difficult* mean? Is it really the client who is difficult? These basic questions need resolution before any discussion can be had about what to do about difficult clients.

Editing is an interesting profession in the sense that there really is little that falls outside the purview of subjective; that is, very few of the decisions an editor makes are objectively made. Should it be *since* or *because*? Does it matter? Hasn't English evolved to the point that *since* and *because* are synonymous? Should the commas be serial or not? Can *their* be both singular and plural? Does copyediting include fact-checking? Reference lookup? Rewriting? And the list goes on.

Yes, we can point to a style guide, but let's not forget that it is just a guide and that it only represents the collective opinion of a group whose members I may or may not recognize as being particularly noteworthy or valid. Besides, style guides change over the years, so what was a style guide *no-no* yesterday is a style guide *yes-yes* today and is likely to be a style guide *perhaps* tomorrow.

I raise this because we have to decide what makes a difficult client. In the first instance, is it the client who refuses to accept your recommendations as regards word choice or how a sentence can be better written? Or how complete a reference is needed? Or whether something is grammatical? Or something else that is really a subjective opinion by you?

Or, in the second instance, is the difficult client the client who hired you to do copyediting but wants you to also do developmental editing as part of the same work for the same fee? Or who wants you to add additional tasks at no charge to the tasks you agreed to perform for the quoted fee? Or who agreed to a delivery and review schedule but now ignores it, yet expects you to meet your portion of it or that you will drop everything else you are doing because the client is now ready to work with you?

Or, in the third instance, is the difficult client the client who refuses to pay for your work for whatever reason? Or is it the client who will pay but, instead of paying within the agreed-upon timeframe, has unilaterally decided to pay over a much longer timeframe?

Or, in the fourth instance, is difficult defined some other way?

In the case of the first instance, I do not think the client is difficult. I know it bruises our professionalism to think that someone has the audacity to insist on describing people as *that* instead of *who*. It bruises our self-esteem to think that we who have devoted our careers to the perfection of the art of language are being dismissed like dirty dishwater by someone whose language skills are questionable. But isn't the truth pretty simple?

We are hired to give our opinions, not to dictate terms. No matter how correct we may be in terms of standard and accepted language conventions, the bottom line is that we are simply being asked for our opinion, which the client has always been free to accept or reject or qualify. We may not like it, but it is the nature of being in business, especially a business such as ours. Consequently, I think if anyone is being difficult in this scenario, it is the editor, not the client. So let's scratch this possible definition.

The second instance does present the possibilities of a difficult client. But even here, I have to ask, what didn't the editor do to nip this type of behavior before it could even bud? Is there a written contract? Is it complete? Does it define both the editor's and the client's responsibilities? Did the editor discuss the relationship with the client before undertaking the project? Or, as is often the case, is it a matter of the editor having done everything correctly before starting the project and client simply choosing not to hear what the editor has said?

Even with a contract, these types of difficulties arise because clients rarely understand the world of publishing. A written contract can help to alleviate some of these problems, but my experience has been that clients tend to ignore the contracts because they think it is not in their interest to follow it. Or, as is too often the case, the client views the editor-client relationship as a personal rather than as a business relationship.

In this second instance, I think an editor's choices are really limited. The editor can grin and bear it and keep working for the client, or the editor can call a halt to the relationship. Over my 30 years of editing, it has been my practice to halt the relationship in such a situation. In the beginning, I chose to grin and bear it, only to learn that, once I took that stance, there was no end to difficulties with the client. Acceding to one request led to a demand for accession to a second, then a third, and so on. After my first such experience, I chose to terminate such relationships early and quickly in similar future situations.

I don't think there is much one can do in second-instance cases other than to talk to the client, explain the editorial process, point to the terms of the contract, ask for more money for additional tasks, and hope for the best.

Why do editors grin and bear it? Because of the money and because they have no other project to fill the void. Yet these are not good reasons, in my opinion, to keep the relationship going. Instead, the editor should view ending the relationship as an opportunity to work on fixing the editor's deficits in obtaining work. Whether to keep or end a relationship is a conundrum that is not easily solved. I suppose that the other alternative is to grin and bear it for this project, but then decline future work from the client.

It is worth noting that an additional problem with the grin-and-bear-it solution is that it sets the client's expectation standard for future work. Once the editor establishes that he is willing to fulfill the client's demands, the client will always expect that her demands will be fulfilled and on the same terms as previously; that is, any agreements will be ignored and the client can demand and obtain additional work at no additional expense. Not a good way to run a business.

The third instance, lack of payment or untimely payment, is not really a definition of a difficult client. It is a business frustration, but not much more. Recourse ranges from chalking it up as a loss and moving on to filing a lawsuit to claiming a copyright interest in the edits you made to the client's manuscript and trying to enforce the copyright interest. But no matter how you cut it, these are just standard, run-of-the-mill business problems.

The fourth instance is so nebulous that it isn't worth discussing.

The real crux of the difficult client is the second instance—the client who wants more, expects more, and ignores the negotiated terms of the relationship. In the end, it boils down to just how much abuse you are willing to accept in exchange for the promised fee. The more desperate you are for work, the more abuse you will be willing to accept. Consequently, the real solution is for you to improve your business to the point that you are willing to say, early in the relationship, "You are fired!"

It is not that difficult to reach that point. And sometimes, even if you are not yet at that point, it is better for you to say goodbye to a client rather than to agonize over every interaction you have with the difficult client. From experience, I can tell you that firing the first client is difficult; subsequent clients become increasingly easy to fire.

83

VETERINARIAN OR EDITOR?

The *New York Times* had an interesting article on February 24, 2013: "High Debt and Falling Demand Trap New Vets." The article made several points that surprised me.

First, the profiled veterinarian had $312,000 in student loan debt solely from veterinary school. Second,

> This would seem less alarming if vets made more money. But starting salaries have sunk by about 13 percent during the same 10-year period, in inflation-adjusted terms, to $45,575 a year, according to the American Veterinary Medical Association.

Third, that fewer vets will be needed in the future and that new vets can expect to see further erosion of starting salaries.

And, finally, fourth, that a vet who is paid $60,000 a year is considered to be well-paid.

I know that I spend a small fortune every year at our veterinarian's office for our dog and cat, let alone the fortune I spend on the food they eat. Had I been asked to guess at the starting salary for a vet, I would have guessed $85,000; for the median salary, I would have guessed $115,000.

If one of my children had asked me whether they should be a veterinarian or an editor, from the strictly income perspective, I would have said veterinarian. Not after reading this article, though.

Interestingly, what is being seen in the world of veterinary medicine is also being seen in other fields. Going to law school or obtaining an

MBA from a business school, although it resulted in high student loan debt ($150,000 to $300,000), meant a good chance at a high-paying career. But not today. Today, law school graduates are struggling to find jobs and those they do find pay $40,000 or less. The same is true of those with an MBA degree. The only ones making money are the schools that offer these expensive programs.

I look at all this costly education and wonder why anyone would choose such a career path—especially when an editor can earn significantly more than these new lawyers and vets and MBAers—only to put themselves in a position where they can never get out of debt and never enjoy the fruits of their labor.

The job market is changing drastically. Consider this article from the February 19, 2013, *New York Times*, "It Takes a B.A. to Find a Job as a File Clerk." As noted in the article,

> Even the office "runner"—the in-house courier who, for $10 an hour, ferries documents back and forth between the courthouse and the office—went to a four-year school.

What will that mean for editors?

I think we will see, in the not too distant future, many universities and colleges offering "advanced" degrees geared to editing, and we will see publishers and authors demanding that editors have such an "advanced" degree—even if the degree is really meaningless. After all, what will the editor study to warrant the cost and time of an advanced degree? We know that the schools will insist on it being at least a one-year, if not a two-year degree.

More importantly for editors, I think we will see a glut of new editors and a further depression of fees based on a tiered system. Those editors with just B.A. degrees will be paid less than those with the advanced degree, even though those with the advanced degree will not be paid very much because of the glut of editors.

As it stands now, editing can be a very good profession economically, even with the depression of fees. But newer and younger editors do not seem to be doing so well in today's editorial market, or at least not as well as those of us who have been in the profession for a decade or two (or more). I am constantly amazed at for how little new editors are willing to work.

In a way, I guess I shouldn't be surprised. Everyone in the "food" chain seems to devalue editorial skills. Authors and publishers will someday face the problem of a shortage of capable editors. The shortage will be the result of the penurious approach to paying for editing skills that is in force today. Just as fewer people are thinking of entering the legal profession, fewer people will think of entering the editing profession if barriers are raised.

These barriers to the editing profession will be the need for advanced degrees and the simultaneous depression of pay. Younger generations are much smarter than my generation when it comes to the need for the cost of education to balance against the financial gain that can be expected as a result of incurring that cost. In my college days, cost was a secondary, if not a tertiary concern—getting the education and degree was what mattered, because the more advanced the degree (generally speaking), the higher the income earnings would be.

Can editors still earn the "big" bucks? I'd like to think so, but I'm not really in a good position to know, because my earnings are derived from a combination of factors, not least of which are 30 years' experience as an editor and consistent application of business principles to what many colleagues consider a craft.

Would I recommend to my children that they become editors? It depends. It depends on how they would approach the profession, how skilled they really are, and what their expectations are.

Would you recommend editing as a profession to your children? Would you do so if an advanced degree were required?

84

What Do Editors Forget Most Often?

In a way, this is a trick question. After all, editors forget lots of things, just like everyone else. But what I have discovered, through very unscientific surveying, is that editors forget three very specific things with astonishing frequency.

Who's Who in the Relationship

The first thing editors tend to forget is their role in the editor-client relationship. Now, I grant that even more egregious forgetting occurs on the client side, having suffered that many times myself, but editors too often set themselves up to "fail" by forgetting their role in the relationship. *An editor's role in the relationship is to either do what the client wants or not undertake the job.*

It's pretty simple, but one of the hardest things for an editor to do. Why? Because we are knowledgeable about our business, have many years of experience in dealing with issues of language and grammar, and—as between the client and the editor—are the "experts" on matters of language. Alas, all that is meaningless.

Were we in a corporate setting and sitting in the chair of the vice president for communication, discussing with a secretary whether the phrase is simply *myriad* or is *a myriad of* or whether it even matters, we know that our decision in favor of one would be binding: The relationship between us and our secretary is such that the secretary has to take the lumping. And so it is in our relationship with our clients: We are in the secretary's position, yet we too often think that is our client's position.

317

Perhaps we know better than our client, but it is the client who is the decider, and we need to either learn to live with it or drop the project and the client.

Is it More than Opinion?

As much as the editor-client relationship power struggle reigns high on the list of things editors tend to forget, the matter of opinion is the sticking point with me.

There is nothing I dislike more than being told by either a colleague or a client that "*Chicago* says" or "*AMA* says" or "Garner says" in a manner that conveys that nothing more needs to be said. Don't misunderstand. It isn't that I don't value their opinions, because I do; rather, it is that I am told what they say as if what they say is gospel from the Mount, a universal truth that can neither be questioned nor ignored nor deviated from.

In a way, this ties in to the editor-client relationship. If a client tells me that I am to follow the dictates of *Chicago 16*, then I either agree to do so or I decline the project. I do not dispute the client's right to dictate whether compound adjectives should be hyphenated or not.

So my gripe is not with the application of the rules as disclosed by these authorities; instead, my gripe is with clients and colleagues who believe that these are truly rules by which we must live and edit, rather than opinions by which we should be guided.

I am of the firm conviction that treatises like *Chicago* are merely suggestions—guides, if you will—to a method that enhances clarity and consistency. It is nice to be able to point to the hyphenation table on page 375 of *Chicago 16* and say to a client that what I did is correct according to *Chicago*. It relieves me of the burden of justifying *my* "decision."

Yet, that is precisely the problem. Reading and understanding the chart is not difficult. It requires little to no discretion on my part. I become just a pencil-pusher, because all that matters is that whatever "decision" I make, I can justify by citing *Chicago* chapter and verse. So why should a client pay me more for my expertise when there really is no "my" in the "expertise"? when the expertise, if any, lies with the team of contributors to the chosen style guide?

Consider, for example, how much discretion an editor has when styling references. None, really. I understand this when applied to references because references are really a more mechanical task than most editorial tasks. But should this mechanical approach also apply to the explanatory text, the main body of the book?

I think an editor has an obligation to remind a client that the style guides are just that—guides, not the holy gospel of editing. A professional editor brings to a project much more than the ability to read and understand a table of hyphenation or the mechanics of styling a reference. A professional editor brings to the project—or should bring to the project—the ability to understand language and make editorial decisions that enhance the author's communication with the reader. And, most importantly, the professional editor should bring the ability to justify those decisions without saying "*Chicago* says" or "*AMA* says" or "*Garner* says." The professional editor should be able to say "I say" to what the if the editor's decision conforms to that of the style guide, the editor should be able to justify that decision by saying "I followed *Chicago*'s suggestion because . . ." In other words, the editor should be the decision maker and should be able to justify the decision made using the style guides as one leg of support, but not the whole support.

Isn't the knowledge to make and ability to justify editorial decisions that fall outside the purview of a guide's opinion the hallmark of the professional editor? This is what editors too often forget. We need to remind ourselves and our clients that, although we often agree with a style guide, we sometimes disagree, and when we disagree, we do so knowledgeably and because we have the client's interest in communicating clearly with readers uppermost in our mind.

Editing is a Business

The third, and final (for this essay), most-often forgotten thing is that editing is a business, not a hobby. Long-time readers of An American Editor recognize this statement: I make it often, and do so because the mantra too often falls on deaf ears or goes in one ear and out the other.

Here the focus is on the freelance or solopreneur editor. Freelancers too often forget that they are a business and that they must view everything from that perspective. It is wonderful that you want to undertake the local SPCA's newsletter as a freebie to give it the professional polish that organization deserves. But that doesn't mean abandoning business principles. No matter how much you love the SPCA, you need to demand that it approach its dealings with you on a business-to-business basis. Payment or lack of payment is not the determinant.

Your time is valuable. You must respect it and the demands made on it; you must also insist that others do the same. A client is a client; a project is a project. Decisions you make should be made exactly the same way whether the client is a charity you love or a corporation you are indifferent about. And charity clients should be subject to firing on the same terms as a noncharity client. Being a business means acting like a business.

Thus, we have three things that are important to editors that editors too often forget: (a) The client is the ultimate editorial decider in the editor-client relationship; (b) that editorial "authorities" such as style guides are simply one opinion in a spectrum of opinions and that the knowledge to make and ability to justify editorial decisions that fall outside the purview of a guide's opinion is the hallmark of the professional editor; and (c) that no matter what project we do, whether a freebie for a local charity or a highly paid corporate document, we do so as a business and all decisions relating to any project need to be made as business decisions.

85

How Do You Know You Are a Good Editor?

Sometimes from out of the blue, a question is asked that causes not just a little hesitation but weeks of pondering. Philosophy and religion are riddled with such questions. Yet editors, too, have such a question to deal with: How do you know you are a good editor?

By *good editor*, I mean a status closer to, or akin to, *great* rather than to adequate or normal or usual or level of the mass of editors. It is not that an adequate editor cannot be good in the ordinary sense of good, and thus an appropriate editor to hire for a project, but rather that a good editor in the sense I mean—and the sense meant by non-editors who ask the question— is closer to the pantheon of editorial gods than to the mass of editors—the cream of editors. Perhaps *good* is a poor word choice, but the question is usually phrased in terms of *good*, not in terms of *great*, by those who want an editor to distinguish him-/herself from all other editors.

The quick answers that will roll off the tongues of most editors are these:

- I've been an editor for x years and I am still busy all the time.

- My clients tell me I'm the best.

- My clients keep coming back.

- My clients refer colleagues to me.

- Fellow editors tell me I'm good.

- I must be good because I make $x.

And the list goes on.

None of these responses really addresses the question except superficially. The heart of the question is beyond such surface responses. After all, how many of our clients are really knowledgeable about editing skills and standards? How many of our colleagues would we really put on a pedestal as exemplary editors we wish we could emulate? What really is the relationship between years of experience and being busy to how good you are? How much of how well we edit is governed by the combination of pay we receive and the schedule we have to live with?

Unlike some other professions, editing lacks an objective group of core standards against which an editor can be judged. And while I do think many of my colleagues are good editors, do I really know that to be true? When was the last time I reviewed a manuscript a colleague edited? And even if I did review such a manuscript, how do I know whether the problems I see are the editor's or the client's fault?

Yet the answer to this question is important. It is important for clients and prospective clients, as well as for the editor him- or herself, and the editor's colleagues.

I suppose there are myriad ways of approaching this problem of how to define what makes an editor a good editor, but none are objective and many, if not all, can only be defined by the editor him- or herself. It is clear to me, however, that a grasp of language and grammar is insufficient on its own to declare a person a good editor, just as being a good business person but lacking language skills would not make a person a good editor even though editing is a business that requires business skills, at least for a freelance editor or an editor with an editing company.

Instead, I think, it is a melding of many attributes that bring a person success as an editor that defines a good editor. I think it is the combination of being a good business person and being facile with language and grammar that can define a good (freelance) editor. The combination brings together the years of experience, client praise, repeat business, referrals, and all the other things that we give as quick answers.

Which roundaboutly brings us back to several things that we have discussed in previous essays, such as the resources we use and have handy, our command of the tools we use, our decision-making process, and whether we can support our decisions other than by saying "Chicago says."

In addition, how our colleagues view us adds to how good an editor we are. Although insufficient on its own, that our colleagues seek our opinion, praise us to others, listen to what we have to say, indicate that others in our profession think we are good editors. The better editors our colleagues are, the more valuable are their opinions of us.

We need to be careful that we do not base our decision on whether a colleague is a good editor on differences of opinion about things like word choice and the other matters with which we deal daily that are subjective rather than objective. It is objective to note whether an editor regularly meets or misses deadlines; it is subjective whether the right word choice is *since* or *because*.

But we do need to base our opinion on an editor's understanding of the basic tools of the editorial trade: language and grammar and the editing process. The editor who constantly misses homophones and homonyms, no matter how good the editor's mastery of the other elements of what makes a good editor, should not qualify as a good editor.

Needless to say, I have avoided two significant questions: Once I ascertain that I am a good editor, how do I communicate that to colleagues and clients? and How does a potential client identify a good editor? I admit that I have no better answers to those two questions than I have to the original question: How do I know I am a good editor?

I am almost tempted to say that I am a good editor because no one has said otherwise. But then, is an editing test that we take but do not pass a comment on our skills? Not really. Because I judge tests, I know that there are lots of reasons why a person does not pass, reasons that may have little to do with language skills, which is what many editors think the sole criterion should be, and more to do with mastery of the editor's tools.

I suppose one sign of my being a good editor is that clients ask me to co-bid with them. I do work for a vendor who bids to provide a package of services to a publisher and that client asks me to prepare the editorial services portion of the bid, expecting me to do the editorial portion of the work if the bid is successful.

But even that doesn't satisfy my editorial soul. There is still something missing. Do you have answers? How would you define a good editor?

86

WHAT MAKES AN EDITOR A PROFESSIONAL?

The world is filled with editors and wanna-be editors. I suspect not a day goes by when, on some forum on the Internet, someone declares their passion for books and how much (and how long) they desire to be an editor. They then go on to ask how to become an editor.

Nearly any college graduate can be an editor—or claim to be one. Editing (setting aside the business aspects of the profession) is more of a knack skill than a taught skill. Yet, even with that ease of entry into the world of editing, there is a difference between a professional editor and any editor.

Consider this: Would you consider an editor to be professional who did not own a dictionary? I wouldn't, because I think one of the differences between a professional editor and an editor is that the professional invests in the tools of her trade. How much more fundamental to editing can something be than a dictionary?

Does the editor have to own the hard-copy version of the dictionary? No, but she should then have a subscription to the unabridged online version of the dictionary. There are lots of dictionaries available, but in my experience, there are only a couple that are generally recognized as being authoritative and not one of them is called *The Free Dictionary*.

Would you consider a person who asks what the differences are between the unabridged and the free versions of a standard dictionary, other than that the unabridged has more words (which one would expect if it is unabridged), to be a professional editor? I wouldn't, and I would wonder what other necessary things they skip or resources they lack. What shortcuts will they take with my manuscript?

324

The standard response is that anything can be found on the Internet. That's true as far as it goes. Anything can be found, but nothing assures that what is found is correct or accurate. Consider the cheap, heavily discounted medicines that you can buy over the Internet. Sometimes you get lucky and the medicine is exactly what it is supposed to be; more often, you have been scammed. The same is true with information resources. Anyone can set up a dictionary on the Internet—it doesn't mean either the spelling or the definition of a word is correct. Editing has "standardized" on certain resources because, over many years, those resources have earned a reputation for reliability and accuracy.

The professional editor recognizes that a resource's reputation is important and that using such resources is also a reflection of the type and level of work a client can expect from the editor. How does that fit with the idea of using the free version of an accepted reference?

What does the editor do if what she is looking for doesn't appear in the free version? After all, we know that it costs money to create and maintain accurate resources; even Wikipedia has to raise millions of dollars annually (have we forgotten so quickly when Wikipedia was on the verge of having to shut down for lack of money?). So we know that the free version of a standard resource is not as complete as the paid-for version. Thus, we know that the editor who relies solely on free versions is not making full use of available resources.

What about someone who won't use the unabridged version of that dictionary because there is a small fee? If an editor skimps on basic, standard resources, what else do/will that editor skimp on to the client's detriment?

The professional editor takes pride not only in her skills but in the quality of her work. Quality is affected by the kinds and extent of resources of which the editor makes use. It is one thing to claim to be an editor, which many people can and do claim, but it is quite another thing to be a professional editor with full access to the basic resources needed to give a quality edit.

When I hire an editor, one of the things I ask for is a list of the resources on which they rely and whether they are using the free or premium version. I want to know because it helps me to "rate" the applicant's professionalism. For example, much of my work is in medical editing. I would expect a medical editor to be a subscriber to medical spell-checking software. I think a medical editor should have, and be using, the two leading medical dictionaries.

I learned to ask these questions the hard way. A client once asked me how it was that the editor of a chapter didn't correct misspellings of several important medical terms. When I asked the editor, I discovered that the editor didn't own a medical dictionary and didn't use spell-checking—either medical or nonmedical. He thought his background as a medical transcriptionist was sufficient and that spell-checking software was distracting. That was a costly lesson to me.

Ultimately, the point is that the professional editor will invest in her business and will have access to the premium versions—whether in print or online—of the basic, standard tools used in the type of editing she performs. The nonprofessional editor will rely on free versions and alternates-to-the-standard resources that are free, or not even use standard resources. The nonprofessional does not run his business as a business; he does not invest in his business; cost governs everything.

To be a professional editor, one must act as a professional and conduct one's business in a professional manner. To be compensated as a professional, one must be—and behave as—a professional. Cheapskating on basic resources is not professional.

87

THE ETHICS OF EDITING

Most professions have a code of ethics that governs what members can and cannot (or should and should not) do. Editing, unlike many professions, lacks a standard code of conduct or ethics. Whatever code governs editing, it is unwritten and unique to the individual.

Consider this issue regarding billing. The editor and the client agree that the editor will be paid on an hourly basis but that the client has a budget. In the course of the negotiations, the editor asks the client what the budget is, and the client tells her. Let us assume that the budget is 100 hours at the agreed-upon hourly rate.

The project goes much more smoothly than either the editor or the client expected, taking the editor 50 hours to complete. The question is: Should the editor bill for 50 hours or 100 hours?

I would have thought the answer was obvious, but in discussions with colleagues, I find that opinion is split. Some editors believe that the agreement was for an hourly fee and thus only 50 hours should be billed; others believe that although the fee was based on an hourly rate, the client expects to pay for 100 hours and the project was completed in less than the budget number because of the skill of the editor, consequently, the editor should bill for 100 hours—the client should not be rewarded for the editor's extraordinary skill.

My follow-up to the latter argument is to ask what would happen if, under these circumstances the editing took 125 hours: Should the editor bill for and the client pay for those additional 25 hours? In this case, there is yet a further split among the editors, this time among those who would charge for the 100 hours. Some say no, the client

327

is not responsible because the editor knew there was an outside limit; others say yes, the client is responsible because the agreement was for an hourly rate, not a project rate.

Setting aside for the moment whether I agree or disagree with any of my colleagues, the bottom-line issue is one of ethics, and editors have no ethical code, outside of their own moral code, to guide them as to which decision is the correct decision. This is a failure of the editing profession and does harm to our clients.

A client really has no recourse against an editor except to not pay the invoice, not hire the editor again, not recommend the editor, or sue the editor. The last option, to sue, is really a weak remedy except in the case of billing disputes. A number either adds up or it doesn't, but word choice and quality of editing are matters of opinion.

In the example at hand, I think the only ethical editor is the one who bills for the 50 hours. When the editor bid her price, she did so knowing her skill level. The editor was in the best position to determine the likelihood of finishing within budget. That the client is getting an unexpected "bargain" as a result of the editor's skills doesn't really play into the equation. After all, doesn't the editor include her skill level in determining her fee rate? Isn't that one of the arguments editors make to justify why they charge more than another editor?

I think the other editors are wrong because the client doesn't expect to pay the budgeted amount; the client expects to pay only for the actual hours the editing took with the budget amount acting as a maximum. In the instance where the editor went over the budgeted time, the editor's underestimating the amount of work involved is not the client's fault or problem; the editor is supposed to be the expert when it comes to editing and have the experience to estimate the time more accurately. Neither charging the client the budget amount nor for additional hours strikes me as justifiable.

That is the problem: They do not strike me as justifiable, but I cannot point to an ethical rule that governs the situation.

The scope of the problem is readily seen when it is understood that there are no guidelines for what constitutes a proper edit; no uniform rule that governs how a page is calculated; no clear outline of what copyediting, for example, includes or excludes; no universally accepted guidelines that have to be met to call oneself a *professional* editor. In terms of professions, editing is a Wild West.

What it means is that each editor should make these things clear to clients, preferably in writing. Doing so serves both the editor and the client because it clarifies the duties and responsibilities of each party and the remedies in case of violation. What is really needed is a code of ethics and conduct to which editors can subscribe and to which they can point clients. With such a code, a body of guiding principles, explanations, and opinions can be created. Essentially, I am talking of the creation of a "style guide" for editor ethics.

Until that happens, however, we are stuck with personal ethics. It is not that personal ethics are necessarily or inherently bad; it is just that no one has an idea what action will be taken until the problem arises and the editor has to apply her personal code of ethics to the problem at hand. By that time, it may be too late; the problem may have gotten out of hand.

I do not know how one finds an editor whose personal code of ethics matches a client's expectations. There are so many possible ethical disagreements that it is impossible to ask about them in advance. In the end, it comes down to trust. Trust can be a very shaky foundation for a business relationship in which the end product is but a collection of opinions, especially as loss of trust can be the result of misunderstanding.

What suggestions do you have?

88

Implied Promises and the Professional Editor

Previously, I have discussed the demand for perfection and the disconnect between expectation and reality. Not discussed then, but of equal importance, is the question of an editor's implied promises.

An implied promise is just that: a promise or warranty that the buyer—in our case, an author or publisher—can reasonably infer from statements or actions made by the editor. It is not something that the editor expressly says to the client. For example, if the editor said to the client, "Your manuscript will be error-free when I am done editing it," the editor would be making an express promise (or warranty) to the client that, in fact, the manuscript will be error-free.

I suspect most of us are shaking our heads and saying to ourselves that no editor would be foolish enough to make express promises like that, but, alas, I see comments all the time from editors who make such statements. Sometimes I think I should hire them and, if they do not deliver, hold their feet to the proverbial fire.

But what worries me more are the implied promises. These are the promises that we do not expressly say to a client but which a client can reasonably infer. Perhaps we use a slogan, such as "Making manuscripts perfect!" or "Nothing slips by my eagle eyes." Maybe it isn't a slogan but a company name that there is an implied promise, as in "Roseanne's Perfect Editing Service" or "The Perfectionist."

As editors, we know that words have meaning and that, if we use a word, it is reasonable to expect the reader to draw a conclusion or inference. This is the ultimate purpose of advertising: the use of words and images to steer an observer down a certain path.

Words carry implied promises. When we hold ourselves out to be professional editors, we are not defining exactly what makes us professional, but we are implying that whatever *professional* means in the context of editors, that meaning includes us. And it is reasonable for a client to do what we have not done—define *professional* in the context of editing and apply it as the standard against which the client will judge us and our editing efforts.

It is this vagary that concerns me. I do not wish to imply that I am not guilty of exactly the same vagueness, because I am. But because we all do it does not mean it is not worrisome.

Clients have certain expectations about what an editor does. That, in fact, we may or may not do those things doesn't matter. Because we rarely define the parameters of our work and because we have no universal working definition of what exactly is a professional editor, we subject ourselves to clients drawing implied promises from our calling ourselves editors.

I have discussed contract terms and how some clients try to take advantage of us with terms that are onerous, such as subjecting us to laws that govern a country in which we do not live and most likely have never even visited. The terms of such contracts are both express and implied standards. It is express in that (assuming we agree to the proffered terms) we subject ourselves to the laws of the foreign country; it is implied that we understand our responsibilities under those laws, because if we didn't, we wouldn't agree to the terms.

And so it is with clients who hire professional editors. We express that we are *professional* and imply all that *professional* encompasses; we imply that both we and the client understand the limits of what *professional editor* means. That we and our clients understand the term differently is both our fault and dangerous for us, because, in the marketplace of opinion, it ultimately will be the client's interpretation that will prevail.

We work with words, so we need to step back and look at the words we use to promote ourselves and to obtain business. What implied promises are we making? Are we implying that we will deliver an error-free manuscript? Or that our rates are the lowest? Or that we are equally skilled at editing science fiction as we are at editing engineering texts?

Or that we are masters of the "standard" style guides and usage books applicable to the area of the manuscript?

We need to deal with author/client expectations just as we would have our expectations dealt with; that is, we need to eliminate as many areas of disharmony as possible by being upfront about what the client can expect when we are hired. We need to explain to the client exactly what role we will play and what the client can expect us to accomplish with the client's manuscript. We must avoid leaving it to the client to imply.

When we choose our business names and slogans, we need to carefully tread the fine line between puffery ("I am the best") and the implied promise ("Because I say I am expert in the *Chicago* style, you can expect your manuscript will conform 100% to *Chicago* style"). A failure to live up to the implied promises as the client sees those promises could be disastrous for our business reputations and our pocketbooks.

The point is that we need to look more carefully at our interactions with clients, to be sure that we are defining terms carefully and minimizing the potential effect of any implied promise. We need to define professional, just as we need to define what constitutes a page and what constitutes an error. We need to prevent the client from developing unwarranted and unreasonable expectations for the measures against which our work will be judged.

Consequently, we need to stop rushing forth with offers that a potential client can accept to our chagrin. For example, when a client tells us that a manuscript is 450 pages, before we rush to quote a price for the project, we need to verify that it is, in fact, 450 pages and not 900 pages. Because when we make our quote based on the client-provided information without verifying it, we are impliedly accepting that the manuscript is that long—even if the client used quarter-inch margins with 7-point type to get that length—and that we can, and will, do the work in the time and at the price we think is appropriate for a 450-page manuscript.

It doesn't matter if you define a page as 250 words and I define it as 1,800 characters; it matters that you have a definition and base your response to the opportunity on that definition, which might well be very different from the reality of the manuscript. That is, it matters if you define a page as 250 words and the client's manuscript shows a page as 600 words.

89

PERSONAL OR EMOTIONAL SATISFACTION
AND THE JOB OF EDITING

On a freelance list to which I subscribe, Carolyn Haley asked me, "Rich, do you get any personal or emotional satisfaction from your work?" The question was asked in follow up to a posting I had made to a thread-opening question posed by colleague Ruth E. Thaler-Carter, asking whether any editors had "joy clients or projects"—that is, clients or projects that brought especial pleasure, as well as income, to the editor. Some responders talked about clients, some about projects, some about teachers.

My response was as follows:

The clients who bring me joy are those who:

1. Pay my asking price on or before the invoice due date

2. Do not disturb me while I'm editing

3. Tell me and all their friends and colleagues that I'm the greatest editor ever

4. Insist that their publisher hire me to edit their book

5. Have my telephone number and e-mail address memorized so they can contact me quickly and often

6. Submit manuscripts that are so clean they require minimal effort to conform to the chosen style (particularly those whose reference lists run to hundreds of references with 99% of the references in perfect format)

7. Call me before calling any other editor to see if I can fit their project into my schedule, especially those willing to wait for me to fit them in

8. Want my services so much that they are willing to accommodate my schedule at the expense of their schedule

9. Do not ask for herculean efforts in exchange for slave wages, do not write in Jabberwockyese, and have a great sense of humor

10. Pay my asking price on or before the invoice due date (a trait well worth repeating)

On the list, I responded to the question as follows:

"... I always get personal satisfaction from every book I edit. If I didn't, I would have long ago found a different career. Of course, there is also the personal satisfaction of running a profitable business, finding ways to beat the constant push to suppress prices, finding ways to become more efficient, etc.

"I also get satisfaction at seeing the number of subscribers to my An American Editor blog increase and to the number of times my essays are liked or tweeted.

"But the truth is that should my business or my blog cease tomorrow, I would not feel any less satisfied—personal or emotional satisfaction—because what truly gives me pleasure and satisfaction in life lies outside those confines.

"Bottom line is that I view what I do as a job, and the reward for doing a good job is making money. My personal and emotional satisfaction quests go toward my children and grandchildren—toward such things as making a cranky baby smile, playing catch with my 15-month-old granddaughter, helping her unload all the plastic containers from a cabinet and throw them on the floor (although the subsequent rewashing and restoring isn't so satisfying), seeing my son admitted to the bar of the U.S. Supreme Court, sitting with a book on location while watching my wife create a new painting, and the like.

"I do not view my editing as anything more than a job/business that I like and at which I am qualified and good. I look forward to going to my office and working, but I look elsewhere for personal and emotional satisfaction. I would find no satisfaction whatsoever in knowing that I did a magnificent editing job, turning a book from junk into literature, [only to find] that I have to struggle to get paid or to pay my bills. Editing is a means to an end, not an end in and of itself."

The question about personal and emotional satisfaction made me wonder about how colleagues view their work and whether there is a correlation between personal and emotional satisfaction and financial success as a freelancer. (I do recognize that each of us has our own definition of success and that not everyone counts financial success as the most important measure of success.)

I have wondered about this before. Years ago, when I was a member of the Editorial Freelancers Association, we had discussions of whether editors are artisans or business people. In those discussions, I was in the very tiny minority—many times a minority of one or two—who said we should be business people first, artisans second. Twenty years later, the discussion appears to not have abated.

Think about painters, actors, writers, photographers, and other artists. How many do you know who are making a comfortable living solely from their art? Don't most of those we know have either another job or a significant other who provides financial support? Think about why that is. Is it because their priority is personal and emotional satisfaction from producing their art rather than the business aspects of the art world? Consider, also, how many of them hire agents to handle the business aspects.

Editors aren't different. We make conscious choices to elevate one aspect of our work over another. There is nothing inherently wrong with this—as long as we are willing to accept the consequences of those choices. For most editors, elevating the creative function over the business function means less income.

Why? Because it becomes difficult to make appropriate business decisions. Do we give a manuscript a second pass, knowing that, if we do, we will find errors that we missed on the first pass, when that second pass will be at our expense, not the client's expense? The artisan says, "Yes, I make that second pass" because it is more important to reach perfection (the personal/emotional satisfaction) than to be adequately paid; the business person says, "Not unless I am compensated for the additional work" because, in the business world, decisions are made on a profit-loss basis.

This is not to say that creative satisfaction does not play a role in the business-first approach or that business does not play a role in the creative-first approach. Rather, it is which is dominant and which approach forms the basis for decisions we make.

I find it interesting that many of the editors who struggle financially are those who are unwilling to place personal and emotional satisfaction from editing second to sound to business practices. They tend to refuse work because it doesn't appeal to them, ignoring the financial considerations. There is nothing wrong with such a decision as long as the editor understands the tradeoff.

And, yes, I do know some editors who successfully place artisan values above business values and succeed. But for every Tom Hanks, there are hundreds (if not thousands) of unsuccessful actors. In editing, it is no different—for every successful editor who places artisanship first, there are hundreds who are unsuccessful. If we could all be exceptions, there would be no rule.

Every morning, I look forward to my editing day—even those days when I am editing a book on colonoscopies—because I know that every day brings me satisfaction. I know that I am an excellent editor, that clients are very rarely displeased, and that my services are in demand. I can look at my bank account and not worry. And I know that, at the end of the day, I will be able to indulge in those activities that bring me personal and emotional satisfaction without worrying about how I will pay my bills.

For me, it is the business approach that has to dominate my editorial services. I need to be able to objectively evaluate clients and manuscripts based on financial return, not on whether a topic appeals to me. The very last thing I want to do is worry about meeting my obligations; the very first thing I want to do is face each day knowing that, at the workday's end, I will be indulging in those things that bring me satisfaction.

I would add one more "wondering." I wonder how many editors who place creative above business have families for which they are the sole financial providers? I suspect that it is easier to choose the creative over the business approach when there is a safety net of some sort or when the only person relying on your efforts is yourself. I admit I have never been in such a situation, which probably partially accounts for my business-first approach.

How about you?

90

TAKING ON TOO MUCH

This past week, I was hired to help on a massive project that had been started by other editors who were now behind schedule. I was given a copy of the stylesheet the other editors had created in hopes that I could adopt it for the material I was asked to edit.

The project, as I said, is massive. The portion I received is nearly 5,000 manuscript pages and the client would like that material edited within six weeks, in hopes of partially salvaging the schedule.

The first problem I faced was what to do about the stylesheet. As provided, it had numerous problems. First, there is no clear pattern to some of the decisions. For example, sometimes the suffix *like* is hyphenated and sometimes not. This is not a problem where the suffix is attached to, for example, an acronym (APA-like), but it is a problem when it is attached to a standard word that doesn't end in the letter l (e.g., boatlike vs. tomb-like; why hyphenate the latter but not the former?).

The hyphenation issue didn't stop with suffixes; it extended to prefixes as well. Sometimes a particular prefix is hyphenated and sometimes it isn't.

To complicate matters, some of the decisions are contrary to the dictionary that governs the project and certainly contrary to the appropriate style manuals.

A second problem with the stylesheet is that it contains spelling errors. Not just one or two, but a significant number. These are errors that should have been flagged if the editors are using specialty spell-checking software. I do not mean to imply that an editor can rely on spell-checking software; rather, spell-checking software serves a purpose and an editor should use specialty spell-check software to flag possible errors so they can be checked and a determination made whether they are, in fact, errors.

The first problem was readily solved by a discussion with the client. It was determined that the most important things for this project are chapters being internally consistent (which makes sense because some chapters are longer than many books) rather than consistent across chapters, and that the schedule be met if at all possible. Consequently, I need to have my team of editors do what they have always done: Strive for chapter consistency first and cross-chapter consistency second (ignoring, of course, chapters we are not editing).

The second problem was also easily solved because my team uses appropriate software, including specialty software and EditTools, to help us with these projects. We are ignoring the stylesheet from the other editors for the most part.

However, this scenario does raise a few questions. First, am I ethically obligated to advise the client of the errors in the other editors' stylesheet? If I do, I am questioning the competency of the editors previously hired and I am creating more work for the client, who now has to either correct edited manuscript in-house or ask proofreaders to do it (or possibly just ignore them). I believe an editor's obligation is to the editor's client and, thus, in this instance, believe that the correct course is to notify the client of the errors. I think, too, this holds true with my own stylesheets should I subsequently discover I have made an error. In the case of my stylesheets, I make it a practice to both update the stylesheet and to alert the client, if I discover an error (or more) made by me or another team editor, that I have corrected the stylesheet and the corrected version is now available for download, and the errors made and their corrections.

The second question that is raised is whether an editor has an ethical obligation to advise a client when a project is too large for the editor early enough in the project's schedule for the client to attempt to salvage its schedule. A companion question is whether an editor has an ethical obligation to tell a client when the editor lacks the skill to properly edit the subject matter at hand so the client can hire an editor with the necessary skill.

Again, I think it is an editor's obligation to let a client know when a project is too big for the editor to edit in a timely fashion. I also think an editor should decline projects for which the editor does not have the requisite skillset.

There is yet another issue involved in projects such as this one: having and using the correct tools to do the proper editing job. It is here that I think many editors fail.

The project in question is a medical tome, as I suspect you have guessed. Should not an editor for such a project have current medical spell-checking software and not rely on either one that is years out of date or on the general spell-checking software that comes with Microsoft Word? Should not an editor have current drug manuals or software? How about specialty word software (or books) and dictionaries? More importantly, shouldn't the editor both have these resources at her fingertips and actually use them?

I also think that editors should have and use all of the tools that are available (and appropriate) to make the editor's work more accurate and more consistent. Yet, I have been told by some editors that, for example, they do not use spell-checking software because they have a "sharp eye for misspellings and we all know that that spell-checking software is not always accurate." I have also heard laments about how the software costs money. (I view such costs as investments in my business and profession, and as part of the requirements to do business.)

When an editor overreaches, both the editor and the client suffer. The editor becomes stressed and jeopardizes his relationship with the client, who is also stressed. In the end, the editor may well lose both the project and the client. I recognize that it is difficult to give up projects that will bring in money, especially a lot of money, but there are times when saying "No" or "I can't" is the better strategy.

In the case at hand, the original editors and the project were a mismatch. Whether the mismatch was one of size or skill or both, I do not know. I wonder whether the client's confidence in the original editors is shaken. I'd like to think that a professional editor would not have been swept up in this scene, that a professional editor would place the client's interests before her own interests.

What would you do in a situation like this? What do you think an editor's ethical obligations are?

91

LOSING THE CHANCE

Editors need work and, because we are self-employed, we cannot wait for work to come to us; we need to aggressively seek it out. That has always been the reality, but, with all the competition that editors face globally today, the editor who doesn't seek out work is likely to have no work—unless something separates him from other editors, enhancing his particular value to clients and bringing them to him without his making an effort.

It is unfortunate that most editors do not understand how to find work. For many, as soon as they apply (inquire) about work availability, they have already lost the chance to gain a new client. There are lots of reasons why the chance is lost, but what follows are seven fundamental errors.

Error 1: Not knowing anything at all about the prospective client. For example, most of my work is medical and I primarily work with publishers and packagers, yet I receive applications from editors who want to edit fiction, or history, or anything but what I do. And when they receive the test they need to take, they send me e-mails asking if there is a different test that they can take that is more in tune with their interests. Why would you apply for editing work from a company that doesn't work in your area(s)? Why would you think that a company that publishes cookbooks would consider hiring someone who makes it clear that she is interested in editing young adult fiction? This first error is a major error, generally fatal, but not on a pedestal by itself.

Error 2: Not understanding the pay parameters. One reason clients and employers ask about pay expectations is to weed the serious applicants from the non-serious applicants. To request a rate of pay that greatly exceeds what a prospective client pays or—more importantly—is itself paid dooms any chance you may have of obtaining work.

When I receive applications, the first thing I do is look at the expected pay. Nearly 95% of applicants have wholly unrealistic expectations. Part of that lack of realism comes about because they are already working in a non-editorial-related field and, in their field, the amounts they state on their applications are reasonable. But when you want to move beyond your field, you need to know what "standard" is in the new field. Unrealistic compensation expectations doom an applicant, if for no other reason than such expectations loudly proclaim that the applicant has no experience. Why would someone hire an applicant whom they know they can't pay? Or whom they know will be unwilling to work at the payscale that comes with the work?

Error 3: Not providing the information requested in the application in the form requested. I ask, for example, for the résumé to be in a particular form. Out of 25 applicants, one will comply. The other 24 simply demonstrate that they either cannot read and follow instructions, in which case, they would not be good for my business, or that they don't care enough about the work to make the effort to comply, in which case, why would I hire them and invite trouble? If they don't care enough to follow my simple request, how can I be certain they will follow client requests? Or that they won't cause clients to take their business elsewhere?

Error 4: Providing the wrong kind of information. If you are seeking work from someone who does mainly medical work, you need to highlight your medical experience or explain why your nonmedical experience is relevant. What you should not do is emphasize your nonmedical work in a vacuum: that is, leave your prospective client wondering if you have the necessary skills. This is especially evidence of poor judgment when it is combined with error 2, asking for wholly unrealistic compensation.

Error 5: Not taking any required test in a timely fashion. Even if a prospective client is discarding your application because you made the first four errors, you have an opportunity, by completing the test, to make the client rethink. I know that, when I have seen an exceptional test from someone who committed any of the first four errors, I have made the effort to contact the applicant and explain the realities; I have discussed the possibilities further with the applicant. A well-done test is a chance at resurrection and salvation—yet most applicants simply do not take the test.

I find this particularly odd because I make it clear that an applicant will automatically receive a copyediting test and that the test is required to be considered. Yet, the applicant who doesn't intend to take the test submits an application anyway. Why do applicants think that prospective clients give any consideration to their applications in the absence of the completed test?

Error 6: Not knowing how to take a copyediting test. There are certain fundamental things an editor is expected to do when editing a manuscript; those same fundamentals should be done on an editing test. The editing test is where you get the opportunity to show a prospective client that you really are a topnotch editor; that you are worth the compensation you requested; that you can do the job without a great deal of supervision; that you understand editing; that you are a professional.

Have you ever wondered how long it takes a client to determine whether an applicant has passed or failed an editing test? I can't speak for everyone, but for me and for several in-house editors who have the responsibility of reviewing submitted tests, the answer is that we can tell if you failed in less than one minute and whether you passed in less than three minutes. I'll go you one better: I can tell you whether you failed my test in 10 seconds. (There are levels of failure. Some things result in an automatic fail, others simply get weighed in the balance, which is why there is the range of time.)

Copyediting tests are designed to assess core skills that the prospective client is most interested in, be it subject-verb agreement, following instructions, knowledge of subject matter lingo; whether certain resources are used; computer skills; or something else. Examiners also have a hierarchy—one or two things that, if you miss them, you automatically fail, whereas other errors are just added to the negative side of the balance.

The bottom line is that you need to know how to take a copyediting test, because a skilled editor will get past the automatic fail and will convey to the examiner that you are a talented, skilled editor.

Error 7: Calling the prospective client out of the blue and saying you want to apply for editorial work. Few clients are appreciative of this or have the time to deal with you. That is why many post information about how to apply for work at their websites. But even if they do not, writing rather than calling is the smarter method of seeking work from new clients. If nothing else, sending an e-mail message gives you a chance to show that you edit your own material to produce accurate copy, while a phone call tells me nothing about your skills.

These are key errors, but not all of the errors, that editors make when seeking work. Correcting these errors is the first step on the path toward new clients and more work for an editor.

92

WHY A COMPANY?

In my essay "Domains and E-mail," I discussed having a company domain name and ended by promising a discussion of why I want to be viewed as a company and not as an individual. In this essay, I'll tackle some of those reasons.

In "Thinking About Invoices," I gave one reason: I like to have the terms of my invoices honored, not dismissed. Dealing with clients on a business-to-business basis seems to make honoring my invoice terms happen with significantly greater regularity than when I was seen—and treated—as merely an individual freelancer (which was when I first started in the business).

Yet there are even more important—to me—reasons why I want to be viewed as a company rather than as an individual.

As I have noted many times, I like to work on very large projects—much larger than one editor working alone could probably handle, especially if the turnaround time is at all tight. I find them financially more rewarding. It is not unusual for me to receive a project that requires multiple editors. In the olden days, on such projects, I would receive a few chapters to edit and some other editors whom I didn't know would also each receive a few chapters. The client then expected us to coordinate our stylesheets—but to do so on our own time.

I don't disagree about the need to coordinate style among multiple editors, but why complicate the situation? Once I began convincing clients that I really was a business and not an individual (I always speak of *we*, not *me*, when speaking about Freelance Editorial Services with clients), clients would send me the whole project and I could determine whether I needed additional editors or not.

If I do need additional editors, then I hire them, not the client. And the client has no input on whom I hire (of course, I am responsible for the job and its ultimate quality; if I make bad choices in whom I hire, the client will complain about poor work and not hire my company again). As a company, I do not discuss personnel issues outside the company. This does not mean that I do not tell the client who the other editors are who are working on a project, if I'm asked, because I do tell them. In fact, because I use an online system to which the client has access, the client can see who all the editors are on a project just by logging on to my website. But I remain in control, which is as it should be.

As a company, I often receive multiple projects from a client simultaneously. Clients rely on me to manage the editing aspect of projects and to deliver a quality-edited manuscript on time. This allows me to increase my revenue flow and helps prevent the most dreaded of all freelance problems: a period of no work!

Being viewed as a company also means that I receive inquiries for work that goes beyond copyediting and into other aspects of the editorial/production process. This gives me the opportunity to expand my offerings and to earn additional income, without sacrificing basic copyediting work because of a lack of time to do the work myself.

Because I'm viewed as a company, clients expect me to have multiple editors available. Consequently, the only inquiry I receive these days is "Do you have an editor available for _____?" Clients do not limit me to what I can actually do myself.

Another matter is perhaps even more important than any of the already-mentioned items: privacy.

How many times have you been asked to produce proof that you are a freelancer? It used to be that I would be asked to produce a copy of my tax return or 1099 forms. I have never provided that information, and won't. I always politely responded that, as a privately held company, such information is not disclosed as a matter of company policy. However, I do say that the company would, I am sure, make an exception if they would provide me the salary information for their employees or a copy of their (i.e., the client's) tax returns. Once you are accepted as a company, it is assumed that, like all other companies, you work for multiple clients. Proof is not requested.

Ultimately, being viewed as a company rather than as an individual means being treated as the client would treat every other company vendor. This means minimal interference with how I conduct business. It also means that I can have company "policies" that I will not violate, which clients, especially corporate clients, understand because they face the same situation. Here is a good example: Have you ever been told that you must sign an agreement prepared by the prospective client or not get any work from the client? Have you tried negotiating the agreement but been rebuffed?

Over the course of my 30 years as an editor, I have had occasion to be presented with these sign-or-no-work agreements. I have always carefully read them and I have always offered counter-terms. The agreements are so one-sided as to be wholly unfair (I remember one that wanted me to file any disputes in a court in a province of India, even though the prospective client had U.S. offices). I make it clear that my company's policy prevents me from signing such agreements without the changes in terms I indicated. Sometimes the prospective client has said sorry, but either sign or get no work, in which case I opt for no work, but more often, they either agree to modify the terms or simply to disregard the agreement as a precondition for work. As a company, and because I always speak of *we* and not *I*, the relationship is viewed as more of one between equals and less of one between master and servant.

Being viewed as a company has yet another advantage. It has opened possibilities to me that would be foreclosed if I were viewed as an individual. For example, a client recently consulted with me about doing a joint bid for a very large project. They made it clear that they were asking me for several reasons, including the quality of my company's work (based on our existing relationship) and because, if our bid were to succeed, they "know" that my company could expand and hire the additional editors needed to complete the work. Whether or not we win the bid is beside the point. The point is that, because I am a company, I was given the opportunity to make the bid. If it was work I wasn't interested in, I could have declined the opportunity, but being seen as a company meant I had the opportunity to bid or not bid. An individual—someone operating as a freelancer rather than a company—would not have been offered the opportunity to bid.

It is important that you not misunderstand the idea of being a company. Being a company doesn't mean that you must have employees other than yourself. It doesn't mean that you must use subcontractors. It is very common to have a company of one. But regardless of whether you are a company of one or several, you do need to act, think, and speak in terms of a company and of *we* rather than *I*. A company is a second persona, distinct from you the person, and you need to act accordingly—just as if you were employed by someone else, rather than self-employed.

Think of being a company as having opportunities that would otherwise be foreclosed to you.

93

Solopreneur or "Company"—Part I

This essay, titled "A Solopreneur's Perspective on Business Models," is a guest essay written by Ruth E. Thaler-Carter, a long-time friend and colleague. Ruth is a freelance editor and writer, as well as host of conferences for freelancers. Ruth and I have discussed numerous times whether it is better to be a solopreneur or a "company." Here she makes her case for solopreneurship.

Rich Adin's blog, *An American Editor,* has seen a number of convincing posts about the value of doing editing as a company with more than one editor on board, rather than working solo, and why that business model might be the wave of the future.

Becoming an editing company makes a lot of sense for anyone who wants to handle large publishing projects, which is the niche for Rich's company, but I'd like to offer my reasons for planning to remain a solopreneur as a freelance editor.

Like many of my editor colleagues, I am comfortable working on smaller projects where the overall funds may not be as attractive as what a huge medical text, for example, might generate. The work can be as profitable when you take into account the different level of effort or scale of project and the fact that, as a solopreneur, I end up with the whole fee in pocket, rather than some of it going to colleagues, employees, or subcontractors.

My editing work involves articles for magazines, newsletters, professional firms, and blogs; book-length manuscripts for trade associations; website content; and other relatively short or small-scale assignments. Most of these projects probably would not be worth doing for a bigger business entity. I enjoy working on them, and I make enough on them to pay my bills and feel good about the income they generate. As an editing company, I might miss out on smaller projects that I really enjoy doing.

Based on what I see in discussion lists, many of my colleagues take a similar view of their editing work. Those who work with MA and PhD students, for instance, or with academic authors trying to submit manuscripts to journals, often do quite well as solopreneurs on projects that might not be big enough for a company or whose authors might not be able to afford the fees of a company.

When he says that it's difficult to find individual clients who will pay enough to be worthwhile for solopreneur editors, Rich also has a good point. It is true that finding individual clients can be a challenge, and that the expanding world of self-publishing may mean there will be more and more authors who don't think they need editors, rather than more and more who understand the importance of editing to make their work its best. But some of us do well in working with such clients, once they find us or we find them; the challenge is more making that connection than whether those clients are comfortable working with us as individual editors rather than as companies or what appear to be businesses.

It is possible that some individual clients/authors might view a company name and identity as more trustworthy and "legit" than an individual freelance editor. That might explain why new authors go to web-based services for editing. However, I think those self-publishing clients who do want editing services also might be scared off by the prospect of working with a company, assuming—perhaps wrongly—that they wouldn't be able to afford the fees that a company would charge. (I'm not necessarily comparing my fees and costs of doing business to those of a company, but companies usually have overhead and other expenses to cover that a solopreneur doesn't have.)

There are when times when it would be easier if I had, or were part of, an editing company with employees or subcontractors already in place. When I've been offered a project much larger than what I normally work on, though, I turn to colleagues who might be comfortable working together.

If I had a business partner or employees/subcontractors, I could and would take on much bigger projects, but I also would have a whole new layer of administrative responsibility—even if some of it can be delegated—that I really don't want. Having an editing company means finding, vetting/testing, hiring, training, overseeing, and paying the people who do some or all of the editing work. Only some of those tasks can be handled by someone other than the head of the company. I would rather spend my time doing the actual editing work; the billing and related aspects of my business are nominal compared with what I assume such administrative activity is for a larger-scale editing company (of course, we all know about the dangers of assuming!).

Some of this decision-making process, of course, is rooted in each individual's personality and comfort zone. Not everyone wants to own and manage a company. Not everyone wants to handle huge editing projects. Not everyone even wants to make a six-figure income—someone might want to have such an income, but not want to do what it takes to earn it.

I'm open to reconsidering how I structure my business over time as the markets evolve. I've adapted to technology over the years in ways I never could have anticipated, so I probably could adapt to a new business model as well. At least for now, though, I don't anticipate morphing into a company. My solopreneur model is working nicely for me, both personally and financially.

SOLOPRENEUR OR "COMPANY"—PART II

In "Solopreneur or 'Company' (I)," Ruth Thaler-Carter made her case for solopreneurship. There are a couple of fundamental points that I want to address.

An underlying premise of Ruth's argument is that she is satisfied with her level of income. Although not stated this way, I think that is an implicit recognition that there is an income-limiting factor that is self-imposed by the solopreneurship. That limiting factor is the focus on the smaller projects.

Consider it from just one angle. When Ruth takes on a 25-page journal article, the work is finished in a (relatively) short period of time and Ruth now needs to find additional work. The nature of dealing with small projects it that there is a frequent cycle of work-no work. Ruth may be able to find another project in a day or a week, but the point is that, because the project is small, it provides a finite return and requires faster return to self-marketing.

When I take on a 6,000-page project, that project could provide work for months, depending on the number of editors needed and the schedule. Large projects limit the work-no work cycle. From a financial perspective, too, the larger project is better because it assures a steady income for a longer period of time.

But that is only one aspect of the large versus small project scenario Ruth discussed. (I am ignoring her statement, "As an editing company, I might miss out on smaller projects that I really enjoy doing." because it assumes—falsely—that only small projects are enjoyable. Personally, I find book-length and longer projects significantly more enjoyable than short projects. It also falsely assumes that an editing company cannot or does not do small projects.) Ruth's foundation is that both the solopreneur and the company work on one project at a time. I think that is more true of the solopreneur than of the company; it certainly is not true of my company where we work on multiple projects—or the equivalent—simultaneously.

The single-versus-multiple project is important only from a revenue-generating perspective. If you can only work on one project at a time—and, let's admit it, an editor can only edit one project at a time even if the editor has three projects in-house for editing; in that case, we edit them sequentially, not simultaneously—and your hourly rate is $30, the most you earn is $30 for one hour of work. On the other hand, if you are able to have work done simultaneously on multiple projects, you can earn that same $30 plus a portion of the other projects.

Another assumption made in the solopreneur argument is that all companies are similarly structured. It does not account for the various arrangements that can be made that can make up a company. The argument confuses the presentation to the world with the arrangement between members of the company. A company can be a traditional employer-employee arrangement or it can be an association or it can be one of myriad other arrangements. But regardless of the arrangement, the presentation to the world of clients is a presentation of unity. It is not safe to assume, as Ruth did, that, depending on the arrangement, she couldn't end up with "the whole fee [for her work] in [her] pocket, rather than some of it going to colleagues, employees, or subcontractors."

Consider one possible arrangement. The agreement between the editors is that the editor who brings in the project receives 25% of the fees generated by the project. In this case, the editor has to do nothing to earn the 25% except find the project and sign it on. But suppose it is a project that requires three editors, and the finder is one of the three editors who will edit the project. In this case, the finder would receive 100% of the fee for the material she edits plus 25% of the fee generated by the editing of the other two editors. Doesn't the finding editor still get "the whole fee in pocket" plus some?

Even if the finding editor received no fee from the other editors' work, she still would be receiving "the whole fee in pocket" for her work, just the same as if the client's in-house editor had divided the project among three editors rather than the finding editor dividing the project.

Another assumption Ruth makes to the company approach is that company fees are higher and authors might not be able to afford them. Just as easily, the fees might be significantly lower than those of the solopreneur. Considering the lack of standardization of fees in the editing industry, I'm not sure how one can draw this conclusion. Ruth's rationale is that companies have overhead and other expenses that solopreneurs don't have.

Again, this depends on how the company is arranged. In the association-type company where one editor finds the work and then subcontracts parts of the work to other editors, the only increase in costs would be the cost of check writing to pay the subcontractors, a very nominal sum in view of the increased work and fee opportunities. Even in a traditional structure company there need not be significantly greater overhead. In fact, based on my own experience, I can see where the overhead of a traditional company could be less, as well as more, than that of the solopreneur. The solopreneur has to bear any health insurance costs, which can be staggering (until recently, e.g., I was paying $1,500 a month), whereas a company doesn't need to offer it at all. On the other hand, companies do have costs that solopreneurs do not have, such as being required to carry worker's compensation and disability insurance and contributing half of the cost of Social Security to anyone receiving wages. I suspect that. in the end, it balances out.

There is no easy, single solution. What it comes down to is trying to predict what the market is going to require in the future. The trends I see increasingly point toward collaboration among editors in some type of arrangement as a company. I think it will become increasingly difficult for the solopreneur to find sufficient amounts of work that pays enough to keep the lights on. The reasons for being a solopreneur will not change but the economics of solopreneurship will.

The argument about solopreneur versus company, however, misses a key point. The primary purpose of a company of editors is to create opportunities to increase work availability and income. This is done by relieving diminishing in-house staff of the responsibility of finding and managing multiple editors. The arrangements between the editors are not what matters; what matters is that a cohesive group of editors who can work together when needed do so and present themselves to potential clients as having that capability. In addition, it enables editors with different areas of expertise to contribute to the group by expanding the areas in which the group can comfortably work.

It is at least something to think about and not dismiss by simply saying, "I became a freelancer so I could work on my own," especially if what you are earning is less than what you would like to earn or need to earn.

95

Solopreneur or "Company"—Part III

In the prior two essays on this topic, the discussion centered around the "what" (what it means to be a solopreneur or a company). As one commenter pointed out, the reality is that even a solopreneur is a "company," with the solopreneur being an employee of that company. But the difference for our discussion lies less in the taxing authority definitions than in commonly understood definitions.

What was missing from the earlier discussions and needs to be addressed is what the future looks like.

To see our future as editors in the context of solopreneurs versus company, we need look no farther than the changes that have come about in the legal and medical professions. Professions like plumbing are not good comparisons because both the worker and the work have to be local; it would be pretty difficult to hire a plumber located in San Francisco to fix a leaking faucet in an apartment in Los Angeles, much less one in New York or Bangladesh. But the limitation faced by the plumber, and at one time thought also to apply to doctors and lawyers, doesn't apply to doctors and lawyers in the global economy. It certainly doesn't apply to editors.

True, there is still a "thriving" solopreneur approach to law and medicine, but if you watch the trends, you will discover that, whereas 90% of doctors and lawyers were once solopreneurs, today that number is rapidly approaching less than 25% with no end in sight as to the decline.

That there will always be some solopreneurs is really just an excuse. What doctors and lawyers have discovered is that solopreneurship is generally not economically feasible. Back in the days when I practiced law, the movement was toward two-person offices. It wasn't long before it was a movement toward three- to five-person offices, and the trend has continued. Globalization and insurance and lack of insurance have made the change happen.

The discussion of solopreneur versus company, when phrased in terms of personal preferences, ignores changing economics—it misses the foundational point of the discussion: survival in one's chosen field; in our case, the field of editing. To choose between solopreneur and company, one needs to answer this question: Am I earning the net amount of money I want or need each year in my current form? If I am, then nothing more needs be discussed. But if I am not, then one of the several things that needs to be thought about is whether I am in the correct "form" to survive.

Another question that has to be asked and answered is this: Where do I fall on the bell curve of working life? For example, in my case, I am on the downslope side; although I continue to work, I am eligible to retire. Consequently, my approach to the solopreneur versus company question is different (or should be different) than that of someone on the upslope side. If I were on the upslope side and not making the income I wanted, I'd be looking at what changes I can make to get me the income I want.

I don't disagree that it is important for an editor to be comfortable in his business model. What I do disagree with is the idea that one needs to sacrifice income for comfort. Each of us has our own strengths and weaknesses. Some of us are better editors than others; some are better businesspeople than others. Some are better editors than businesspeople and vice-versa. The idea of collaboration—or a company—is to take advantage of the strengths of each of the people who collaborate (make up the company).

I understand the reasons for solopreneurship, but I do not understand making it a god so that one clings to it even in the face of not making a sufficient income.

When it comes to professions that are reluctant to change, I think editing is one of the most reluctant. We tend to cling to what has worked because it has worked, even if it once worked for us but no longer works for us. Many of us still edit as if we are editing using paper and pencil—even though we are editing using a computer. (I even know a few editors who still refuse to edit or proofread except on paper—and they have clients who agree!)

The Internet has brought a sea change to editing. Before the Internet, we knew our competition. With the Internet, our competition is anyone and everyone, and that competition has acted as a brake on pricing. The other sea change has been the number of people who want to become editors to supplement their income or because "it looks easy to do." These "editors" also are a brake on the professional editor's income.

When we think about solopreneur versus company, we need to think about these economic factors, how they affect us, and what model—taking into account our business skills and interests—will best serve to maximize our incomes and best be able to deal with the sea changes of the future. Just as lawyers and doctors have realized that, to correct the mismatch between their income expectations and income realities, they have had to move away from the solopreneur model, editors, too, may have to come to that realization.

It is not enough to say that there will always be a place for the solopreneur editor. Although true, it fails to account for the ease of entering the profession and the growing number of people who are competing for that same group of clients. It also fails to account for the growing globalization of editing.

The most important thing is not to be quickly dismissive of the company model. Your future may be at stake.

96

"I Can Get It Cheaper!"

Perhaps the toughest issue to deal with as an editor is the prospective client (or existing client) who contacts you about a project, asks for a quote, and responds with, "I can get it cheaper!" Dealing with such a statement should bring out the editor's professionalism (and business savvy). How do you discuss pricing in the face of resistance?

The most common responses are to tell the client about your experience—"I've been editing this type of manuscript for 30 years. Can the other editor match my experience?"—or to relate how happy your clients have been. Or any number of other general responses that don't really highlight why you should be hired at any price.

The second most-common response seems to be an attempt to lower one's price to bring it in line with the lower price the client says another editor quoted.

In both instances, I think the response is the wrong response.

Under no circumstance, once you have quoted a price, should you lower the price (subject to an exception to be discussed later). If you are not worth the price you quoted, why did you quote it? If you are worth the quoted price, why lower it to less than you are worth? And why would you start a bidding war with yourself—a war that you can only lose and even lose repeatedly, once the client learns that all it has to do is say "Lower your price" and you jump to do so. I make it an absolute rule never to lower a price once given, except in a circumstance to be discussed later. You may be a great editor, but I am the greatest of all editors—and I let clients know that in many ways, not least of which is that I do not lower my price.

If the client insists, I suggest that it would be best for them to hire the other editor and call me when the editing needs fixing.

The exception is this: when I also reduce the services to be provided. In other words, I make pricing a companion to services: More service equals higher price; less service equals lower price. But even then, there is a limit to how little I am willing to do and to how low a price I am willing to quote. Which brings me to the nonfinancial response.

Having years of experience is a great selling point, but it doesn't mean anything in the face of a client's budget. What does matter are the services to be provided. My first response to the client is, "Do you have the quote in writing?" If yes, which is the usual case in these e-mail-negotiation days, I ask for a copy of the quote. (At this juncture, I haven't said yes or no to whether I will lower my price, so the client still has hope.) I am usually provided with a copy and then I start on my rebuttal. (When asked why I need a copy of the quote, I say I need to verify the terms and conditions of the price I am being asked to match or beat so that any quote I provide matches those terms and conditions. Although not said, I also want to verify that the person who made the quote is capable of delivering the promised quality and work—and that the client really has gotten a lower bid.)

If I'm dealing with a prior client who should be familiar with my work and pricing, I ask why, knowing my pricing and having this quote in hand, they contacted me for a quote. What I want to do is draw the client into admitting that they like my editing and would prefer that I do the work than to hire someone else. This is important because it starts to draw the client toward my way of thinking about fees.

If this is a new or one-shot client, I have to take a different approach, so I ask what is most important to them as regards the project. Is it cost? Quality of the edit? Experience? Something else? If the answer is cost, I stop the discussion and suggest that they try someone else. I tell them that I take too much pride in the quality of my work to denigrate it by lowering my price to where I cannot justify taking on the work or would earn so little that my only concern would be getting the project done. If they ask for names of other editors, I tell them that I do not know any *professional* editors whose quality of work or pride in that quality is such that they would be willing to match or underbid the quote they already have and that I make it a policy not to provide names of *nonprofessional* editors whose work I cannot vouch for.

If they give me an answer other than cost, then I ask about what services are included in the other editor's quote. Rarely are those services spelled out—the client doesn't know what is included except "copyediting" or "editing," which can mean anything. Usually the quote reads "copyedit of xyz at/for $abc." If the quote is based on an hourly rate, I also ask if it includes a limit on the number of hours (usually not), and what happens if the editing is not done when that limit is reached (definitely never spelled out).

Once I have drawn all this information out of a client, I can begin my "defense." This is where a professional editor can shine. Explaining what is included and what is not included in editing helps the client define precisely what work the client wants. As I go through the various options and the client says yes or no, I begin to build a quote. What I want the client to grasp is that, when the client hires me, she knows exactly what services she will get for the money. There is no gambling on what will be done or not done.

Importantly, it makes the client a part of the quoting process. If the quote is still too high for the client, I can now say, "If we eliminate this service, the price would be $xyz." It is picking from the buffet and creating one's own version of editing.

I also only quote a project or per-page fee, *never* an hourly fee. I explain to the client how this can save them money and is competitive with that lower bid they received. More importantly, I explain that it assures the client that a complete job will be done and that no additional money will be paid by the client to have the job done and done right.

What I am doing is making the client confident that the only smart decision is to hire me as a professional editor. I try to get a client to compare apples to apples, which the client cannot do with a quote that simply says "copyedit of xyz at/for $abc," especially if the quote is based on an hourly rate with no limit to the hours and no explanation of what happens should the limit be reached with the editing incomplete.

There are other things I do as well, but the important point is to be professional and make the client see the value of hiring a professional editor.

How do you deal with the client who says, "I can get it cheaper!"?

97

THE DISAPPEARING CLIENT

I've been a freelance editor for nearly 30 years. Over those years, I have seen clients come and go. I remember the first time I "lost" a major client. I nearly had a heart attack—I had thought an editor-client relationship, where the client was a big publisher, could and would last until the day I retired.

When that first client disappeared, I faced losing between $50,000 and $70,000 a year in income. True, it was not my only client, but it was my biggest client at the time.

Fortunately, I had my business experience to fall back on (as well as other clients). My business experience had taught me never to rely on existing clients but to keep trying to add new clients. The real issue was not what to do—find new clients—but how to do it.

From the beginning of my freelance career, I have made it a point to promote my services and my company constantly. During times of plenty, I would be less aggressive in my promotion; during times of stress (i.e., when a client disappeared), I would become aggressive in my promotional efforts.

The two keys underlying the search for and finding of clients are these:

1. Market/promote yourself constantly, both when your plate is full and when it is leaning toward empty.

2. Find clients before they think they need you, not when they are looking for an editor.

Those two points really sum up the effort that any business person needs to make.

Clients disappear for lots of reasons. Sometimes it is because they no longer think you are a good fit; sometimes it is because you start working with a new in-house person and your personalities clash; sometimes it is because the client goes out of business; sometimes it is because the client is bought by a non-client who has its own stable of editors. There are myriad reasons.

I have lost clients over the years for just about every possible reason. One long-time client decided to cut the ties with me on the grounds that its authors were complaining about the copyediting I was doing. When asked for examples of the complaints so I could figure out how to improve my editing, the client was unable to give me any. Ultimately, I learned that the real reason was the client could get the work done for half my price. That became important to the client because, as a small publisher, it wanted to reduce its costs to make itself more attractive for purchase by a larger publisher.

I have also lost clients as the result of mergers and buyouts. That was the story with my first disappearing client. It merged with another publisher who, shortly after the merger, began laying off staff from my client and kept freelance editors who worked with my client only if they would accept a much-reduced fee, something I was unwilling to do at the time.

As I said earlier, it is important to always be on the search for new clients—*before* they know they need your services. My objective is not to contact a potential new client and immediately get work (although that would be nice), but to make the new client aware of me so that, when the next project comes up, it thinks of me.

I know we live in the Internet age and networking and socialization is done over the Internet, but I stand before you as a dinosaur and say that, if you rely solely on such networking to find clients, you will never fully succeed—unless your clients are individual authors as opposed to businesses.

The networking that can be done over the Internet does put you in contact with individual authors who would otherwise be hard to locate, but, even in this case, there are methods you can follow to reach them other than by networking. For example, if the people you want to work with are lawyers or doctors, you could both Internet-network and place an ad in a journal or newsletter that targets them or on a website they are likely to visit.

The point is that you need to expand the avenues you take to promote yourself and not rely solely on Internet networking. You may get the occasional inquiry and job via LinkedIn, but remember that there are thousands of editors looking for work the same way. There is probably nothing that makes you stand out. But combining that effort with more "traditional" methods might be the difference between your being one of the crowd and being remembered.

In my efforts at promoting my business, I spend a good deal of time, money, and effort on using traditional marketing methods. I know editors who seek work by sending an e-mail. The problem with an e-mail is that other editors are taking the same approach; the recipient probably gets hundreds of these solicitations, and likely to quickly hit the delete or spam button on seeing an e-mail solicitation from someone he doesn't know.

In my experience, people tend to first read, even if just by skimming, material that comes via standard mail. They are less annoyed by standard mail than by e-mail, and thus are more likely to respond. However, this is not to say that e-mail does not have a role; rather, I am saying that you need to think about the various approaches, what you hope to accomplish, and whether your intended audience is likely to respond in the manner you hope when you adopt a marketing approach.

Disappearing clients are the norm in the business of editing. Some editor-client relationships last many years—I had several that lasted more than 20 years—but things change in the business world and you need to be prepared to deal with those changes.

One way to successfully deal with such changes is to constantly market yourself to your target audience. When you are swamped with more assignments than you can handle, go gently; when you have gaps in your schedule, become aggressive. In both cases, go after clients before they know they need your services, and keep after them. Remember that the goal is to implant your name in the client's mind so that, when a project does arise, your name is at the top of the to-be-called list.

Marketing is not an as-needed project; marketing is an always-needed project.

98

WORKDAYS AND SCHEDULES

Every business has business hours. Some businesses are open 24 hours a day, 7 days a week, 365 days a year. In the Internet age, people too often assume that, because they can access your website at any time, they can contact you at any time and get a response. Unfortunately, I have seen an increase in the number of clients and prospective clients who pay no attention to day or hour and calculate editing schedules as if an editor works 24/7/365.

When I am hired to edit a project, I make it a point to discuss schedule. This is important for many reasons, the most obvious one being an assessment of whether I can take on a project based on the expected starting date or whether it conflicts with current commitments.

A "perk" of being self-employed is that I can set my own work hours. The reality is that I am not wholly free to do as I please when it comes to setting my work hours. For example, once I accept a project, I commit to meeting the deadlines that accompany it and so my freedom to determine my work hours is curtailed to the extent that I need to accommodate the project schedule. In addition, if I want to remain in business, clients have to have some idea of when they can reach me.

Yet I am a business and I want to be treated as a business. At the same time, I want to make it clear to clients that I—not they—determine my work hours. Consequently, I always have the schedule discussion.

Editors are effective for a limited number of hours a day. Some editors can effectively edit for five hours a day, some can do more, some can do less, but the longer the editing workday, the more likely errors will be missed or introduced. Productivity and efficiency are subject to the bell curve phenomenon.

I have set my workday hours to be 10 a.m. to 4 p.m. Eastern Standard Time, Monday to Friday, excluding holidays. That doesn't mean I am not in the office at other hours or on holidays (alas, I usually am at my desk much earlier than 10 a.m.); rather, it means that a client can expect to be able to reach me during my business hours.

Having those hours is, of course, less important these days because most communication is done electronically and the expectation is that, if you are available, you will respond promptly; if you are not available, you will respond as soon as you become available. But those hours are important—very important—for project scheduling. They establish a standard against which expectations can be measured.

I scrutinize schedules that I receive from clients. I make sure that clients understand that the normal workweek for an editor—or, anyhow, this editor—is five hours a day, Monday through Friday, exclusive of holidays. Thus, the client who wants a "heavy" edit of a manuscript and wants the first 500 pages returned in one week is told that such a schedule is impractical for a single editor. It would require a churn of 20 pages an hour, which is much too high for a "heavy" edit.

I also make it a point to explain clearly to the client that I cannot require editors to work on weekends in the absence of extra compensation. Too many clients just pull schedules out of the air. I want clients to see me as an equal, as a partner. To reinforce that view, I make sure that I act as an equal, as a partner, as a business. One way I do that is by having established business hours and by making it clear that, when I consider a project's schedule, I weigh the proposed schedule's demands against my established standard workweek.

The standard workweek is also important when negotiating the rate of pay for a project. The worst bargaining tactics that can be employed are those that have an aura of desperation about them. A client who knows you are desperate for work is less likely to negotiate pay or schedule. But a client who wants you to do the work and knows that you are willing to say no as readily as you will say yes is more willing to negotiate. Again, this status of negotiation with an equal is one that is gained by making it clear that you are a business, an equal, a partner, and by reinforcing that impression each and every time you speak with a client or potential client.

Even one day matters. A client recently approached me to edit a book. The end date for the project was scheduled for July 31 and the start date was to be July 8. The first chapter had to be edited and submitted by July 12. I replied to the client, thanking them for asking my company to undertake this project, but saying that I had to decline. I would not have an editor available until July 15 and I would need until August 5 to complete the project.

The client came back the next day and, after stating they wanted us to do the editing, said they could modify the schedule so that the end date would be August 5 with a July 15 start date, but that they needed the first chapter by July 16. The first chapter was 84 manuscript pages. I pointed out that it was not possible for me to guarantee to meet that deadline, and countered with my own deadline for the first chapter. In my counter, I explained, yet again, that we work a five-hour day, Monday through Friday, and that I could not assume that we would be able to edit the 16 pages an hour that would be required to meet the one-day deadline. Until we actually start on the project, we have no idea of how well or badly written the manuscript is or whether such things as references are in proper format or need to be modified to meet the style. If it is well-written and if the references are in proper format, it might be possible to meet the deadline; if not, then more time will be needed. Consequently, any deadline has to accommodate the possibility of problems.

In the end, we got the project with a modified schedule that fit my needs. But we got it because the client negotiated with us as an equal. I was as willing to turn down the project as to accept it. More importantly, when I explained our workweek to the client, it was the umpteenth time they had heard the explanation. I have been consistent over time as to what constitutes our workweek and workday. Similarly, I am consistent about the cost of working weekends and holidays. Even if a client is prepared to pay for such work, I make it clear that doing so is voluntary, not something I can require an editor to do.

The reality is the editors who work for me, and I, set our own work schedules based on the time we need to devote to a project to meet the deadlines. But those are schedules we set; they are not imposed on us. That may seem like a small difference, but it is not. It is the difference between being regarded by a client as a business and, thus, as an equal and a partner, or not being regarded as a business but as someone to whom the client can dictate.

The first step toward negotiation equality is to have well-established business hours that you faithfully maintain, and repeatedly letting the world know what those hours are.

Part VI

THE FUTURE

"As efficient as your process is, it is not efficient enough!"

—*Richard H. Adin, An American Editor*

The world of publishing, and the role of editing within that world, is changing every day. For those considering entering the field and those already established, it's worth taking some time to think about where our profession is likely to be going. The essays in this section provide thought-providing insights into the future—even the viability—of editing as both a business and a profession.

99

Viewing the Future of Publishing

Sometimes all the discussion that can be had about publishing's future can be boiled down to a few minutes of video:

www.youtube.com/watch?feature=player_embedded&v=hirlekjqkdQ

Although humorous, the video does illustrate the confused state of publishing. No one knows how to accommodate all the different needs that each of the characters in the video represent.

What is clear, however, is that none of the pundits, none of the publishers, none of the technologists—no one—has a clear vision of tomorrow's publishing landscape. Some commentators predict that ebooks will soon be 25% of all publishing; others predict they will soon be 50%. But those predictions are really unhelpful without a plan for maintaining publishing standards while moving to a more standard-less medium.

Everyone says that publishers need to adapt and change. Easy enough to proclaim, but without firmer guidance as to what adaptation is needed, what changes to the industry must be accomplished, and how all the various competing interests can be reconciled, the pronouncement is like spitting into the wind.

Before the ease of computer-to-Internet ebook publishing, the book market was inundated with new books, many of which could be classified as a waste of time, effort, money, and paper primarily because finding a particular book (without guidance to the book) was like finding a needle in a haystack of needles. Too many books were being published for any person to rummage through. Now the problem is compounded as the number of books brought to market has quadrupled with ebooks and the direct-from-computer-to-Internet model—and it will continue to grow, because, with ebooks, there is no need for any book to go "out of print." Now it is like looking for a sliver of a needle in a haystack of needles.

The one thing no one wants to hear is that the more books that are available, the fewer will be read and the less valuable books become. In the marketplace, it is scarcity that causes prices to rise, not abundance. It is true that marketplace forces have had little effect in list pricing of books before the Age of eBooks, but there was definitely an effect on actual selling pricing—at least until agency pricing. And it has been true that certain authors could lead a price increase that "trickled down" to books of all authors, but this required that the certain authors were authors of such repute that they were instant million sellers.

Alas, this is all changing under the new regime. As difficult as it was to find financial gems among 250,000 books published traditionally in 2009, imagine how much more difficult it will be to find those gems among 1 million-plus books, especially as that 1 million grows to 2 million and more in the Age of eBooks.

With such increases in numbers of books available, the only way to get one's needle to be seen in the haystack of needles will be price. Consequently, ebooks will lead the spiral of pricing downward. As that happens and as there is less money to divide among multiple parties, there will be lots of negative effects on the publishing industry:

- A publisher who can only sell an ebook for $2.99 (or less) will be unwilling—if not unable—to spend money on production and marketing, thereby gradually eliminating the publisher's role altogether, which will make a chaotic market even more chaotic

- An author who has to sell his or her work for $2.99 (or less) has to rethink the whole artistic endeavor and has to consider 100% self-publishing as the only viable way to earn a return

- Such pricing and self-publishing will also put downward pressure on production quality, so even more corners will be cut by necessity than are currently cut, leading to a downward trend in quality

- Readers will continue to exert a downward pressure on pricing because readers are, for the most part, author-agnostic; that is, they are less interested in who the author is than in a story they enjoy, the consequence being that they will look for lower-priced ebooks to try

- Third-party book producers—the editors, the marketers, the printers, the designers, etc.—will struggle to keep afloat in a world that wants to pay less for fewer of their services, adding to the overall decline in quality

The future of publishing—once we get past the notion of quantity and instead focus on the notion of quality—as a structured enterprise appears bleak in the eBook Age. I, for one, have difficulty imagining a survivable structure focused on quality in the absence of an easing of pressure on pricing. Consequently, I am like the other pundits—I know that there has to be adaptation and change, but I can offer no guidance on how to accomplish either, not even for my role in the production process. Will historians of the future look at the 20th century as the epitome of publishing?

100

EBOOKS AND THE FUTURE OF FREELANCE EDITORS

Here's the tough question: Is there a future for freelance editors in the eBook Age? To which we can add this question: If there is, what kind of future will it be?

There are few things that freelance editors can be certain of, but here are some of those few things:

- Every day, our numbers increase as increasing numbers of people turn to freelance editing as a full-time career or for a second income

- Every day, colleagues, including those with years of experience, are trying to find in-house work and give up freelancing

- Every day, there are fewer jobs available for a larger pool of editors

- Every day, another author or publisher decides that editing can be bypassed because readers simply don't care

- Every day, another editor lowers his or her price, reducing the value of professional editing and making it harder for the professional editor to earn a living wage

We also know that there is no true professional organization for freelance editors that is actively seeking to lobby on our behalf or to find new employment opportunities for us. And we also know that computers were the first modern revolution in our business, the Internet was the second, and ebooks will be the third.

We've got trouble right here in Edit City!

eBooks are bringing a new kind of revolution to freelance editing as a consequence of the direct-from-author's-computer-to-Internet model that some publishers and many authors are adopting.

Editors have always faced the problem of authors and publishers being unwilling or unable to pay our fees and of authors and publishers doing without our services, with authors instead asking friends and neighbors to give their manuscripts a once-over. But this has become more common and more problematic with the advent of ebooks and the proliferation of the belief that anyone can be an author (and anyone can be an editor).

The underlying problem, I think, is acceptance of the good-enough standard for publishing in lieu of the much-higher threshold that existed when I first began my editorial career more than a quarter-century ago. This lower standard is a combination of industry consolidation, ease of access via the Internet, increased competition, and a desire to lower costs, with intangible costs, such as editing, being a prime target for cutting. I've even heard one publisher say that paying for editing is a waste of money because most readers don't know the difference between *whole* and *hole*. Based on some of the ebooks I have read, I'm not sure that publisher doesn't have a point.

The good-enough standard is rapidly becoming the de facto standard for editing. When I started as an editor, my role was strictly limited to editing. I was expected to be careful and thorough and focused like a laser on copyediting. As time passed, the laser focus became more of a shotgun focus and other jobs became part of the expectations. And then came the need for speed. Not only was I expected to do more work for less money, but I was expected to do it faster. Where at one time a page rate of three to four pages an hour was the expectation, today the expectation is often 10 to 12 pages an hour, sometimes coupled with the request for a "heavy edit." And where in the beginning I could expect a yearly increase in my fee, now many publishers are unwilling to pay more than they paid in 1995, yet demand more work be done for that pay than they demanded in 1995.

The good-enough standard is both the rationale and the justification for bypassing the editor. As this becomes the actual standard against which an ebook is judged, the expectations of the reader also become less—soon the reader accepts *whole* when *hole* is meant, *seen* when *scene* is meant. And as this happens, authors and publishers sell their work for less, almost as if dumbing-down readers and lower pricing are handcuffed together.

The ripple effect is that, as reader quality expectations decline along with a concurrent lowering of price, there is both less need and less money available for editing, which ripples into less editing being done and declining work for editors. Admittedly, the other scenario is that more authors and publishers will have money available for editing and will want editing services, but at a price that parallels the sales price of their ebooks. This is equally devastating to freelance editors because there is a point at which one cannot afford to work as an editor.

eBooks are the great field opener for authors and publishers but, I fear, they will be the harbinger of doom for freelance editing as a profession for skilled editors. It is a never-ending downward spiral whose downward thrust is reinforced by the incessant consumer demand for lower pricing.

I'm open to suggestions on how to reverse the trend, but I think the future for freelance editors in the eBook Age—at least from the current view—is bleak. The need for ebooks to be professionally edited isn't changing, only the opportunities for professional editors to do that work and earn a living wage.

101

THE TIMES ARE CHANGING!
WILL EDITORS CHANGE WITH THEM?

Everyone knows that time doesn't stand still, except in science fiction and fantasy. Time keeps marching on, even for the publishing world.

The first pebble in the pond appears to be Dorchester Publishing. I admit I hadn't heard of the company, but then its focus is on mass market romance books, not a category I read (although I have always wondered why the cover models romance books so often use should be physically what I should aspire to in order to have that "hot, passionate, romantic adventure of a lifetime"). Dorchester announced the firing of its seven-person sales force and, most importantly for Bookville, that it was going 100% digital—only ebooks and POD (print on demand).

Although there is speculation as to what was the impetus for this move by Dorchester, it really doesn't matter. Dorchester's move to all-digital is a portent of the change that will overcome publishing during the next decade. Sales figures indicate that the two media of growth in publishing have been hardcover books and ebooks, with ebooks showing triple-digit increases nearly every month.

Why does this matter to editors? It matters because, just as the introduction of the personal computer altered our world, so will the move to all-digital publishing. When PCs (used generically to mean personal computers, not Windows OS computers) became commodities, nearly every editor was expected to own one, to have mastered the necessary software (remember WordStar and WordPerfect?), and to change how editing was done.

379

I remember how I promoted myself when I started offering my services as an editor to publishers 26 years ago. Every editor was doing paper-based editing and minimal coding. I advertised my services as online only—I wouldn't accept paper-based editing projects—with a willingness to do more extensive coding (largely SGML, Standard Generalized Markup Language) that would enable a publisher to bypass the typesetting stage, all for a small premium over what my paper-based colleagues were charging. And it worked when I gave small demonstrations of how using my services could save publishers thousands of dollars in production costs.

But to do that, I had to learn new and different skills and adapt them to the editing process. Today, those skills are minimally required of any editor, so I am constantly looking for ways to differentiate my services from that of my colleagues and to justify a higher price (at which I am not always successful).

As seismic as the change from paper-based to online editing was for professional editors in the 1980s, this change to all-digital publishing, as it overtakes the publishing industry, could be cataclysmic for professional editors. The question is whether professional editors will be better prepared this time.

Dorchester's switch to all-digital is just the first pebble being tossed into the massive pond of publishing. Its ripple is barely noticeable, but, like the shamans of old, I find it to be a sign of a vast change that is about to overwhelm professional editing like a tsunami, and one for which few editors are well-prepared. I expect to see a rapidly increasing number of small publishers follow Dorchester's lead, with medium- and large-size publishers not too far behind. But an even larger force in the tsunami will be the author-driven market.

The trend will, I expect, follow this path: Increasingly, authors will "abandon" the large publishing houses and strike out on their own. In the beginning, they will believe they can do it all themselves, with the help of a few friends, and they will be encouraged to believe so by their organizations, such as SWFA (Science Fiction and Fantasy Writers of America). But as fewer authors succeed in making a living from their writing, the trend will begin to alter and authors will start seeking professional help.

When should editors start preparing for the trend changes? My belief is that they should start as soon as they identify the change that is coming.

To devise a strategy to address the coming changes and to become proficient in the techniques that will be needed to ride the change waves takes time and effort. The earlier the start, the more likely the success.

The switch from pbooks to ebooks won't happen tomorrow, but it will happen in the next decade, perhaps even in the next five years. There are too many pluses to going digital from the perspectives of consumers, authors, and publishers, even though all are currently struggling to find the right path through the current morass. But once that "right" path is found, movement will go from a turtle's pace to rocket speed as everyone tries to maximize their experience.

Which brings me to my original question: Will editors help lead the various groups through the current morass or will editors simply be followers who react, as they have done in the past? Will editors change with the changing times? I can only speak for myself, but I'm already working on the problem; how about you?

(The topic of professional editors in an ebook world was part of my discussion at the Communication Central conference "Finding Your Niche/Expanding Your Horizons." If you are interested in joining the discussion and learning more about the effects of all-digital publishing on professional editing, join me and other editing professionals at the next Communication Central conference; www.communication-central.com.)

102

THE DECLINE AND FALL OF THE AMERICAN EDITOR

In past essays, I have bemoaned the decline in language skills that I see in many younger editors and in authors. My bemoaning was revitalized by an article in the December 1, 2012, issue of *The Economist* ("Higher Education: Not What It Used to Be," pp. 29–30), which said:

> A federal survey showed that the literacy of college-educated citizens declined between 1992 and 2003. **Only a quarter were deemed proficient**, defined as "using printed and written information to function in society, to achieve one's goals and to develop one's knowledge and potential." Almost a third of students these days do not take any courses that involve more than 40 pages of reading over an entire term. Moreover, students are spending measurably less time studying and more on recreation. "Workload management," however, is studied with enthusiasm—students share online tips about "blow off" classes (those which can be avoided with no damage to grades) and which teachers are easiest going. [Emphasis supplied.]

Only 25% of college-educated U.S. citizens are literate! How depressing is that? The article went on to note that "[a] remarkable 43% of all grades at four-year universities are As, an increase of 28 percentage points since 1960," which means that students are being rewarded for being illiterate. Makes me wonder if their professors are literate.

Unfortunately, a confluence of many factors is resulting in the dumbing down of the editorial and authorial classes in America. The decline in newspaper readership is but one symptom of this decline. It is not enough to say that readers are getting the same information from sources other than newspapers, unless you can also say that the information that is contained in a multipage newspaper article is equally comprehensively conveyed by a 140-character tweet.

Discussions that I used to have about current events with neighbors have hit a dividing line. Those of my generation still engage in detailed discussions regarding topics of local interest and are informed about those topics; those of the younger generation can only discuss, at most, the headline.

eBooks are both a blessing and a curse as regards promotion of literacy. That anyone who has access to a keyboard can suddenly become an author is a curse; that readers pick up and read a lot of the produced drivel is a curse; that these same readers and authors do not recognize the difference between, for example, *your* and *you're* is a curse; that readers are more interested in being distracted from reading than from actually reading is a curse.

On the other hand, ebooks make material to read more accessible to more people at a lower cost, which is definitely a blessing. In addition, because ereaders offer such things as instant dictionary access and online access to websites like Wikipedia where more information is available about a topic, ebooks can be viewed as spreaders of knowledge, which is also a blessing.

Alas, for the blessings to truly *be* blessings, the reader has to be open to taking advantage of them. With the trend of using nondedicated ereaders to read ebooks, however, combined with the trend to read only a very few ebooks during the course of a year, it is difficult to get the blessings to outweigh the curses.

The more insidious trend that ebooks promote is the acceptance of incorrect language use. The more often a child sees "while your driving the car," the more ingrained it will become that *your* is correct. The fewer authors who hire qualified professional editors to fix grammar errors, the more standard becomes the misuse of language and the more such misuse is learned and accepted.

Compounding the problem is the discouragement qualified professional editors receive from authors and publishers. There is no reward, only punishment, for being a qualified professional editor in today's market. The punishment is on several levels. On the most basic level, it is the downbeating of pricing. Authors and publishers rarely accept the pricing that a professional editor would charge were the editor's services valued. Rather, the mantra is lower pricing. And, to force the market to lower pricing, authors and publishers too often search the Internet for best pricing, rather than best editing.

The consequence of this downbeating of pricing is that those of the younger generations with the requisite language skills to provide top-notch editorial services do not enter the profession, or do so in a very limited way. That means that the ranks of editors are being filled by those who lack proficiency in the very skills they seek to provide. When an author whose ebooks is riddled with homophonic errors tells me that the ebook has very few such errors because they paid to have the book edited, it tells me that both the author and the editor lack necessary and fundamental language skills and that neither can recognize that lack, so both accept substandard work as standard. If you are a young learner and are subject to reading hundreds of such substandard books, you soon begin to believe that they are correct and replicate the errors in your own writing.

If you do not think repeated exposure to erroneous language use will lead to that erroneous use becoming accepted as correct, look no further than the argument regarding the age of Earth (6,000 years of age vs. millions of years of age). Or consider how advertising works (repeat exposure to a message is designed to get a viewer to believe the message's verity; this is most clear when looking at political advertising).

The illiteracy noted by *The Economist* above bodes ill for American editors becoming or remaining a valued profession. It is difficult to uphold high values when you cannot recognize high values. When America's most educated class—its university graduates—are reading-challenged and language-challenged/-deficient, how much expectation can there be for the proficiency of those not in that "educated" class? (And think about those of the "educated" class who become the teachers of our children. Considering where most teachers are in class standing at university, how likely is it that your child's teacher will be one of the literate 25%?) Considering that professional editors today generally come from the university-educated class of workers, how likely is it that the literacy level demanded of the printed word a few decades ago will survive to future decades? When the income levels of qualified professional editors are in a state of perpetual decline and when authors increasingly avoid using qualified professional editors, preferring to self-edit or to have "beta" readers provide the editorial review, how likely is it that the high editorial standards of past decades will carry forward to future decades?

Will we soon be reading *The Decline and Fall of the American Editor* in Twitterese? What do you think? Are you concerned?

103

Is Editing a Future Safe Harbor?

One of the newspapers I read had an article discussing the future workplace and what kinds of jobs will be lost to technology. The article pointed out that both white-collar and blue-collar jobs are subject to loss as technology advances and gave some examples.

One example it gave was the truck driver. As automated cars and driving are perfected, will there be a need for the truck driver? The article concluded no, but I'm not so sure. Perhaps there will be no need for a person to actually do the driving, but there will still be a need for someone to make sure that the items are delivered correctly. In other words, the role may change but the need for a real person may not.

The article got me thinking about editors. I know we've discussed the future of editing before, but not from the perspective of technological advances.

With each passing year, computer software gets smarter. Increasingly, the tasks that editors perform are being performed by software. Consider just spell-checking and grammar software. I remember when the software first appeared and how limited it was. Now it offers suggestions that were unimaginable 15 years ago—and it is increasingly accurate when it suggests *whom* instead of *who*.

It wasn't so long ago that spell-checking software was only found in word processing programs; now programs like Acrobat and InDesign include spell-checking software and third-party vendors sell enhanced versions.

I don't want to get hung up on a particular type of software because what editors do is so much more than just spell checking and grammar. Yet the issue remains: Do editors face technological extinction?

386

I think that, if we do, it is yet many decades in the future. It is not because our routine skills cannot be emulated by a computer, but because of nuance. If the only thing that mattered was that there are no spelling mistakes in a document, editors would be far down the path to being jobless. But the real key to being a successful editor is nuance competence—that is, the ability to understand the subtleties of language and language choice and what those subtleties communicate.

Consider this example: "Up to 20% of fractures are missed on plain film." Both the spelling and the sentence are correct and so should pass muster if a computer is evaluating it. Yet an editor should note a problem: What does the sentence really mean? It simply isn't clear. Does it mean that the radiologist will miss these fractures even though they appear on the plain film or does it mean that the imaging technique itself doesn't display (i.e., misses) these fractures? The difference is one of nuance, but is also one of great importance.

If it is the radiologist who will miss the fractures, then it is one type of problem that needs resolution. Perhaps better training or perhaps a second or third set of eyes to review the film, or maybe something else. If it is the imaging technique that misses these fractures, then what other technique should be used, either instead of or as supplemental to the plain-film technique, or is there no technique currently that will image these fractures? In both instances, questions of treatment are raised. This is a nuance that only a human (at least for now) can provide.

Consider this second example: "Left-handedness, above average weight and height for age, family history and spondylolysis or spondy-lolisthesis are associated with Scheuermann disease." Again, nuance is important. The editor should be asking whether *family history of* or *family history, and* is meant. Each is a possibility and each leads to a different conclusion and perhaps affects treatment. How likely is it that computer software will be able to identify the problem and ask the pertinent question?

Because editing is more than just rote spelling and grammar, because it involves nuance and understanding of possibilities, it is likely that, for the foreseeable future, editing will be a safe harbor while technology advances. Although some forms of white-collar work will disappear as technology advances, and even though some of the functions that editors currently perform may fall to technological advances, it is likely that editing as a profession will remain viable.

A companion question to viability, however, is whether potential clients will believe that there is a need to go beyond what computer software can do. This problem is one that editors face today. A goodly number of publishers and self-publishing authors believe that Microsoft Word's built-in spell-checking and grammar software are all that is needed; the eye of the professional editor can be bypassed.

I recently received an "ad" from a new author for his new fantasy ebook. Although I found the summary in the notice a bit confusing, I decided to look at a sample of the ebook. Perhaps the summary got garbled but the ebook was fine. Within the first three pages, I discovered a dozen problems, so I privately wrote to the author and mentioned a few, suggesting that it would be worth his while to hire a professional editor. The response I got was that he would take care of the problems himself.

My thought was: If you didn't catch these types of error before you published the ebook, what makes you think you will find them now?

His response is the response I increasingly see as publishers and authors fall into the trap of believing that technology is the savior. Increasingly, no one thinks about the nuances of language. The consequence is that the story is not well-communicated and readers (and authors) are made poorer for that lack of communication.

To combat the rise in reliance on technology, editors need to discuss nuance and to focus prospective clients on the nuances of writing—the things that technology is not adept at finding. This is truly our value. I expect that, in the not-too-distant future, software will be able to accurately distinguish between the proper and improper use of, for example, *your* and *you're*, but not the nuances that choosing one word over another may entail. This is the editor's strength and what should be pushed as we fight to maintain our relevance in the future.

104

GROUP SOURCING?

Recently, several authors have commented that they have turned to group sourcing for their editing needs. I have also read of a couple small publishers who are trying crowd-source editing in lieu of hiring professional editors. For the past week or so, I have been pondering whether this is the future of editing.

The immediate problem I see with this approach is that you have no idea of what skill level the participants bring to the editing. A professional editor might offer to edit a friend's manuscript for free, but I can't see someone at the professional level offering to provide free editing to all comers.

The second problem is how one determines which edits to keep and which to discard when the editing is group sourced. One person changes *which* to *that* and a second changes *that* to *which*. Which change does the author see? How does the author decide which to keep and which to reject?

The third problem that rushes to the forefront involves improvement of the manuscript's structure and text, not just the basic grammar and spelling; that is, the developmental edit. Does the crowd scour the manuscript with the idea of offering suggestions for improvement or of outlining gaps? From what I have seen of group-sourced editing, this is a real weakness of the system, almost like the blind leading the blind.

A fourth problem is how well the author has prepared the materials for the crowd-source edit. For example, a professional editor will take the time to create a character list and description so that each time the editor comes across the character Betsy, the editor can make certain that Betsy is described the same way. Preparing such stylesheets is time-consuming and not something that can be expected to be performed by someone working for free. If not prepared by the crowd, it needs to be prepared by the author and distributed. From conversations I have had with authors who have tried crowd-sourced editing, they do not distribute stylesheets, often not having prepared detailed ones for their own use.

There are other problems with crowd sourcing of the editorial function, but there are also good things that can come of it *if* crowd sourcing occurs after a traditional professional edit and proofread but before final publication. For example, it never hurts to have feedback from the target audience. Has the author successfully communicated with his or her target audience? Are there errors that still remain that can be fixed before release?

What attracts authors to crowd-source editing are the cost savings and the belief that nearly anyone can edit—the "I can read, therefore I can edit" syndrome. Admittedly, it is hard for professional editors to combat the cost issue as there is a wide gap between whatever the professional would charge and the "free" of crowd sourcing. The strongest argument in favor of professionals is the debunking of the myth that anyone who can read can be an editor.

As those of us who are professional editors (in the sense that we earn our livelihoods from freelance editing) know, there is a lot more to editing than just reading a manuscript and fixing spelling and grammatical errors. We have developed techniques and skills over years of doing such work, and have a collection of resources that we consult when questions arise. Yet the idea that all we do is correct spelling and grammar is what most people believe when they think "editing."

Group-source editing can have a place at the editorial table if properly used to supplement the work of a professional editor, but not if it is a substitute for professional editing. The challenge professional editors face in the coming years is educating authors and publishers that crowd-source editing is not a substitute for professional editing. Whether we are up to the challenge remains to be seen.

105

Missing the Editorial Boat

Here's the question of the decade—at least for us editors: Are editors missing the editorial boat?

I can hear you mumbling, "What in heck is he talking about?" I'm talking about the changes that have occurred in editorial work between the 1970s and the 2000s, and whether editors are still stuck in LP mode while the rest of the world has moved to CDs and MP3s.

In the 1970s (and before, as well as into the early 1980s), most of the larger U.S. publishers were American owned and had a stable of freelance American editors that they called on. In addition, the Internet was still being birthed and the world was a faraway place. This invited and encouraged many of us to give up corporate jobs, especially low-paying publishing jobs, and become our own bosses. And many freelancers touted on any number of forums that they were free and would never work for someone else as an employee again.

Yet the world moved on. Many of the American publishers bought other American publishers and eventually were absorbed into even larger conglomerates that were based in Europe. These American publishers now had different masters with different outlooks. No longer was the outlook American-centric; it became global and increasingly driven by the need to increase short-term returns for global investors.

Many experienced editors who have worked through these decades have commented on the changes seen in editorial quality as the push came to lower costs and increase profits. Where American publishers hired American editors at reasonable rates in the beginning, the pressures created by bottom-line thinking changed that so that publishers increasingly were no longer hiring editors directly but outsourcing the complete production cycle. The rise of the packager.

Packagers, who now dominate the editorial process, get their business by providing low-price bids to publishers that include the complete production package—editing, composition, and even printing. Yet these packagers usually only do the latter two functions in-house; they out-source to freelance editors the editorial aspects.

All of this is OK until one thinks about how the packager's bid is aligned. If the packager outsources the editorial function but keeps in-house the rest of the production process, the packager, like other businesses, wants to maximize the profit of the in-house work and minimize the loss of the outsourced work. Yet the packager has to create an attractive price to win the publisher's work. So the method is to externally provide a bundle price but internally separate out the allocations to outsourced and in-house functions.

The result is that minimal sums, as minimal as can be gotten away with, are allocated to the outsourced editorial function. And, of the sum allocated, the packager keeps a portion as its profit, as packagers are unwilling to either take a loss or simply break even on any facet of the work.

With this going on in the background, what changes have been seen in the world of freelance editors? As I look at my colleagues, what I see is exactly the same approach to business today as was the approach in the 1980s. In this regard, I think editors are missing the editorial boat.

Yes, we have changed in that we now work using computers rather than editing on paper, but that really isn't much of a change. It's like changing from goose quills to ballpoint pens—the tool has changed but not the approach. But even that change is only a partial change. Most freelancers have rudimentary knowledge of the tools they use and refuse to spend any money on tools that are not absolutely required.

The largest hurdle that freelancers have to surmount is the idea that working alone is the way to work. Packagers have gained their stran-glehold because they offer a single stop for a publisher. The publisher's costs are reduced because the packager handles all of the production aspects and the publisher no longer needs to maintain high staff levels. Freelancers need to learn and adopt the packager lesson: Freelancers need to think in terms of working as a group and offering their services as a competitive group. Freelancers need to make themselves attractive to publishers by becoming low cost-low maintenance, yet high-quality service, providers.

If freelancers think downward price pressure is a burden now, the further behind the editorial boat leaves us, the greater the downward pressure will become, especially as editorial skills are increasingly thought of as a commodity.

Something to think about as we contemplate our editorial futures, and something to address in the new year.

106

MISSING THE EDITORIAL BOAT REDUX

I received several private comments regarding my Missing the Editorial Boat essay, with all demonstrating that the primary point is being missed.

What is it that packagers offer American publishers? They offer (1) complete (or near-complete) production services at a price that is less than what it would cost the American publisher to do the same work in-house and (2) convenience. It appears that readers grasped the first concept but not the second, yet it is the second that is the most important for editorial freelancers.

Traditionally, an in-house production editor would have x number of books to shepherd through the production process in a year. As the publishing industry consolidated in the 1990s, the in-house production editor's workload increased. Instead of having to occasionally hire a freelance editor, for example, hiring freelance editors became the norm, a necessity even—yet the in-house production editor had to monitor each hired freelancer's work. What happened is that the role played by the in-house editor changed from editing to managing.

This workload increased greatly as the years passed and the demand for more profit by the parent company had to be met. It reached a point where the in-house production editor could no longer manage all of the titles for which he or she needed to be responsible and still meet the corporate bottom-line goals, in the sense that the production editor could no longer properly manage all of the individual freelancers needed to be hired to get the work done. In addition, freelancer costs were rising.

The solution was the packager, who offered to undertake the management burden as well as the production burden, at a price that was often less than the publisher's current costs. The packager's lower cost came about in two ways: first, by moving the mechanical production outside the United States to developing countries where costs were significantly lower, and second, by putting the burden of meeting that lower cost on the freelancer; after all, the packager's in-house costs, although less than that of the publishers it dealt with, was/is still a fixed cost. The cost of the freelancer, however, was/is a flexible cost.

Conversations with publishers tell me that the packager situation is less than ideal and that quality of output has declined, but there is no viable alternative for the publisher. Publishers are still being squeezed between costs and profit demands, so they are trying to publish more books with fewer in-house staff. And it certainly is less than ideal for editorial freelancers who get price-squeezed. But the **convenience factor**, when added to the lower bid price of the packager, makes packaging a sensible choice for publishers. Take away the convenience factor, and the packager is not necessarily the best alternative.

Just so it is clear, the convenience factor is the convenience of having a third party manage all of the freelancers the publisher needs to get the books edited. Packagers have undertaken the role of the in-house production editor in this regard, and now, when a publisher sends a book or several books to a packager, the publisher only needs to speak with one person even if there are 15 freelance editors working on the publisher's books. This is convenience, as well as a lower cost to publishers.

The idea behind partnering is to level the playing field as regards convenience. There still needs to be price competition, but that is another matter. To get to that point, freelancers first need to overcome the hurdle of convenience.

Think about the editorial boat essay in that light.

107

THE EDITORIAL WORLD—
WILL IT PASS EDITORS BY?

When I presented at the 2011 Communication Central conference, *Editorial Entrepreneurship in the 21st Century*, in Baltimore, MD, I not only spoke about making money as an editor and marketing, I also gave the keynote address, which was a prediction of what the editing world will be like in 2015. Knowing that I had committed myself to speaking, I began thinking about how my editorial world continues to change and whether I and my colleagues are cognizant of the changes going on about us and are adapting to the changes.

The true impetus for my giving thought to this question was an article in the May 7, 2011, *The Economist* titled "A Less Gilded Future," whose theme, interestingly, was repeated in a June 3, 2011, *New York Times* article, "Where Lawyers Find Work." (As an aside, although the *New York Times* article's contents are identical, the titles are different for the print and online versions. I have used the print title.)

Editors have been facing the outsourcing problem (in which outsourcing = offshoring) for years now; doctors have been facing the phenomenon in recent years; and now lawyers. Offshoring seems to be moving up the food chain. Of great interest to me is that the offshoring for each of the three markets is to the same geographic area, largely India.

If doctors and lawyers are facing this phenomenon, what hope is there for editors to reverse the longstanding offshoring trend? I guess we could become plumbers and electricians because you do have to be on the spot to fix a plugged toilet or wire a new wall outlet.

As with all major problems, there is no easy solution. Entry to the medical and legal fields is, relative to entry to the editorial field, very difficult—perhaps comparable to a climb up Mount Hood versus a walk across an open, flat meadow. The ease of entry into the editorial field compounds the offshoring problem for editors. After all, what does it really take to hang out a shingle and say "I'm an editor and open for business!"?

(For some interesting data regarding editors in the United States, see Occupational Employment and Wages, May 2010: 27-3041 Editors, from the U.S. Bureau of Labor Statistics.)

The freelance editorial profession—developmental editors, copyeditors, technical editors, proofreaders—in the United States has multiple failings as regards self-preservation. One, of course, is that there is no organization that looks out for the *political and financial* interests of editors—no lobbying group dedicated to improving the business life of the freelance editor. The organizations that do exist are socially oriented, generally of local interest, and not well-managed, and the core members who exert control are rarely interested in looking out for the political and financial welfare of the profession as opposed to having a social outlet for themselves. There might be, for instance, a job service – but it's reactive, with no proactively going after jobs for members. Or group health insurance, but only on a very limited level.

The consequence is that freelance editors think and speak the party line of having become a freelance editor to be free of corporate bondage, to be able to set one's own work hours and schedule, to live free and work free—and all of the other trite pap that we can think of as justification for working outside the corporate box. Oh, I hear you screaming at me already—"Trite pap! How wrong you are." And the reasons follow.

Alas, it is pap unless you are one of the fortunate few who can view working as a freelance editor as a hobby—the extra income is nice but not really needed. It pays for a fancier vacation or car, but is not necessary for putting bread on the table or for paying bills.

I've been in the business—and yes, freelance editing is a business and needs to be treated as a business—since 1984, although some days it seems like forever. In my case, editorial work was/is needed to put bread on the table and to pay household bills. It wasn't/isn't supplemental income, it is primary income—always has been and always will be—which means that I need to watch trends and adapt my business to those trends, or see my business shrivel and die.

Because my editorial business is my primary income, I cannot emulate the ostrich and hope that today's negative trends will suddenly reverse themselves and become positive trends for me on their own. If anything, I need to push them in the direction I want to go and, if I can't do that, then I need to rework my business to account for the trends.

Most editors don't view freelance editing through the same lens I view it. Most editors I know will defend until their economic death the status quo, the idea that they chose to become a freelance editor to be free of all corporate bonds, to be wholly independent, to be ... whatever. I think that, to survive, one needs to alter how one thinks about freelance editing.

The result of offshoring has been a depression in freelance wages and jobs for the homegrown freelance editor. Jobs haven't wholly dried up; rather, they have changed and the source of the jobs has changed. Whereas in 1984, domestic publishers needed freelance editors and hired them directly at a relatively decent rate of pay, in 2010, most of those domestic publishers have been absorbed into a few mega-corporations that are outsourcing (offshoring) editorial work because they view it in the same global dimensions as they view accounting. The accounting thinking is that rules of profit and loss are the same regardless of location.

Unfortunately, that global accounting thinking is also being applied to editorial processes. It is true that, at some level, one can think globally about the editorial process, but it is not true at most levels. Although English is the most universally used and taught language, it is not a universal language in the sense that, for example, rules of grammar, spelling, conventions, and idioms are universal. Yet publishing conglomerates act as if English is no different in Britain than in Australia, in America than in India. And this hurts local editors by denying the editors opportunities to ply their trade.

The result is that accountants cannot see the value in hiring local when hiring nonlocal can be so much less expensive. So the editorial work is farmed out to nonlocal low bidders who now have to hire local talent to fulfill the contract but do so on a depressed wage scale. It is the imposition of the nonlocal wage scale on the local talent that ultimately is the problem, and most editors simply throw up their hands in surrender to "the inevitable."

And this is why I wonder whether the future editorial world will pass editors by. Adaptation to the current offshoring and its depression-level economics is not a viable solution. A viable solution would be one that makes it uneconomical to offshore what should be local, just as it is uneconomical to hire a nonlocal plumber to unclog your kitchen sink. Will editors come up with such a viable solution or will the editorial world pass us by? That is the question that must be answered in the near term by local editors everywhere.

108

COMPETITION GETS KEENER:
AGENTS, AUTHORS, AND PERSEUS

The world of editing is a tough, competitive world that is getting tougher and more competitive. The toughness and competitiveness I refer to is that of finding paying work as a professional editor. The Perseus Books Group has created yet another new wrinkle for the professional editor.

Previously, if a major publisher wasn't interested in an author's work, the author was on his or her own. For some authors, agents who believed in the project would act as publisher, but this option was limited. One problem with agents for freelance professional editors is that the agents often do their own editing of client manuscripts. This is not to say that an agent never hires the freelance professional editor, just that it occurs with less frequency than traditional publisher hires.

For professional editors, Perseus is changing the editorial world. It has created a new unit, Argo Navis Author Services, and is offering the agent-represented author whose agency has signed on with the unit an alternative to wholly self-publishing ebooks. Argo Navis is offering marketing and distribution services—key items in the world of self-publishing—to such an author, even as the author remains the ebook's publisher. It is a hybrid of traditional and nontraditional publishing.

This is good for authors, but makes it significantly more difficult for professional editors to connect with new clients. Argo Navis is not offering editorial services; each author is responsible, along with the author's agent, for obtaining such services independently.

The setup shifts the production burden. In exchange, the revenue split is 70% author/30% distributor. (I'm not quite clear on whether this is

70% of 70%, as the retailer needs to get its cut, too.) The traditional publisher no longer provides the author with financial support, and what services the publisher does provide are fewer than under a conventional publishing contract.

We knew this was coming. There had to be a change in the way business was conducted because top-tier authors see self-publishing as a way to maximize their revenues and publishers need a way to capture a part of those revenues while simultaneously cutting costs. When cutting costs, the first thing to go is editorial services.

Editorial services are the invisible services. They have no perceived value on the publisher's spreadsheet because no one can point to a particular book and say: "This book sold better than expected because of the high-quality editing" or "This book sold fewer copies because of a lack of editing." The average reader is numb, for example, to homonym error—the difference between *seam* and *seem* doesn't register high on the annoyance scale for most readers; *there, their, were, where, your, you're* are just interchangeable words that mean what they mean to the reader in context. ("'When *I* use a word,' Humpty Dumpty said, in rather a scornful tone, 'it means just what I choose it to mean—neither more nor less.'" Lewis Carroll, *Through the Looking Glass* [Raleigh, NC: Hayes Barton Press, 1872, p. 72].)

With this new role for a traditional publisher, the professional editor will have a harder time finding clients. Where under the traditional model, 100 agents funneled 300 author manuscripts to one publisher and editors sought work on those 300 manuscripts by discussion with the one publisher, editors now will need to find and approach the 100 agents *and* the 300 authors, and hope that the agent doesn't already provide editorial services, which many do, in-house.

It isn't clear to me how to approach this changing market. What is clear, however, is that it not only needs to be approached if professional editors expect to survive the transition to ebooks and the world of self-publishing, but that professional editors need to rethink their compensation, as agents have a worldwide reach and professional editors will be competing globally, not locally.

109

Does the Future of Editing Lie in Tiers?

One of the things that struck me about the "saving" of the American auto industry was the new union contracts that created two wage tiers. The idea of tiers is also invading public employee contracts.

Then a new project came to me that was conditioned on my accepting a lower per-page rate than I customarily charge. The tradeoff was the size of the project and the extra long schedule. Yet that made me wonder: Does the future of editing lie in tiers?

We have already seen the changes in pay that were brought about by globalization of the editor's job. Whereas when I first started in editing, 28 years ago, I had to overcome publishers wanting editors who were very local—that is, editors who could pick up and deliver the hard-copy manuscripts—today, I have to overcome publishers who are price-focused and globally oriented. That global orientation has already caused a depression in rates that publishers will pay.

I thought that the rate pressure had hit bottom until this project was offered. Now I see it hasn't and that it may be taking a more insidious form—the form of tiering.

I called the client to discuss the pricing and discovered that the rate they were offering was their new top-tier rate, given only to very experienced editors and only for the most problematic projects. I was informed that most of the freelance professional editors who worked for this client were in one of two even-lower-paying tiers.

I understand the pressure that publishers are under. Competition is getting keener, with agents starting their own presses and with booksellers venturing into the publishing end of the book process. Yet the race to the bottom means everyone loses.

Right now, the bulk of the competition for American editors lies in India-based editors and in newly minted American editors, both of whom are willing to work for low wages (i.e., low based on the American lifestyle). Newly minted American editors think that taking a job at any price is better than not having any work at all and also that it gives a foot in the door. That was reasonable thinking a few decades ago, but not today, with globalization and with publishers viewing editorial services as being of questionable value for their bottom lines.

Alas, although such thinking is no longer reasonable, I am unsure what reasonable thinking is when it comes to pay. I am also wondering what the effect would be should I decide to accept this project at the proffered price. I am weighing multiple factors as I consider the effects.

First, even at the proffered price, the project would be profitable to me. Because of efficiencies in how I run my business, the proffered price is not a breakeven or worse price, yet it is not as good a price as I expect for a project with the problems this one has.

Second, I wonder if acceptance would set a precedent. Would I be more willing to accept lower-paying projects in the future? Will this client expect to pay even less next time?

Third, I wonder how this will affect other facets of my business. Will I be able to accept projects from other clients or higher-paying projects while working on this one? How will it interfere with work over the next few months (the proffered project is expected to last six or seven months of near-full-time editing).

There are other concerns, but perhaps the most important concern is this: Is this project a portent of the future of editing in which low and tiered pay will become the norm, with editors having no control over the tier to which they are assigned? This may seem farfetched now, but the future is not so far away that we can ignore what is or may be coming. The time to plan counterstrategies to these possibilities is now; waiting until they are universal is too late.

It is at times like these that I lament the lack of a useful, viable, forceful national association for professional editors that is something more than a social club. The one lesson that publishers have absorbed, and that freelance editors shore up by their actions, is the divide-and-conquer lesson. American editors stubbornly refuse (generally speaking) to coalesce into anything that smacks of giving up some independence.

Ultimately, that reluctance to give up any of our freedom will be our downfall.

Sadly, I think tier pricing for editors will be the norm in a few years, not a few decades. I think when that occurs, it will be too late for editors to join together to fight it. The ease of entering the field—all one need do is hang out a shingle that proclaims he or she is ready for work—and the very minimal financial investment needed to do so work against us in this time of globalization, just as it worked for us when we started our own careers.

How many of us would choose this career path today should we be given the opportunity to restart our career lives? I know I would have to think carefully about my choice.

THE CRYSTAL BALL SAYS . . .

The May 4, 2013, edition of *The Economist* reported that the British Research Councils will begin requiring taxpayer-funded research to be published in journals that make the research available free within one year of publication, if not sooner ("Academic Publishing: Free-for-all"). This mirrors the White House's executive order to the same effect and a bill in Congress that would set the time limit at six months. Not to be left behind, the European Union is moving in the same direction.

The crystal ball sees these as a positive trend for taxpayers, but a worrisome trend for authors and editors, especially when you realize where this leads: to the extension of self-publishing to research papers.

It doesn't take much effort to recognize that a journal cannot survive if it is paying all the costs of production and marketing but cannot charge for the content. Publishers, being businesses, would have to shift the economic burdens, and the only place to which they can be shifted is onto author shoulders.

It is true that, now, many researchers hire editors at their own expense to help them prepare research articles for submission to journals. The authors see this as an investment because they are trying to be published in journals whose reputations will boost the authors' reputation—the honor and prestige of being published in a journal known to reject 90% or more of submissions is calculable in the academic world. Getting published by *Nature* or *Science* is an academic plum; the same cannot be said for articles published in *PLoS*, which accepts 80% or more of the articles submitted to it.

The future seems to be that authors will not only have to bear the burden of the editorial costs, but also the production costs, which will be wrapped into a publication fee: "Want to have your article published in our journal? You need to pay us $x." In other words, the vanity press model of publishing is the likely model that publishers of journals will adopt. As long as you are willing to pay to be published, you will be published.

Setting aside the ramifications such a system has for the reputation of the open-access journal and, thus, the reputation of the author published in the open-access journal, and setting aside the potential benefits to society of researchers having full access to these research articles, we need to consider the impact it will have on us in the performance of the work we do as editors and authors.

The boom in self-publishing of ebooks has not transferred its momentum to either editors or to authors. Although some editors have seen an uptick in work received from authors, most editors have not; many editors have seen, instead, a decline. More importantly, perhaps, is that editorial standards have declined as authors increasingly decide they can self-edit or that having their nephew's kindergarten teacher (or the nephew himself!) do the editing for free or minimal cost is sufficient. Of course, it does not help that readers are buying error-riddled ebooks and often are unaware of the errors. (It is hard to convince someone who believes *gr8* is an acceptable spelling of *great* that *gr8* is erroneous.)

This momentum toward self- and nonprofessional editing also puts downward pressure on professional editors fees. We are in the race to the bottom!

A bright spot in editing has been academic editing. It hasn't been financially bright, but work-wise, it has been shining when compared to the offshoring of "standard" editorial work. But that is because there have been several parties who were interested in achieving excellence, an excellence that is not represented by either most self-editing efforts or editing by nonprofessionals.

Yet I foresee a coming change as a result of the open access requirements. Researchers who are already hard-pressed to financially support their research and who now pay for a preliminary submission edit, knowing that, if accepted, the journal will provide additional editing, will be rethinking whether to self-edit or have a nonprofessional do the editing, and whether to put pressure on professional editors to reduce fees, all because these authors will have to pay publication fees to the journals in addition to those fees they have already been paying.

According to *The Economist* article, the journal *Nature* claims it costs $40,000 per published paper to cover all of the production and review costs. I have no reason to doubt the number, but it makes me wonder who will bear—and pay—such cost in the open-access model of publishing. How many authors would willingly pay even 25% of that cost? How many authors could afford to absorb such costs?

If the journal is not absorbing the cost, then the ripple has to move downstream. It has to keep moving until it is finally stopped at the place where the cost is absorbed or until it no longer has momentum because either the costs to be absorbed have greatly diminished or no longer have someone to absorb them. How much of that ripple will editors have to absorb by way of lower prices?

(Something to note: "Lower prices" doesn't necessarily mean reducing, for example, an hourly rate from $45 to $35. It can also mean leaving the rate as is but increasing the scope and amount of services provided. The effect is the same in both instances: It is a lowering of price.)

I also wonder when we will see this open-access publishing model extend to all of academic publishing, not just to journals. I expect that publishers, once they wrap themselves in open-access publishing and see that charging a fee to be published can be profitable, will apply this model to academic books. University presses are already financially in trouble; the open-access model of having the author pay the costs could reduce their financial stress. However, it would also mean less opportunity (or less money) for professional editors as authors strive to reduce their cost burden.

I think the future for authors is one of more costs and less prestige. More costs because the financial burdens will shift from journals and university presses to the authors. Less prestige because the quality of presentation of the research will decline and because a pay-to-publish scheme will reduce the selectivity of the journals and publishers—as long as you can pay, you will be published.

I think the future for professional editors is one of lower prices and less work. Lower prices because authors will pressure for lower fees, or a broadened scope of work, or both, and editors will not be able to resist that pressure because it will come from all directions. Less work because as the costs to publish rise, authors will try to self-edit or find colleagues or students or friends or relatives or other nonprofessionals to do the editing as a way to reduce their financial burden, with the result that there will be less work for professional editors.

My crystal ball says authors and editors need to begin thinking about how they will adapt to what the future portends.

111

WHO SPEAKS FOR THE FREELANCE EDITOR?

The title asks the question; the answer is no one. What brought this to mind is a commentary in *BusinessWeek*, "Misrepresenting Small Business," which asks the question more broadly.

When I began my editorial career, I searched for an organization that could help me launch my career, look out for my interests on a national level, and help me find work. Remember that this was in the early days of the Internet, so socialization online was still in its infancy and online searching was unlike today. At that time, I had little success.

Subsequently, I discovered the EFA—Editorial Freelancers Association—a New York City-based group that had the right name and was, semi-conveniently, near my backyard (I live in upstate New York, a mere train ride away from the Big Apple). So I joined the EFA with high hopes and expectations, only to discover that it failed on many counts, with its big strength being a place to schmooze over the water-cooler. I was a member for many years until I realized that the return wasn't worth the investment.

From conversations with several colleagues who are members today, what I considered faults in the EFA years ago remain what I consider faults today, yet the organization continues to draw new members to replenish the ranks of those who leave it.

So, I ask the question again: Who represents the interests of American freelance editors? It seems that, although the need for a viable, national group that addresses the shortcomings of being self-employed is even of greater importance today than ever, there is a vacuum. I suspect the vacuum has many causes, not least of which is either the unwillingness or inability of many freelance editors to fund such an organization with high annual dues. Yet I remain convinced that not only is such an organization viable and needed, but that, once it is established and demonstrates its prowess at representing freelance editors, membership would bloom.

What should such a group do? There are numerous things, not least of which is to create a national certification program and tie that program in with jobs. Finding work is one of the hardest things the self-employed do. Some of us are good at it; others could be good if they could overcome their shyness; others will never be good at self-promotion even though they may well be the best editors available.

Here are some things that a quality national organization should provide for freelance editors:

- Hire full-time staff whose jobs revolve around making connections for trained editors and for training editors to high standards.

- Negotiate group discounts with software companies like Microsoft—most editors use Microsoft Word; why couldn't, for example, the organization negotiate a volume license?

- Provide a software help desk—not on how to install the product but on how to use the product most efficiently.

- Provide continuing education courses around the country in various editing specialties.

- Lobby for state and national legislation that addresses our needs, including appropriate tax legislation.

- Provide legal advice, especially about contracts.

- Combat the movement of work based solely on labor costs.

- Educate the publishing industry so that the value of members is both understood and appreciated as reflected in a payscale that isn't retrogressing to the early 1990s but is moving forward to the 2020s.

- Provide a social outlet for members.

- Anticipate changes in the publishing industry and help prepare members for those changes.

- Provide a first-class magazine filled with how-to articles, along with more general articles.

- Teach members new skills so that members can expand their services.

- Provide business advice.

- Negotiate discounts with service providers such as FedEx and UPS.

There are lots more "things" that a quality national editorial association could do for editors. All one needs to do is look at what other successful organizations provide members. But the big thing is to have an association that is focused on our needs as a group and not on the needs of the few who run it.

Now all we need to do is find someone to start it. Any volunteers?

112

ONE IS THE LONELIEST NUMBER

I had been doing a lot of thinking recently about being a freelancer. Much of my thinking was in preparation for delivering the keynote address at the *Editorial Entrepreneurship in the 21st Century* conference (sponsored by Communication Central, held in Baltimore, MD, in 2011), along with the sessions in which I am involved. When I think of my years as a freelance editor, I often think of the Three Dog Night song from 1969 titled "One."

Over the years, I have heard many reasons why someone became a solo freelancer; not once have I heard as a reason the opportunity to make more money. Invariably the reasons focused on other issues, such as hating the corporate environment, hating having to deal with inferior bosses, wanting to be able to set one's own schedule, the ability to choose to accept or reject work, and so on. Although there is some commonality to the reasons given, there is significantly more commonality when freelancers are asked about the negatives of going solo. The most oft-given complaint is loneliness—that is, the loss of water-cooler socialization. Thus, one is the loneliest number for solo freelancers.

It is because of this social loneliness that solo freelancers jump at chances to participate in online social groups nowadays—the substitute water cooler. Yet these substitutes have their own negatives, primarily that a freelancer can spend—and often does spend—too much time socializing online, so much so that the socializing interferes with earning a living. I'm not sure that there is an easy resolution to this problem; the balancing act that is required is not an easy one to master.

Yet forced change may be what lies in the future.

I've noticed on several of the online lists in which I participate that the number of solo freelancers who are seeking or accepting full-time employment with corporate denizens is increasing. Whereas a few years ago it was rare to find a freelancer who was actively (as opposed to passively) seeking to change career paths, today the active seeking is much more common.

None of the active career-path-change seekers bluntly says, "These are the reasons why I am making [*or* want to make] the career switch," but I suspect that the top reasons are social loneliness, inability to afford health insurance, low earnings, and inability to set aside money for retirement, perhaps even in that descending order. Being a solo freelancer places a lot of heavy burdens on one's own shoulders, burdens that are shouldered by corporations in the usual employer-employee relationship.

As I see it, every problem that the solo freelancer faces coalesces around the singular problem of loneliness, of not having that colleague in the next cubicle with whom one can share a cup of tea and the problems of the moment. The more time one needs to devote to staving off loneliness, the less time one has to spend working and earning and thus the less money one has to purchase health insurance, to set aside for retirement, to use for vacations, to pay life's daily bills. Which makes me wonder whether going solo is really the right choice for most freelancers.

Not much thought, and even less acceptance, is given by solo free-lancers to the idea that perhaps they should combine forces with other solo freelancers—not in an online forum but in an actual business relationship. The excuses given are myriad and although usually of molehill size, made into mountains. But our editing world is changing, its needs are different today than what they were just five years ago, let alone a quarter-century ago when I started my solo career, and maybe greater consideration needs to be given to putting aside the imaginary wonderful world of solo freelancing and to thinking about ways to go from one to more than one.

Yes, as the song says, two can be as lonely as one, but it is much easier for two to not be lonely than it is for one. We solo freelancers are quick to dismiss anything that might suggest that what we are doing is less than ideal; this has been true for the 27 years that I have been a freelancer. Yet what was once true, correct, and sustainable is no longer true, correct, or sustainable. Not only has time marched on, but so has the way we need to conduct business, especially if making money is a key goal. If we do not recognize these changes and begin to address them, we can expect that we will be, for better or for worse, joining the ranks of those who now say, "Once upon a time, I was a solo freelancer." There is no reason why "One" must be our theme song in perpetuity.

113

WORKING ALONE—OR NOT?

This essay is by Ruth E. Thaler-Carter. Ruth is the owner of Communication Central, the sponsor of an annual conference for freelancers, as well as a freelance editor and writer. Ruth's essay is a response to my recent essay, "One Is the Loneliest Number." Needless to say, I will respond to Ruth's essay. Ruth argues for the solo freelancer remaining solo.

As my favorite professional time of year approaches—time for the Communication Central conference—I've been thinking about the meaning of being an editorial entrepreneur; a freelancer, in less-lofty parlance.

Colleagues have talked here about the nature of freelancing in terms of someone working alone versus as part of a larger entity or partnership, perhaps even with subcontractors or employees. Many colleagues believe that the future of editorial freelancing is in grouping together and functioning as teams or even companies with employees, or at least subcontractors. Some colleagues believe that the day of the one-person freelance operation is approaching its nadir; others see a continuing future for the one-person business—as long as that person has a network of colleagues to make it possible to find and accept more complex projects.

I'm firmly in the camp of being and remaining a sole practitioner—doing all the activity required of a freelance writing, editing, proofreading, desktop publishing, and speaking business myself. I like being hands-on for my business, knowing my own skills and working around any limits I might have, controlling when and how I work—all aspects that make freelancing deeply appealing, and being a sole practitioner is an ideal way to exercise those preferences. I've never felt a need to partner formally with another colleague.

415

But this doesn't mean that I work in a vacuum, or would want to. I'm certainly not antisocial; I'm one of the most extroverted, gregarious people you'll ever meet. I may not want to share my projects and profits with colleagues as a permanent business model, but I often partner with colleagues: a graphic designer who can bring artistic skills to a project, a tech writer who can create content on a level that's beyond me, a photographer on a professional basis. I still get to do what I love doing—the writing, editing, proofreading, layout, etc.—and can take on projects that otherwise I would have to turn down, or at best do less of and profit less from. Having colleagues to turn to for such partnerships means that I can take on projects that would otherwise be beyond me. Most of those partnerships have turned out well, but not well enough to tempt me into changing the structure or nature of my editorial business. I still prefer to position myself as not just an entrepreneur, but a sole practitioner.

I do interact regularly with colleagues through professional organizations. I'm a huge fan of networking, in person and, nowadays, electronically. As some readers of this blog know, I'm very active in several membership associations. This is the main way that I overcome the potential isolation of being a one-person shop and connect with other people. Not just clients, but colleagues, many of whom have become friends as well.

I look forward to the Communication Central conference because I think that an in-person gathering of colleagues is a valuable—perhaps even invaluable—resource for any freelance writer, editor, proofreader, website developer, graphic artist, indexer, etc. We're all trying to succeed in an increasingly competitive world for editorial professionals, as publishing contracts, e-publishing expands, and outsourcing continues to drive down prices in some areas. We need each other more than ever these days—even those of us who intend to retain a solo business structure.

It's ever-more-important to meet and learn from each other, and occasionally work with each other. Maybe not as ongoing formal business partners, but at least as backup or added value for specific assignments and projects, as well as for advice and even a shoulder to lean or cry on. It's important just to know that there are people available to turn to when an intriguing project is on the horizon that you can't tackle alone.

We also need to expand our perception of how and where to market our skills. We can learn about marketing without fear from each other and without necessarily poaching on each other's territory or client base.

Meeting in person is also a great opportunity to learn from each other about the tools we need, how they work, and how to make the most of them.

There's just something special about putting faces, voices, and personalities to those e-mail addresses, Twitter handles, and other electronic networking environments of our current era!

I might have developed a business model that combines the best of both worlds: the sole practitioner and the partnership or group. I'm committed to retaining my identity as a one-person shop, but I still see interacting with colleagues as a key element of the success of my editorial business. The advice and insights, and occasional project participation, of colleagues help me maintain my solo business and keep it growing.

114

Is the Editorial Freelancer's Future
a Solo Future?

In a previous essay, "Working Alone—Or Not?," guest author Ruth E. Thaler-Carter discussed the positives of being a solo freelancer. Although a well-argued position and a position that most freelancers believe in, I think the future lacks promise for the solo freelancer and will demand that editorial freelancers think about, and form, group practices.

Current views of freelancing hearken back to the days of craft guilds. In the craft guilds, each guild member was an artisan whose work was protected. One couldn't work, for example, as a scribe unless a member of the scribe's guild. The guild offered a monopoly for the craftsperson and assured quality to the consumer.

But such thinking, which had at least some validity into the late 1980s, is no longer valid. The entry requirements to become a freelance editor are so minimal as to be nonexistent. Whereas the guilds imposed classes and apprenticeships and maintained a required minimum-level skillset, today anyone can proclaim him- or herself to be a freelance editor at the moment of his or her choosing—no specialty education required.

This change was brought about by the dynamic of consolidation in the publishing industry—the transformation from numerous "small" publishing houses to a handful of multinational mega-corporations. The transformation brought with it a philosophical change in the approach to publishing—a change from quality first to profits first. It is this change that the guild-minded freelancer has yet to grapple with; rather than guild thinking, the editorial freelancer must move to business thinking.

Notably, Ruth's essay neglected to discuss income. It seems to me that not discussing income is to look at editorial freelancing through rose-colored glasses. After all, isn't that the bottom-line motivator for most of us—the earning of an income sufficient to enable us to work for ourselves without worrying each day whether we have the wherewithal to financially survive?

In my discussions with colleagues, I am constantly hearing about their struggles to find clients and earn a decent wage. It is not that a few editorial freelancers do reasonably to very well financially; rather, it is that the vast majority do not. Part of the problem is skill level and types of skills. For example, too many editorial freelancers whose livelihood is based on using Microsoft Word have little mastery of the software program. The lack of mastery makes every job that much harder and longer and lower paying.

But I think a larger part of the problem, if not the largest part, is that too many editorial freelancers work solo and cling to guild thinking rather than moving to business thinking. When they are too sick to work, there is no income; there is no one to share the marketing burden with; it is difficult to take on the multi-editor jobs that have the potential to be more lucrative; it is difficult to accept new work on top of the work one already has because there aren't enough hours in a day for the solo freelancer to work; the solo freelancer has insufficient financial resources to invest in the future of their business.

The trend in the publishing industry is to outsource to full-service production companies, and this trend has been accelerating. Publishers have reduced in-house production staff while increasing the number of publications expected to be published and that each retained production editor must handle. Unlike when I started my editorial career in 1984, a time when most editorial work was still done in-house and on paper, today most editorial work is done out-house and electronically.

In the days of guild hegemony, clients could not go far astray. I remember seeing ads for freelance editors that included the requirement that the freelance editor live locally so that the editor could easily pick up and drop off manuscript. The advent of overnight delivery services and the Internet, combined with the change from paper to electronic editing, did away with that restriction. Now it is as easy to use an editor who lives 3,000 miles away as it is to use one who lives next door.

Consequently, those who cling to guild thinking fail to compete with their competition, which is the world.

Today, in-house production staff are responsible for more projects than they were just five years ago. As part of these responsibilities, they have to monitor numerous freelance editors, unless they assign the projects to a full-service company, in which case, they deal with a single contact and it is the outside company's problem to monitor the cadre of editors.

Think of it like a pyramid. At the pyramid's peak is the in-house production editor. Just below the production editor are the freelance editors. The more freelancers the production editor has to be involved with, the shorter the pyramid and the wider its base (picture short and squat). But, if the production editor can delegate to one or two people who, in turn, can delegate to several freelance editors, then the taller the pyramid and the narrower the base that the production editor has to worry about.

The point is that, increasingly, in-house staff look to find editorial groups to whom they can delegate the work because finding a group means that numerous projects can be sent to the group, but there need be only a single contact point that the production editor needs to monitor. Monitoring of editors moves down the chain of responsibility.

This is important because (a) it enables the publisher to schedule more projects as the in-house editor can handle more, and (b) the group can take on more work than can the solo freelancer because the group has the resources to handle the volume. Taking on more work means less downtime and increased income. Plus, there is not the worry about losing work due to illness, emergency, difficult projects, etc. An editorial group means help with all aspects of the freelance business.

There is yet another consideration: the rate of compensation. There has been a downward pressure on rates. In my early years, it was not uncommon for a publisher to raise the rate it would pay a freelance editor based on the number of years the freelancer had worked with the publisher and the quality and quantity of the freelancer's work. In my experience, those days are long gone. Instead of increasing, the rate has remained steady or declined.

The solo editorial freelancer is rarely in a position to bargain over the rate. The competition for the work is simply too fierce; there are hundreds, if not thousands, of freelancers who are willing to work for the offered rate or even less, especially with the worldwide marketplace that the Internet has birthed. Part of why the solo editorial freelancer lacks bargaining power is that he or she offers nothing more than the barebones editorial work. In contrast, a group offers, in addition to the editorial work, management and other skillsets, relieving the client of those responsibilities.

I think the future for editorial freelancers is in grouping, not in remaining solo; shifting from guild thinking to business thinking. Although working solo has its attractions, I think those attractions are rooted in guild thinking and ultimately will lead to a dry work-well in the not-too-distant future.

WANT TO KNOW MORE?

As with all good things, there must come an end, so the book ends. But that does not mean you and your colleagues can't extract more information from Ruth E. Thaler-Carter, Jack Lyon, or Rich Adin.

Each is available, either individually, in pairs, or as a trio to speak to groups of freelancers on a variety of topics. If your local group of freelancers would like to have us conduct a seminar or conference, either in person or via webinar, please contact us through Communication Central at conference@communication-central.com.

In addition, even considering the depth and length of this book, it has only touched the surface of the many issues facing the professional editor who strives to make a success of an editing business. We plan to publish additional collections of *An American Editor* essays in the future.

To continue the conversation, do consider subscribing to and commenting at An American Editor (www.americaneditor.wordpress.com).

ABOUT THE AUTHOR AND THE EDITORS

Richard H. Adin has a BA and a JD degree. He practiced law for seven years before joining Matthew Bender as an executive editor in 1984. In 1984, Richard started Freelance Editorial Services (www.freelance-editorial-services.com) as a part-time business to provide copyediting and desktop publishing services to publishers. In 1989, he joined Prentice Hall as managing editor, and was involved in electronic and desktop publishing. In 1991, Richard left Prentice Hall to devote full-time to Freelance Editorial Services.

In addition to providing editing services to publishers, in the mid-1990s, Richard was CEO of Rhache Publishers Ltd., a small press. His duties included negotiating author contracts, day-to-day management, editing, design, and the myriad other things that are needed to be done to publish and market a book.

Richard has also taught continuing education classes on book publishing, editing, and marketing for small businesses.

In 2006, Richard formed wordsnSync Ltd (www.wordsnSync.com) to market his EditTools collection of macros and as a future site to house his patent-pending Max online stylesheet. Rich remains president and CEO of wordsnSync and continues to improve and add to his EditTools collection of macros for editors.

In 2010, Richard started his now-acclaimed blog, *An American Editor*, from which the material in this book is drawn. Through his blog and through appearances as a presenter at conferences, Richard has shared his business and editorial knowledge with colleagues from beginning to very experienced editors.

Richard can be reached through any of his websites: Freelance Editorial Services (www.freelance-editorial-services.com), An

American Editor (www.anamericaneditor.com), and wordsnSync Ltd (www.wordsnSync.com).

Ruth E. Thaler-Carter (www.writerruth.com) is a long-time, successful freelance writer, editor, proofreader, desktop publisher, and speaker whose motto is "I can write about anything!"® She has been published locally, regionally, nationally, and internationally in newspapers, magazines, newsletters, magazines, websites, and books, including as coauthor of a popular book on eldercare and author of two booklets on freelancing, "Get Paid to Write! Getting Started as a Freelance Writer" (self-published) and "Freelancing 101: Launching Your Editorial Business" (Editorial Freelancers Association, www.the-efa.org/res/booklets.php). Her copyediting and proofreading work includes magazines, newspapers, newsletters, websites, journals, law and marketing firms, a virtual PR firm, tech companies, and other businesses.

She is known as a queen of networking and presents workshops on freelancing, basics of editing and proofreading, websites for freelancers, and the modern portfolio for organizations such as Writers and Books, the Editorial Freelancers Association, Society for Technical Communication, American Copy Editors Society, National Association of Independent Writers and Editors, Association for Women in Communications, and more.

Thaler-Carter is also the owner of Communication Central (www.communication-central.com), which hosts an annual conference for freelance communications professionals at which Rich Adin and Jack Lyon have been frequent presenters.

Jack M. Lyon is a book editor who got tired of working the hard way and started creating programs to automate editing tasks in Microsoft Word, eventually founding the Editorium to make those programs available to others (www.editorium.com). He has worked in the publishing field for thirty-five years, editing on the computer as early as 1985. For many years the managing editor at a trade publishing house in Salt Lake City, he now owns and operates Waking Lion Press (www.wakinglionpress.com). He is the author of several books, including *Microsoft Word for Publishing Professionals* and *Macro Cookbook for Microsoft Word*. He is also the coauthor of a business book, *Managing the Obvious.*

INDEX

accuracy as concern. *See* quality considerations

acknowledgments, value of, 304–6

acronyms
consistency and editing process, 189–91
copyediting stage, 170
macros overviews, 78, 79, 134–36

Adin, Richard. *See also* EditTools
background of book, xvii–xviii
key resources, xix
for more information, 423

agencies, future of editing, 374, 400–401

AMA style dataset, 102–3

Amazon cloud computing, 118–19

An American Editor blog
background of book, xvii–xviii
for more information, 423

The American Heritage Dictionary of the English Language, 66, 69, 105

The American Heritage Guide to Contemporary Usage and Style, 57, 66, 70

American judicial system, business rule regarding, 157

The American Language, 57, 70

annual bookkeeping, 243–45

annual price increases, 254–55

Antec case, 138

antimalware software, 122, 139–40

antivirus software, 109, 119, 122, 139–40

APA Dictionary of Psychology, 66

APA's Publication Manual, 70

Apple computers, 79, 121, 137–38, 140. *See also* Mac computers

applying for work. *See* hiring considerations

arbitration clauses, 210–11

arbitration of claims, 153

Argo Navis Author Services, 400–401

artificial or arbitrary schedules, 181–84. *See also* schedule considerations

artisans, editors as, 335–36, 418

associations for editors. *See* professional organizations

attorney-in-fact clauses, 153

audience for book as consideration, 58

author alteration (AA) charges, 195, 196

author commandments
creation of, 35
thou shalt treat editors as partners, 44–46, 50
thou shalt use a professional editor, 40–43

author-created stylesheets, 106

author-editor relationship. *See also* expectations; *specific aspects*
artificial schedules, 183
author as final arbiter, 13
authorial and editorial processes, 178–80
burning bridges, 307–9
copyright interest and payment, 145
editors as partners, 44–46
"professional" resources and, 88–90
unwritten rules and, 47–50
what editors need from authors, 192–94

author queries, 12, 49, 125–28

Backup4All, 139
backup considerations, 119, 121–24, 138–39
The BBI Dictionary of English Word Combinations, 57, 70
bell curve phenomenon, 364
best price bids, 232–34
bibliographic references. *See* references (bibliographic)
bids. *See* estimates
billing. *See* collection of payments; rates *headings*
Bing, reference books vs., 110
BitDefender Internet Security, 139
bookkeeping, yearly, 243–45
bookmarks, Macro Express overview, 77
book prices, 374
bookshelves of editors. *See* reference books
buyouts and mergers, 362

callouts, 77, 166–67, 247
Carbonite, 138–39
career of editing. *See also* professionalism considerations; *specific aspects*
acknowledgments, value of, 304–6
burning bridges, 307–9
company vs. solopreneur question, 344–47, 348–50, 351–54, 355–57
difficult clients, 310–13
disappearing clients, 361–63
editing tests overview, 289–91
ethics of editing, 327–29
fee schedule, posting of, 240–42, 301–3
good editors, defining, 321–23
how not to get work, 295–96
"I can get it cheaper," 358–60
implied promises of editors, 330–32
in-house work, freelancers moving to, 413
new clients, losing chance for, 340–43
other careers vs. editing, 314–16
pricing self out of market, 292–94
professional editors, identifying, 324–26
reference books overview, 297–300
satisfaction from editing, 333–36
taking on too much, 337–39
what editors forget most often, 317–20
workdays and schedules, 364–67
cell phones, 122–23

certificate of insurance, 143
certification program, need for, 410
certified mail, copyright interest notice, 145
Chambers Dictionary of Etymology, 66
characters per page formula, 269
charges for services. *See* profit considerations; rates *headings*
The Chicago Manual of Style
client requirements, 297
lack of familiarity with, 55
opinion and style choices, 318–19
prevalence of use, 298
in professional editor's library, 70
versions compared, 299
child clauses, 157
churn rate, expectations and compensation, 36–37
citations. *See* references (bibliographic)
client cost considerations. *See* rates *headings*
client-editor relationship. *See also* expectations; *specific aspects*
burning bridges, 307–9
difficult clients, 310–13
disappearing clients, 361–63
implied promises of editors, 330–32
interacting with prospective clients, 240
liability insurance requirements, 141–43
Rule of Three, 223–25, 242, 243–44
satisfaction from editing, 333–34
types of "employers," 292–93
what editors forget most often, 317–20
client expectations. *See* expectations
cloud computing, 118–20
code of ethics. *See* ethical considerations
coding in macros. *See* macros
cold calls to prospects, 342–43
cold reading, 24–26
collection of payments. *See also* rates *headings*
copyright interest and payment, 144–47, 212, 308, 312
difficult clients and, 311
domains and e-mail, 129, 131, 344
ethics of billing, 249–52, 327–29
invoicing methods, 246–48
late payment as concern, 246–47, 307–8, 311–12
lawsuit remedy, 153
nonpayment as concern, 210–12, 293, 307–8, 311–12

yearly bookkeeping, 245
college costs and career choices, 314–16
commandments for authors
    creation of, 35
    thou shalt treat editors as partners,
        44–46, 50
    thou shalt use a professional editor,
        40–43
Communication Central as resource, xix,
    381, 416, 423
company name
    company vs. solopreneur question, 349
    domains and e-mail, 129–32, 248, 344
    implied promises and, 330, 332
company slogans, implied promises and,
    330, 332
company vs. solopreneur question, 344–47,
    348–50, 351–54, 355–57. *See also*
    group practices vs. solo freelancing
compensation for services. *See* profit consid-
    erations; rates *headings*
competition considerations. *See also specific*
    aspects
    agencies and, 400–401
    best price bids, 233–34
    changing face of editing, 19
    disappearing clients, 361–63
    editing roles and downward pressure on
        price, 21–22
    editing tests and, 291
    education costs and career choices,
        315–16
    "I can get it cheaper," 358–60
    low rates and competition, 229–31
    pricing self out of market, 292–94
    raising prices, 253, 255
    reducing prices, 227–28, 257–58
    solo freelancing vs. group practices,
        419–21
    tier pricing, 402–3
Composition of Scientific Words, 57, 66, 70
composition/typesetting, editing roles and
    outsourcing, 25–26
computer hardware. *See* hardware
computer software. *See* software
confidentiality considerations, 9, 149,
    156–59. *See also* privacy considerations
consistency
    copyediting stage, 168–69
    ensuring, 188–91

paper-based vs. online editing, 197
"professional" resources and, 89
contracts. *See also specific aspects*
    copyright interest and payment, 144, 146
    difficult clients and, 311–12
    editor beware, 148–51
    handshake agreements vs., 47, 146, 152,
        210
    implied promises of editors, 331
    liability insurance requirements, 141–43
    long-term, accepting, 240–42
    nondisclosure agreements, 156–59
    nonpayment as concern, 210–12
    relationships and unwritten rules, 47
    sign-or-no-work agreements, 346
    as slippery slope, 152–55
copyediting. *See also* process of editing; spe-
    cific aspects
    changing face of editing, 18–20
    copyediting by any other name, 24–27
    copyediting stage, 165, 167, 168–72
    expectations and compensation, 36–37,
        39
    light, medium, or heavy as terms, 28–31
    processing stage, 165, 166–67
    proofing stage, 165, 173–75
    relationships and unwritten rules, 48, 50
    role comparison, 11–13
    tests, 24–25, 216–17, 289–91, 340–42
Copy Editing List, 114, 115, 116
copyright interest and payment, 144–47,
    212, 308, 312
craft guilds, 418
crowd-source editing, xvii, 389–90
CSE's *Scientific Style and Format,* 70, 299
custom-built computers, 82, 121–24,
    137–38. *See also* hardware
custom "keyboards," 74, 77
custom word lists, 174

deadline considerations. *See* schedule con-
    siderations
decision-tree process, 111–13
defamation as concern, 141–43
definition of editing
    copyediting by any other name, 24–27
    editing roles and downward pressure on
        price, 22
    education of editors, 5–7
    good editors, defining, 321–23
    light, medium, or heavy as terms, 29

professional editors, identifying, 324–26
degree costs and career choices, 314–16
developmental editing. *See also specific aspects*
    changing face of editing, 18–20
    editing tests and, 290
    expectations and compensation, 36–37, 39
    group sourcing and, 389
    light, medium, or heavy as terms, 29, 30
    relationships and unwritten rules, 48, 50
    role comparison, 11–13
dictionaries
    editing tests and, 290–91
    grammar skills and, 51–52
    macros overview, 79
    online editing resources, 108–10
    professional editors and, 57, 65–66, 69–71, 299, 324–26
Dictionary of Americanisms, 57, 66
Dictionary of Theories, 70
Dictionary Pro package, 110
digest mode, 117
digital books. *See* ebooks
directory structure, 133–34
disability insurance, 353
disappearing clients, 361–63
disaster preparedness, 123–24, 137–40. *See also* backup considerations
discounting prices, 226–28, 232, 255, 257–59
dispute resolution clauses, 210–11
distrust, contracts and, 153, 154–55
domains and e-mail, 129–32, 248, 344
Dorchester Publishing, 379–81
Dorland's Illustrated Medical Dictionary, 66, 69, 109

ebooks
    acknowledgments, value of, 306
    agencies and, 400–401
    authorial and editorial processes, 179
    blessings vs. curses, 383–84
    citing as sources, 176–77
    Dorchester changes as harbinger, 379–81
    expectations as recipe for disappointment, 209
    future of freelance editors, 376–78
    future of publishing, 373–75
    open-access model and, 406
    schedules and client expectations, 186

    self-editing and, 388
    WYSIWYG conundrum, 14
economies of scale concept, 259
editing tests
    living in a dream world, 216–17
    new clients, losing chance for, 340–42
    overview of, 289–91
    roles and outsourcing, 24–25
editor alteration (EA) charges, 195, 196
editor-author relationship. *See* author-editor relationship
editorial boat, missing, 391–93, 394–95
Editorial Commandments
    creation of, 35
    thou shalt treat editors as partners, 44–46, 50
    thou shalt use a professional editor, 40–43
Editorial Freelancers Association, 114, 195–96, 264, 335, 409
Editorium macros. *See also specific macros*
    key resources, xix
    macros overview, 76, 77–78
    mastering macros, 94
    processing stage, 166–67
    query macro, 125–28
    wildcard macros and money, 236
Editor's Toolkit Plus, as key resource, xix
Editor's Toolkit Ultimate, as key resource, xix
EditTools. *See also specific macros*
    consistency and editing process, 189–91
    copyediting stage, 167, 168–72
    creation of, 255
    intellectual property concerns, 158
    key resources, xix
    large project logistics, 198, 199–200
    macros overviews, 76, 78–79, 133–36
    mastering macros, 94–96
    planning macros, 111
    processing stage, 166–67
    publisher agreement regarding callouts, 247
    publisher search for savings, 221
    wildcard macros and money, 236–39
education of editors
    career choices and, 314–16
    decline and fall of the American editor, 382, 384
    grammar skills and, 52–53

in philosophy and law, 5–7
professional organizations and, 410–11
EFA. *See* Editorial Freelancers Association
effective hourly rates. *See* rates, effective
   hourly
Effective Onscreen Editing (Hart), 92–93, 94
efficiency and profits. *See* profit considerations
electronic editing. *See* online editing
electronic stylesheets. *See* stylesheets
e-mail
   contacting prospective clients via, 343,
      363
   copyright interest notice, 145
   discussion lists, 114–17
   domains and, 129–32, 248, 344
   password security, 140
   work hours and, 364
emotional satisfaction from editing, 333–36
Employer Identification Number, 131, 248
English language, quest to standardize, 55
Enhanced Search, Count, and Replace, 133,
   135–36
equipment, computer. *See* hardware
error read, copyediting read vs., 220
errors and omissions insurance, 141–43
errors as concern. *See* quality considerations
ESCR. *See* Enhanced Search, Count, and Replace
estimates. *See also* profit considerations;
   rates *headings*
   best price bids, 232–34
   changing face of editing, 17–20
   co-bid requests, 323
   "I can get it cheaper," 358–60
   implied promises of editors, 332
   joint bids, 346
   levels of editing, 30
   minimum acceptable pay, 217–18
   number of pages, calculating, 268–69
   packagers and, 392
   publisher search for savings, 222
   Rule of Three, 223–25
   workdays and schedules, 365–66
ethical considerations
   billing methods, 249–52, 327–29
   Higgs boson of editing, 33–34
   large projects, 198
   taking on too much, 338–39
etymological books, 66, 71

Excel, Microsoft, 245, 248, 271
exhibits attached to contracts, 154
expectations. *See also* author-editor relationship; *specific concerns*
   burning bridges, 308–9
   changing face of editing, 17–20
   compensation and, 36–39
   demand for perfection, 260–63
   difficult clients, 310–13
   implied promises of editors, 330–32
   liability insurance requirements, 141–43
   light, medium, or heavy as terms, 28–31
   as recipe for disappointment, 207–9
   schedules and, 185–87
   work samples and, 10
   WYSIWYG conundrum, 14–16
expenses
   calculating EHR, 265–66, 276–77
   tracking of, 243
expert opinion, "professional" resources
   and, 89–90
eyewitness identification, 15

fees. *See* profit considerations; rates *headings*
fiction projects. *See also specific aspects and
   concerns*
   acknowledgments, value of, 304–5
   consistency as concern, 188, 191
   cost considerations, 41, 229
   demand for perfection, 262
   schedules and client expectations, 186
   Toggle and, 168–69
   what editors need from authors, 192–94
   WYSIWYG conundrum, 15–16
FileCleaner, 78, 166
file directory structure, 133–34
Find and Replace (Word)
   caution in using, 134
   copyediting stage, 170
   macro-writing example, 80–87
   processing stage, 167
finding a professional editor, 8–10
finding clients, 115, 117, 340–43, 361–63.
   See also hiring considerations; marketing of services
firewall software, 139–40
firing clients. *See* client-editor relationship
Fitzgerald, F. Scott, 179
foreign laws and courts, requirements regarding, 150, 156–57

40-hour work week, as basis for EHR, 265, 267, 276
Fowler's Modern English Usage, 70, 299
F&R. *See* Find and Replace (Word)
The Free Dictionary, 299, 324
freelance status, proving, 143, 148, 246, 345
free resources, being wary of, 109, 122, 325–26. *See also* online resources
future of editing. *See also specific aspects*
    agencies and, 400–401
    decline and fall of the American editor, 382–85
    Dorchester changes as harbinger, 379–81
    ebook Age and, 376–78
    editing as potential safe harbor, 386–88
    editorial world as passing editors by, 396–97
    group sourcing, 389–90
    missing the editorial boat, 391–93, 394–95
    open-access model, 405–8
    price tiers, 402–4
    professional organizations, 409–11
    publishing world changes, xvii, 373–75
    solo freelancing vs. group practices, 392–93, 412–14, 415–17, 418–21
    solopreneur vs. company question, 355–57
future of publishing, xvii, 373–75. *See also specific aspects*

Garner's Modern American Usage, 57, 66, 70, 110, 299
Gateway computers, 121
global accounting thinking, 398–99
global market. *See also* outsourcing
    agencies and, 401
    editing roles and, 21–22
    editing tests and, 291
    low rates and competition, 230
    missing the editorial boat, 391–93, 395
    raising prices, 255
    solo freelancing vs. group practices, 419–21
    tier pricing and, 402–4
gmail, 129
God particle of editing, 32–35
going rate as concept, 264–65. *See also* rates *headings*
Google, reference books vs., 110

grammar guides, professional editors and, 57, 67, 70, 299
grammar skills, as missing ingredient, 51–53
The Gregg Reference Manual, 67, 70
gross income, target, 263, 267
group practices vs. solo freelancing, 392–93, 413–14, 415–17, 418–21
group sourcing, 389–90
guilds. *See also* professional organizations
    guild thinking, 418–20
    need for, 151

Haley, Carolyn, 304, 333
handshake agreements vs. contracts, 47, 146, 152, 210
hard drives, 119, 121–24, 138–39
hardware
    custom-built computers, 82, 121–24, 137–38
    monitors, 72–73, 74, 107
    mouse, programmable, 75
    removable drives, 119, 121–24, 138–39
    XKeys, 73–74
Hart, Geoff, 92–93, 94
health insurance costs, 353
heavy edit, use of term, 28–31. *See also* levels of editing
Hemingway, Ernest, 179
Higgs boson of editing, 32–35
higher education costs and career choices, 314–16
hiring considerations
    company vs. solopreneur question, 345
    editing test overview, 289–91
    how not to get work, 295–96
    minimum acceptable pay, 216–18
    new clients, losing chance for, 340–43
    pricing self out of market, 292–94
    resource material familiarity, 68–69, 325–26
holidays, working on, 365, 366
hot-swappable drives, 119, 121–24, 138–39
hourly rates. *See* rates, hourly
hours of business, setting, 364–67

If . . . Then . . . process, 111–12
income, tracking of, 243. *See also* profit considerations; rates *headings*
InCopy, 100

independent status, proving, 143, 148, 246, 345
InDesign, 100, 166
Indian judicial system, requirement regarding, 150, 156, 346
in-house production editors, role changes for, 394–95
in-house work, freelancers moving to, 413
Insert Query macro, 125–28
insurance, 141–43, 353
Integrated Taxonomic Information System, 108
intellectual property concerns, 144–47, 158, 212
interim schedules, 181–84. *See also* schedule considerations
Internal Revenue Service, 143, 148, 246. *See also* tax considerations
The International, 307
Internet resources. *See* online resources
interpretation clauses in contracts, 154
invoices. *See also* collection of payments; rates *headings*
   copyright interest notice and payment, 145–46
   domains and e-mail, 129, 131, 344
   ethics of billing, 249–52, 327–29
   evaluating clients, 307–8
   methods overview, 246–48
   yearly bookkeeping, 245

journal publishing, cost considerations for, 405–7
Journals (macro)
   copyediting stage, 170–71
   large project logistics, 200
   macros overview, 79
   mastering macros, 96, 101–3
   mastering Word, 99
Joyce, James, 305
joy derived from editing, 333–36

"keyboards," custom, 74, 77
key combinations, XKeys and, 74. *See also* macros

Lakme, 178, 180
language usage guides. *See* usage guides
large projects. *See also specific aspects*
   artificial schedules, 181–84
   best price bids, 232–34

company vs. solopreneur question, 344–47, 351–52
   logistics of, 198–201
   mastering macros, 101
   online editing vs. paper-based editing, 91
   taking on too much, 337–39
   yearly bookkeeping, 244–45
late payment as concern. *See* collection of payments
law, education in, 5–7
LCD monitors, 72–73
legal concerns. *See also* contracts
   American judicial system, rule regarding, 157
   copyright interest and payment, 144–47
   Indian judicial system, requirement regarding, 150, 156, 346
   lawsuit remedy, availability of, 153
   lawsuits and difficult clients, 312
   liability insurance requirements, 141–43
   nonpayment and contracts, 210–12
legal profession
   editorial career vs. legal career, 314–16
   outsourcing and, 396–97
   solopreneurs in, 355–57
levels of editing
   editing role comparison, 11–13
   editing roles and downward pressure on price, 21–23
   ethics of billing, 249–52
   handshake agreements vs. contracts, 146
   light, medium, or heavy as terms, 28–31
   rate schedule and, 264
   relationships and unwritten rules, 48
   schedules and client expectations, 186
   schedules and workdays, 365
Levenger, paper from, 111
liability, limitation of, 153
liability insurance requirements, 141–43
libraries of editors. *See* reference books
licensing considerations, cloud computing and, 119–20
light edit, use of term, 28–31, 48. *See also* levels of editing
limitation of liability clause, 153
linguistics, education in, 5–7
LinkedIn, 114–17, 229, 363
Lippincott Williams and Wilkins, 91, 118
ListFixer, 78, 166
literacy, decline in, 382–85

Logitech programmable mouse, 75
loneliness, solo freelancing and, 412–13, 416
losing clients, 361–63
lowering prices, 226–28, 232, 255, 257–59
Lyon, Jack. *See also* Editorium macros
    background of book, xviii
    key resources, xix
    Macro Cookbook for Microsoft Word, 87, 94, 96, 104, 113
    macros overview, 76, 77–78
    Microsoft Word for Publishing Professionals, 87, 94
    for more information, 423
    wildcard macros and money, 236

Mac computers, 76, 79, 99, 138, 139. *See also* Apple computers
Macro Cookbook for Microsoft Word (Lyon), 87, 94, 96, 104, 113
Macro Express
    consistency and editing process, 189
    macros overview, 76–77
    use with XKeys, 74
macros. *See also specific packages*
    artificial schedules, 183–84
    consistency and editing process, 189–91
    copyediting stage, 167, 168–72
    Editorium macros overview, 76, 77–78
    EditTools overview, 76, 78–79
    key resources, xix
    large project logistics, 199–200
    Macro Express overview, 76–77
    macros overview, 76–79, 133–36
    macro-writing example, 80–87
    mastering macros, 94–97, 101–4
    mastering Word, 98–100
    online stylesheets overview, 106–7
    PerfectIt overview, 76, 78
    planning macros, 111–13
    processing stage, 166–67
    publisher agreement regarding callouts, 247
    publisher search for savings, 221
    query macros, 124–28
    wildcard macros and money, 235–39
    XKeys and, 74
market, competition in. *See* competition considerations
marketing of services
    calling vs. e-mailing, 342–43

    disappearing clients, 361–63
    networking and, 417
    professional organizations and, 410
Max stylesheet, 158
ME. *See* Macro Express
medical abbreviation software, 118
medical dictionaries
    editing tests and, 291
    online editing resources, 109
    professional editors and, 66, 69, 326
medical profession
    outsourcing and, 396–97
    solopreneurs in, 355, 357
medical spellcheck software, 68, 291, 326
medium edit, use of term, 28–31. *See also* levels of editing
MEDLINE, 108
MegaReplacer, 78
The Merck Index, 66, 299
mergers and buyouts, 362
Merriam-Webster online, 105
Merriam Webster's Collegiate Dictionary, 66, 67, 69
Merriam Webster's Dictionary of English Usage, 57, 66, 70
MFR. *See* MultiFile Find and Replace
Microsoft antivirus software, 140
Microsoft cloud computing, 118–19
Microsoft Excel, 245, 248, 271
Microsoft PowerPoint, 112
Microsoft Visual Basic Applications
    applications based on, 76
    custom-built computers and, 138
    macros overview, 77
    macro-writing example, 80–87
    mastering VBA, 100, 167
Microsoft Windows
    Apple vs., 138
    macros overview, 76, 79
    Windows 7, 122–23
    Windows 8, 122–23
Microsoft Word. *See also* macros
    changing face of editing, 19
    future of editing and, 388
    invoicing methods, 248
    large project logistics, 200
    macros overview, 77, 79
    Mac versions, 99
    mastering macros, 94–97
    mastering Word, 98–100, 419

online editing background, 91
paper-based vs. online editing and, 195, 197
processing stage, 166–67
query macro, 125–28
reference books for, 87, 91–93, 94, 96, 104, 113
use of as prerequisite, 68–69
Windows 7 and, 123
Word 2003, 99, 119
Word 2007, 99
Word 2010, 99, 119
XKeys and, 74
Microsoft Word for Publishing Professionals (Lyon), 87, 94
monitors, computer, 72–73, 74, 107
mother clauses, 157
mouse, programmable, 75
mugwump, definition of, 58
MultiFile Find and Replace, 133–34, 136, 169–70

National Library of Medicine, 101, 108
network-attached storage box, 138–39
networking (interpersonal), 114–17, 362–63, 416–17
Never Spell Word
    consistency and editing process, 189–91
    copyediting stage, 170
    large project logistics, 199–200
    mastering Word, 99
    for prospective changes, 134
The New Fowler's Modern English Usage, 57
newspaper readership, decline in, 382–83
nondisclosure agreements, 156–59
nonpayment as concern. *See* collection of payments
NoteStripper, 78, 166
nuance, future of editing and, 387
number of pages, calculating, 268–69

offshoring. *See also* global market
    editing roles and, 24–27
    editorial world as passing editors by, 396–99
    schedules and client expectations, 185–86
O'Moore-Klopf, Katharine, 301
1and1 (registrar), 130, 140
online communication. *See* e-mail
online editing. *See also specific aspects*

background of, 91–92
editing roles and outsourcing, 26
mastering macros, 94–97, 101–4
mastering Word, 98–100
online resources, considerations for, 108–10
paper-based editing vs., 91–92, 121, 195–97, 356–57, 380
planning macros, 111–13
query macro, 125–28
reference books for, 87, 91–93, 94, 96, 104, 113
stylesheets overview, 105–7
online networking (interpersonal), 114–17, 362–63
online resources
    citing ebooks and Internet, 176–77
    cloud computing, 118–20
    discussion groups, 114–17, 412–13
    as online editing tool, 108–10
    reference books vs., 54, 67, 69, 70, 108–10, 324–26
online stylesheets. *See* stylesheets
open-access publishing model, 405–7
opinion
    defining good editors, 321–23
    editing as governed by, 260–63, 310–12
    "professional" resources and, 89–90
    what editors forget most often, 318–20
organizations, professional. *See* professional organizations
outsourcing. *See also* global market; packagers; third-party vendors
    editing roles and, 24–27
    editorial world as passing editors by, 396–99
    missing the editorial boat, 392
    schedules and client expectations, 185–86
    solo freelancing vs. group practices, 419–21
The Oxford Dictionary of Word Histories, 66
Oxford English Dictionary, 66, 108
Oxford University Press, 110

packagers. *See also* third-party vendors
    long-term contracts, 242
    missing the editorial boat, 392–93, 394–95
    one price doesn't fit all, 242
    reducing prices, 227

types of "employers," 292–93
page count
 calculating, 268–69, 332
 tracking, 244–45
Page Number Format, 166–67, 201
page rates. *See* rates, per-page
pages, calculating number of, 268–69, 332
paper-based editing, online editing vs., 91–92, 121, 195–97, 356–57, 380
paper-based macro planning, 111–12
partnering with colleagues, 415–17. *See also* group practices vs. solo freelancing
partners, authors and editors as, 44–46
password security, 140
patterns in macros. *See* macros
payment for services. *See* collection of payments; profit considerations; rates *headings*
PC Tools, 139
PDF files, 25, 248
perfection as expectation. *See* expectations; quality considerations
PerfectIt, 76, 78, 173–75
Perkins, Maxwell, 179
per-page rates. *See* rates, per-page
Perseus Books Group, 400–401
personal satisfaction from editing, 333–36
philosophy
 education of editors, 5–7
 Higgs boson of editing, 32–35
phones, 122–23, 248, 342–43
PowerPoint, Microsoft, 112
pricing of services. *See* profit considerations; rates *headings*
printed reference books. *See* reference books
print on demand model, Dorchester changes as harbinger, 379–81
privacy considerations, 345. *See also* confidentiality considerations
processing stage of copyediting, 165, 166–67
process of editing. *See also* roles of editors; *specific aspects*
 authorial and editorial processes, 178–80
 best price bids and, 233–34
 changing face of editing, 17–20
 citing ebooks and Internet, 176–77
 consistency considerations, 188–91
 copyediting read vs. error read, 220

copyediting stage, 165, 167, 168–72
 difficult clients and, 310–13
 "I can get it cheaper," 359–60
 large project logistics, 198–201
 paper-based vs. online editing, 91–92, 121, 195–97, 356–57, 380
 processing stage, 165, 166–67
 production line of editors, 281–82
 proofing stage, 165, 173–75
 schedule considerations and, 181–84, 185–87
 what editors need from authors, 192–94
process serving, setting up, 211–12
production line of editors, 281–82
productivity and profits. *See* profit considerations
productivity studies, 72
professionalism considerations. *See also* career of editing; *specific aspects*
 artificial schedules and, 183
 authorial and editorial processes, 179–80
 domains and e-mail, 129–32, 248, 344
 editors as partners, 40–43
 finding a professional editor, 8–10
 Higgs boson of editing, 34
 "I can get it cheaper," 358
 identifying professional editors, 324–26
 implied promises of editors, 330–32
 invoicing methods overview, 247–48
 low rates and competition, 229–31
 minimum acceptable pay, 216–18
 online discussion groups, 114–17
 "professional" resources, 88–90
 reducing prices, 227
 reference books, use of, 54–56, 57–59, 65–67, 68–71, 297–300, 324–26
professional organizations
 author organizations and publishing trends, 380
 future of editing and, 376, 397, 409–11
 need for, 151, 255, 409–11
 online forums and, 114, 116
 solo freelancing vs. group practices, 416
 tier pricing and, 403–4
profit considerations. *See also* rates *headings*
 best price bids, 232–34
 calculating EHR, 213–15, 265–66, 267–70, 276–79
 company vs. solopreneur question, 344, 348–50, 351–54, 356–57

demand for perfection, 260–63
determining actual hourly rate, 276–79
editorial world as passing editors by, 397–98
ethics of billing, 249–52, 327–29
expectations as recipe for disappointment, 207–9
going rate as concept, 264–65
invoicing methods overview, 246–48
low rates and competition, 229–31
mastering macros, 96, 101–3
minimum acceptable pay, 216–18
nonpayment and, 210–12
one price doesn't fit all, 240–42
paper-based vs. online editing, 195–97
publisher search for savings, 219–22
raising prices, 253–56
reducing prices, 226–28, 232, 255, 257–59
Rule of Three, 223–25, 242, 243–44
satisfaction from editing, 334–36
schedules and client expectations, 185–87
solo freelancing vs. group practices, 419–20
tracking EHR, 271–75, 280–83
utility of EHR, 280–83
what to charge, 264–66, 267–70, 271–75, 276–79, 280–83
wildcard macros and money, 235–39
yearly bookkeeping, 243–45
programmable mouse, 75
programmers, hiring to write macros, 103–4, 113
project lists, 8–9
project rates. *See* rates, project
proofing stage of copyediting, 165, 173–75
proofreading
      editing roles and downward pressure on price, 21–22
      editing roles and outsourcing, 24–26
      low rates and competition, 230
      relationships and unwritten rules, 49–50
      stylesheets and, 25, 105, 199
Publication Manual (APA), 70
publishing, future of, xvii, 373–75. *See also* future of editing; *specific aspects*
PubMed, 102, 108, 119, 200
purchase orders, 146

quality considerations. *See also* professionalism considerations
      acknowledgments, value of, 304–6
      compensation and expectations, 36
      contract considerations, 150–51
      copyediting read vs. error read, 220
      demand for perfection, 260–63
      ebooks and future of editing, 377–78
      editors as partners, 44–46
      expectations as recipe for disappointment, 207–9
      future of publishing, xvii, 375
      good editors, defining, 321–23
      implied promises of editors, 330–32
      low rates and competition, 229–31
      paper-based vs. online editing, 197
      PerfectIt overview, 78, 165, 173–75
      posting prices and, 301–2
      professional editors, identifying, 325
      publisher search for savings, 220–22
      reducing prices and, 258–59
      relationships and unwritten rules, 48–50
      taking on too much, 337–39
queries, author, 12, 49, 125–28
QuickBooks Pro, 245

raising prices, 253–56
rates (generally). *See also* profit considerations; *specific rate types*
      changing face of editing, 17–19
      downbeating of pricing, 383–84
      ebooks and future of editing, 376–78
      editing roles and downward pressure on price, 21–23
      editing roles and outsourcing, 24–27
      editing roles and unwritten rules, 50
      editors as partners, 41–43
      education costs and career choices, 315–16
      expectations and compensation, 36–39
      going rate as concept, 264–65
      group practices vs. solo freelancing, 420–21
      group sourcing and, 390
      how not to get work, 295
      "I can get it cheaper," 358–60
      levels of editing overview, 28–31
      liability insurance requirements, 143
      low rates and competition, 229–31
      minimum acceptable pay, 216–18
      minimum universal price, lack of, 228

missing the editorial boat, 391–93, 394–95
new clients, losing chance for, 340–41
one price doesn't fit all, 240–42
open-access model and, 405–8
posting prices on website, 240–42, 301–3
price tiers, 402–4
pricing self out of market, 292–94
raising prices, 253–56
reducing prices, 226–28, 232, 255, 257–59
rush charges, 247, 309, 365, 366
schedules and expectations, 185–87
schedules and workdays, 365
tier pricing, 402–4
what to charge, 264–66, 267–70, 271–75, 276–79, 280–83
rates, EFA schedule of, 264
rates, effective hourly
calculating, 265–66, 267–70, 276–79
EditTools creation and, 255
macros overview, 133
mastering macros, 96
query macro, 128
reducing prices, 258
tracking, 214–15, 243–44, 271–75, 280–83
utility of, 280–83
rates, hourly
company vs. solopreneur question, 352
demand for perfection, 262
determining actual hourly rate, 276–79
ethics of billing, 249–52, 327–29
expectations and compensation, 37–38
how not to get work, 295
"I can get it cheaper," 360
mastering macros, 101
mastering Word, 100
minimum acceptable pay, 216–18
one price doesn't fit all, 240–42
posting prices on website, 301–2
pricing self out of market, 292
publisher search for savings, 220–22
raising prices, 253
reducing prices, 258
rates, per-page
calculating EHR, 213–14, 268–69
ethics of billing, 249, 251
expectations and compensation, 38
"I can get it cheaper," 360

low rates and competition, 229–31
macros overview, 133
mastering macros, 96, 101–3
mastering Word, 100
meeting EHR, 278
minimum acceptable pay, 217
one price doesn't fit all, 241–42
posting prices on website, 302
pricing self out of market, 292
publisher search for savings, 220–22
reducing prices, 227–28
tier pricing, 402–3
tracking EHR, 272–73
yearly bookkeeping, 244
rates, project
calculating EHR, 268
ethics of billing, 249, 251, 328
expectations and compensation, 38
"I can get it cheaper," 360
mastering macros, 101
meeting EHR, 278
one price doesn't fit all, 241–42
yearly bookkeeping, 244
reducing prices, 226–28, 232, 255, 257–59
reference books
grammar skills and, 51–52
for Microsoft Word, 87, 91–93, 94, 96, 104, 113
online resources vs., 54, 67, 69, 70, 108–10, 324–26
professional editors and, 54–56, 57–59, 65–67, 68–71, 297–300, 324–26
"professional" resources, 88–90
what editors forget most often, 317–20
references (bibliographic)
artificial schedules, 182
copyediting stage, 170–71
ebooks and Internet as sources, 176–77
editor's discretion in styling, 318–19
large project logistics, 200–201
macros overview, 79
macro-writing example, 80–87
mastering macros, 95–96, 101–3
mastering Word, 98
processing stage, 166–67
wildcard macros and money, 235–39
references (for job applicants), 9
Registry Mechanic, 139

relationship considerations. *See* author-editor relationship; client-editor relationship
removable drives, 119, 121–24, 138–39
resource libraries of editors. *See* reference books
RoboForm, 140
roles of editors. *See also* process of editing; *specific roles and concerns*
    blurring of roles and pricing down, 21–23
    changing face of editing, 17–20
    copyediting by any other name, 24–27
    developmental editor vs. copyeditor, 11–13, 29
    difficult clients and, 310–13
    editorial commandments, 35, 40–43, 44–46, 50
    education and, 5–7
    expectations and compensation, 36–39
    finding an editor, 8–10
    grammar skills, 51–53
    Higgs boson of editing, 32–35
    in-house production editors, 394–95, 420
    light, medium, or heavy as terms, 28–31
    production line of editors, 281–82
    professionalism considerations overview, 54–56, 57–59
    relationships and unwritten rules, 47–50
    WYSIWYG conundrum, 14–16
Rule of Three, 223–25, 242, 243–44
rush charges, 247, 309, 365, 366

safe deposit boxes, 123, 138
samples of work, 9–10
Samsung monitors, 73
satisfaction from editing, 333–36
"satisfactory" contract wording, 153
schedule considerations
    artificial or arbitrary schedules, 181–84
    ebooks and future of editing, 377
    ethics of billing, 249–52, 327–29
    expectations and compensation, 36–39
    expectations and schedules, 185–87
    levels of edit and, 30
    online discussion groups and, 114–15, 117
    paper-based vs. online editing and, 196–97
    relationships and unwritten rules, 48
    taking on too much, 338–39
    tier pricing and, 402–3

    workdays and schedules, 364–67
    yearly bookkeeping, 243–44
schedule of rates (EFA), 264
Scientific Style and Format (CSE), 70, 299
Search, Count, and Replace
    macros overview, 78, 79
    mastering macros, 95
    overview of, 133, 135–36
self-editing trends, xvii, 388, 405–8
self-publishing
    agencies and, 400–1
    future of publishing, xvii, 374
    open-access model and, 406
service of process, setting up, 211–12
signature for e-mails, 130–31, 248
sign-or-no-work agreements, 346
Simenon, Georges, 186
since/because, 32–33, 52
smart phones, 122–23
social media, 114–17, 229
Social Security contributions, 353
Social Security number, 131, 248
software. *See also* macros; *specific packages and types of software*
    antivirus, 109, 119, 122, 139–40
    cloud computing and, 119
    disaster preparedness and, 138–40
    editing as future safe harbor, 386–88
    editing tests and, 291
    Editorium macros overview, 77–78
    EditTools overview, 78–79
    free resources, 109, 122, 325–26
    grammar skills and, 51–52
    key resources, xix
    Macro Express overview, 76–77
    online editing background, 91–93
    PerfectIt overview, 78
    taking on too much, 338–39
    use of as hiring consideration, 68–69
solo work
    solo freelancing vs. group practices, 392–93, 412–14, 415–17, 418–21
    solopreneur vs. company question, 344–47, 348–50, 351–54, 355–57
specialty reference books. *See also* reference books
    editing tests and, 291
    online editing resources, 109
    professional editors and, 66, 69–70, 299, 326

spellcheck software
    editing as future safe harbor, 386–88
    editing tests and, 291
    large project logistics, 200
    medical, 68, 291, 326
    as not used by some, 68, 339
    reliance on, 51–52
spelling skills, as missing ingredient, 51–53
stages of editing. *See* process of editing
state laws, as governing contracts, 211
Stedman's Medical Dictionary, 66, 69, 109
Stedman's Medical Spellchecker, 291
Storyboard paper, 111–12
structure-oriented nature of editing, 5–7, 29
style manuals
    editing tests and, 290
    Higgs boson of editing, 34
    online discussion regarding, 115–16
    professional editors and, 54–56, 57, 65,
        70–71, 297–300
    "professional" resources, 88–90
    usage guides vs., 88
    what editors forget most often, 317–20
stylesheets
    backup considerations, 140
    editing process and, 188–91
    editing tests and, 290–91
    group sourcing and, 389–90
    large project logistics, 199
    Max Stylesheet, 158
    monitor setup and, 73, 107
    online stylesheets overview, 105–7
    proofreading and, 25, 105, 109
    taking on too much, 337–39
subject-matter expertise, changing face of
    editing, 17–19
Superscript Me, 166–67
swappable drives, 119, 121–24, 138–39

tax considerations
    company vs. solopreneur question, 345
    contract purpose, 148
    insurance coverage, 143
    invoicing methods, 246
    taxpayer-funded research, access to, 405
team concept, 198. *See also* group practices
    vs. solo freelancing; large projects
technological advances and future of edit-
    ing, 386–88. *See also specific aspects*
telephone number, on invoices, 131
telephones, 122–23, 248, 342–43

templates
    changing face of editing, 18
    mastering macros, 96
    mastering Word, 98
    online editing background, 91
10 Editorial Commandments
    creation of, 35
    thou shalt treat editors as partners,
        44–46, 50
    thou shalt use a professional editor,
        40–43
tests
    editing roles and outsourcing, 24–25
    living in a dream world, 216–17
    new clients, losing chance for, 340–42
    overview of, 289–91
Thaler-Carter, Ruth E.
    background of book, xviii
    contracts, 150
    job satisfaction, 333
    key resources, xix
    LinkedIn and editors, 114–17
    for more information, 423
    solo freelancing vs. group practices,
        415–17, 418
    solopreneur vs. company question,
        348–50, 351
that/which, 52
there/their, 52
thesauruses, 70
third-party vendors, 149–52. *See also* out-
    sourcing; packagers
tier pricing, 402–4
time considerations. *See* estimates; schedule
    considerations
Timeless Time and Expense, 271
time tracking methods, 271–75
Toggle
    consistency and editing process, 189–91
    copyediting stage, 168–69
    frequency of use, 134
    macros overview, 78
    mastering macros, 95
tools for editors. *See also specific tools*
    cloud computing, 118–20
    contract considerations, 148–51, 152–55
    copyright interest and payment, 144–47
    disaster preparedness, 137–40
    domains and e-mail, 129–32
    editing tests and, 290–91

hardware overviews, 72–75, 121–24
key resources, xix
liability insurance requirements, 141–43
LinkedIn, 114–17
macros overviews, 76–79, 133–36
macro-writing example, 80–87
mastering macros, 94–97, 101–4
mastering Word, 98–100
Microsoft Word reference books, 87, 91–93, 94, 96, 104, 113
missing the editorial boat, 392
nondisclosure agreements, 156–59
online editing resources, 108–10
online stylesheets overview, 105–7
planning macros, 111–13
professional editor's bookshelf, 54–56, 57–59, 65–67, 68–71
"professional" resources, 88–90
query macro, 124–28
removable drives and Windows 8, 119, 121–24
software overview, 76–79
taking on too much, 338–39
Track Changes
    changing face of editing, 19
    consistency and editing process, 190
    copyediting stage, 169
    mastering Word, 99–100
    paper-based vs. online editing, 195, 197
trade secrets, 156–59
translated books, editing, 227
trust, contracts and, 153, 154–55
typesetting/composition, editing roles and outsourcing, 25–26

Ulysses (Joyce), 305
URLs, citing, 176–77
usage guides
    editing tests and, 290
    grammar skills and, 51–52
    online editing resources, 110
    professional editors and, 57–59, 66, 69–70, 299
    "professional" resources, 88
    style manuals vs., 88
venue clauses, 210–11
veterinarian vs. editor as career choice, 314–16
Visual Basic Applications, Microsoft. *See* Microsoft Visual Basic Applications

waiver of rights (in contracts), 153
warranties for computers, 123
warranty, implied promise as, 330–32
web design pricing example, 253–54
web resources. *See* online resources
websites for editors
    checking out before applying for work, 295
    company vs. solopreneur question, 345
    domains and e-mail overview, 129–32
    online stylesheets and, 73, 106, 140
    password security, 140
    posting prices on, 240–42, 301–3
    work hours and, 364
weekends, working on, 247, 365, 366
Whose Grammar Book Is This Anyway?, 70
Wikipedia, 54, 67, 177, 299, 325, 383
Wildcard Find and Replace, 201, 236–39
wildcard macros
    basics of VBA, 76
    copyediting stage, 167
    large project logistics, 201
    macro-writing example, 80–87
    profit considerations, 235–39
Windows, Microsoft. *See* Microsoft Windows
Word, Microsoft. *See* Microsoft Word
word books, 66, 70
word lists, custom, 174
wordnSync programs. *See* EditTools; *specific programs*
Word Parts Dictionary, 57, 66, 70
WordPerfect, 91, 195
words per page formula, 269
Worker's Compensation, 143, 353
"work for hire" contract wording, 153
work hours, setting, 364–67
working alone. *See* solo work
work samples, 9–10
work week (40-hour), as basis for EHR, 265, 267, 276
written contracts. *See* contracts
WYSIWYG conundrum, 14–16

XKeys, 73–74, 76–79
XyWrite, 91

yearly bookkeeping, 243–45
yearly price increases, 254–55

CPSIA information can be obtained at www.ICGtesting.com
Printed in the USA
BVOW08s0111160116

433130BV00003B/118/P